# Pichi Pichi Pitch 1

## Manga by Pink Hanamori
## Scenario by Michiko Yokote

Translated and adapted by William Flanagan

Lettered by Min Choi

**DEL REY**

BALLANTINE BOOKS • NEW YORK

[7]

A Del Rey Trade Paperback Original

*Pichi Pichi Pitch, volume 1* copyright © 2003 by Michiko Yokote, Pink Hanamori, Kodansha Ltd., and We've.

English translation copyright © 2006 by Michiko Yokote, Pink Hanamori, Kodansha Ltd., and We've.

Published in the United States by Del Rey Books, an imprint of The Random House Publishing Group, a division of Random House, Inc., New York

DEL REY is a registered trademark and the Del Rey colophon is a trademark of Random House, Inc.

Publication rights arranged through Kodansha Ltd.

First published in Japan in 2003 by Kodansha Ltd., Tokyo.

ISBN 0-345-49196-3

Printed in the United States of America

www.delreymanga.com

9  8  7  6  5  4

Translator/Adaptor—William Flanagan
Lettering—Min Choi
Original cover design—Akiko Omo

# Contents

# Honorifics

Throughout the Del Rey Manga books, you will find Japanese honorifics left intact in the translations. For those not familiar with how the Japanese use honorifics, and more important, how they differ from American honorifics, we present this brief overview.

Politeness has always been a critical facet of Japanese culture. Ever since the feudal era, when Japan was a highly stratified society, use of honorifics—which can be defined as polite speech that indicates relationship or status—has played an essential role in the Japanese language. When addressing someone in Japanese, an honorific usually takes the form of a suffix attached to one's name (example: "Asuna-san"), or as a title at the end of one's name or in place of the name itself (example: "Negi-sensei," or simply "Sensei!").

Honorifics can be expressions of respect or endearment. In the context of manga and anime, honorifics give insight into the nature of the relationship between characters. Many translations into English leave out these important honorifics, and therefore distort the "feel" of the original Japanese. Because Japanese honorifics contain nuances that English honorifics lack, it is our policy at Del Rey not to translate them. Here, instead, is a guide to some of the honorifics you may encounter in Del Rey Manga.

-san:   This is the most common honorific, and is equivalent to Mr., Miss, Ms., Mrs., etc. It is the all-purpose honorific and can be used in any situation where politeness is required.

-sama:  This is one level higher than "-san" and it is used to confer great respect.

-dono:  This comes from the word "tono," which means "lord." It is an even higher level than "-sama," and confers utmost respect.

-kun:   This suffix is used at the end of boys' names to express familiarity or endearment. It is also sometimes used by men among friends, or when addressing someone younger or of a lower station.

-chan: This is used to express endearment, mostly toward girls. It is also used for little boys, pets, and even among lovers. It gives a sense of childish cuteness.

Bozu: This is an informal way to refer to a boy, similar to the English term "kid" or "squirt."

Sempai/senpai: This title suggests that the addressee is one's "senior" in a group or organization. It is most often used in a school setting, where underclassmen refer to their upperclassmen as "sempai." It can also be used in the workplace, such as when a newer employee addresses an employee who has seniority in the company.

Kohai: This is the opposite of "sempai," and is used toward underclassmen in school or newcomers in the workplace. It connotes that the addressee is of lower station.

Sensei: Literally meaning "one who has come before," this title is used for teachers, doctors, or masters of any profession or art.

[blank]: Usually forgotten in these lists, but perhaps the most significant difference between Japanese and English. The lack of honorific means that the speaker has permission to address the person in a very intimate way. Usually, only family, spouses, or very close friends have this kind of permission. Known as *yobisute,* it can be gratifying when someone who has earned the intimacy starts to call one by one's name without an honorific. But when that intimacy hasn't been earned, it can be very insulting.

THERE ARE SEVEN MERMAID
PRINCESSES AND
SEVEN PEARLS.
THEY EXIST TO PROTECT
THE SEVEN SEAS.

THE REASON I SING IS
TO CONVEY MY LOVE.
THE REASON THE PEARL
SPARKLES IS TO
BRIGHTEN UP THE SEA.

And so,
I can never forget . . .

. . . . . . the sound of
the waves or
the warmth of the s

And someday . . .

. . . I'll remember!

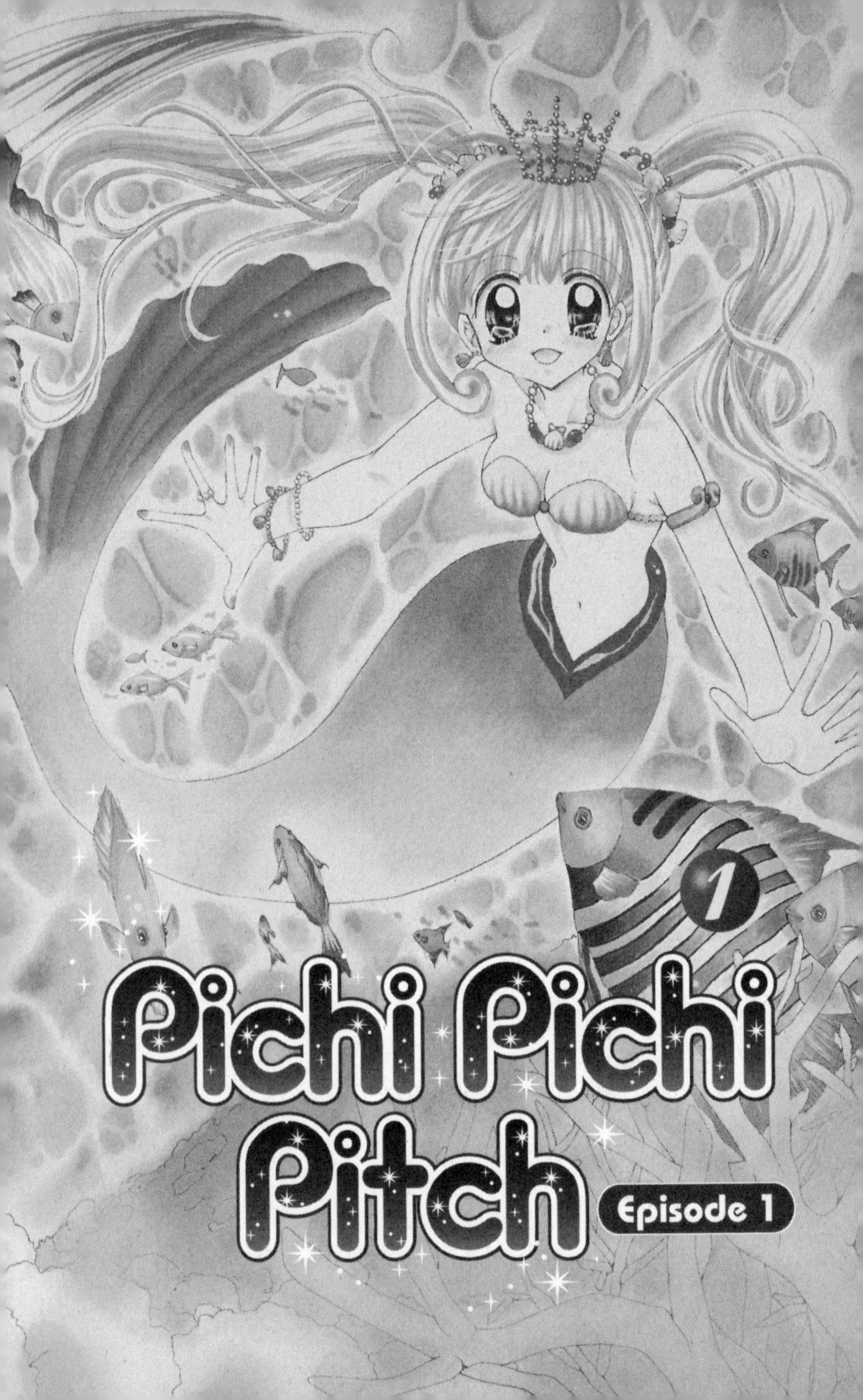
1
Pichi Pichi Pitch
Episode 1

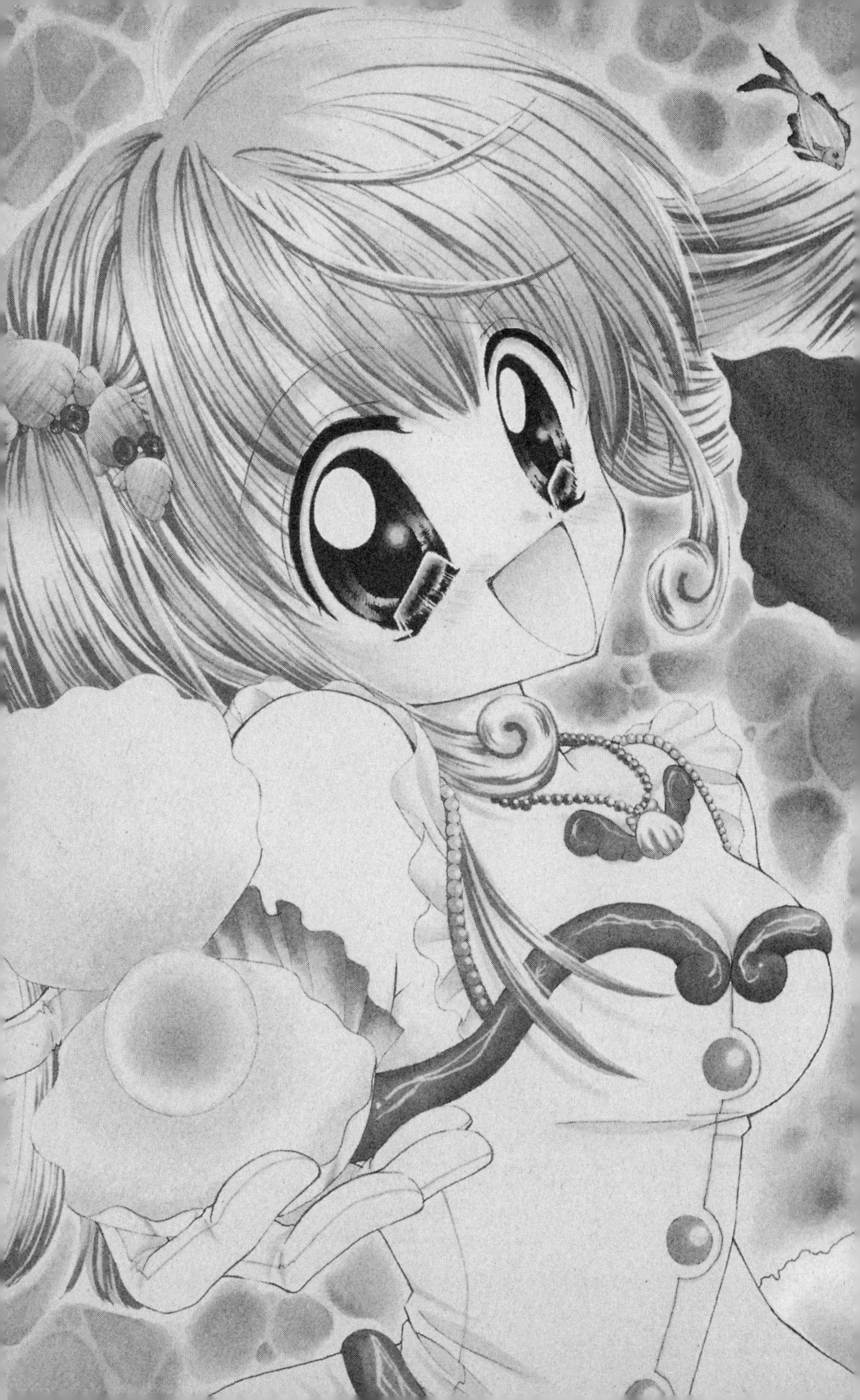

## GREETINGS!

LIPS

NICE TO MEET YOU.
I'M PINK HANAMORI. (IT'S A PEN NAME)
THIS IS HANAMORI'S VERY FIRST COMIC.
THANK YOU FOR PICKING IT UP.
IT'S ONLY FIVE MINUTES BY CAR FROM MY HOUSE
TO THE SEA. SEE LIKE THIS...
I LIKE JOHNNYS. I LIKE VARIETY SHOWS. I LIKE TO LAUGH. I LIKE SNACKS. I LOVE TO SLEEP.
I LIKE ANIMALS (ESPECIALLY THE FURRY ONES).

SELF-NTRODUCTION

| | |
|---|---|
| NAME | PINK HANAMORI |
| BIRTHDAY | NOVEMBER 5TH |
| BIRTHPLACE | SHIZUOKA PREFECTURE |
| BLOOD TYPE | AB |
| DÔBUTSU URANAI | MONKEY |
| FAMILY | YOUNGEST OF THREE CHILDREN |

*THAT'S WHAT I'M ABOUT.*

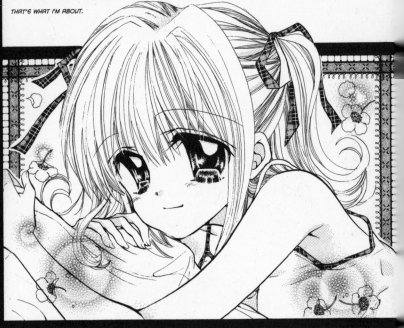

THE MEANING OF LIPS REFERS TO SEVERAL THINGS, INCLUDING HANAMORI'S VERY FAVORITE FLOWER—TULIPS—AND THE LIPS ON A PERSON'S MOUTH. IN OTHER WORDS, I WANT TO CHAT WITH YOU ALL IN A WAY THAT'LL BE FUN FOR EVERYBODY! I KNOW THAT IN THESE FREE SPACES, IT'LL JUST BE ME TALKING (THIS IS A BOOK, AFTER ALL), BUT I'M APPROACHING IT WITH THE FEELING THAT WE'RE TALKING BACK AND FORTH. MY NEWSLETTER (FREE CHAT AND ILLUSTRATIONS) THAT I USED TO SEND TO PEOPLE WHO WERE NICE ENOUGH TO WRITE ME A LETTER, AND THE HOME PAGE THAT A GOOD FRIEND MADE FOR ME, ARE BOTH CALLED LIPS, SO IF YOU JUST SEARCH FOR PINK HANAMORI, YOU'LL BE ABLE TO FIND ME. PLEASE DROP BY THE SITE! AND TELL ME WHAT YOU THINK OF IT! (SORRY, THE WEBSITE IS IN JAPANESE ONLY!)
← NOW, STARTING ON THE NEXT PAGE, PLEASE READ MY MANGA WITH A LIGHT "PICHI PICHI" HEART!

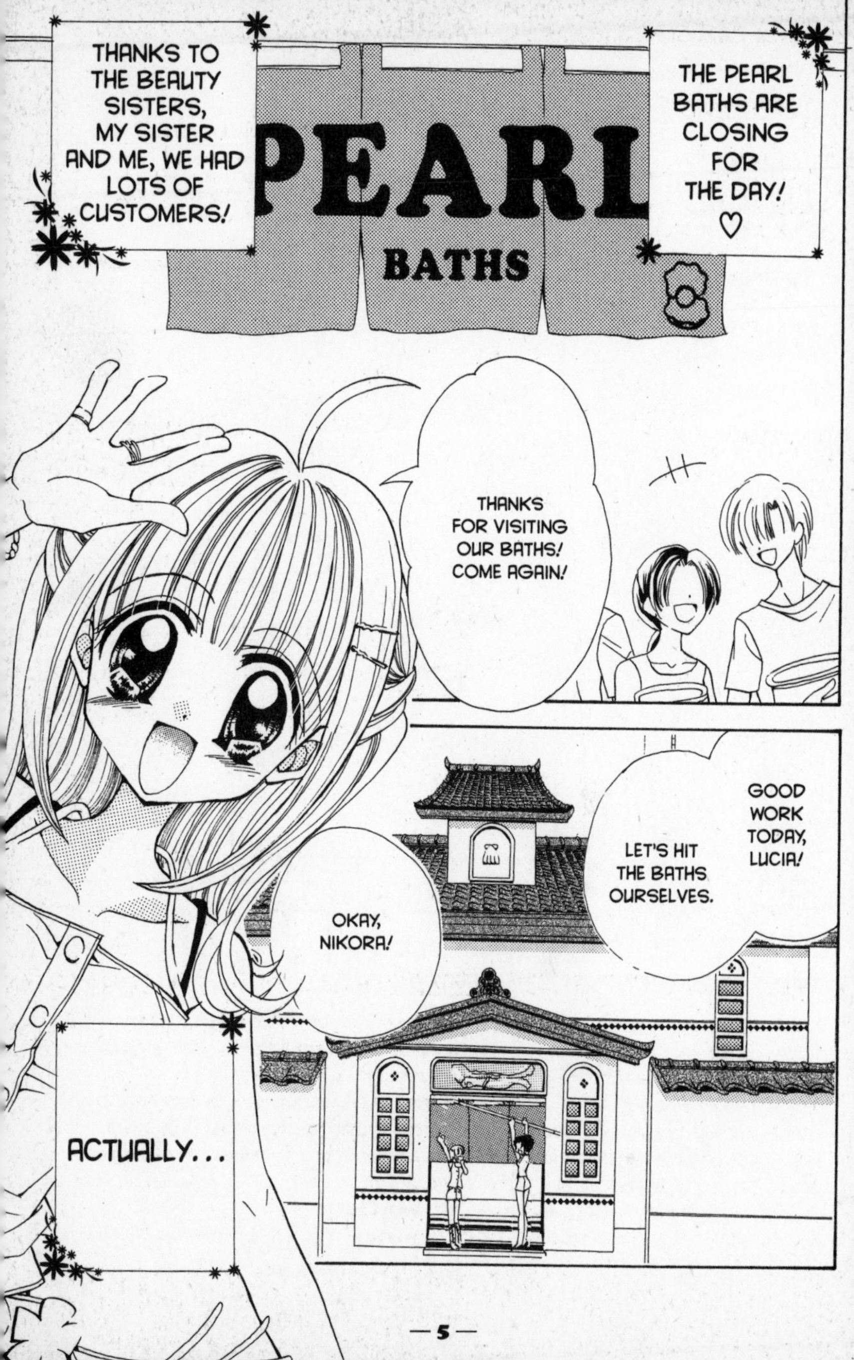
PEARL
BATHS
THE PEARL BATHS ARE CLOSING FOR THE DAY! ♡
THANKS TO THE BEAUTY SISTERS, MY SISTER AND ME, WE HAD LOTS OF CUSTOMERS!
THANKS FOR VISITING OUR BATHS! COME AGAIN!
GOOD WORK TODAY, LUCIA!
LET'S HIT THE BATHS OURSELVES.
OKAY, NIKORA!
ACTUALLY...

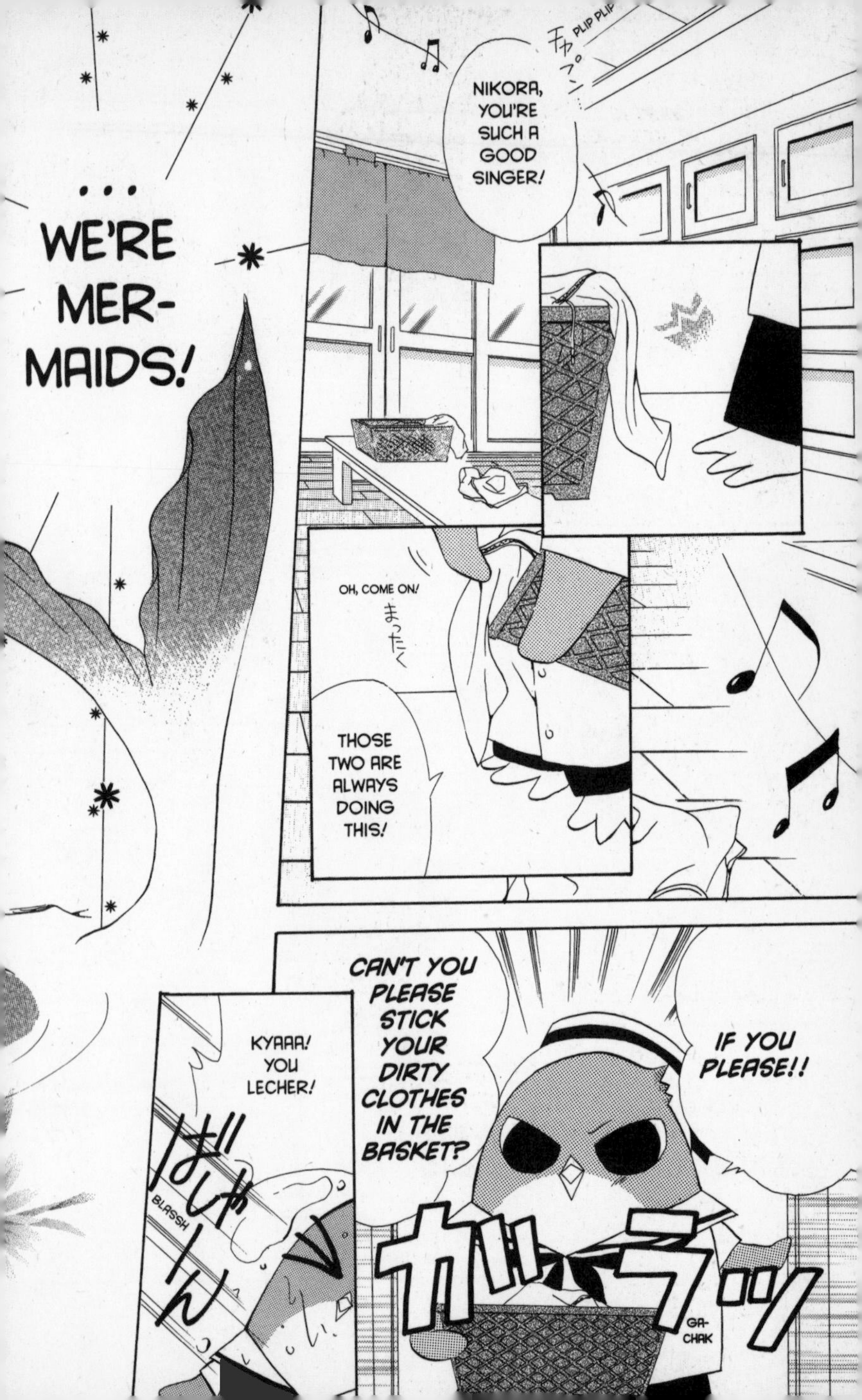

チカプン
PLIP PLIP
NIKORA, YOU'RE SUCH A GOOD SINGER!
OH, COME ON!
まったく
THOSE TWO ARE ALWAYS DOING THIS!
... WE'RE MER-MAIDS!
CAN'T YOU PLEASE STICK YOUR DIRTY CLOTHES IN THE BASKET?
IF YOU PLEASE!!
カッラッ
GA-CHAK
KYAAA! YOU LECHER!
ばしゃん
BLASSH

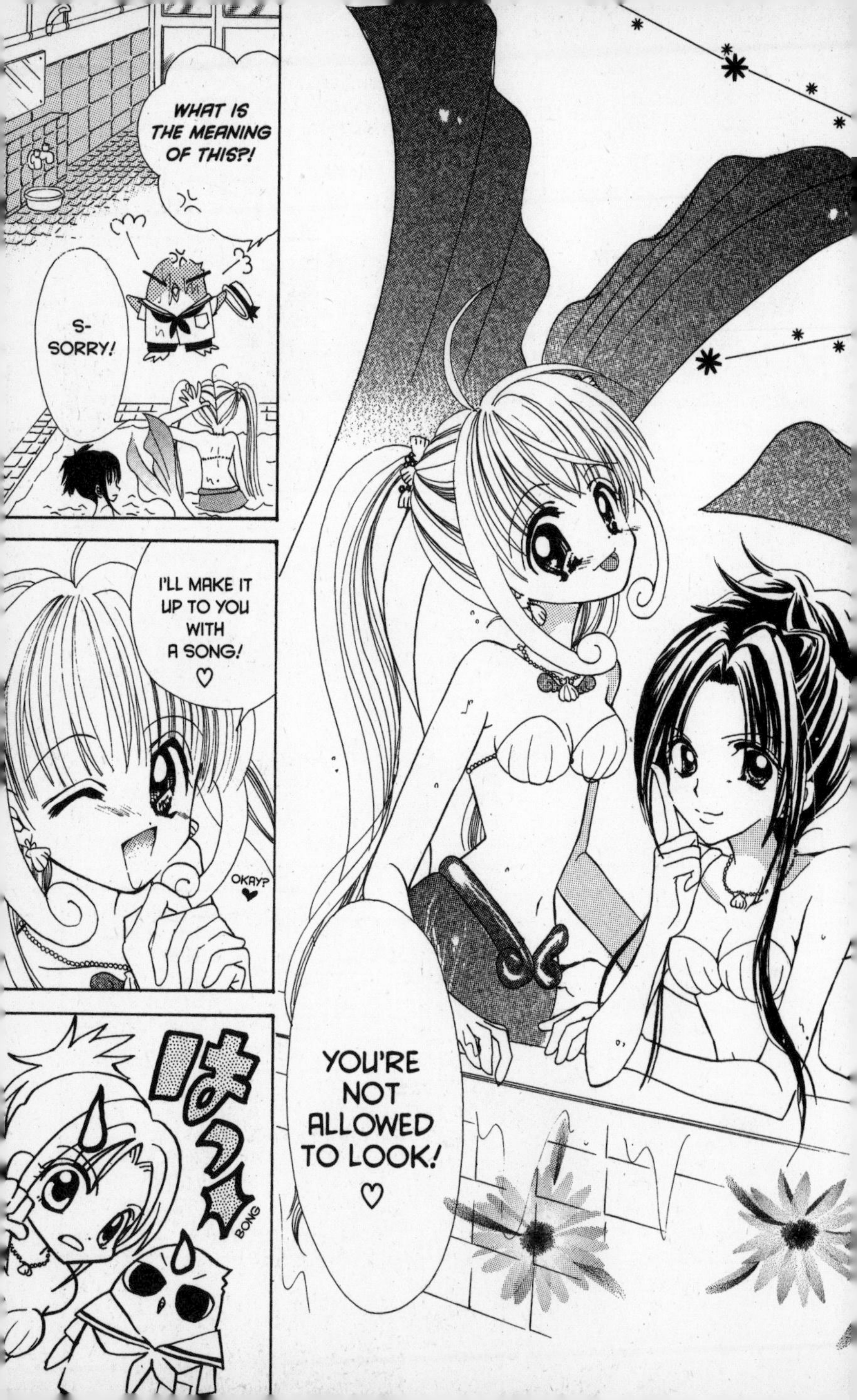

YOU'RE NOT ALLOWED TO LOOK! ♡
WHAT IS THE MEANING OF THIS?!
S- SORRY!
I'LL MAKE IT UP TO YOU WITH A SONG! ♡
OKAY? ♥
はっ
BONG

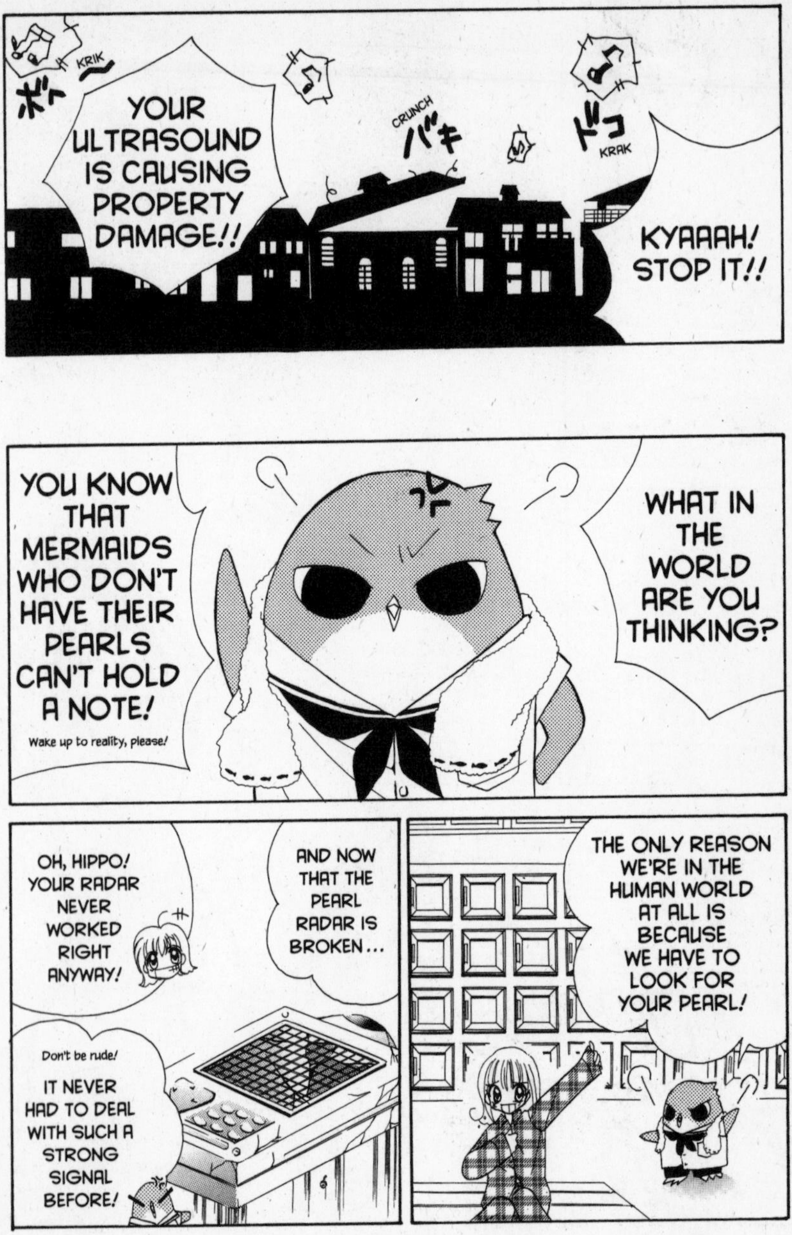

ドコ
KRAK
KYAAAH! STOP IT!!
CRUNCH
バキ
KRIK
YOUR ULTRASOUND IS CAUSING PROPERTY DAMAGE!!
WHAT IN THE WORLD ARE YOU THINKING?
YOU KNOW THAT MERMAIDS WHO DON'T HAVE THEIR PEARLS CAN'T HOLD A NOTE!
Wake up to reality, please!
THE ONLY REASON WE'RE IN THE HUMAN WORLD AT ALL IS BECAUSE WE HAVE TO LOOK FOR YOUR PEARL!
AND NOW THAT THE PEARL RADAR IS BROKEN...
OH, HIPPO! YOUR RADAR NEVER WORKED RIGHT ANYWAY!
Don't be rude!
IT NEVER HAD TO DEAL WITH SUCH A STRONG SIGNAL BEFORE!

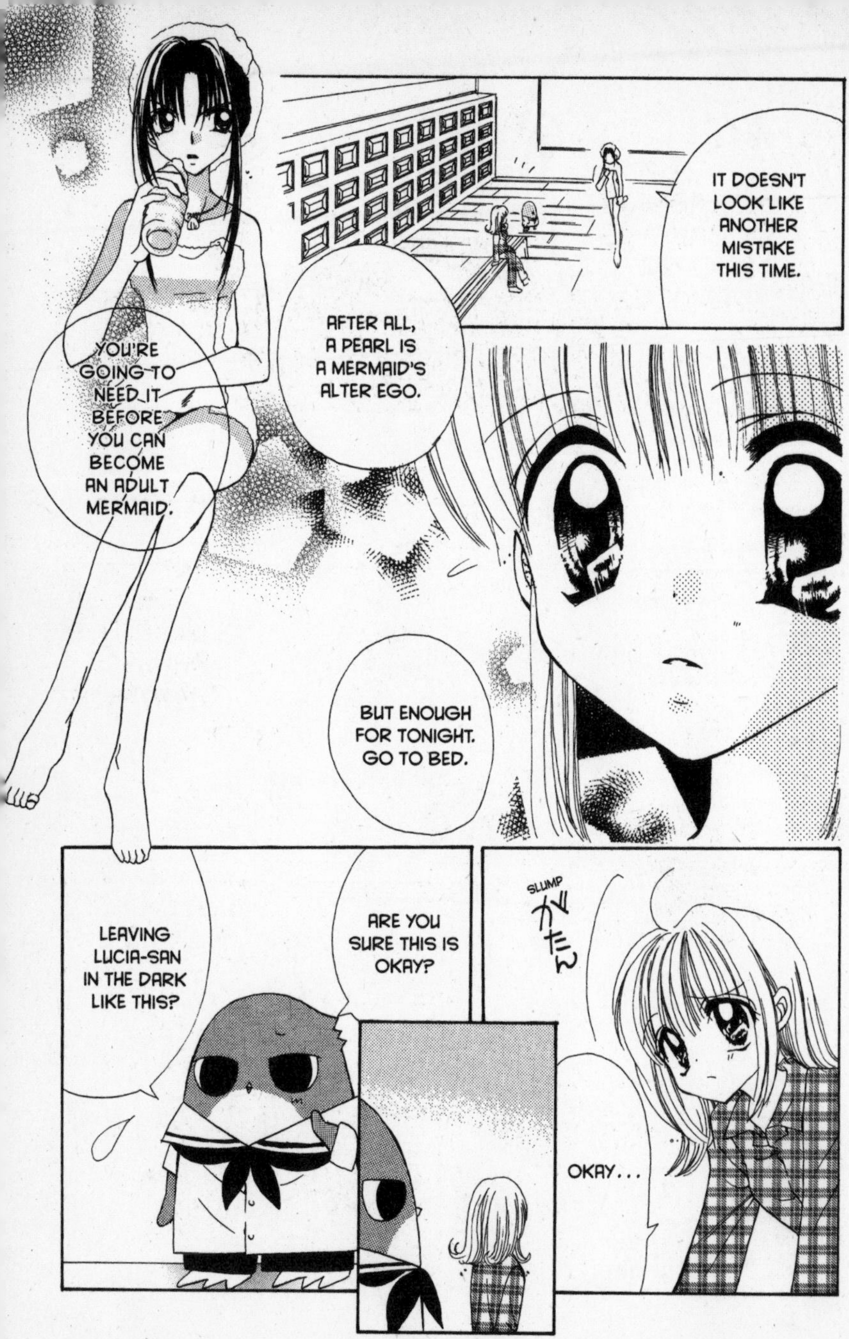
IT DOESN'T LOOK LIKE ANOTHER MISTAKE THIS TIME.
AFTER ALL, A PEARL IS A MERMAID'S ALTER EGO.
YOU'RE GOING TO NEED IT BEFORE YOU CAN BECOME AN ADULT MERMAID.
BUT ENOUGH FOR TONIGHT. GO TO BED.
SLUMP
がたん
OKAY...
ARE YOU SURE THIS IS OKAY?
LEAVING LUCIA-SAN IN THE DARK LIKE THIS?

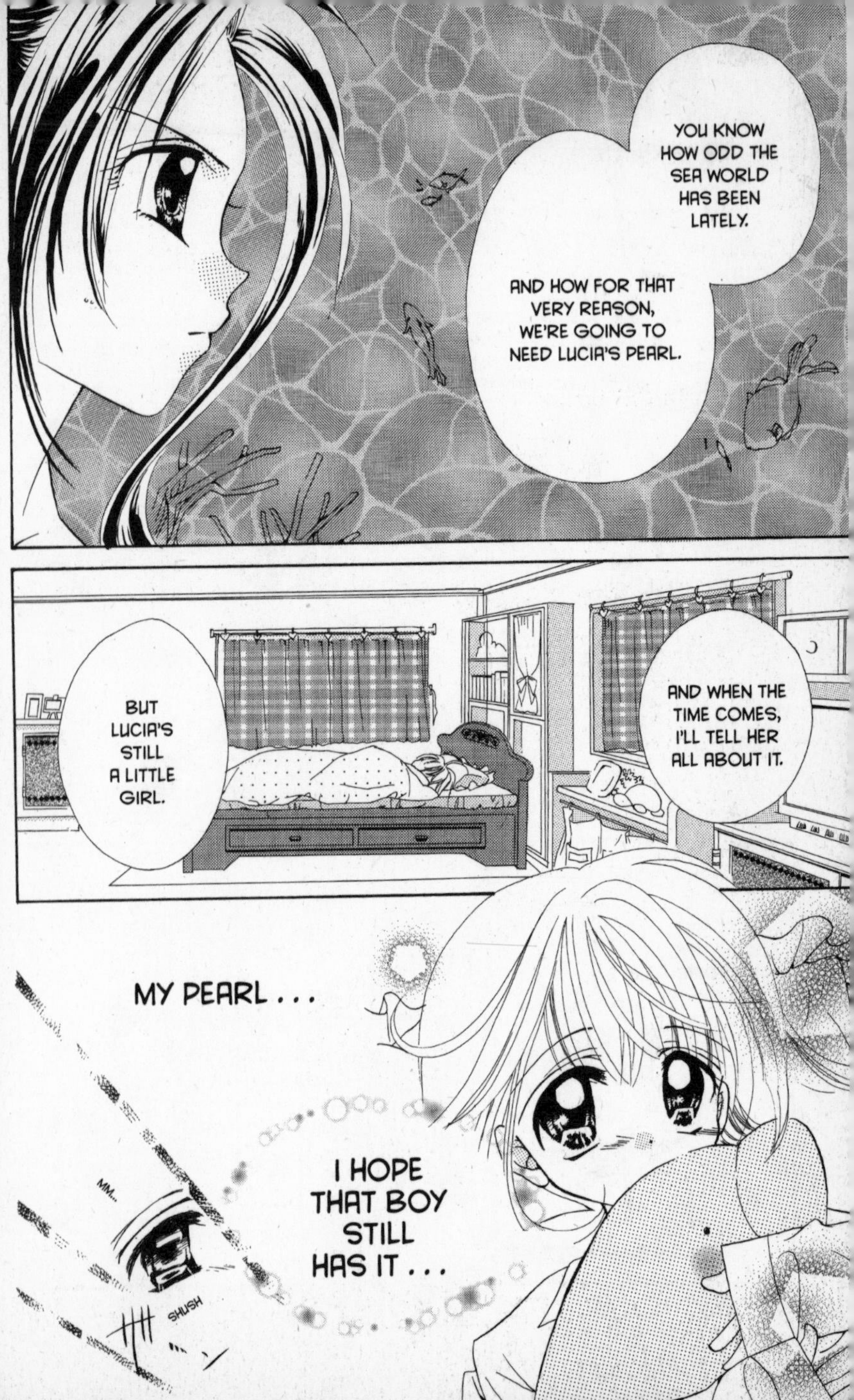
YOU KNOW HOW ODD THE SEA WORLD HAS BEEN LATELY.
AND HOW FOR THAT VERY REASON, WE'RE GOING TO NEED LUCIA'S PEARL.
AND WHEN THE TIME COMES, I'LL TELL HER ALL ABOUT IT.
BUT LUCIA'S STILL A LITTLE GIRL.
MY PEARL . . .
I HOPE THAT BOY STILL HAS IT . . .
MM...
SHUSH

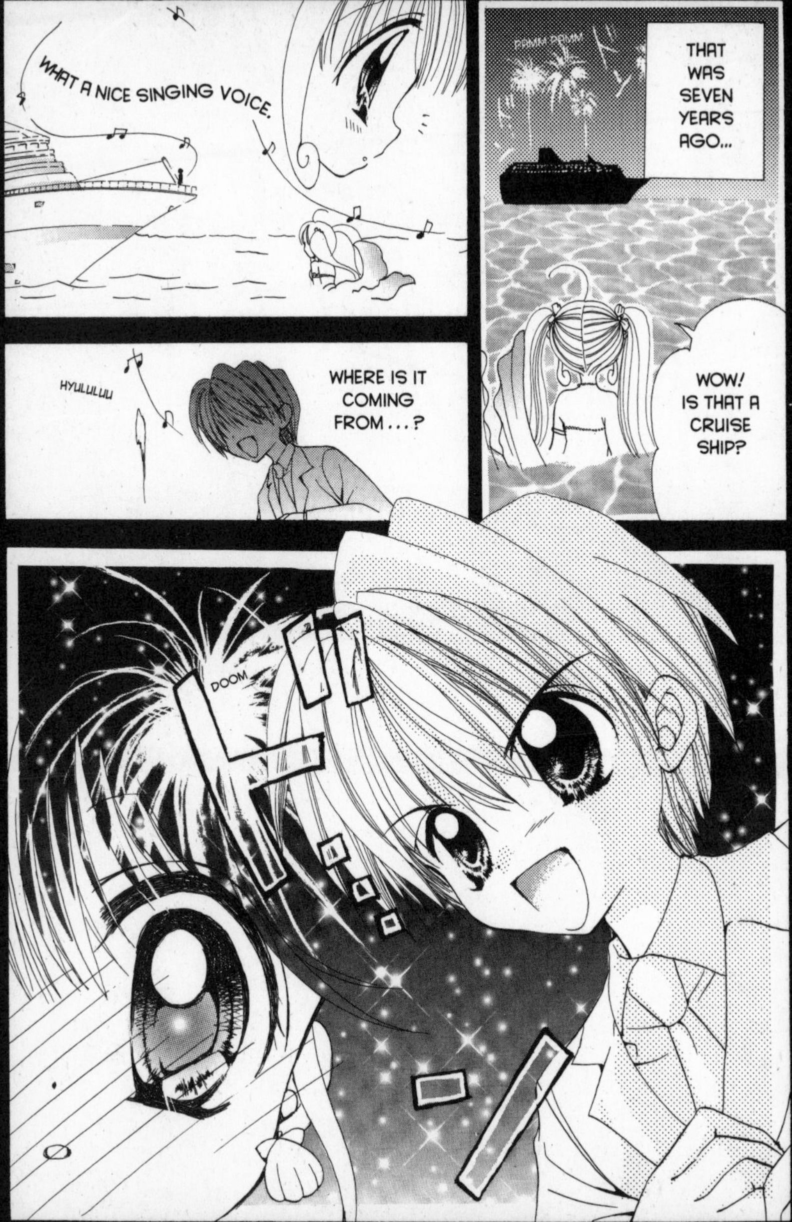
PAMM PAMM
THAT WAS SEVEN YEARS AGO...
WOW! IS THAT A CRUISE SHIP?
WHAT A NICE SINGING VOICE.
WHERE IS IT COMING FROM . . . ?
HYULULUU
DOOM

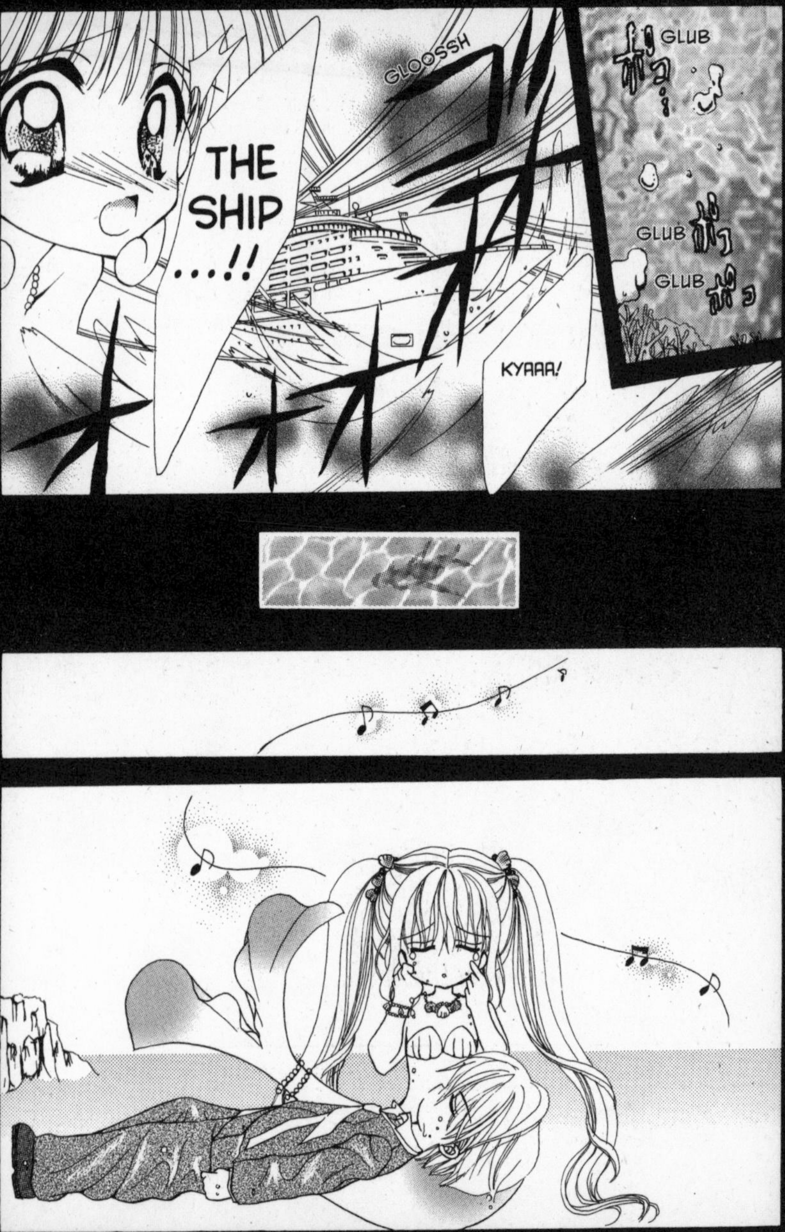
GLUB
GLUB
GLUB
GLOOSSH
THE SHIP ...!!
KYAAA!

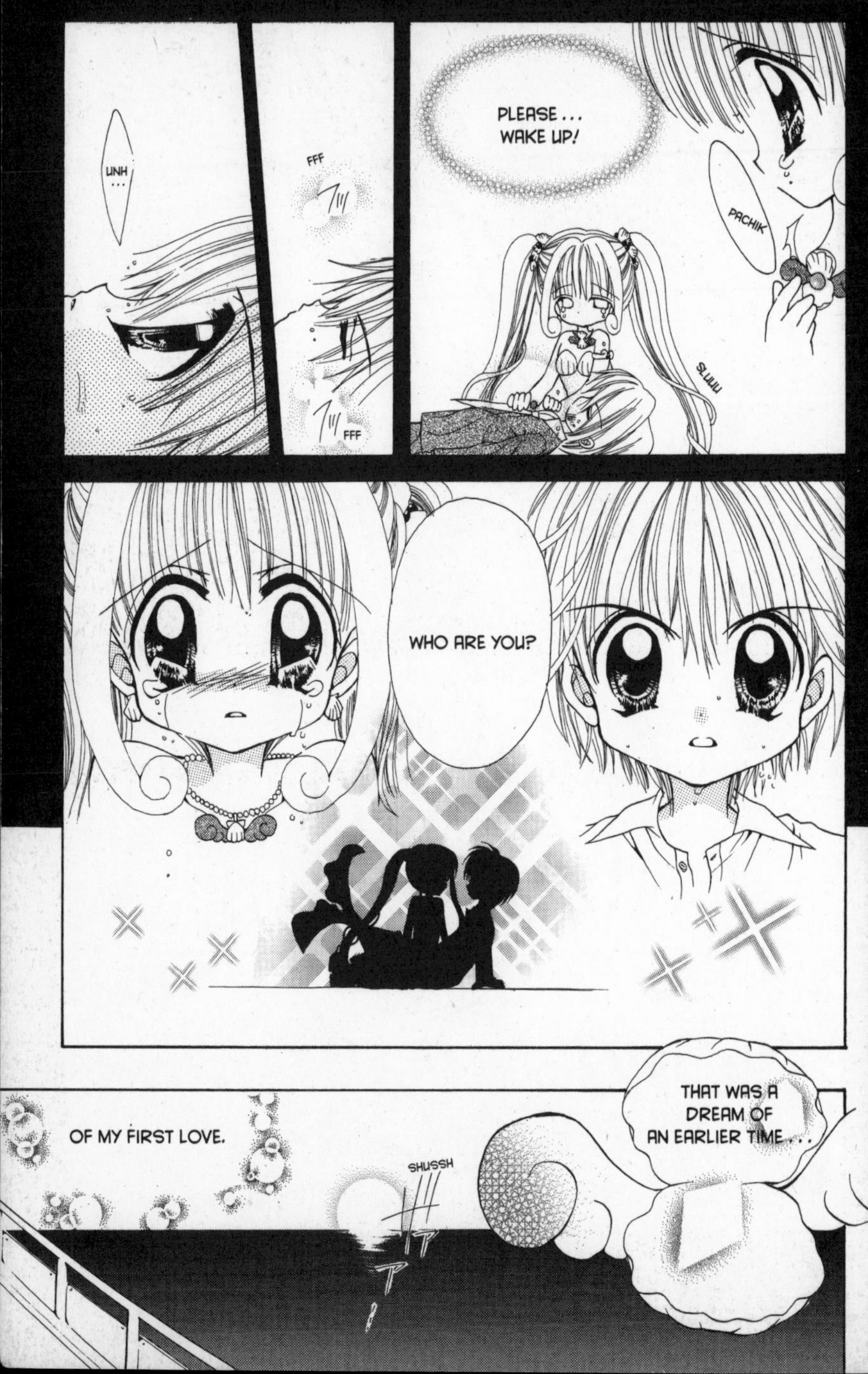
PLEASE... WAKE UP!
PACHIK
SLUUU
FFF
FFF
UNH...
WHO ARE YOU?
THAT WAS A DREAM OF AN EARLIER TIME...
SHUSSH
OF MY FIRST LOVE.

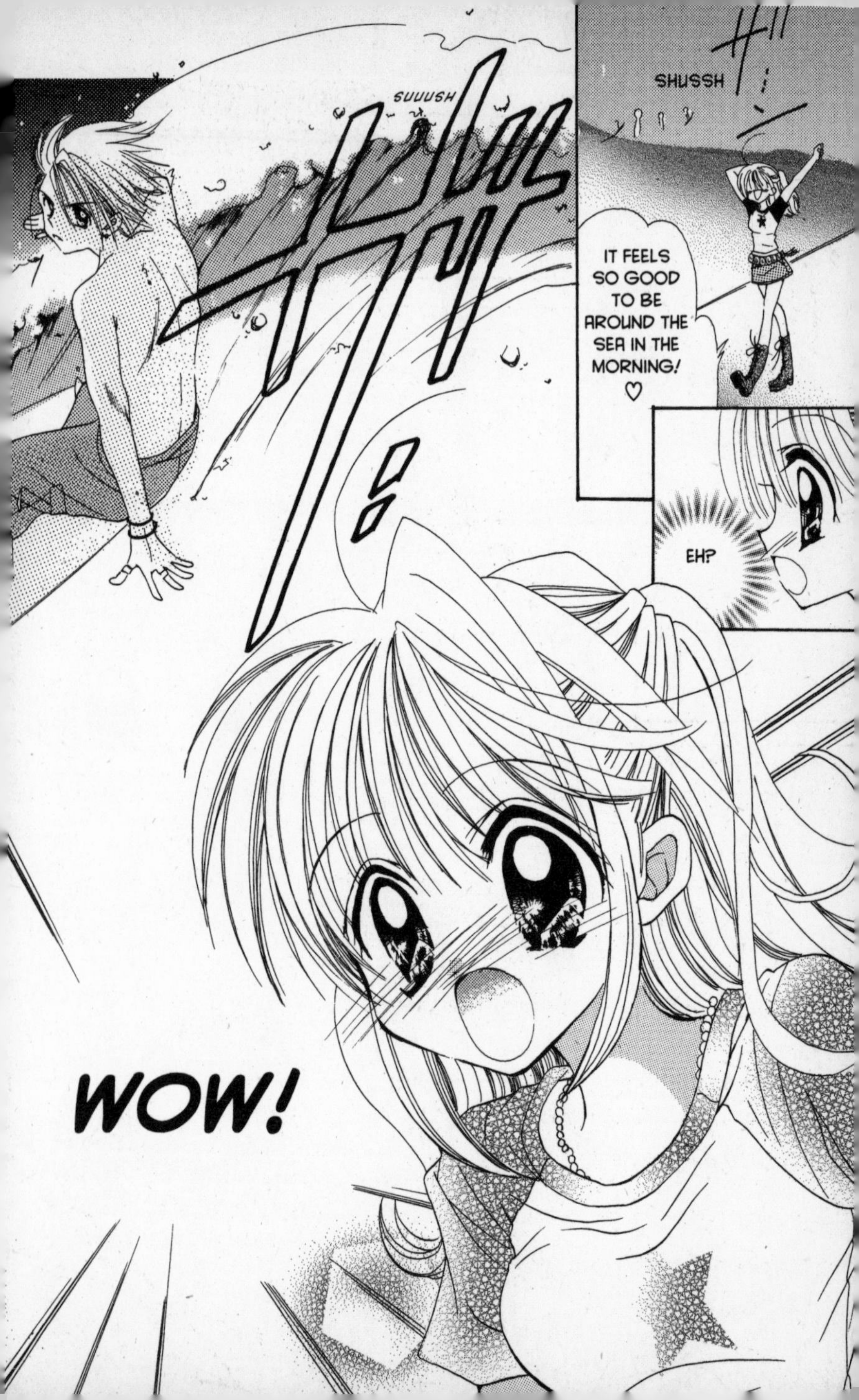
SHUSSH
IT FEELS SO GOOD TO BE AROUND THE SEA IN THE MORNING! ♡
EH?
SUUUSH
WOW!

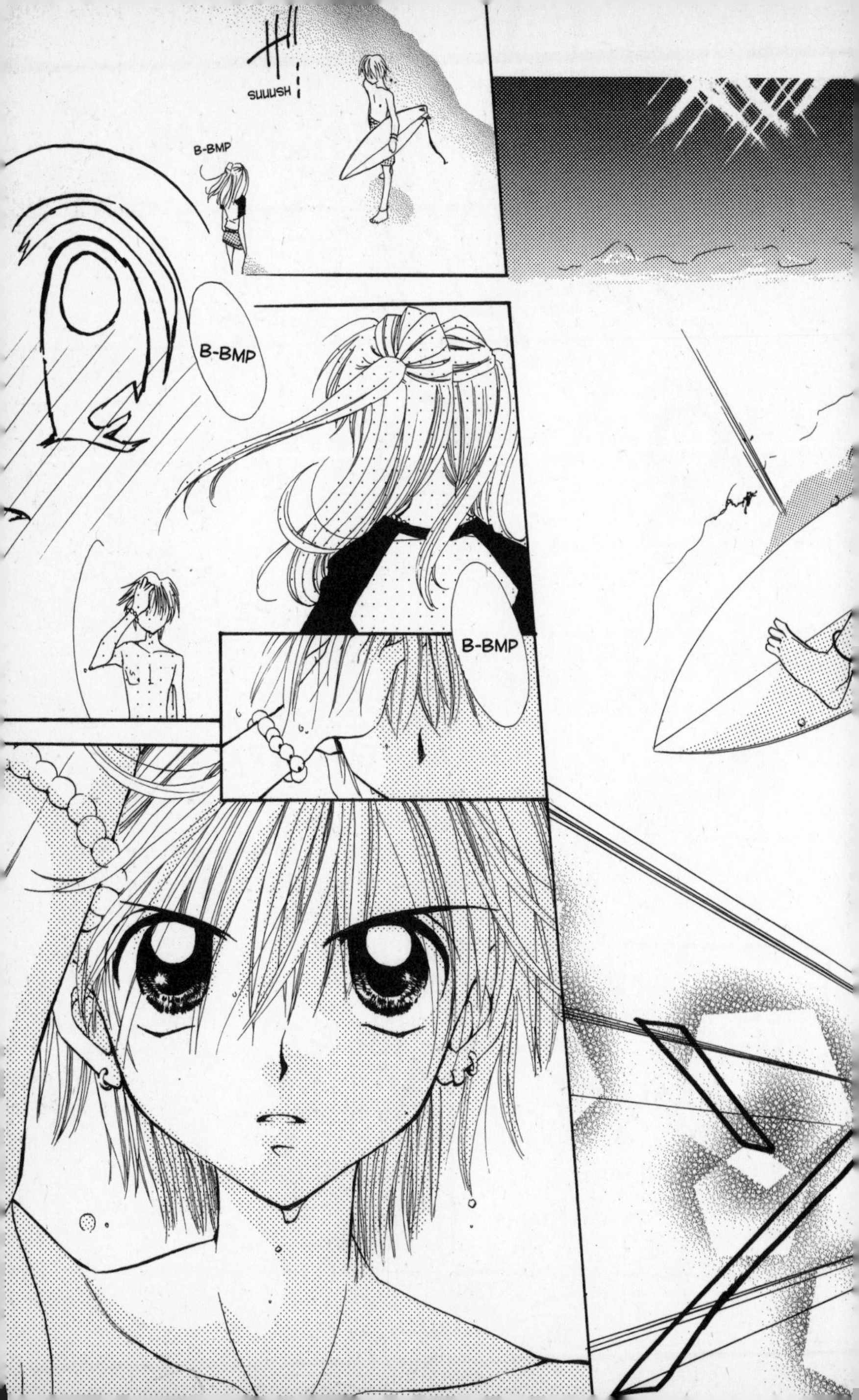
SUUUSH
B-BMP
B-BMP
B-BMP

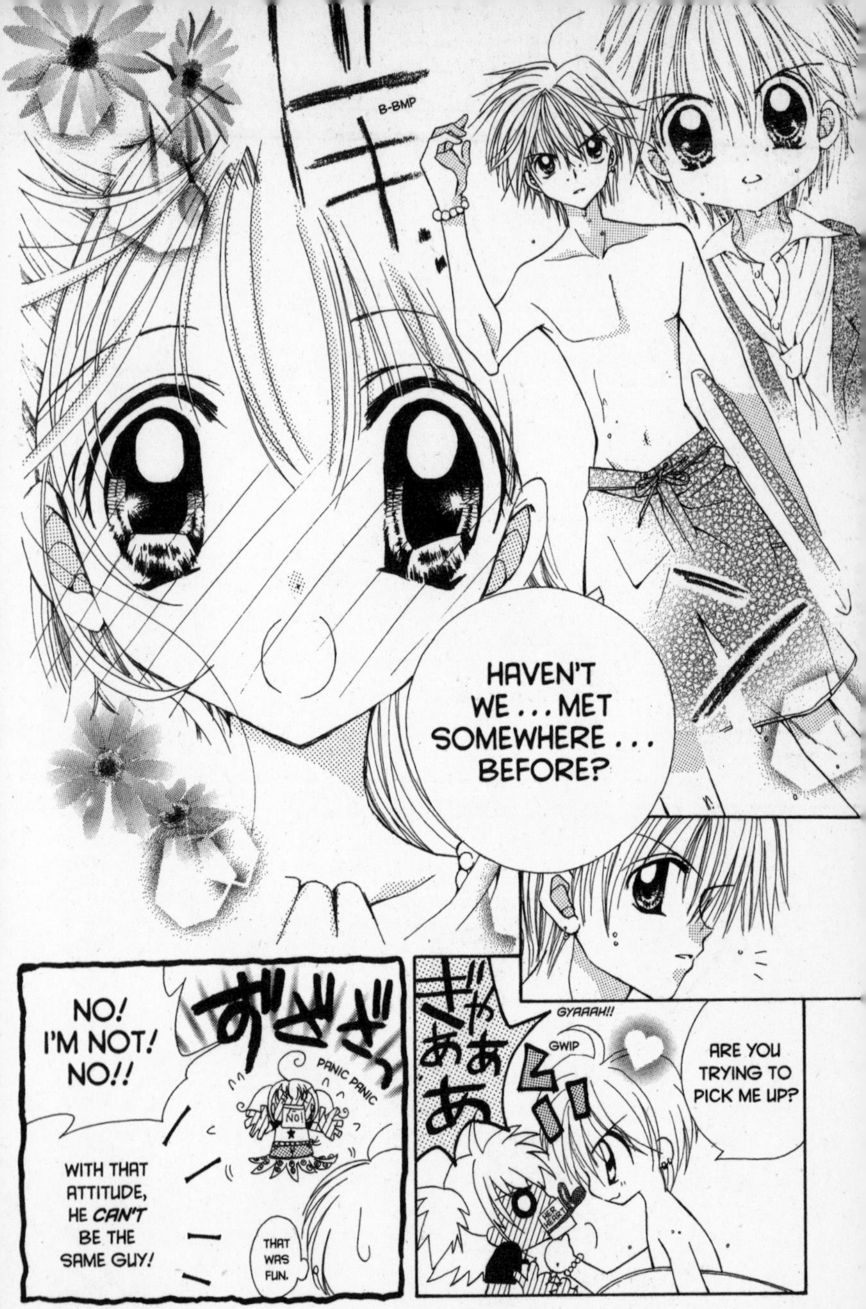
B-BMP
HAVEN'T WE . . . MET SOMEWHERE . . . BEFORE?
ぎゃあああ
GYAAAAH!!
GWIP
ARE YOU TRYING TO PICK ME UP?
HER HEART
NO! I'M NOT! NO!!
PANIC PANIC
NO!
WITH THAT ATTITUDE, HE *CAN'T* BE THE SAME GUY!
THAT WAS FUN.

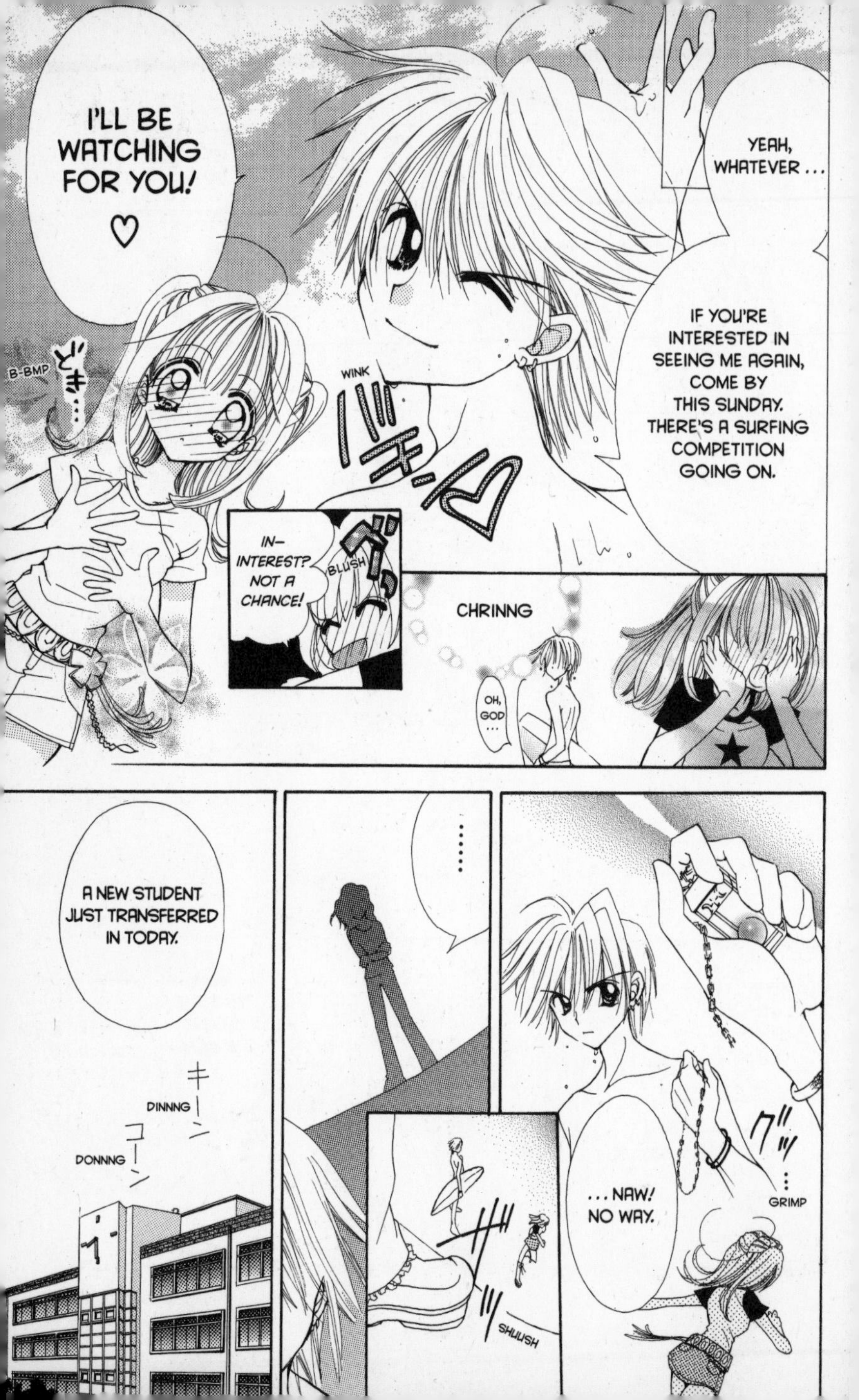
YEAH, WHATEVER . . .
IF YOU'RE INTERESTED IN SEEING ME AGAIN, COME BY THIS SUNDAY. THERE'S A SURFING COMPETITION GOING ON.
WINK
I'LL BE WATCHING FOR YOU! ♡
どき…
B-BMP
CHRINNG
OH, GOD . . .
IN– INTEREST? NOT A CHANCE!
BLUSH
GRIMP
. . . NAW! NO WAY.
SHUUSH
. . . . . .
A NEW STUDENT JUST TRANSFERRED IN TODAY.
キーン
DINNNG
コーン
DONNNG

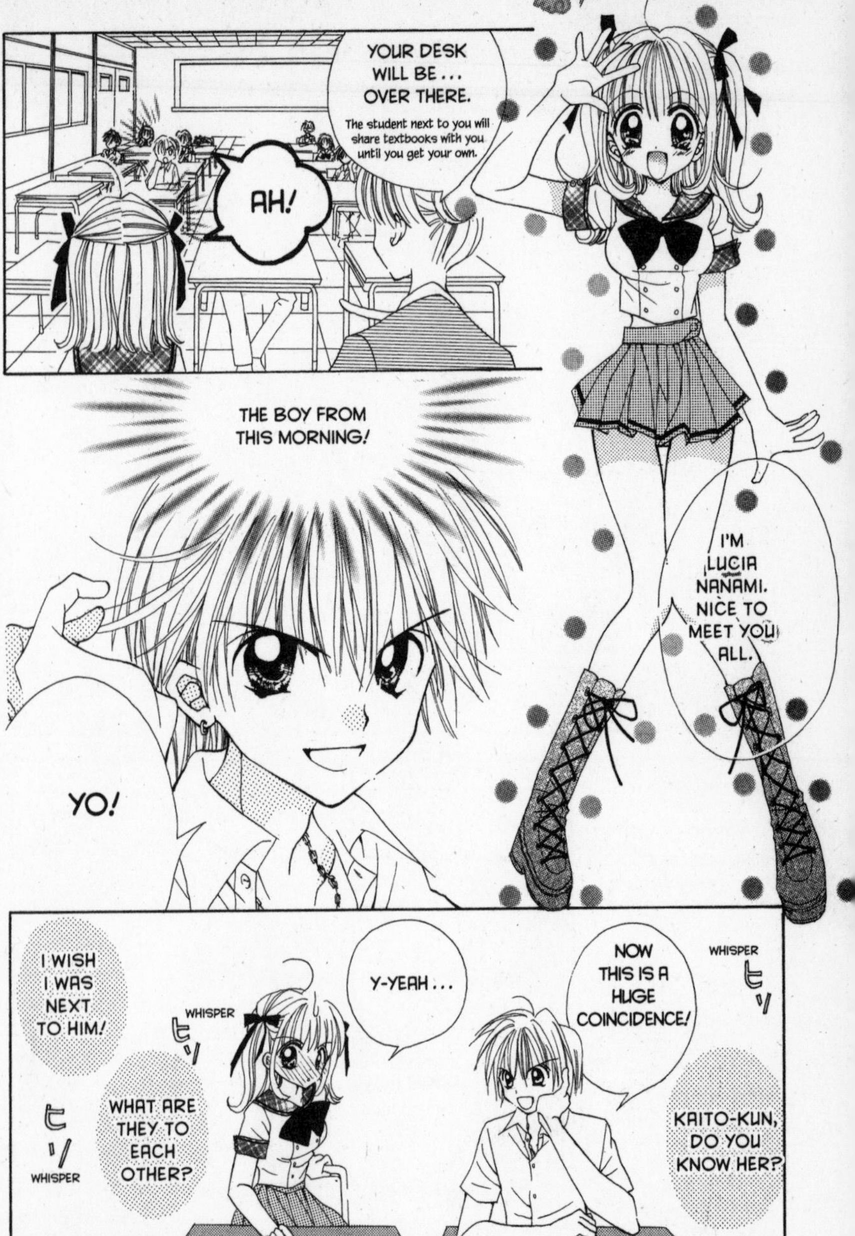
I'M LUCIA NANAMI. NICE TO MEET YOU ALL.
YOUR DESK WILL BE . . . OVER THERE.
The student next to you will share textbooks with you until you get your own.
AH!
THE BOY FROM THIS MORNING!
YO!
WHISPER ヒソ
NOW THIS IS A HUGE COINCIDENCE!
KAITO-KUN, DO YOU KNOW HER?
Y-YEAH . . .
WHISPER ヒソ
WHAT ARE THEY TO EACH OTHER?
I WISH I WAS NEXT TO HIM!
ヒソ WHISPER

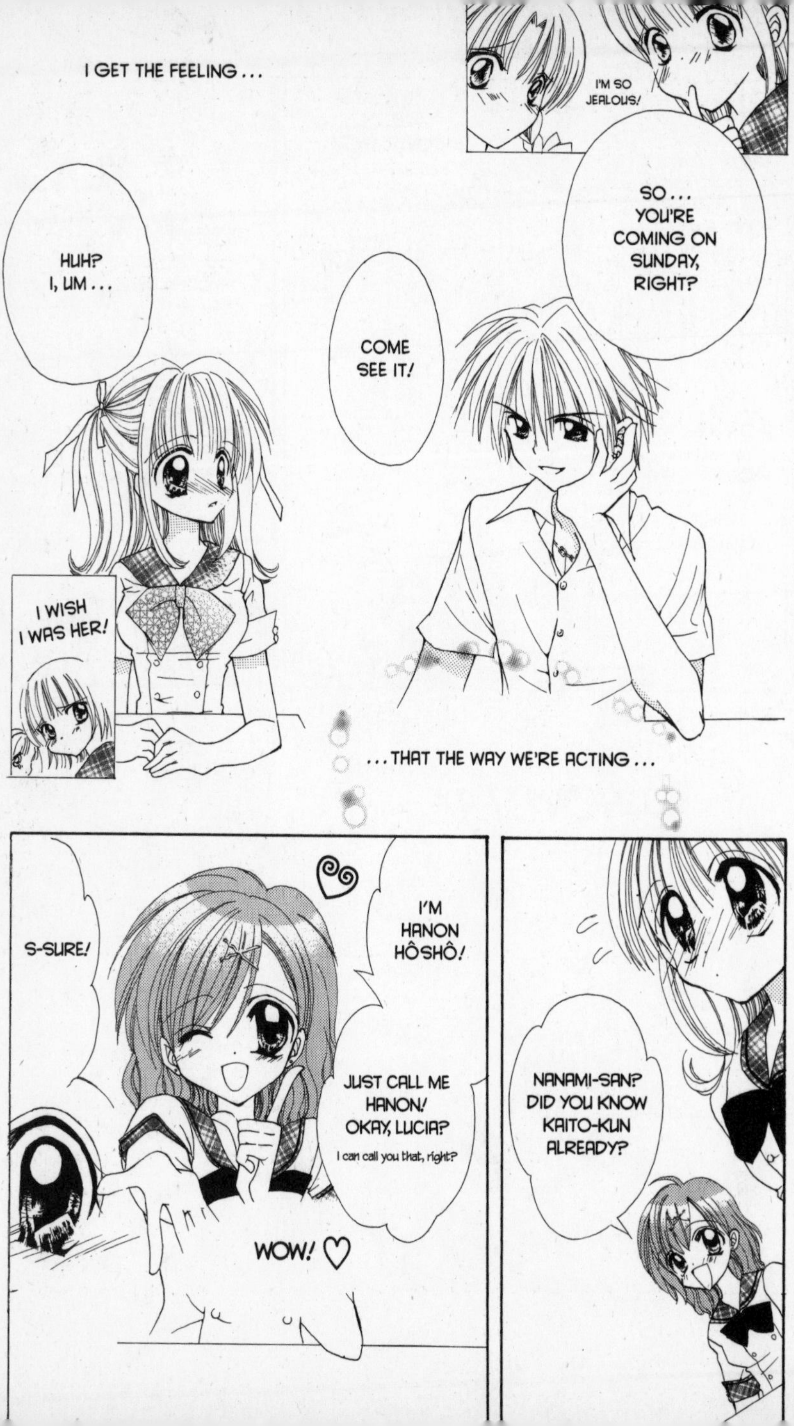

I'M SO JEALOUS!
SO... YOU'RE COMING ON SUNDAY, RIGHT?
COME SEE IT!
I GET THE FEELING...
HUH? I, UM...
I WISH I WAS HER!
...THAT THE WAY WE'RE ACTING...
NANAMI-SAN? DID YOU KNOW KAITO-KUN ALREADY?
I'M HANON HÔSHÔ!
JUST CALL ME HANON! OKAY, LUCIA?
I can call you that, right?
S-SURE!
WOW! ♡

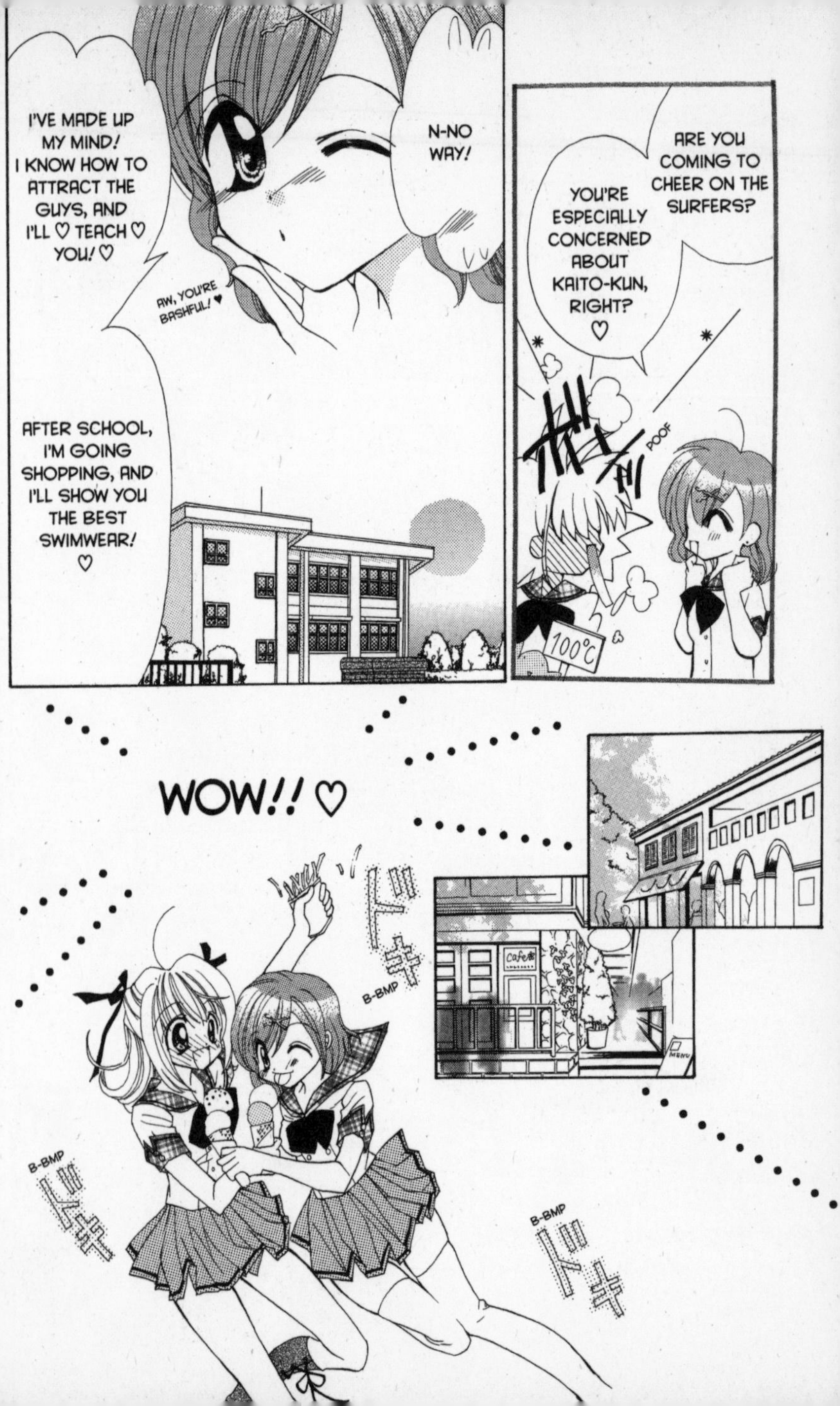
ARE YOU COMING TO CHEER ON THE SURFERS?
YOU'RE ESPECIALLY CONCERNED ABOUT KAITO-KUN, RIGHT? ♡
POOF
100°C
N-NO WAY!
I'VE MADE UP MY MIND! I KNOW HOW TO ATTRACT THE GUYS, AND I'LL ♡ TEACH ♡ YOU! ♡
AW, YOU'RE BASHFUL! ♥
AFTER SCHOOL, I'M GOING SHOPPING, AND I'LL SHOW YOU THE BEST SWIMWEAR! ♡
Cafe
MENU
WOW!! ♡
B-BMP
B-BMP
B-BMP

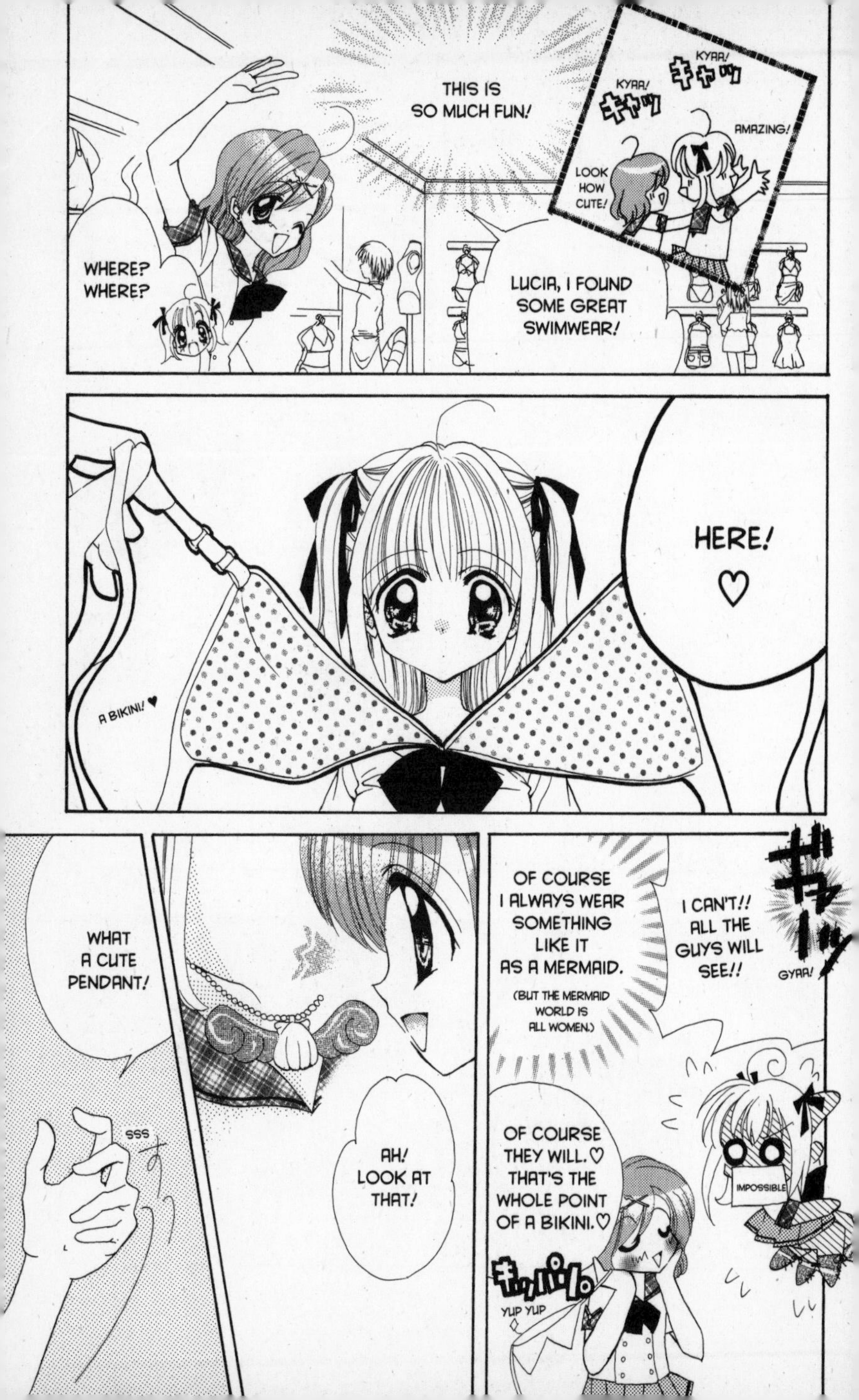
KYAA!
キャッ
KYAA!
キャッ
AMAZING!
LOOK HOW CUTE!
THIS IS SO MUCH FUN!
LUCIA, I FOUND SOME GREAT SWIMWEAR!
WHERE? WHERE?
HERE! ♡
A BIKINI! ♥
GYAA!
I CAN'T!! ALL THE GUYS WILL SEE!!
OF COURSE I ALWAYS WEAR SOMETHING LIKE IT AS A MERMAID.
(BUT THE MERMAID WORLD IS ALL WOMEN.)
IMPOSSIBLE
OF COURSE THEY WILL.♡ THAT'S THE WHOLE POINT OF A BIKINI.♡
YUP YUP
AH! LOOK AT THAT!
WHAT A CUTE PENDANT!
SSS

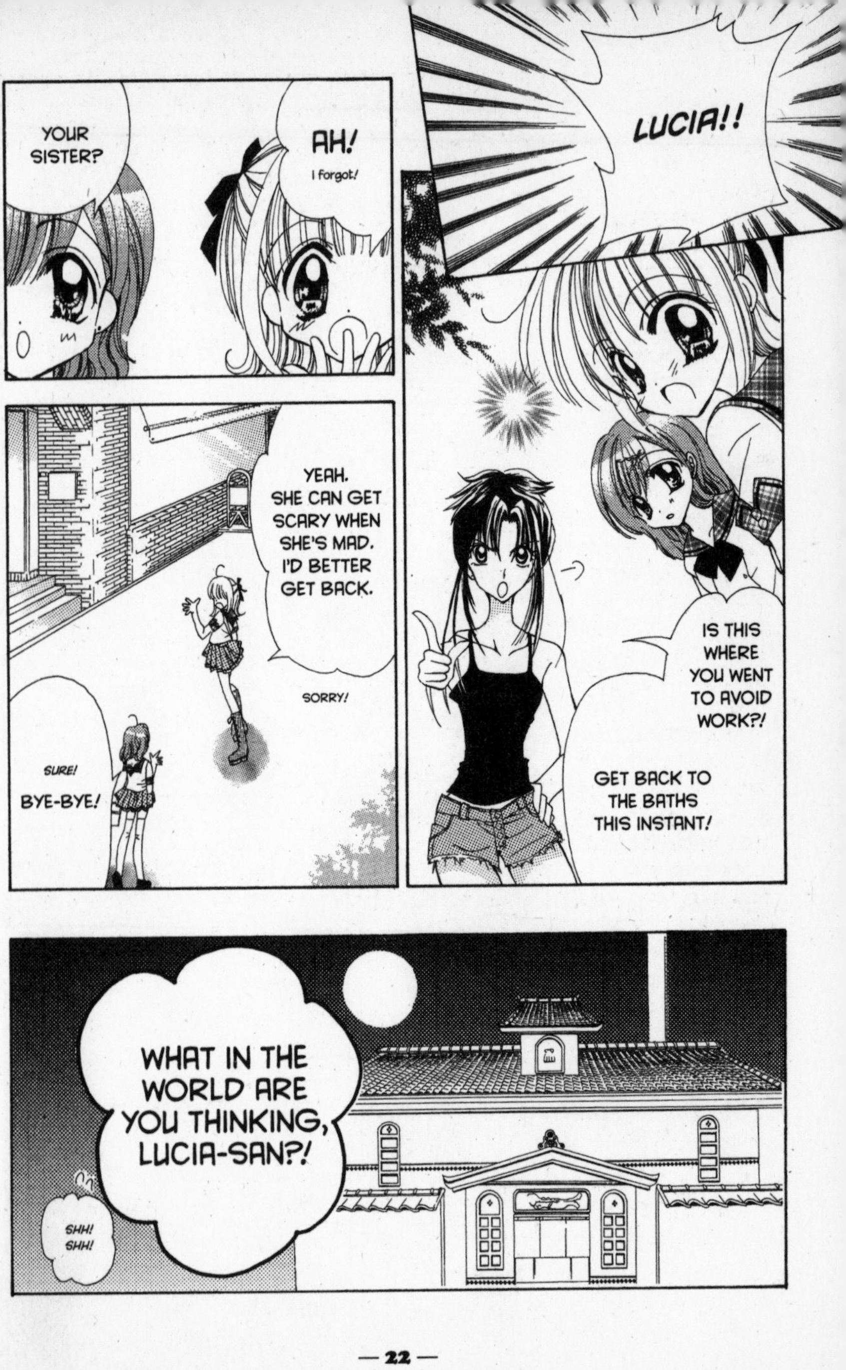
LUCIA!!
IS THIS WHERE YOU WENT TO AVOID WORK?!
GET BACK TO THE BATHS THIS INSTANT!
AH!
I forgot!
YOUR SISTER?
YEAH. SHE CAN GET SCARY WHEN SHE'S MAD. I'D BETTER GET BACK.
SORRY!
SURE!
BYE-BYE!
WHAT IN THE WORLD ARE YOU THINKING, LUCIA-SAN?!
SHH! SHH!

♣ ABOUT PICHI . . .
WHEN I TALK ABOUT "MERMAID MELODY, PICHI PICHI PITCH," I JUST CALL IT "PICHI." SO WATCH OUT FOR THAT IN THE FUTURE.

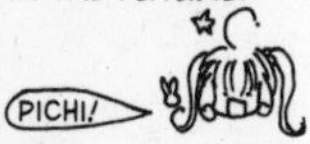
PICHI!

♣ HMM... I WONDER WHAT I SHOULD TALK ABOUT FIRST... THERE'S JUST SO MUCH TO SAY! PICHI IS MY FIRST CONTINUING STORY AND THE FIRST JOB I HAD WHERE I WORK FROM YOKOTE-SHI'S SCENARIO. AND IT'S THE FIRST TIME I'VE WORKED WITH SO MANY EDITORS. (UP TO NOW, IT'S ALWAYS BEEN ONE PERSON, BUT NOW IT'S THREE!!) AND THERE'S EVEN TALK OF TURNING IT INTO AN ANIME! BUT IT STILL DOESN'T FEEL REAL YET . . . IT'S ALL TOO MUCH! EEEE! ANYWAY, THESE ARE ALL FIRSTS FOR ME!

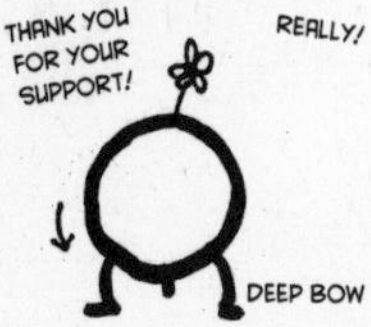
THANK YOU FOR YOUR SUPPORT!
REALLY!
DEEP BOW

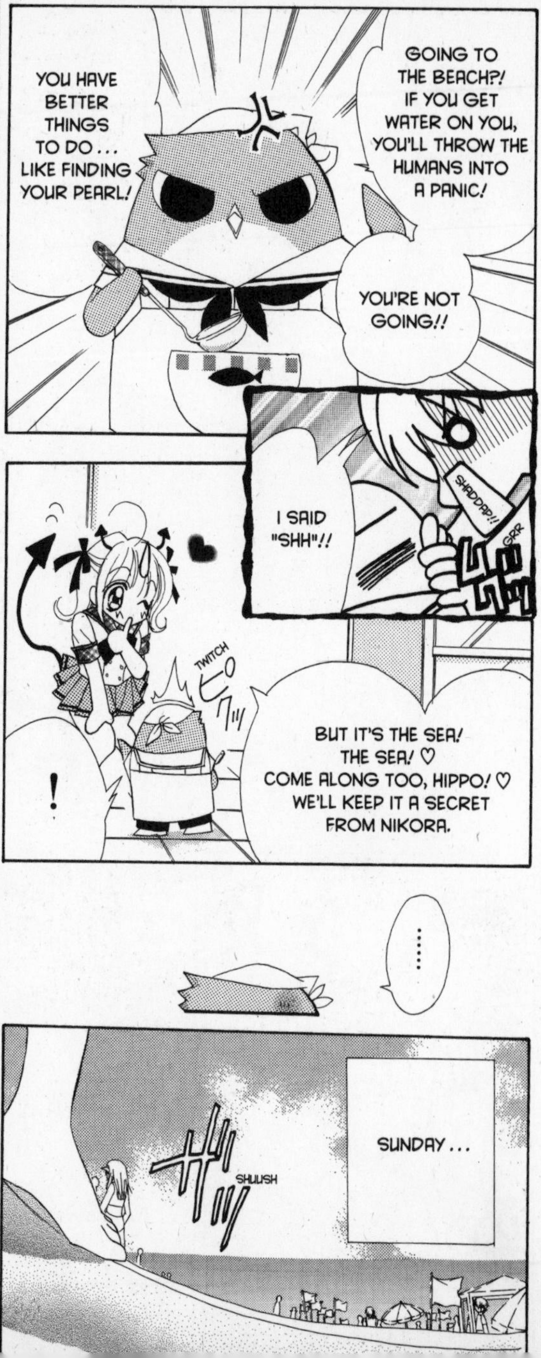
GOING TO THE BEACH?! IF YOU GET WATER ON YOU, YOU'LL THROW THE HUMANS INTO A PANIC!
YOU HAVE BETTER THINGS TO DO . . . LIKE FINDING YOUR PEARL!
YOU'RE NOT GOING!!
SHADDAP!!
GRR
I SAID "SHH"!!
TWITCH
BUT IT'S THE SEA! THE SEA! ♡ COME ALONG TOO, HIPPO! ♡ WE'LL KEEP IT A SECRET FROM NIKORA.
......
SUNDAY . . .
SHUUSH

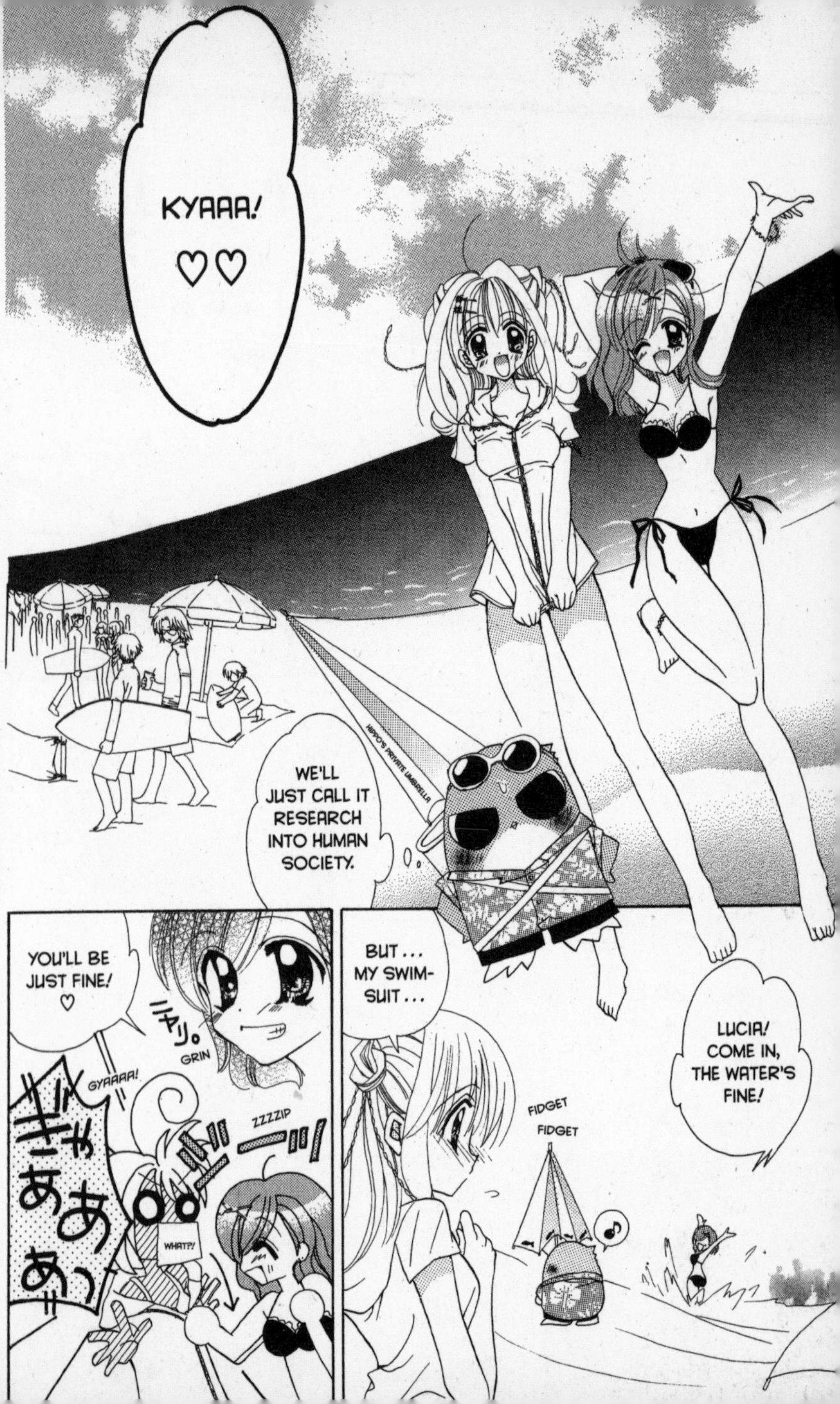
KYAAA! ♡♡
HIPPO'S PRIVATE UMBRELLA
WE'LL JUST CALL IT RESEARCH INTO HUMAN SOCIETY.
LUCIA! COME IN, THE WATER'S FINE!
FIDGET FIDGET
BUT... MY SWIM-SUIT...
YOU'LL BE JUST FINE! ♡
ニヤリ。
GRIN
ZZZZIP
ぎゃあああっ
GYAAAA!
WHAT?!

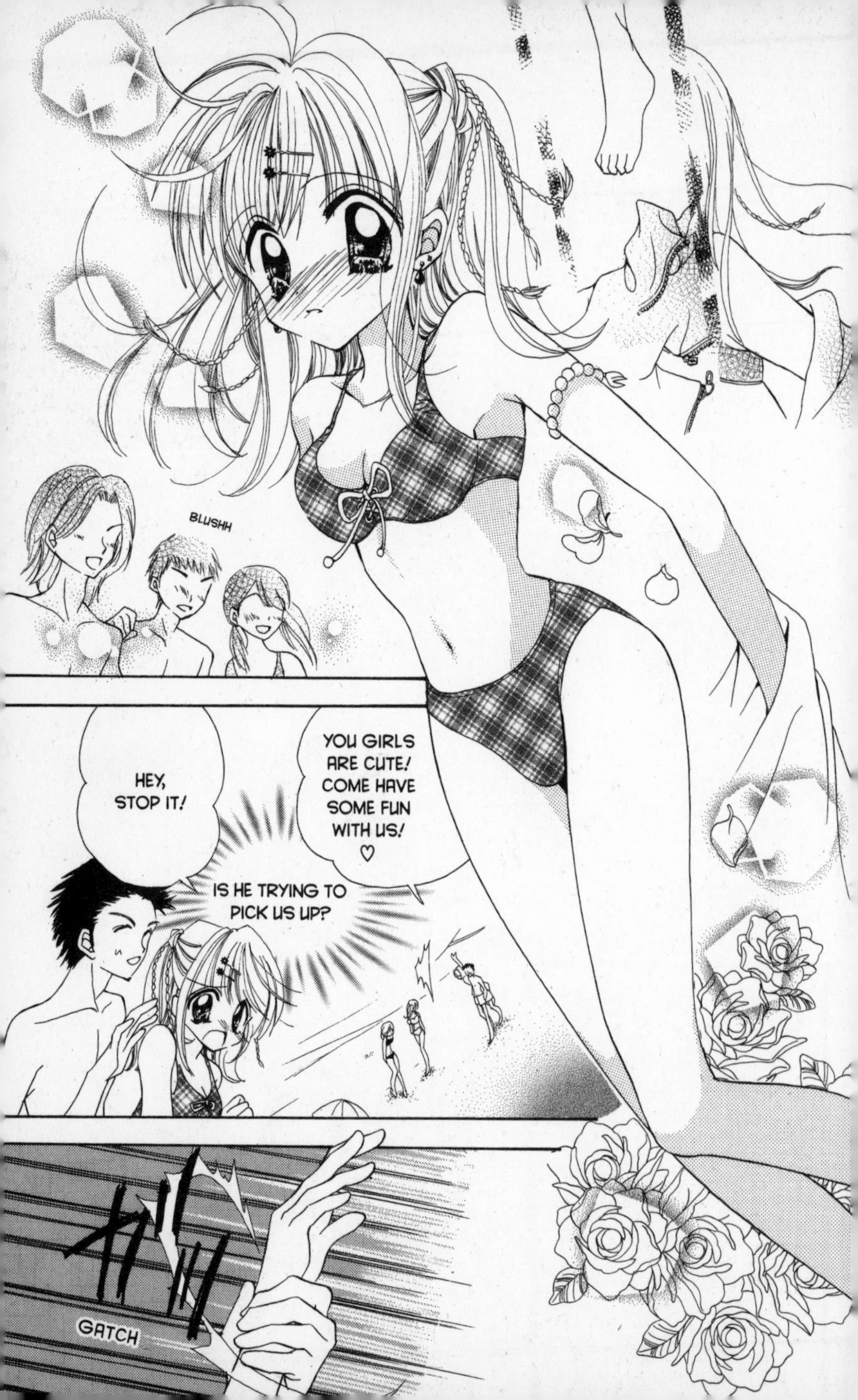
BLUSHH
YOU GIRLS ARE CUTE! COME HAVE SOME FUN WITH US! ♡
HEY, STOP IT!
IS HE TRYING TO PICK US UP?
GATCH

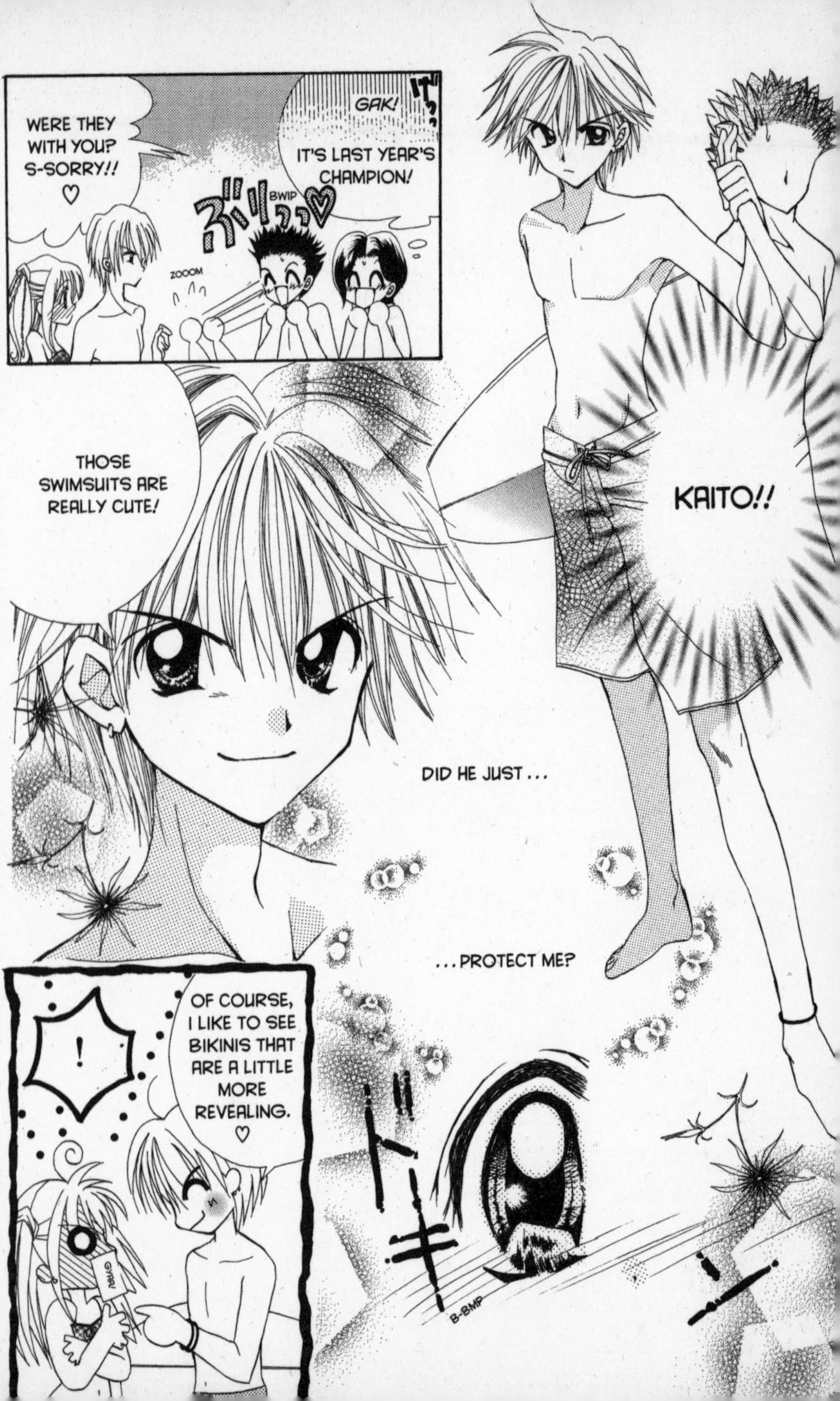
KAITO!!
GAK!
IT'S LAST YEAR'S CHAMPION!
BWIP
WERE THEY WITH YOU? S-SORRY!! ♡
ZOOOM
THOSE SWIMSUITS ARE REALLY CUTE!
DID HE JUST...
...PROTECT ME?
B-BMP
OF COURSE, I LIKE TO SEE BIKINIS THAT ARE A LITTLE MORE REVEALING. ♡
!

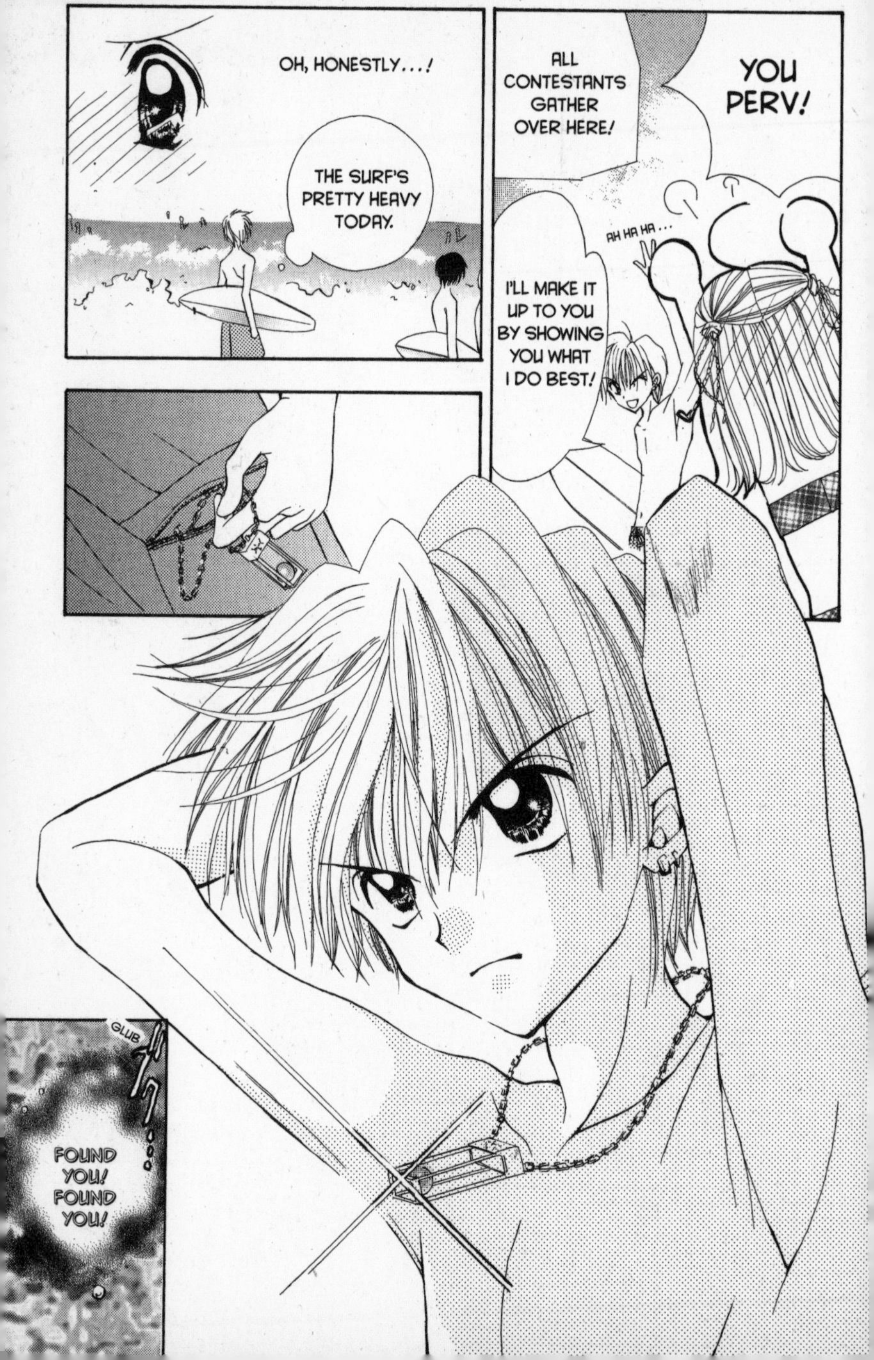
YOU PERV!
ALL CONTESTANTS GATHER OVER HERE!
AH HA HA...
I'LL MAKE IT UP TO YOU BY SHOWING YOU WHAT I DO BEST!
OH, HONESTLY...!
THE SURF'S PRETTY HEAVY TODAY.
GLUB
FOUND YOU! FOUND YOU!

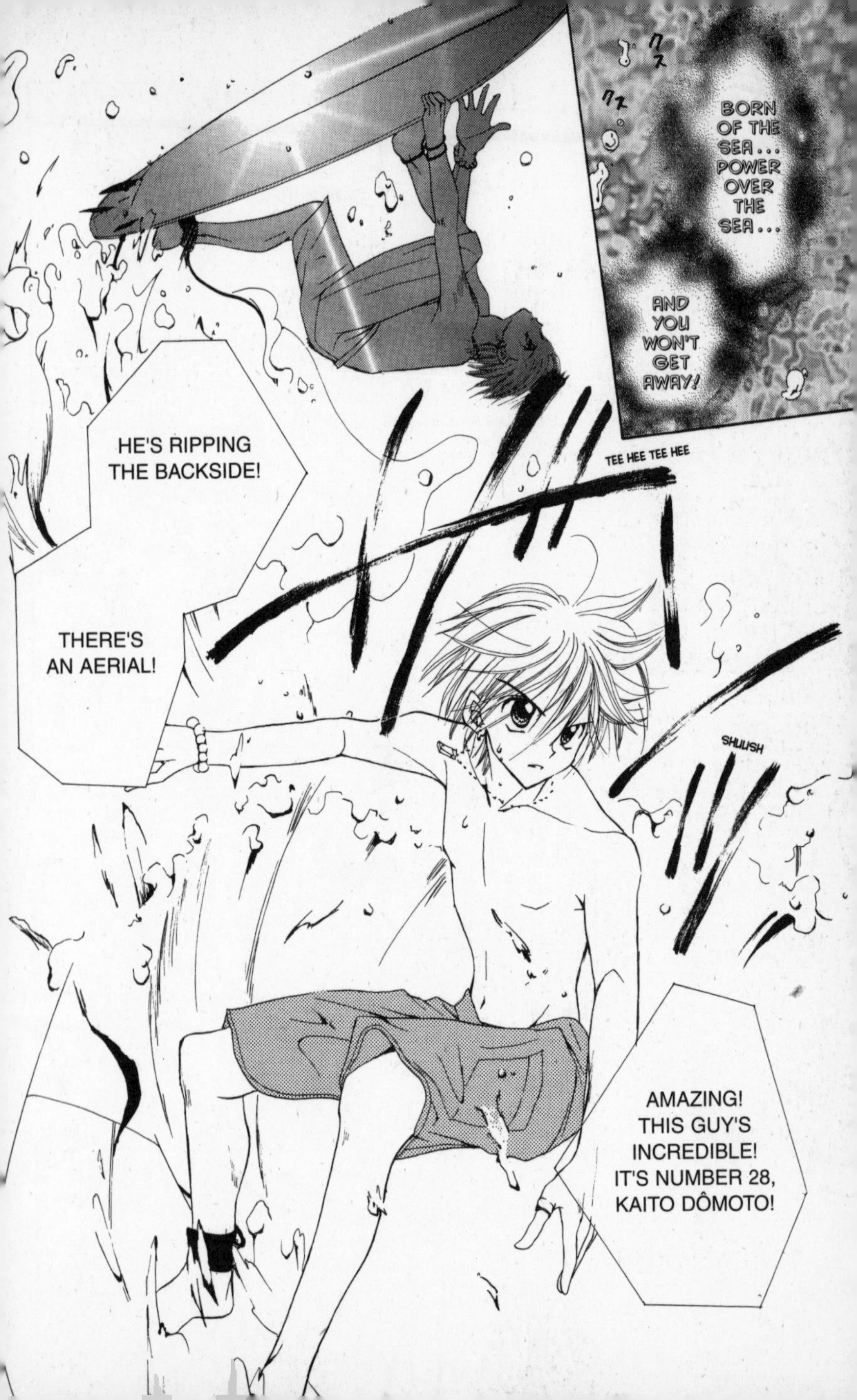
BORN OF THE SEA... POWER OVER THE SEA...
AND YOU WON'T GET AWAY!
TEE HEE TEE HEE
HE'S RIPPING THE BACKSIDE!
THERE'S AN AERIAL!
SHUUSH
AMAZING! THIS GUY'S INCREDIBLE! IT'S NUMBER 28, KAITO DÔMOTO!

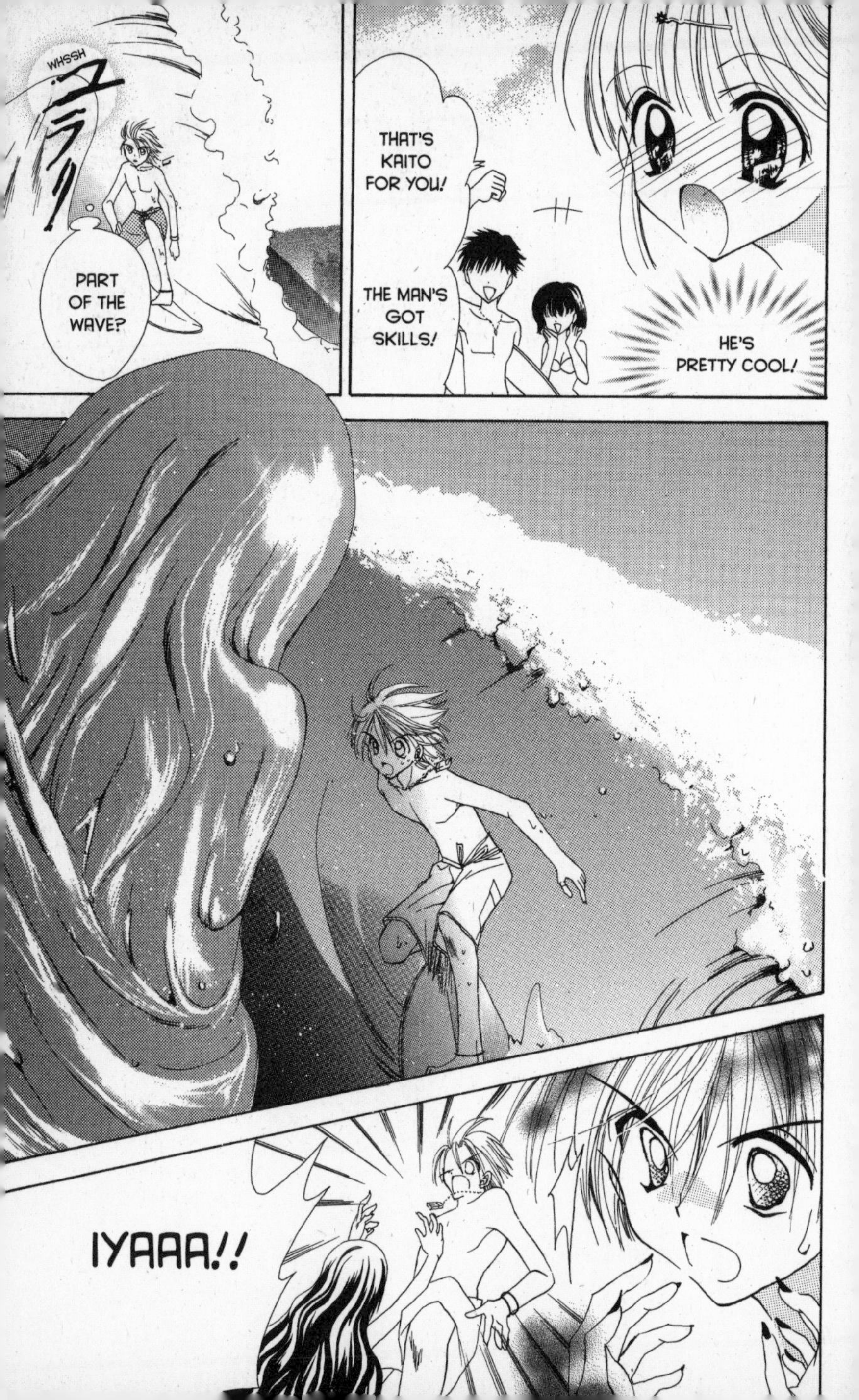
THAT'S KAITO FOR YOU!
HE'S PRETTY COOL!
THE MAN'S GOT SKILLS!
WHSSH
PART OF THE WAVE?
IYAAA!!

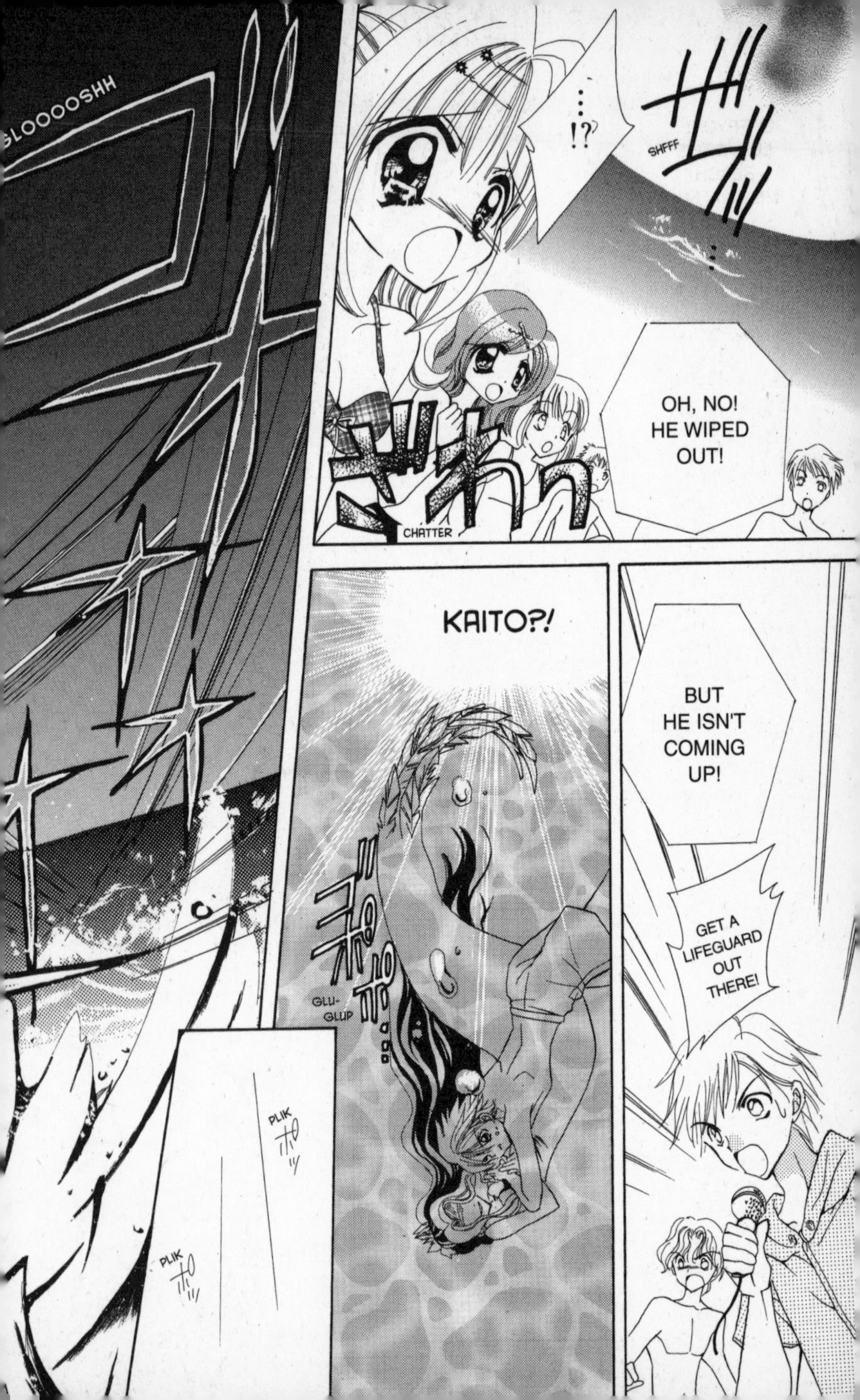
SHFFF
...!?
OH, NO! HE WIPED OUT!
CHATTER
BUT HE ISN'T COMING UP!
GET A LIFEGUARD OUT THERE!
KAITO?!
GLU-GLUP
GLOOOOSHH
PLIK
PLIK

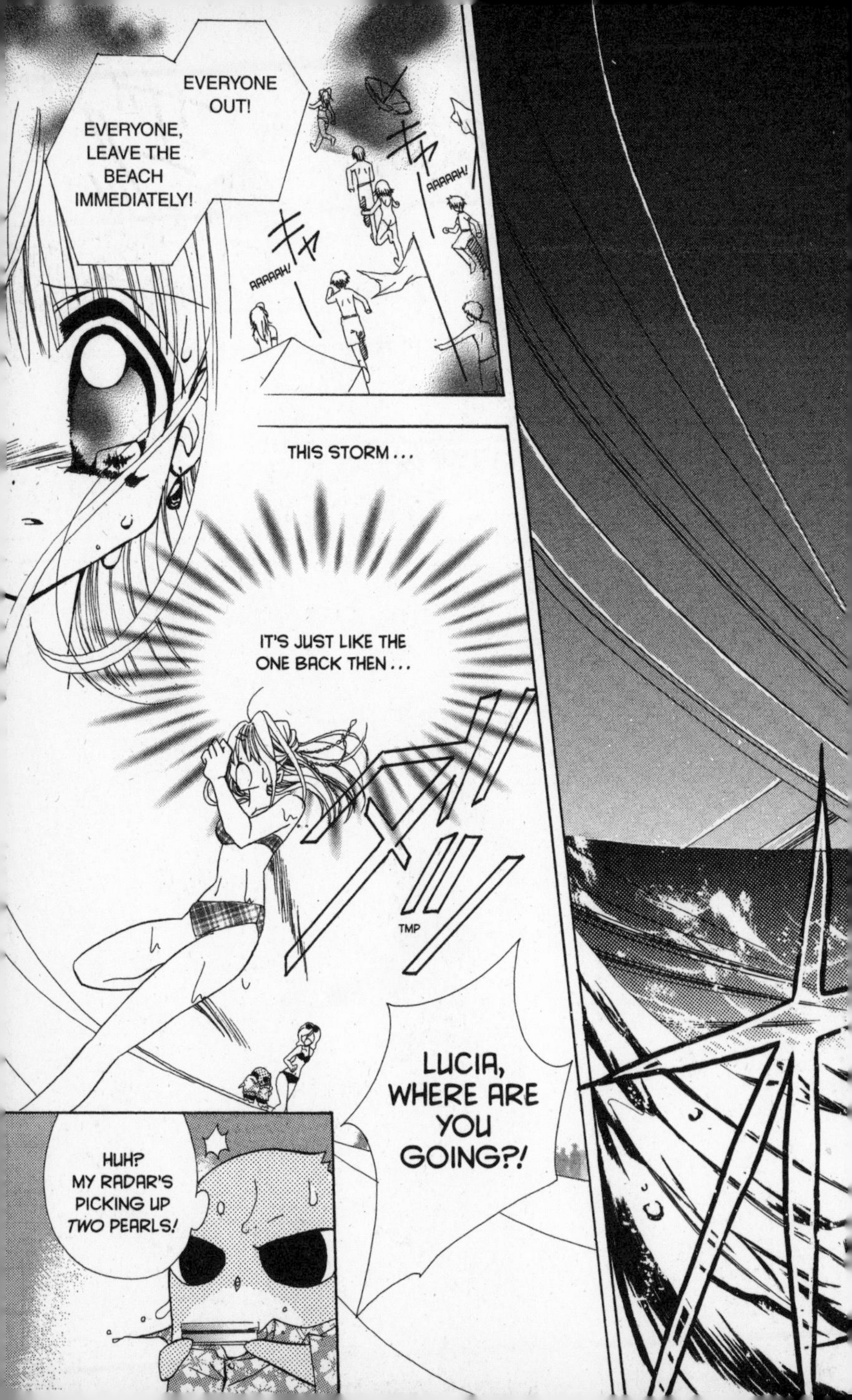

EVERYONE OUT!
EVERYONE, LEAVE THE BEACH IMMEDIATELY!
キャー
AAAAAH!
キャー
AAAAAH!
THIS STORM...
IT'S JUST LIKE THE ONE BACK THEN...
TMP
LUCIA, WHERE ARE YOU GOING?!
HUH? MY RADAR'S PICKING UP TWO PEARLS!

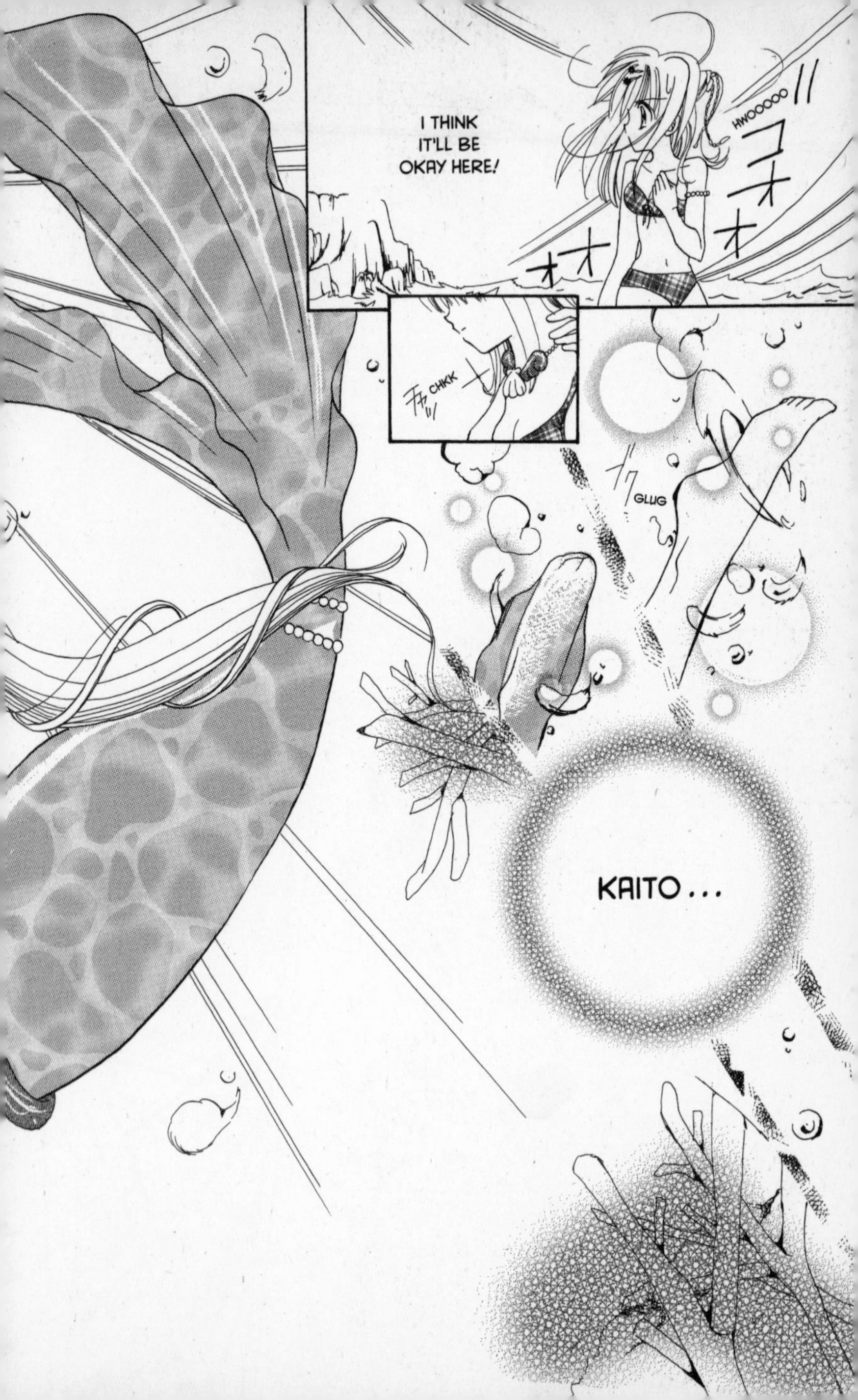
HWOOOOO
コオオオオ
I THINK IT'LL BE OKAY HERE!
CHKK
チャリ
ゴク
GLUG
KAITO . . .

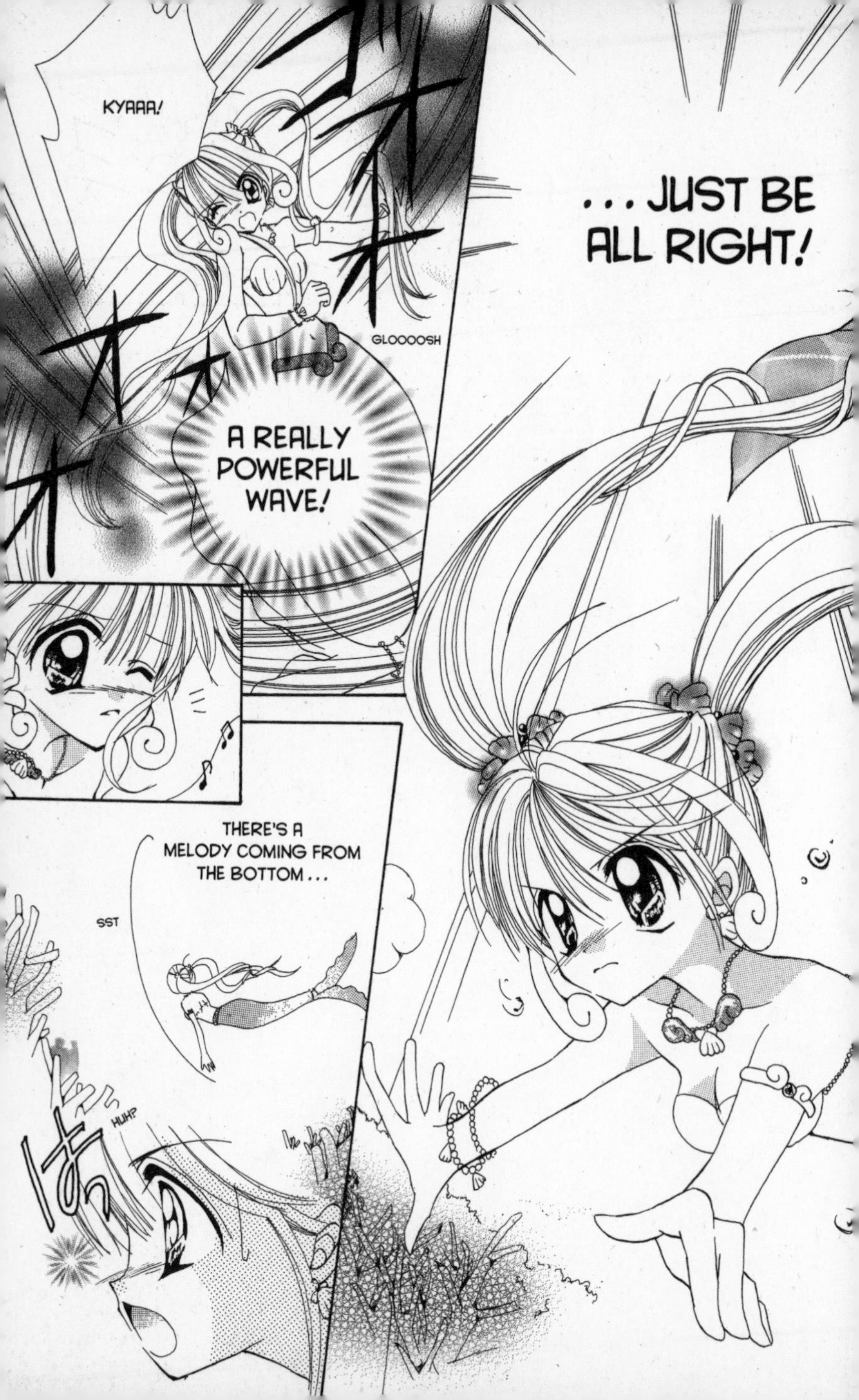

... JUST BE ALL RIGHT!
KYAAA!
GLOOOOSH
A REALLY POWERFUL WAVE!
THERE'S A MELODY COMING FROM THE BOTTOM ...
SST
HUH?

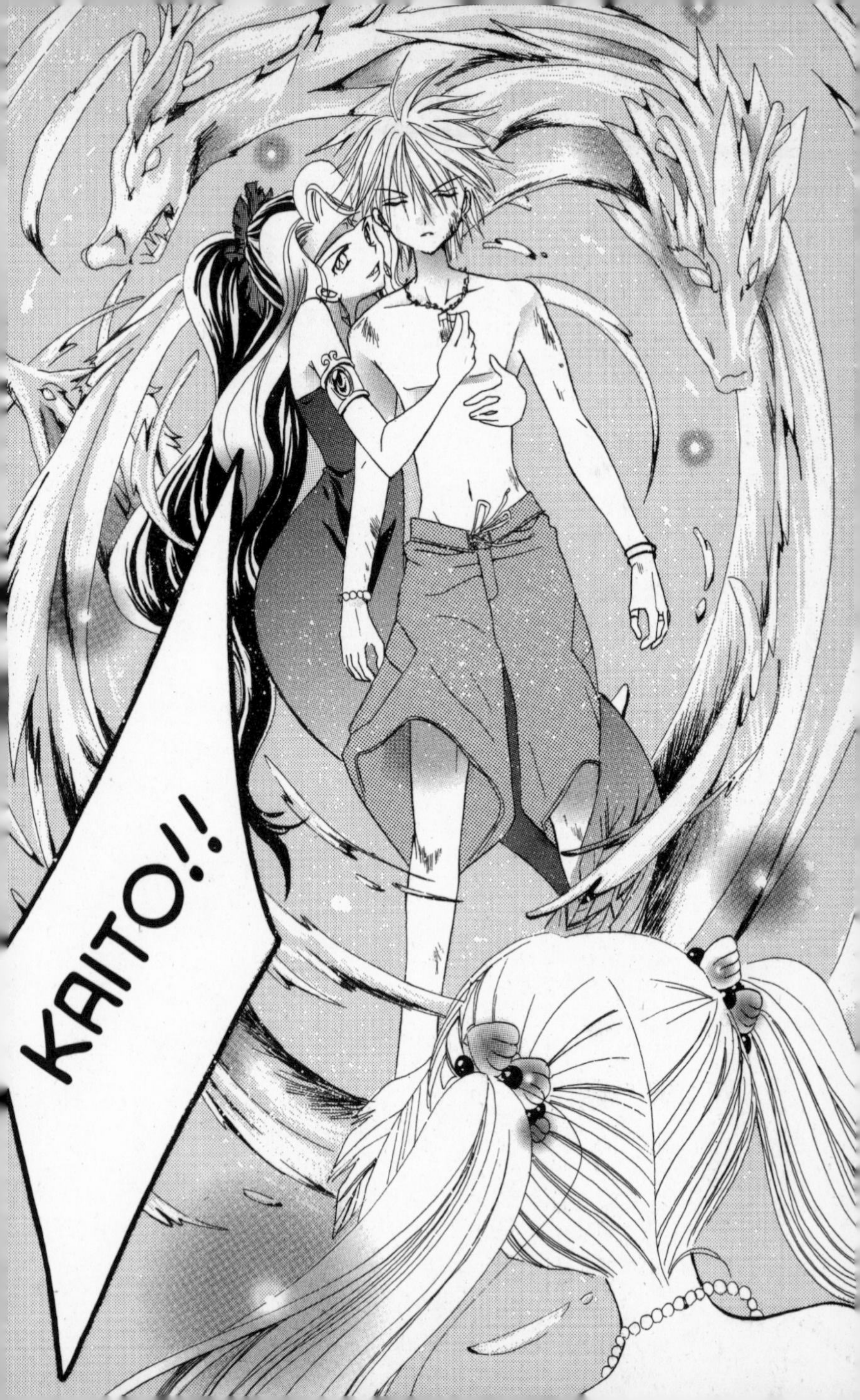
KAITO!!

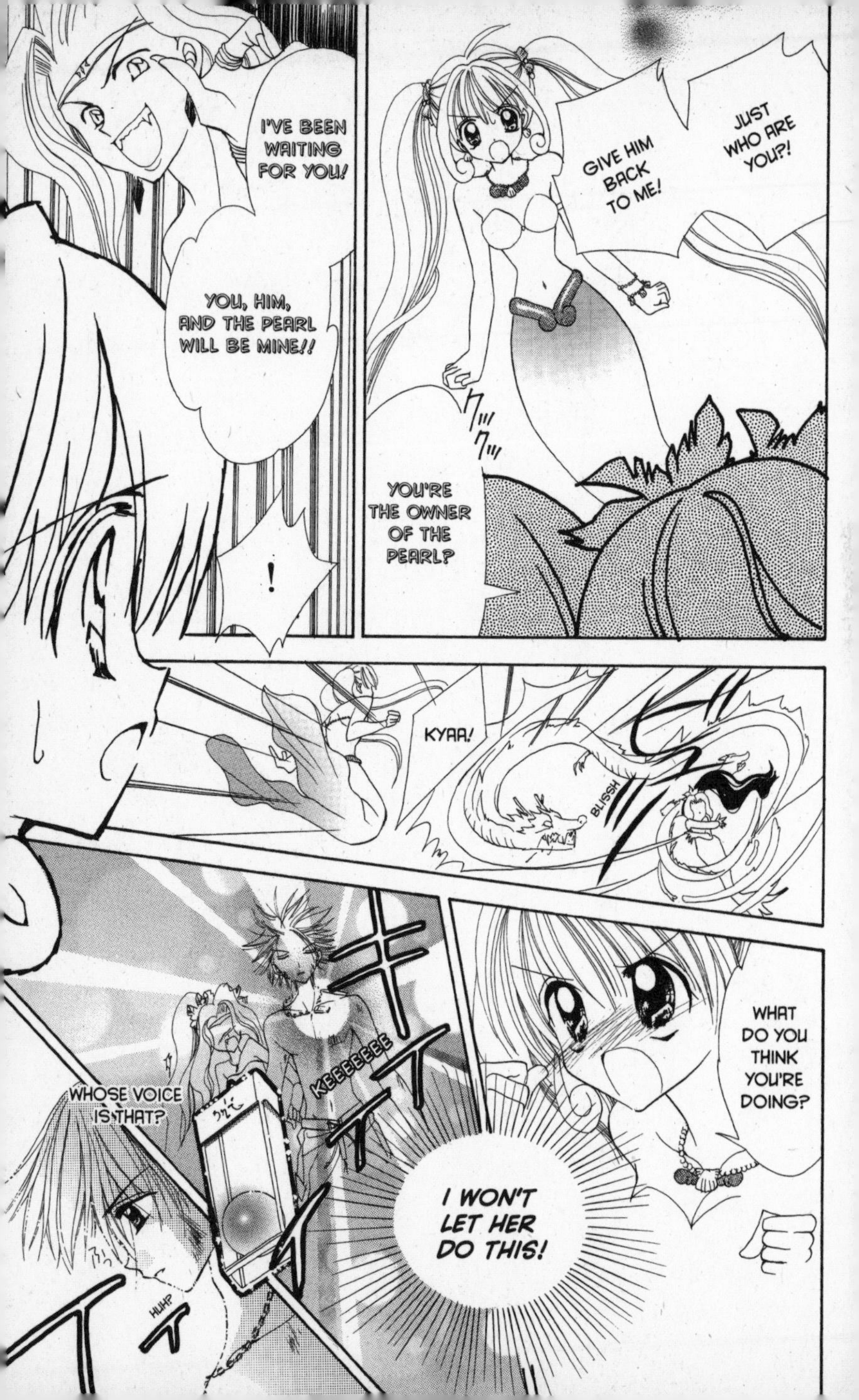
JUST WHO ARE YOU?!
GIVE HIM BACK TO ME!
YOU'RE THE OWNER OF THE PEARL?
I'VE BEEN WAITING FOR YOU!
YOU, HIM, AND THE PEARL WILL BE MINE!!
!
KYAA!
BLISSH
WHAT DO YOU THINK YOU'RE DOING?
KEEEEEEE
I WON'T LET HER DO THIS!
WHOSE VOICE IS THAT?
HUH?

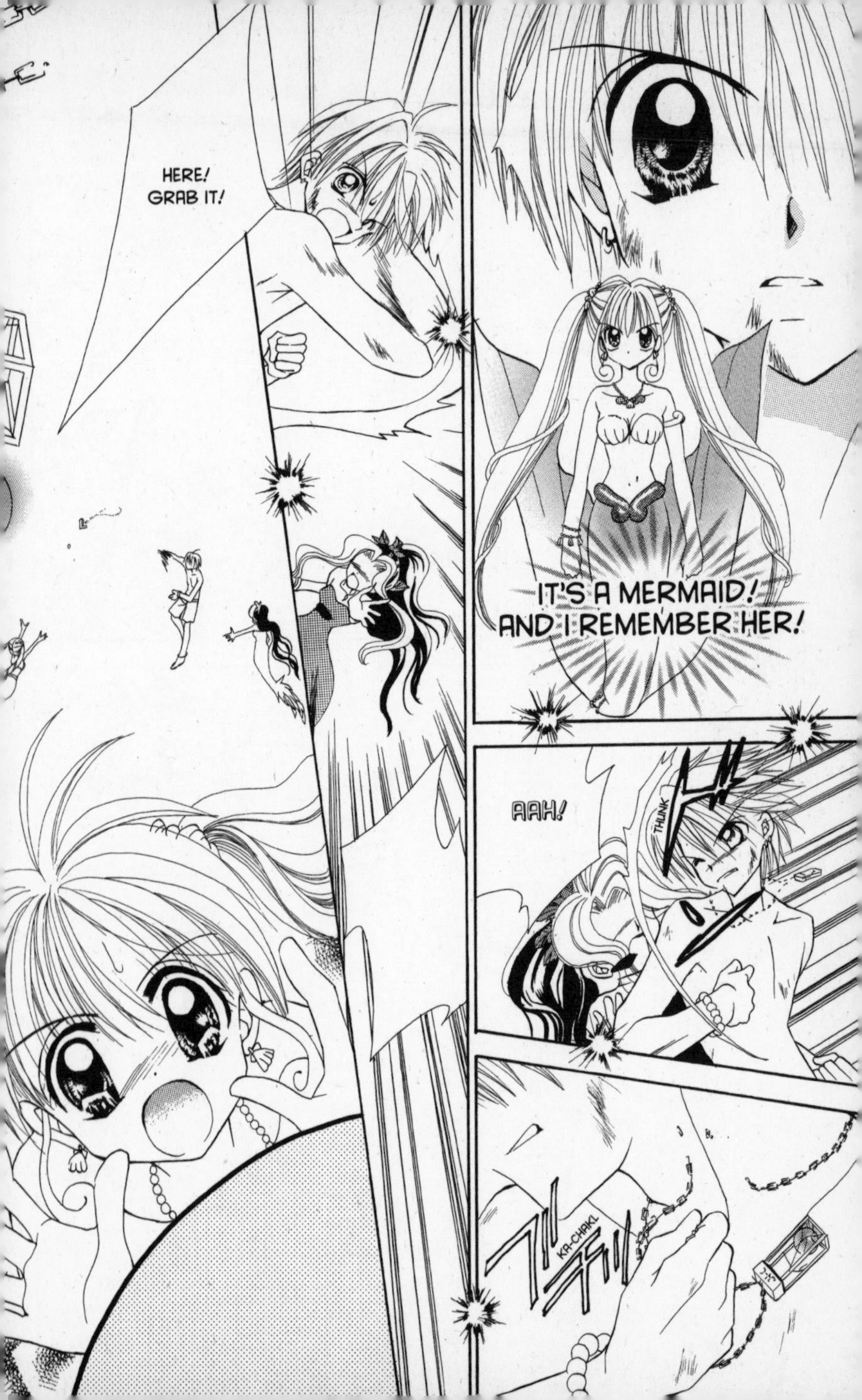
IT'S A MERMAID! AND I REMEMBER HER!
THUNK
AAH!
KA-CHAKL
HERE! GRAB IT!

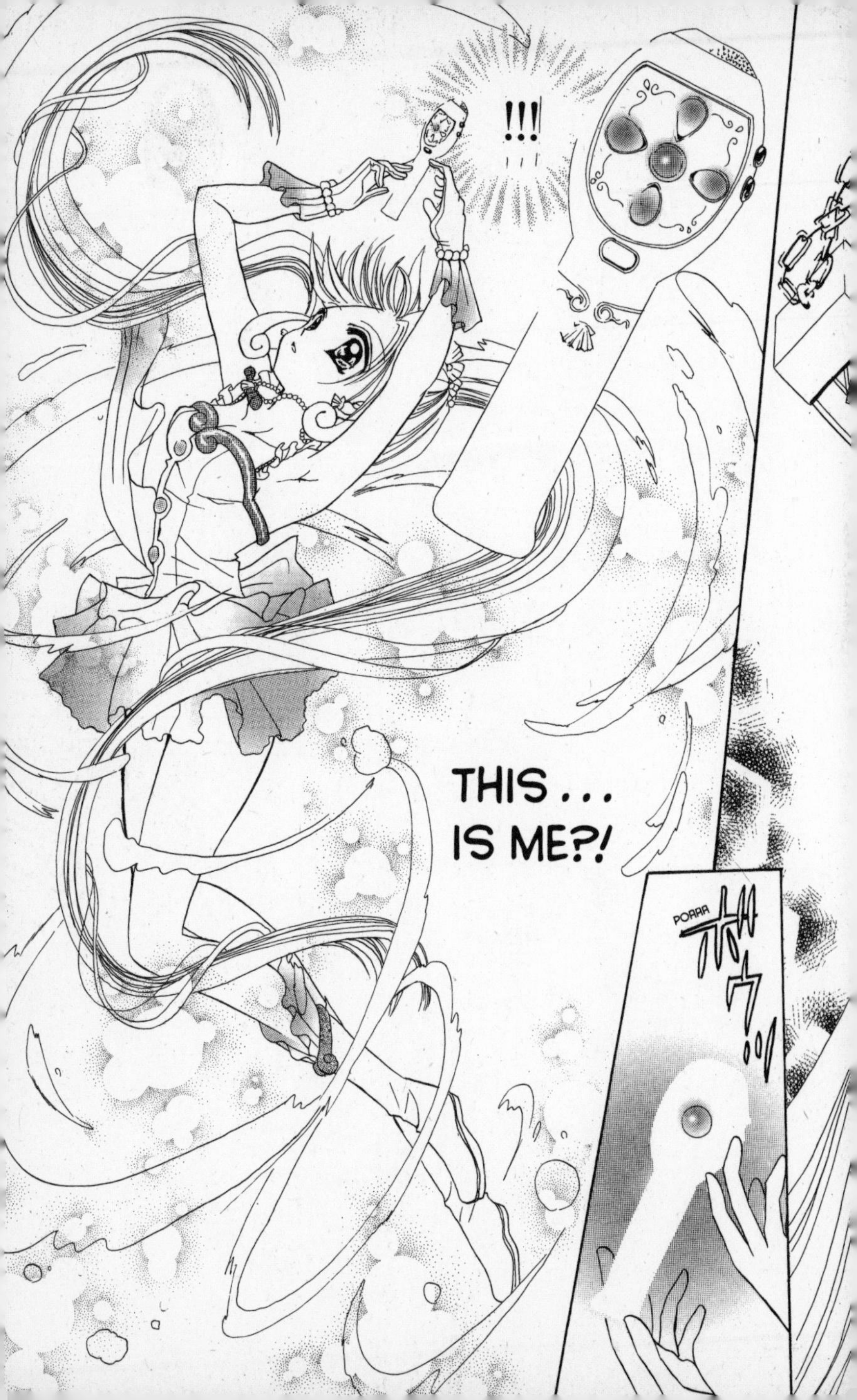
!!!
THIS . . .
. . . IS ME?!
POAAA

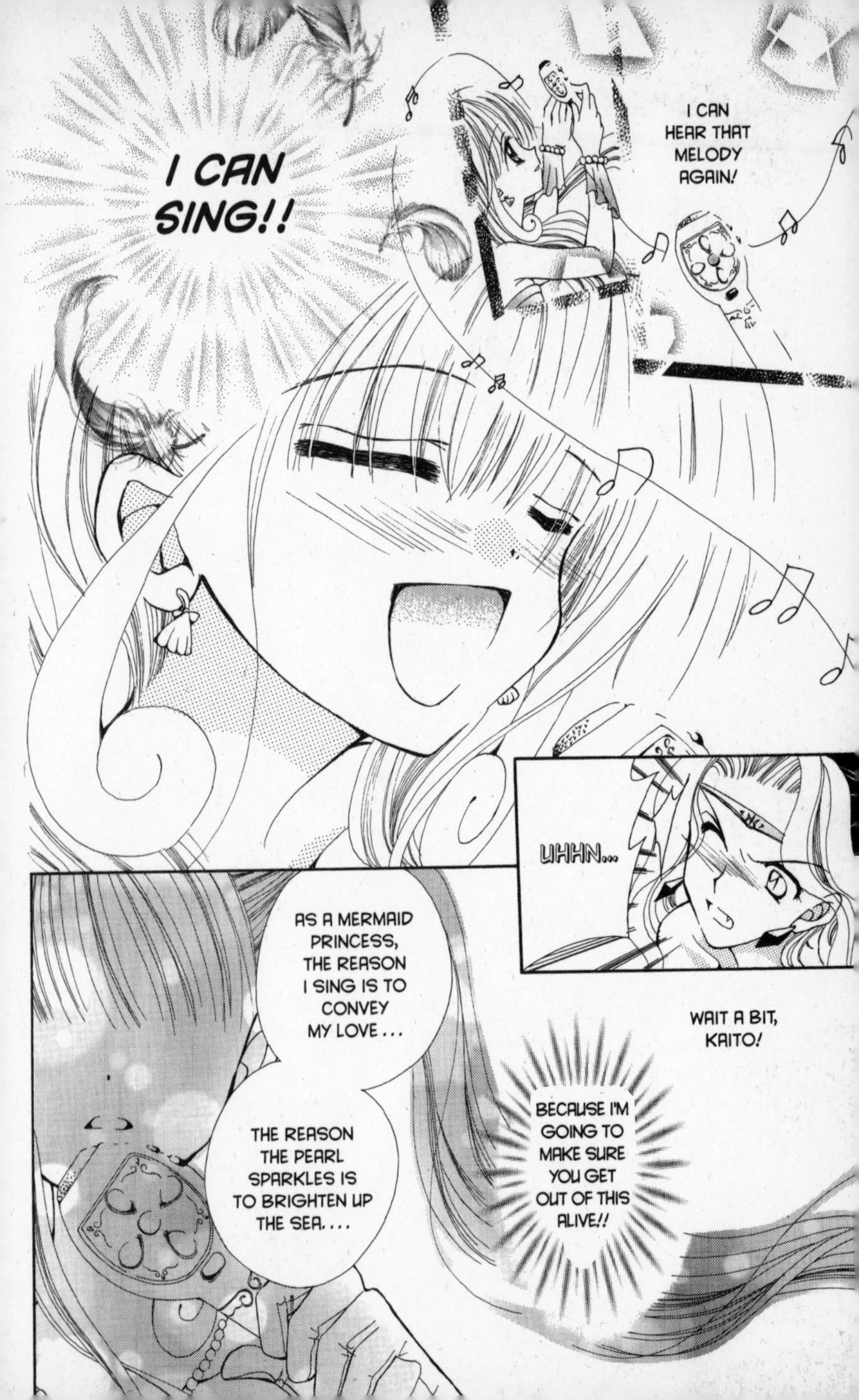
I CAN HEAR THAT MELODY AGAIN!
I CAN SING!!
UHHN...
WAIT A BIT, KAITO!
BECAUSE I'M GOING TO MAKE SURE YOU GET OUT OF THIS ALIVE!!
AS A MERMAID PRINCESS, THE REASON I SING IS TO CONVEY MY LOVE . . .
THE REASON THE PEARL SPARKLES IS TO BRIGHTEN UP THE SEA. . . .

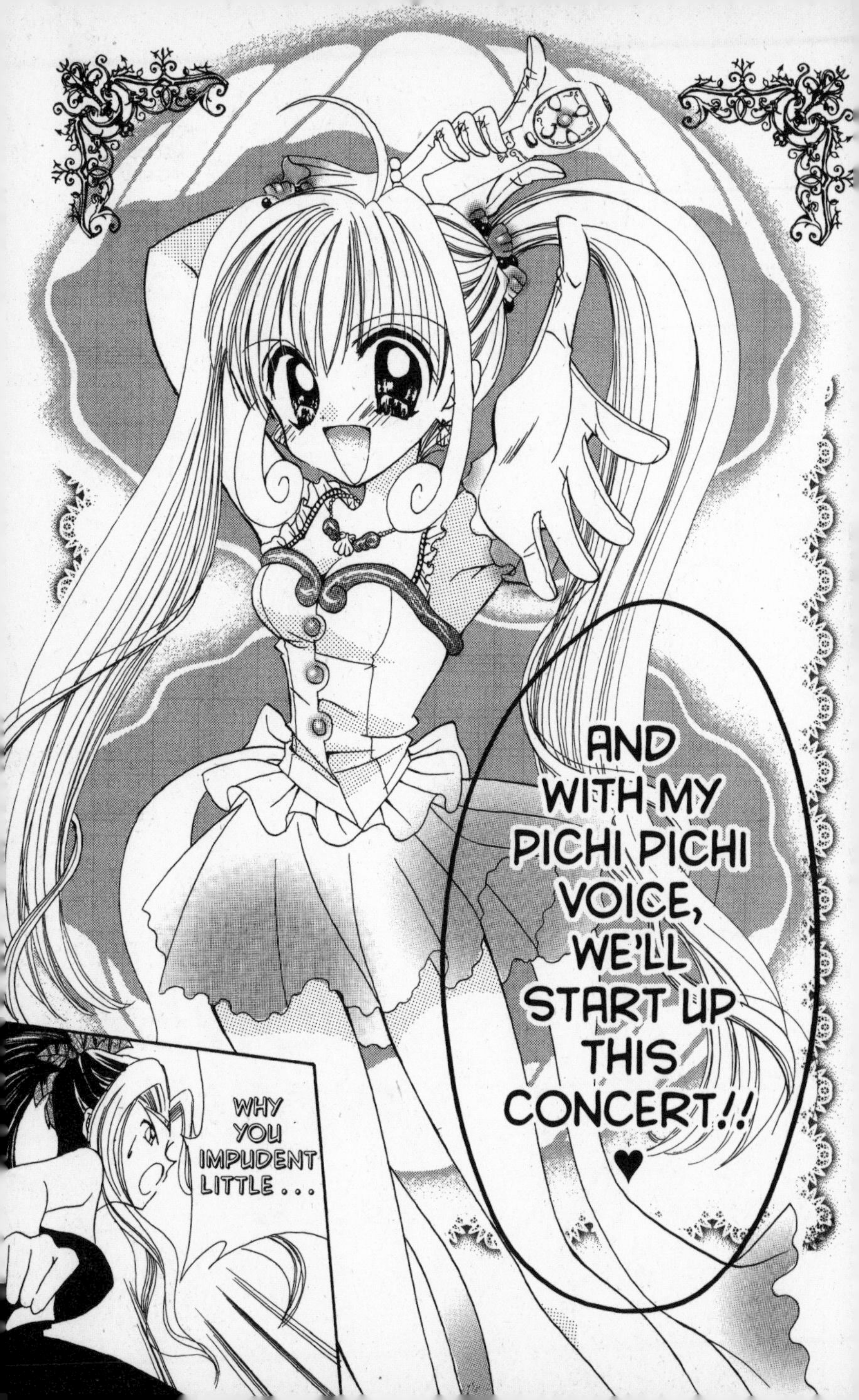
AND WITH MY PICHI PICHI VOICE, WE'LL START UP THIS CONCERT!! ♥
WHY YOU IMPUDENT LITTLE . . .

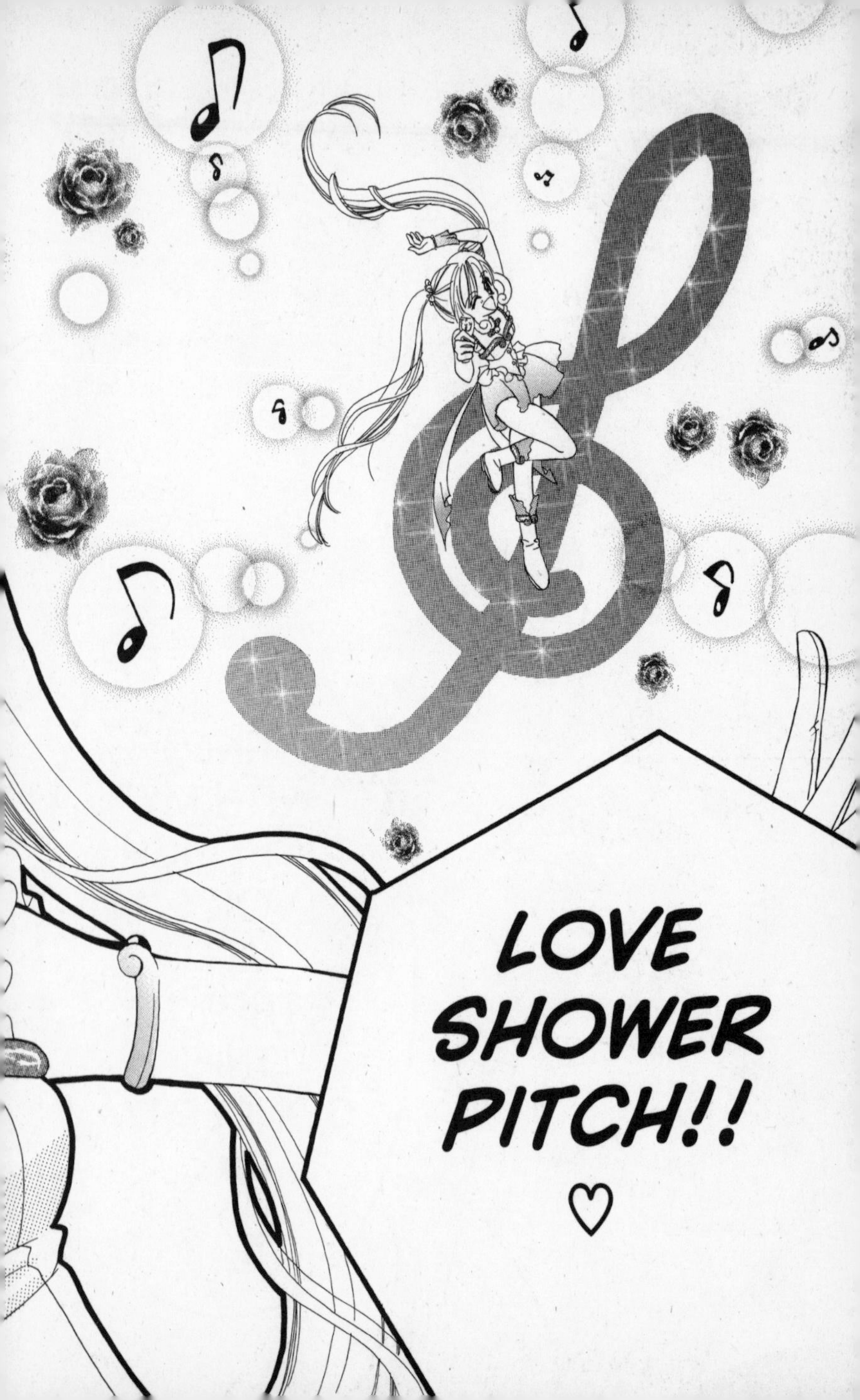
LOVE SHOWER PITCH!! ♡

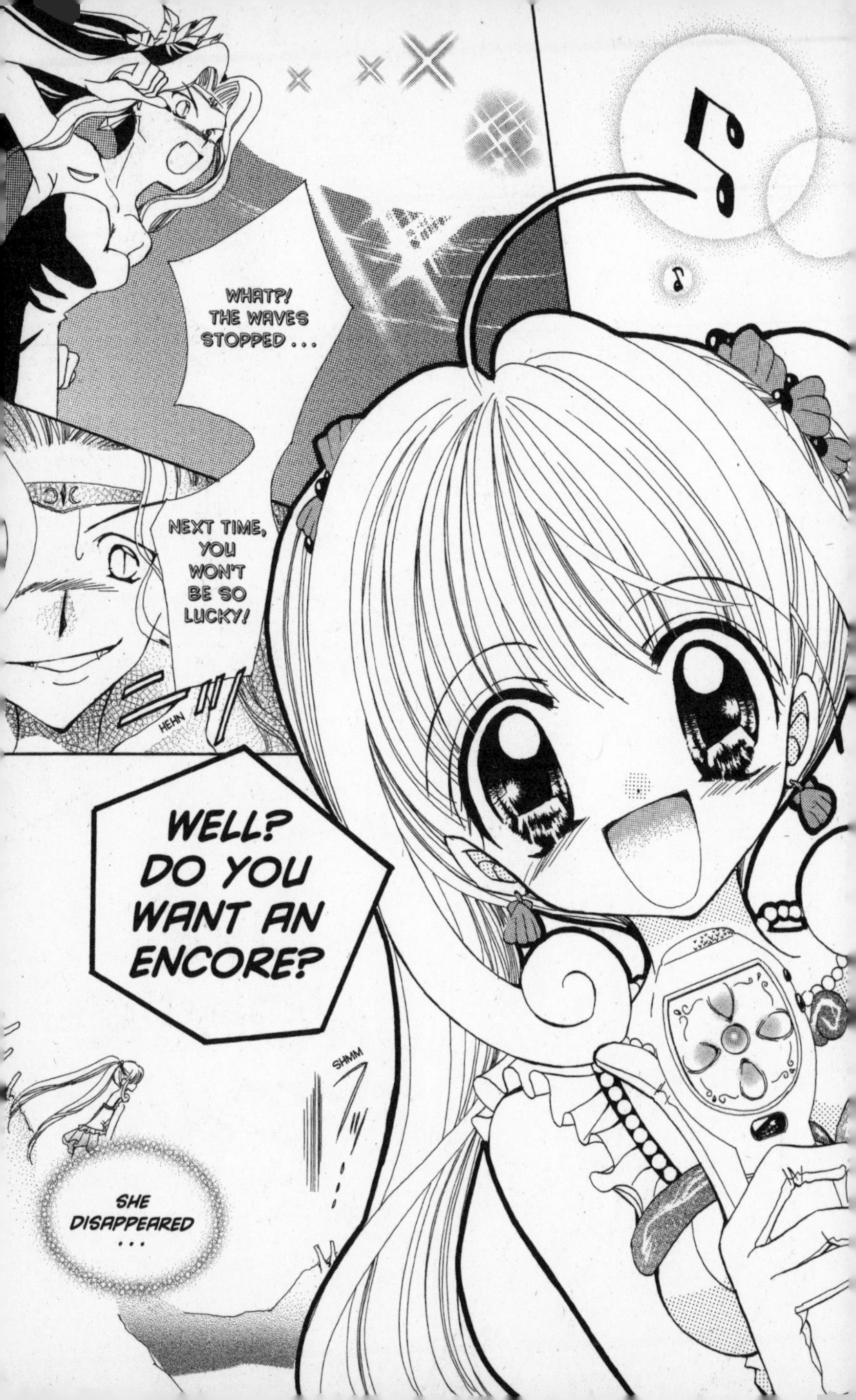
WHAT?! THE WAVES STOPPED . . .
WELL? DO YOU WANT AN ENCORE?
NEXT TIME, YOU WON'T BE SO LUCKY!
HEHN
SHMM
SHE DISAPPEARED . . .

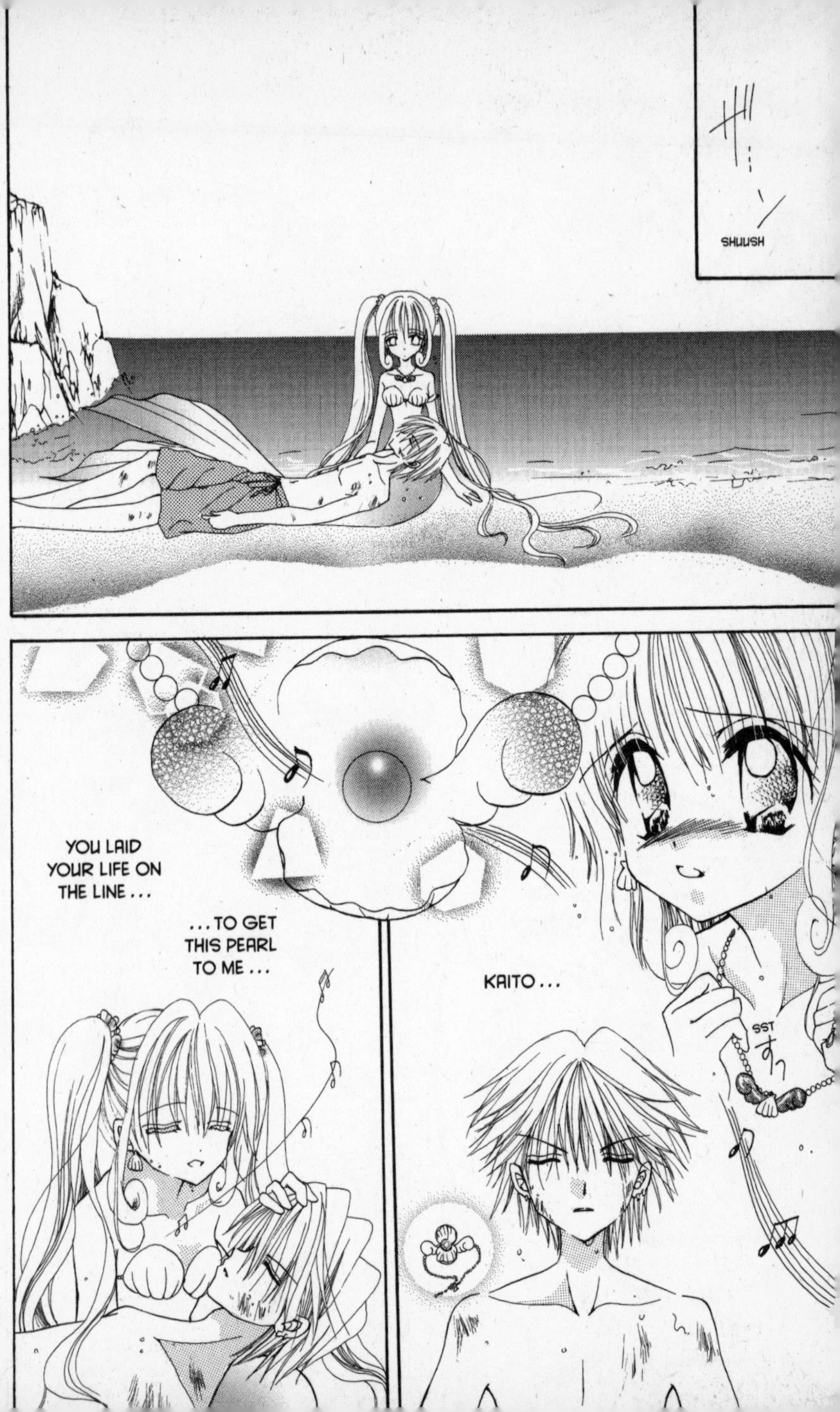
SHUUSH
KAITO...
SST
すっ
YOU LAID YOUR LIFE ON THE LINE...
...TO GET THIS PEARL TO ME...

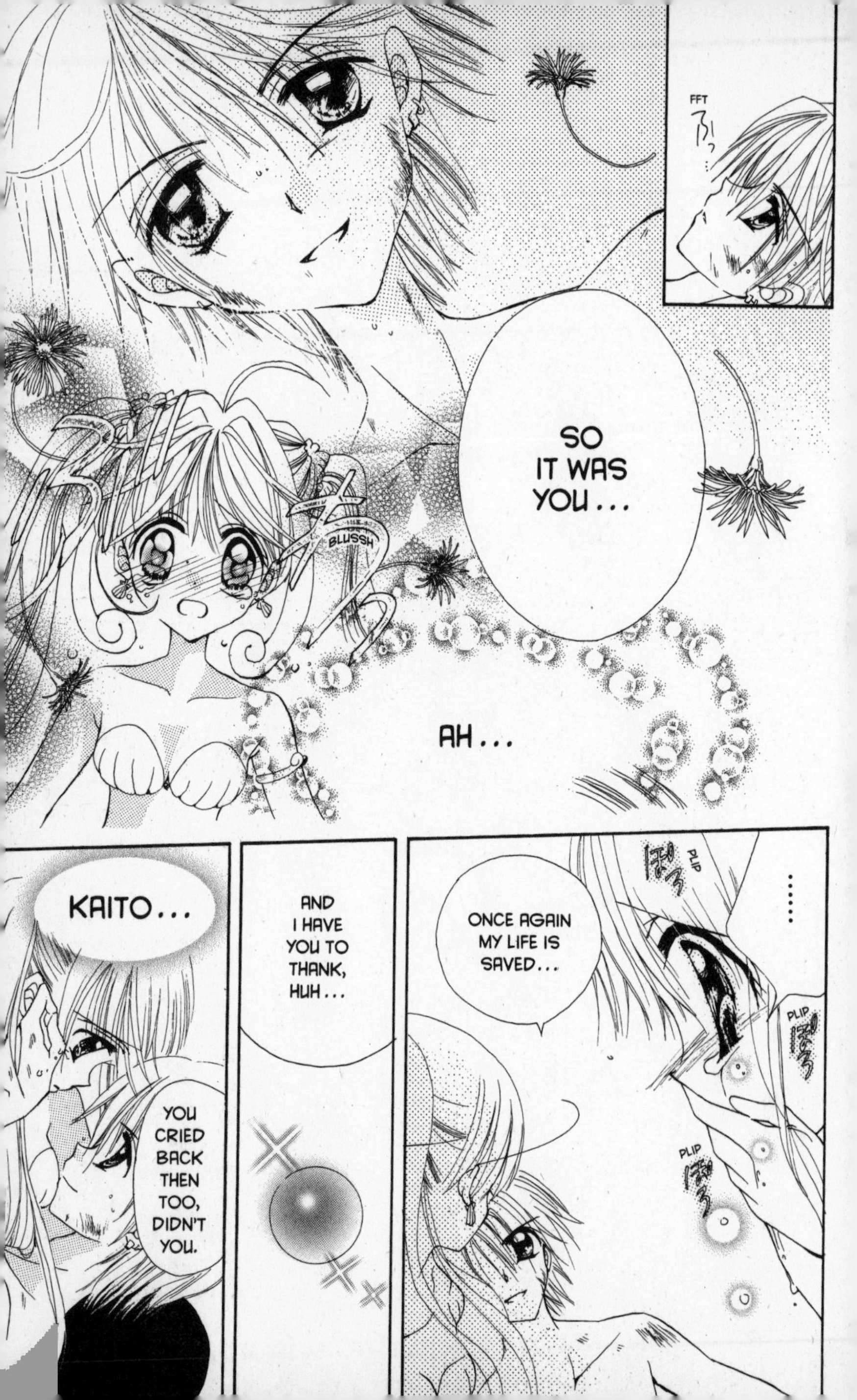

FFT
SO IT WAS YOU...
BLUSSH
AH...
......
PLIP
ONCE AGAIN MY LIFE IS SAVED...
PLIP
PLIP
AND I HAVE YOU TO THANK, HUH...
KAITO...
YOU CRIED BACK THEN TOO, DIDN'T YOU.

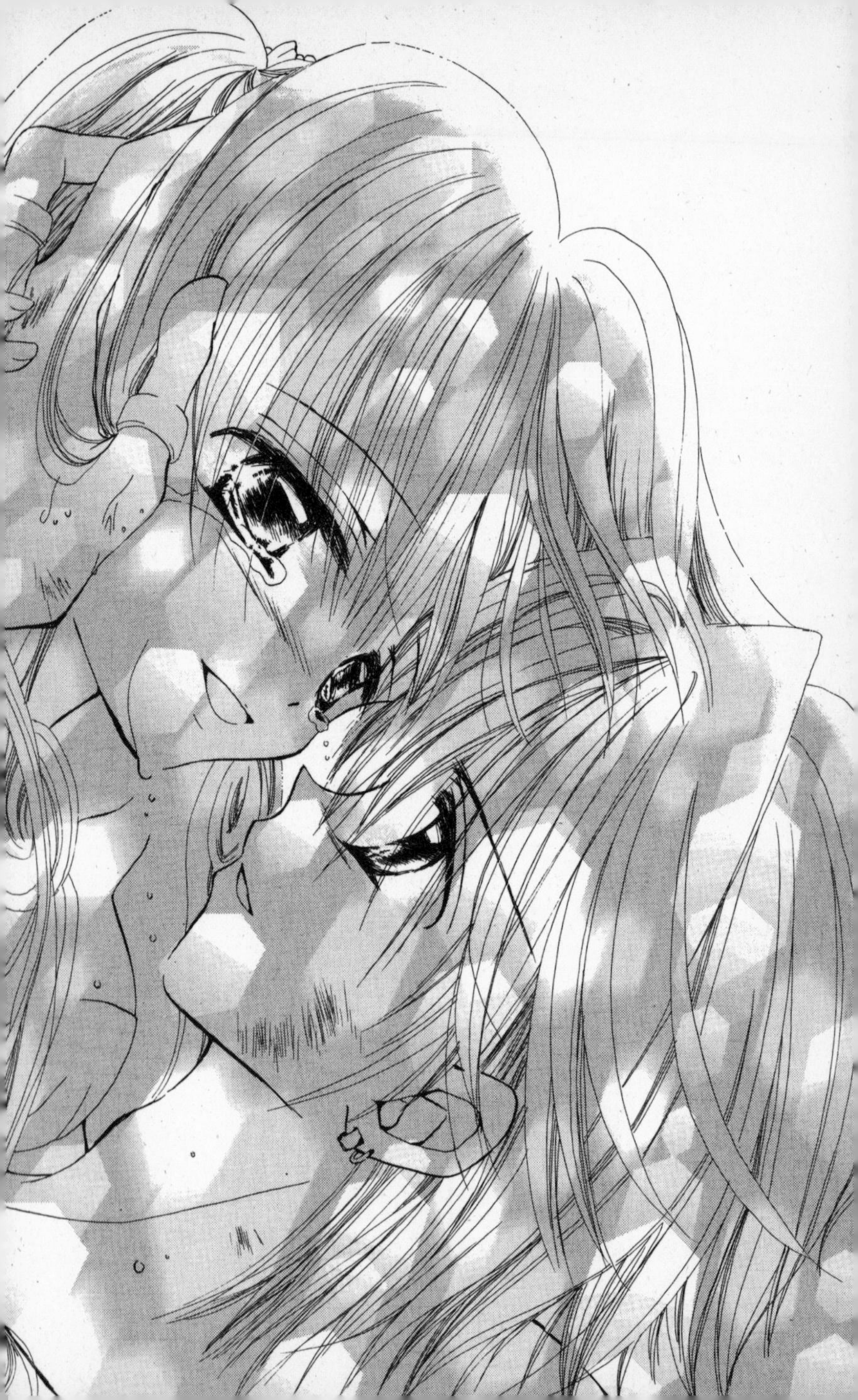

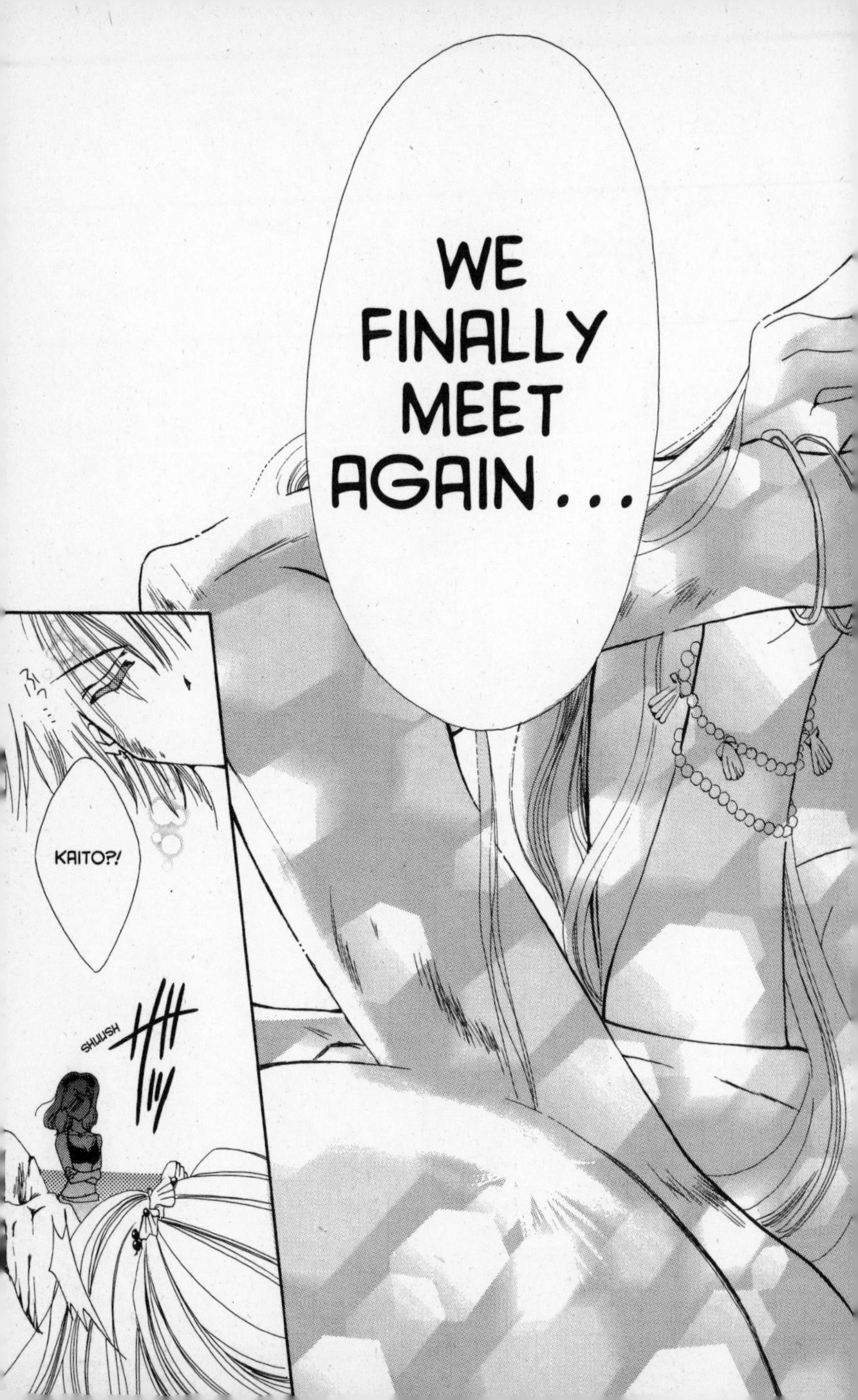
WE FINALLY MEET AGAIN...
KAITO?!
SHUUSH

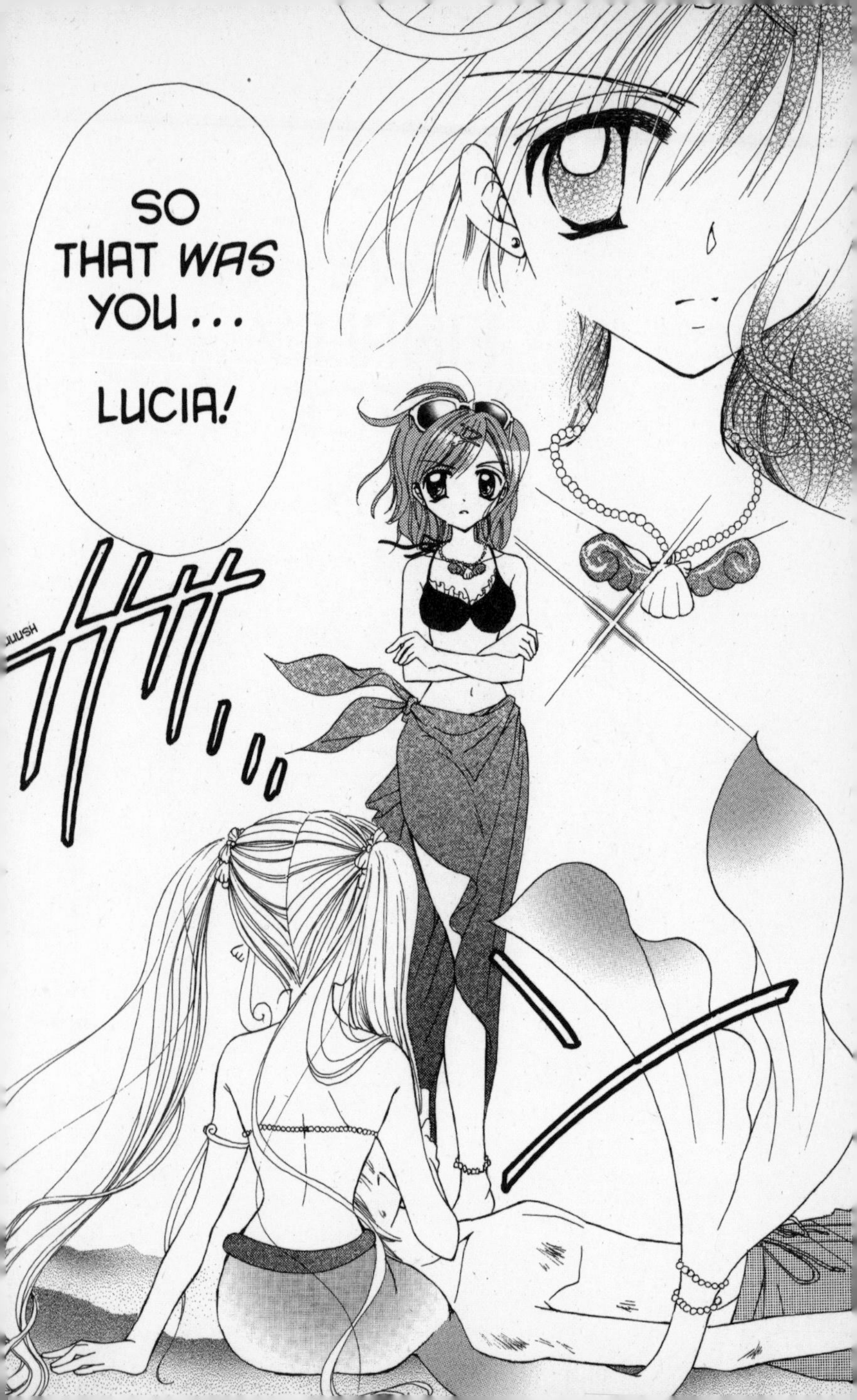
SO THAT WAS YOU... LUCIA!

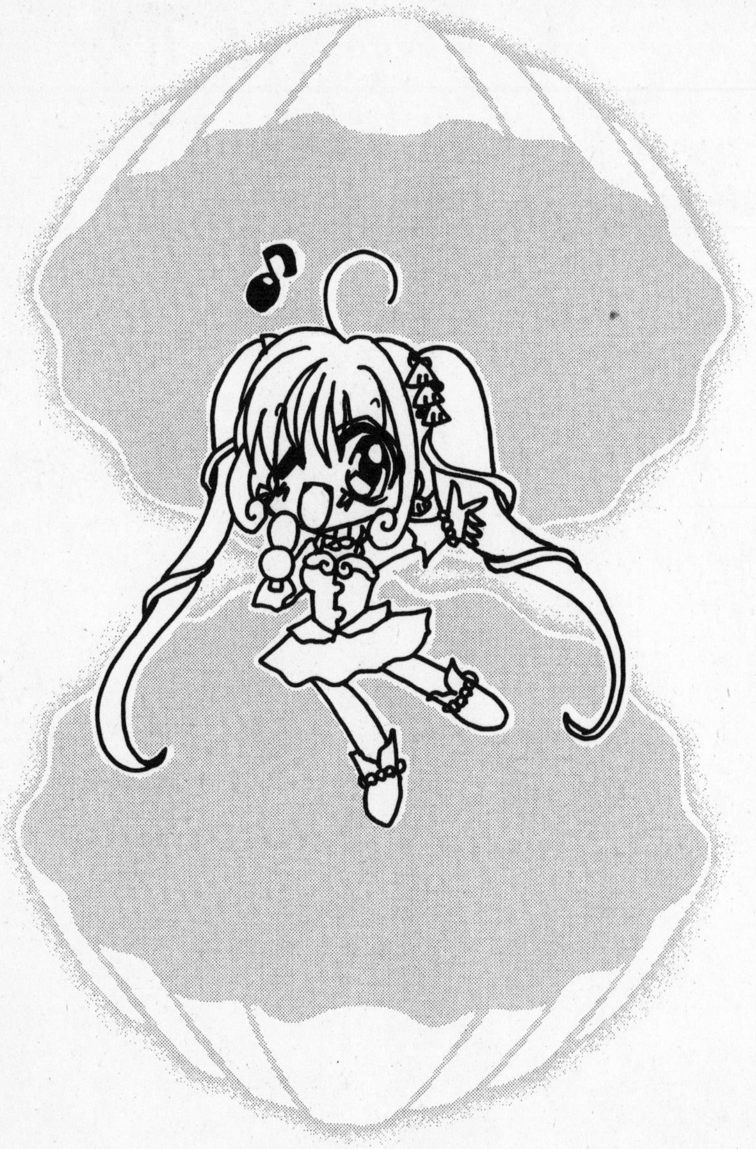

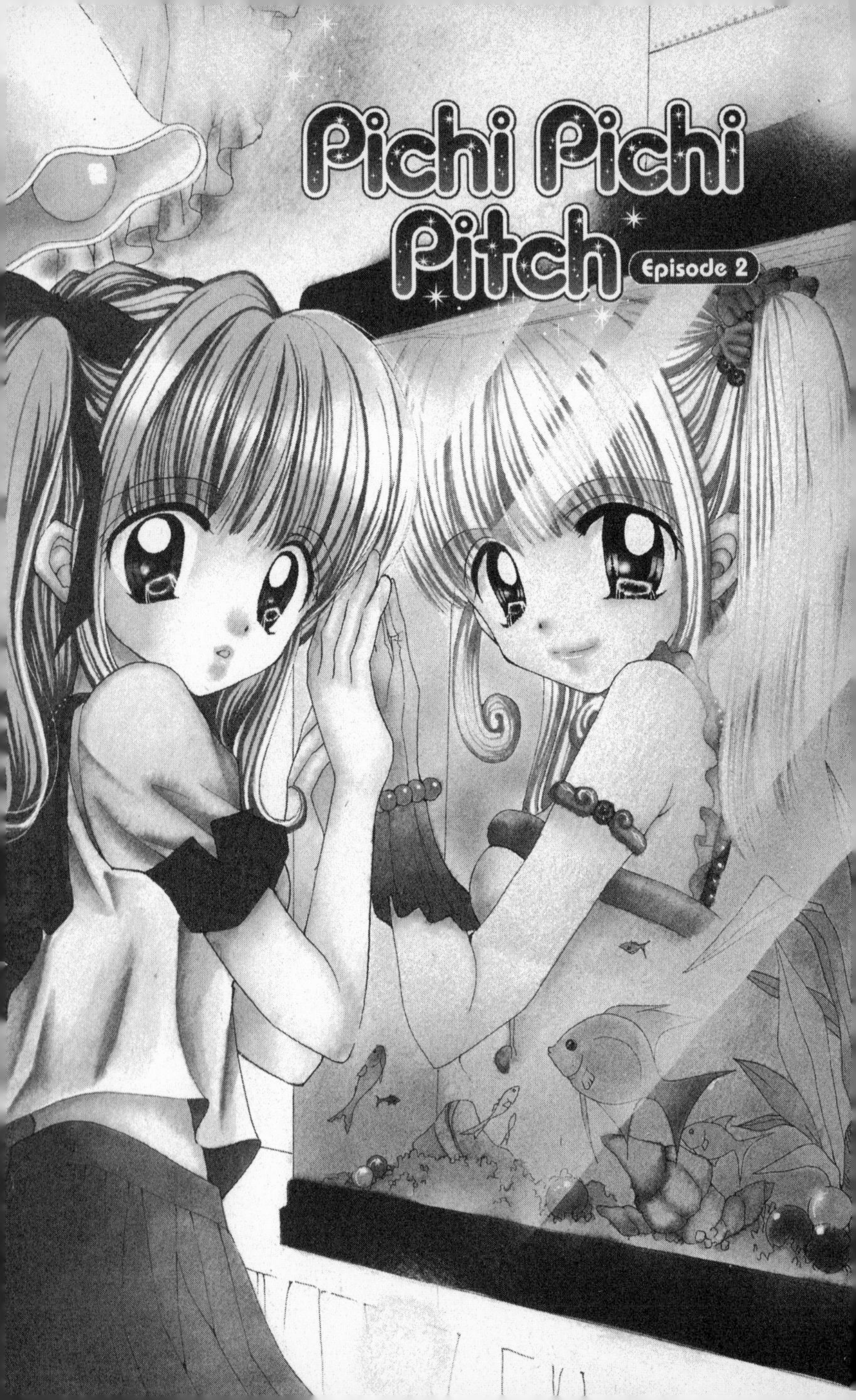
Pichi Pichi Pitch
Episode 2

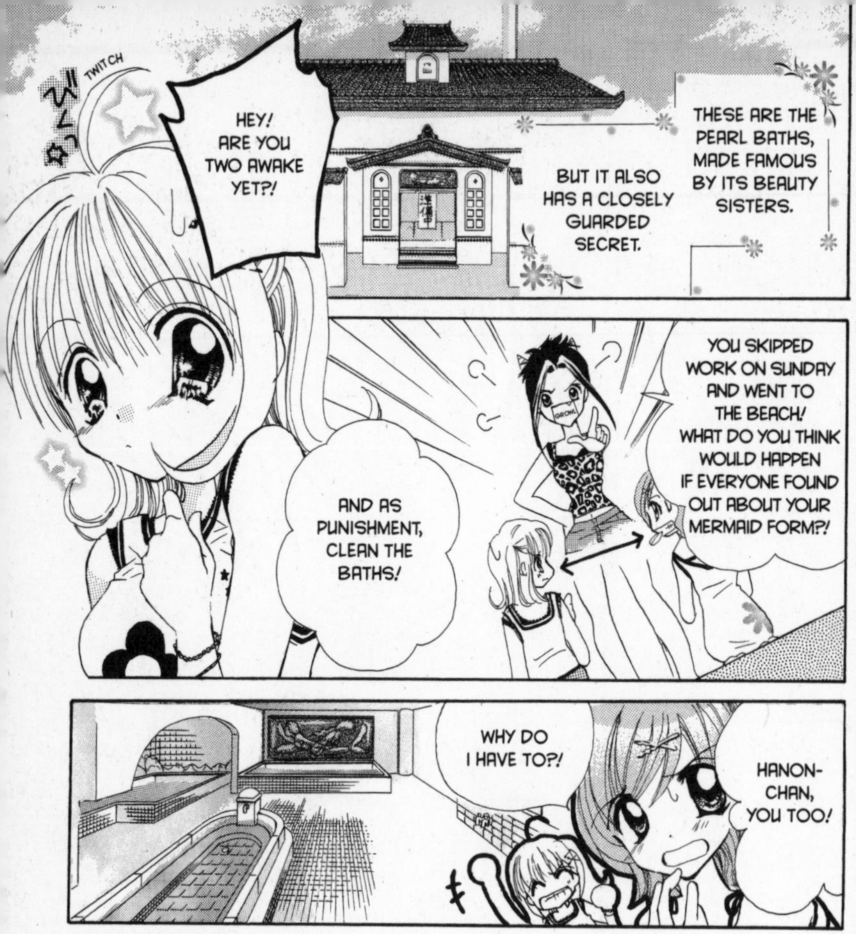
THESE ARE THE PEARL BATHS, MADE FAMOUS BY ITS BEAUTY SISTERS.
BUT IT ALSO HAS A CLOSELY GUARDED SECRET.
TWITCH
HEY! ARE YOU TWO AWAKE YET?!
YOU SKIPPED WORK ON SUNDAY AND WENT TO THE BEACH! WHAT DO YOU THINK WOULD HAPPEN IF EVERYONE FOUND OUT ABOUT YOUR MERMAID FORM?!
GROWL
AND AS PUNISHMENT, CLEAN THE BATHS!
HANON-CHAN, YOU TOO!
WHY DO I HAVE TO?!

(EPISODE 1) THE OPENING SPLASH PAGE WAS DRAWN ON PAPER THAT'S ABOUT A2 [ABOUT 16" X 23"] SIZE. IT'S HUGE! IT WAS THE VERY FIRST TIME I EVER DREW A PICTURE IN SUCH A LARGE SIZE. I TRIED TO SEND IT TO THE PUBLISHER BY WRAPPING IT AROUND A POLE THAT HOLDS UP THE CLOTH OPEN-FOR-BUSINESS SIGN, BUT IT WOULDN'T FIT THROUGH THE MAIL SLOT.

(EPISODE 2) THIS HAPPENED DURING THE MAKING OF EPISODE 1 TOO, BUT I REALLY RELIED ON THOSE NUTRITION DRINKS! EVEN AFTER I FINISHED THE WORK, I DRANK SO MUCH OF THE STUFF, MY BODY HAD GOTTEN USED TO IT. (WHAT'S THAT? DON'T DRINK SO MUCH?) BUT FROM EPISODE 3 ON, I COULD ALMOST SAY THAT I HAVEN'T DRUNK ANY! AND SOMEHOW I GET THE MANGA DONE UNDER MY OWN STEAM. HANON AND ERIRU HAVE TURNED OUT TO BE VERY POPULAR!!! WHEE!

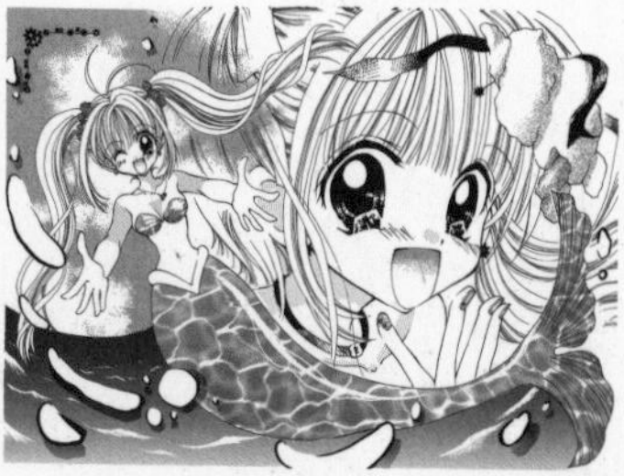

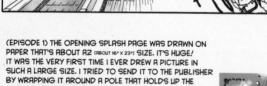

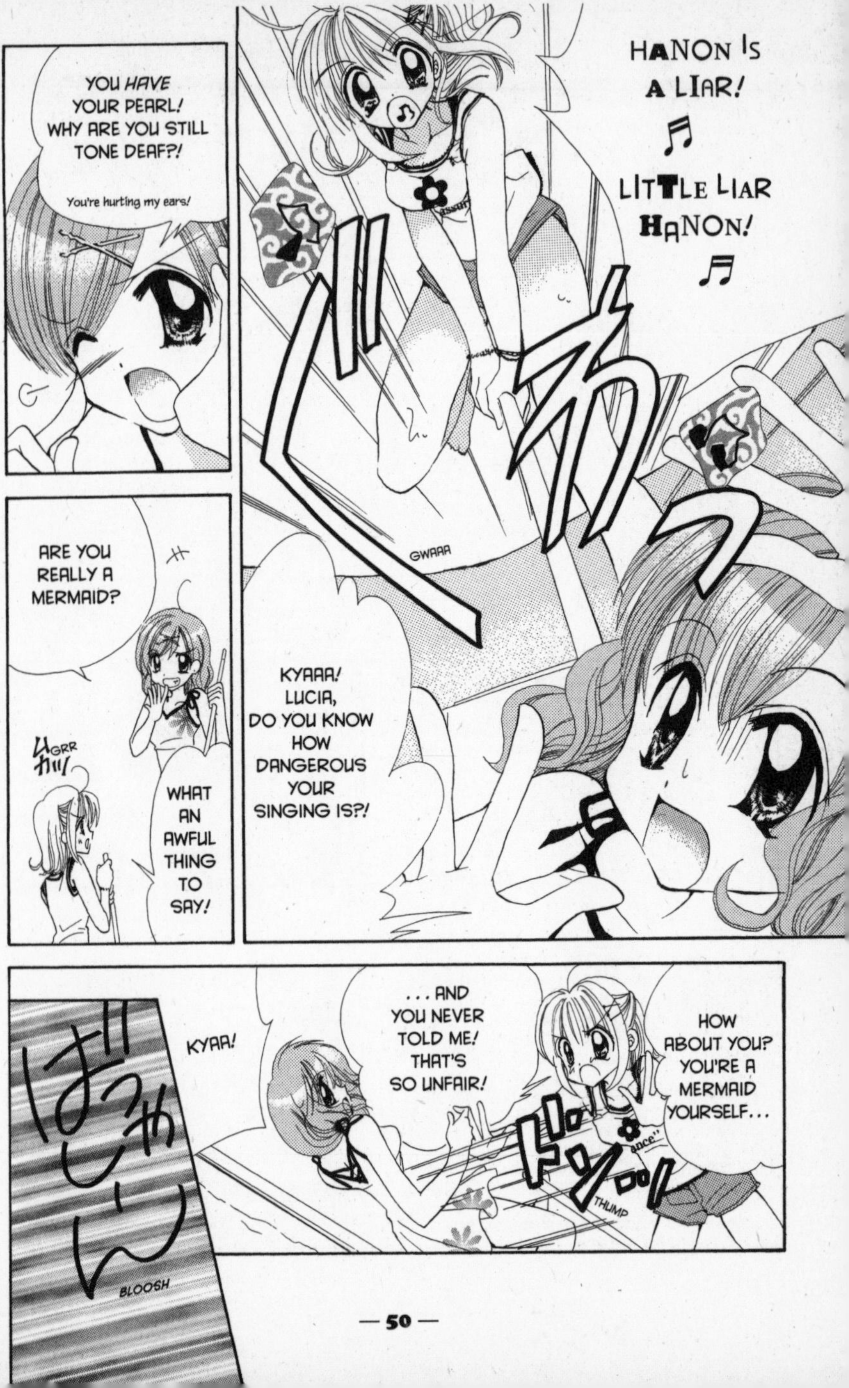
HANON IS A LIAR! ♬ LITTLE LIAR HANON! ♬
GWAAA
KYAAA! LUCIA, DO YOU KNOW HOW DANGEROUS YOUR SINGING IS?!
YOU HAVE YOUR PEARL! WHY ARE YOU STILL TONE DEAF?!
You're hurting my ears!
ARE YOU REALLY A MERMAID?
GRR
WHAT AN AWFUL THING TO SAY!
HOW ABOUT YOU? YOU'RE A MERMAID YOURSELF...
THUMP
...AND YOU NEVER TOLD ME! THAT'S SO UNFAIR!
KYAA!
BLOOSH

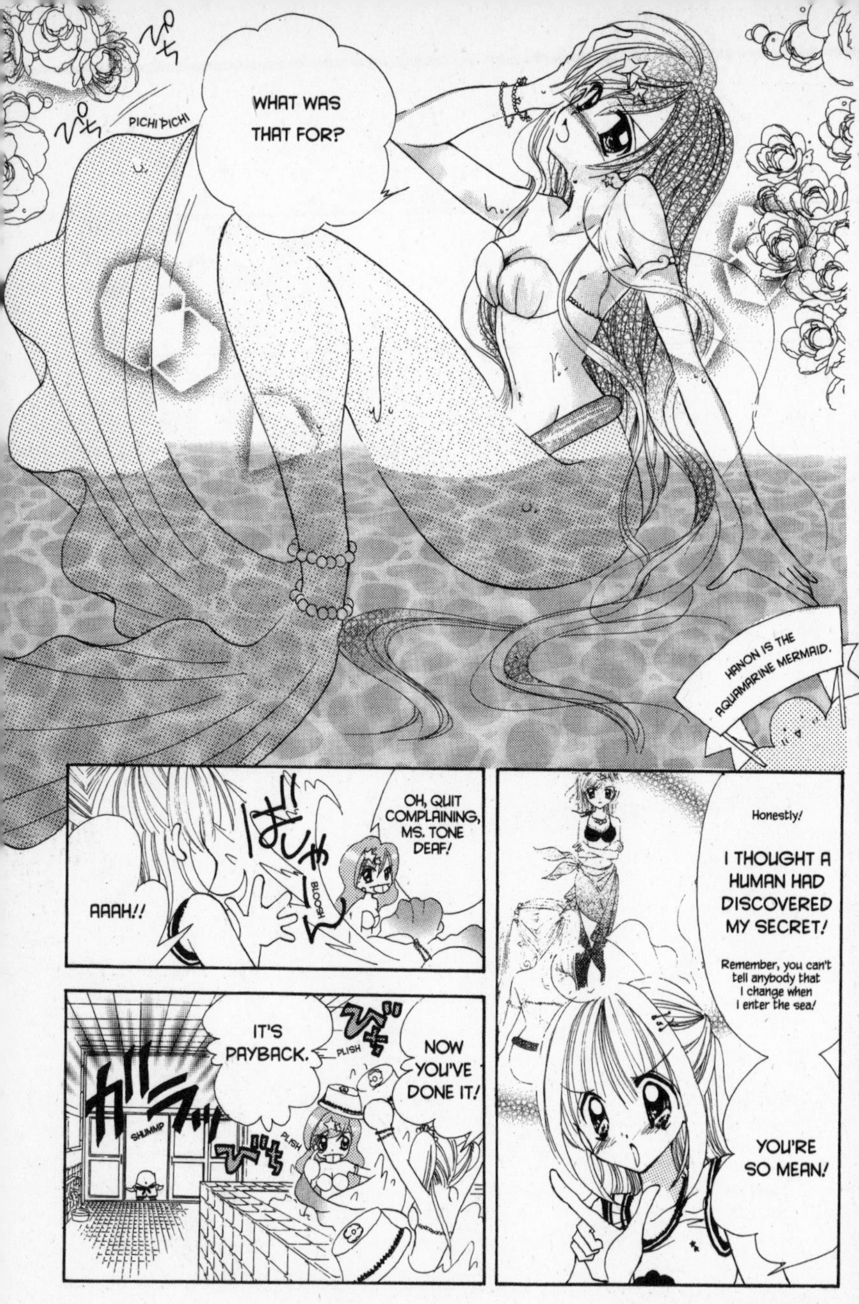
PICHI PICHI
WHAT WAS THAT FOR?
HANON IS THE AQUAMARINE MERMAID.
Honestly!
I THOUGHT A HUMAN HAD DISCOVERED MY SECRET!
Remember, you can't tell anybody that I change when I enter the sea!
YOU'RE SO MEAN!
OH, QUIT COMPLAINING, MS. TONE DEAF!
BLOOSH
AAAH!!
NOW YOU'VE DONE IT!
PLISH
IT'S PAYBACK.
PLISH
SHUMMP

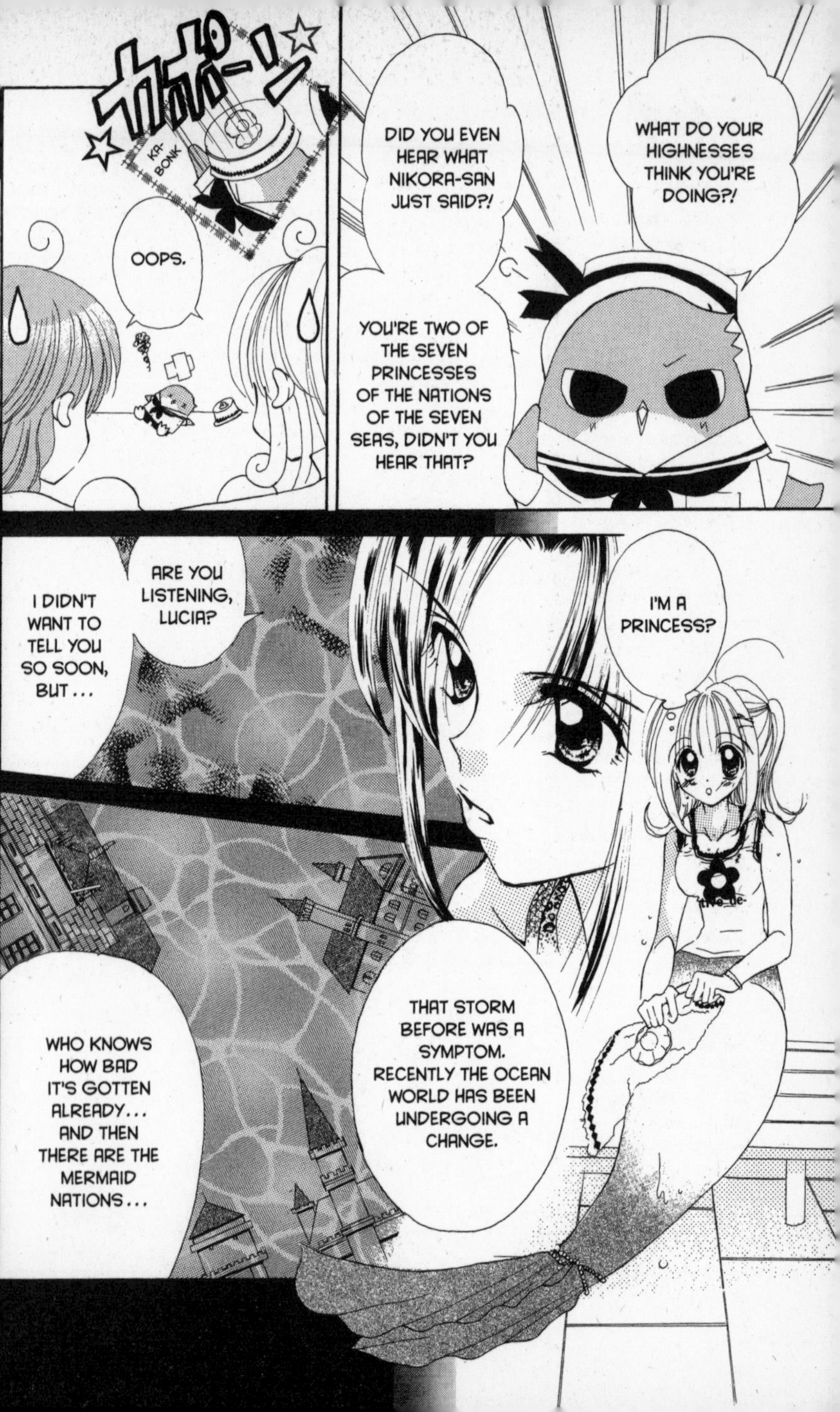
WHAT DO YOUR HIGHNESSES THINK YOU'RE DOING?!
DID YOU EVEN HEAR WHAT NIKORA-SAN JUST SAID?!
YOU'RE TWO OF THE SEVEN PRINCESSES OF THE NATIONS OF THE SEVEN SEAS, DIDN'T YOU HEAR THAT?
カポーン!
KA-BONK
OOPS.
I'M A PRINCESS?
ARE YOU LISTENING, LUCIA?
I DIDN'T WANT TO TELL YOU SO SOON, BUT ...
THAT STORM BEFORE WAS A SYMPTOM. RECENTLY THE OCEAN WORLD HAS BEEN UNDERGOING A CHANGE.
WHO KNOWS HOW BAD IT'S GOTTEN ALREADY... AND THEN THERE ARE THE MERMAID NATIONS...

✱ CONTINUED...

I'VE ALWAYS HAD MEETINGS WITH EDITORS 1 ON 1, BUT THE FIRST TIME I HAD A 3 ON 1 MEETING...

PINK. → DESK ← IT WAS LIKE THIS.

...I WAS SO NERVOUS, I COULD HARDLY EVEN CATCH MY BREATH. (REALLY!) MY HEAD WAS SUCH A TOTAL BLANK THAT I DON'T EVEN REMEMBER WHAT I SAID! (HEY!)

NOW I'VE GOTTEN USED TO IT (I THINK), AND NOW THEY CAN'T SHUT ME UP. EDITORS, YOKOTE-SAMA, AND EVERYONE ELSE INVOLVED, I'M SO SORRY FOR THE TROUBLE I'VE CAUSED! AFTER EVERY MEETING, I ALWAYS RETURN HOME AND REALIZE JUST HOW MUCH I GOT CARRIED AWAY! LOTS OF REGRETS! I'M A SAD CREATURE (WAAAH!) WHO CAN'T LIVE UNLESS I'M BABBLING ABOUT SOMETHING.

ONE TIME I DECIDED TO BE A GOOD GIRL AND STAY QUIET, BUT EVERYONE STARTED WORRYING ABOUT ME AND ASKING IF I FELT ALL RIGHT. (YEAH...) WHY? I THINK I KNOW WHY...

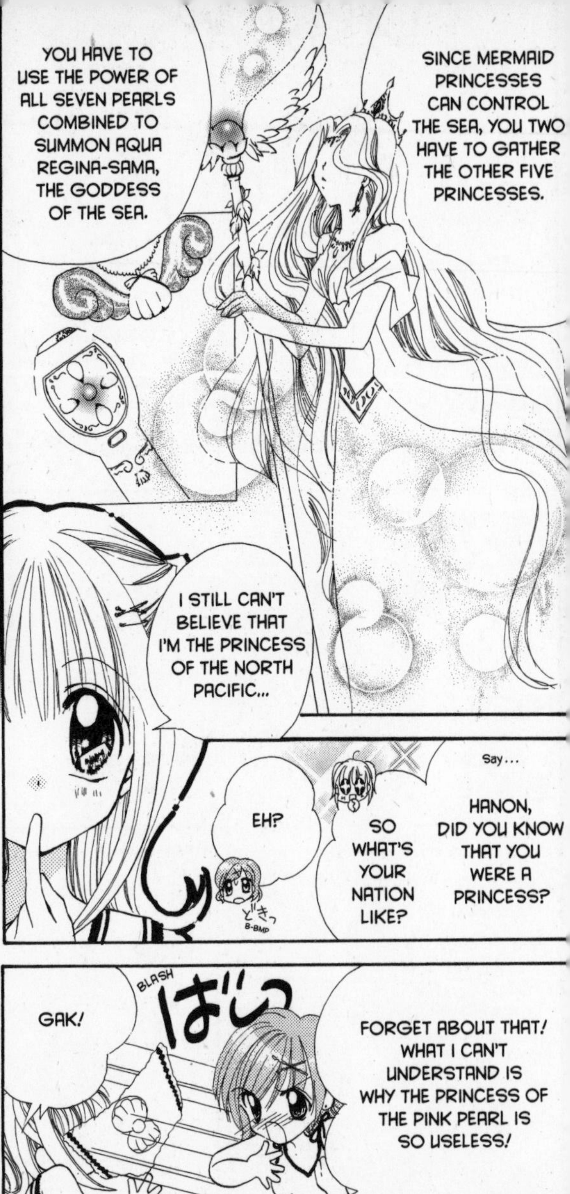
SINCE MERMAID PRINCESSES CAN CONTROL THE SEA, YOU TWO HAVE TO GATHER THE OTHER FIVE PRINCESSES.
YOU HAVE TO USE THE POWER OF ALL SEVEN PEARLS COMBINED TO SUMMON AQUA REGINA-SAMA, THE GODDESS OF THE SEA.
I STILL CAN'T BELIEVE THAT I'M THE PRINCESS OF THE NORTH PACIFIC...
Say...
HANON, DID YOU KNOW THAT YOU WERE A PRINCESS?
SO WHAT'S YOUR NATION LIKE?
EH?
どきっ B-BMP
FORGET ABOUT THAT! WHAT I CAN'T UNDERSTAND IS WHY THE PRINCESS OF THE PINK PEARL IS SO USELESS!
ばこっ BLASH
GAK!

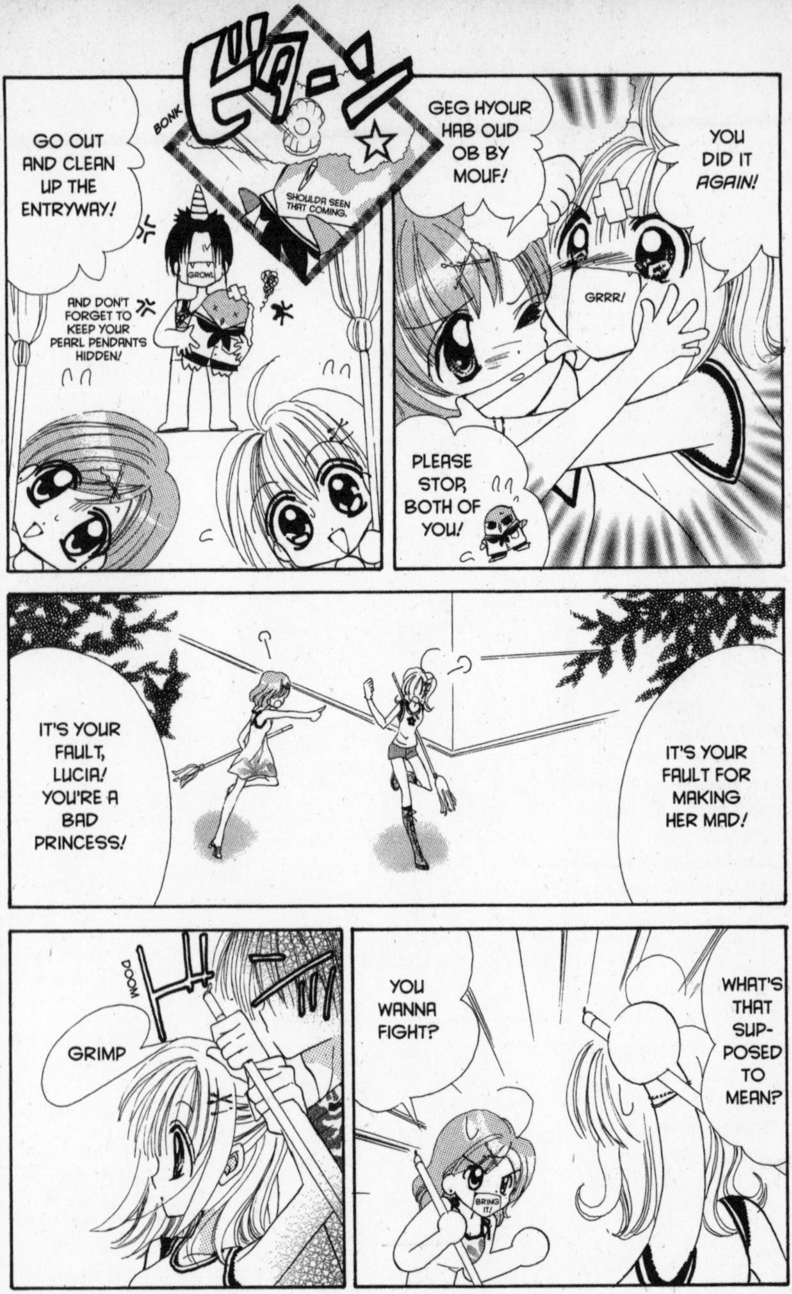
YOU DID IT AGAIN!
GEG HYOUR HAB OUD OB BY MOUF!
GRRR!
PLEASE STOP, BOTH OF YOU!
BONK
SHOULDA SEEN THAT COMING.
GO OUT AND CLEAN UP THE ENTRYWAY!
GROWL
AND DON'T FORGET TO KEEP YOUR PEARL PENDANTS HIDDEN!
IT'S YOUR FAULT FOR MAKING HER MAD!
IT'S YOUR FAULT, LUCIA! YOU'RE A BAD PRINCESS!
WHAT'S THAT SUP-POSED TO MEAN?
YOU WANNA FIGHT?
BRING IT!
DOOM
GRIMP

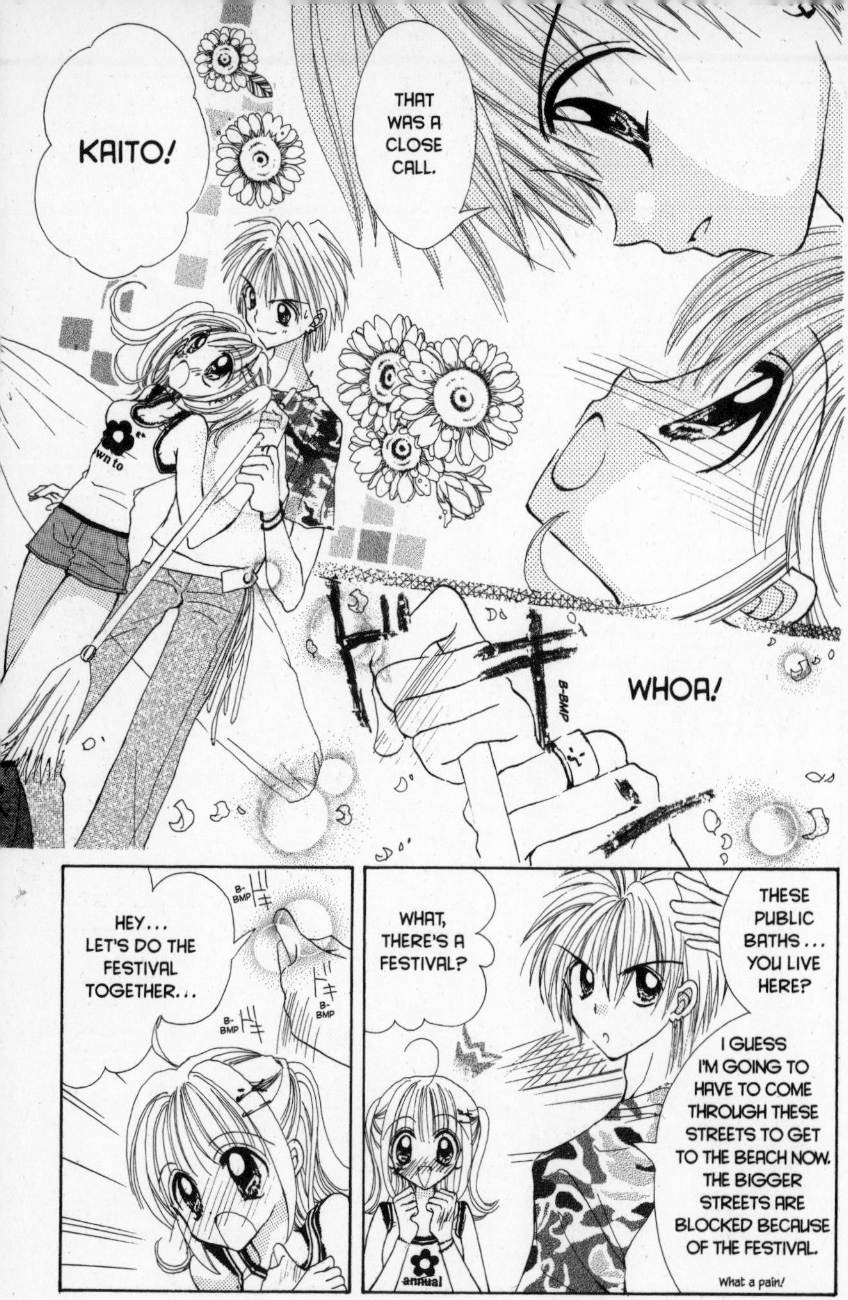
THAT WAS A CLOSE CALL.
KAITO!
WHOA!
B-BMP
THESE PUBLIC BATHS . . . YOU LIVE HERE?
I GUESS I'M GOING TO HAVE TO COME THROUGH THESE STREETS TO GET TO THE BEACH NOW. THE BIGGER STREETS ARE BLOCKED BECAUSE OF THE FESTIVAL.
What a pain!
WHAT, THERE'S A FESTIVAL?
B-BMP
HEY . . . LET'S DO THE FESTIVAL TOGETHER . . .
B-BMP
B-BMP

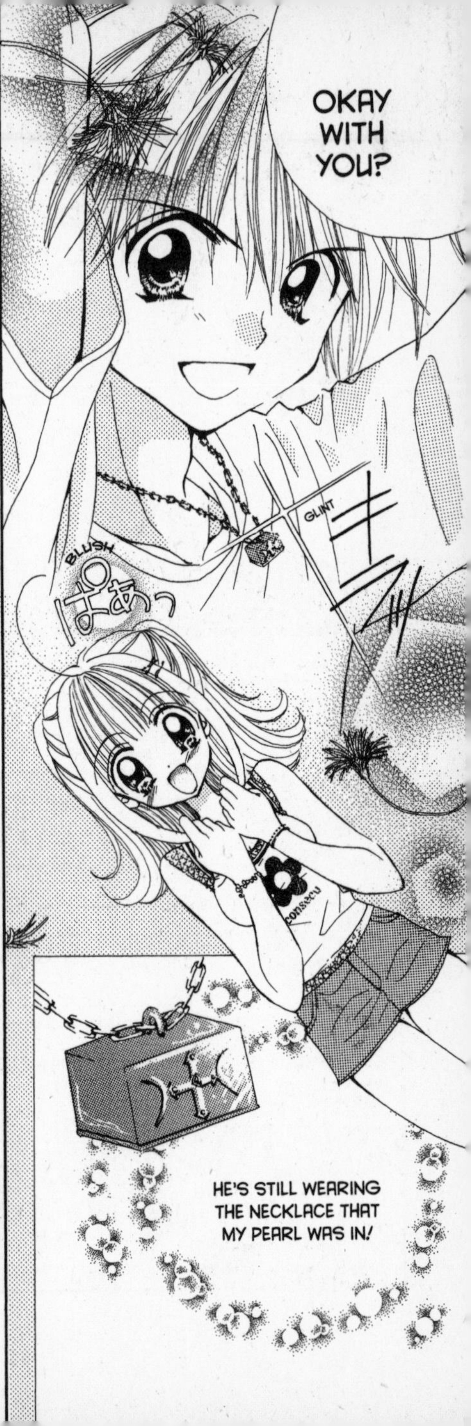
OKAY WITH YOU?
GLINT
BLUSH
ぱあっ
HE'S STILL WEARING THE NECKLACE THAT MY PEARL WAS IN!

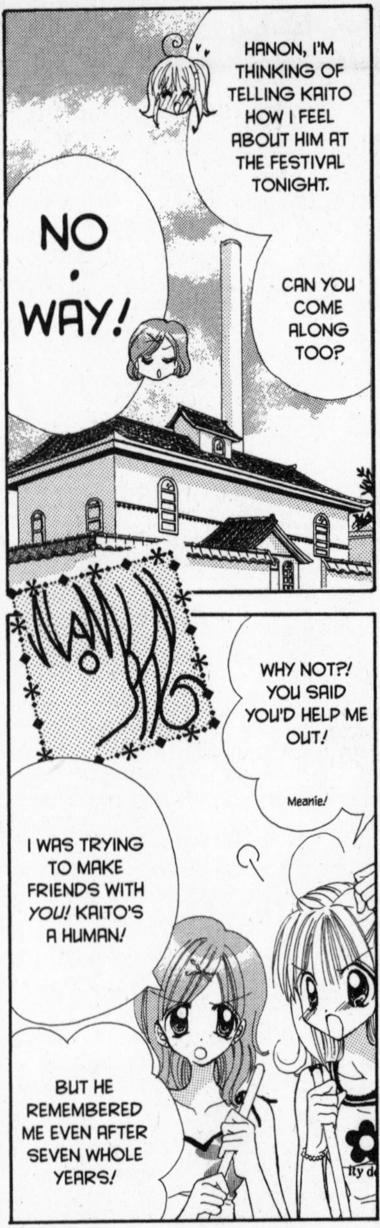
HANON, I'M THINKING OF TELLING KAITO HOW I FEEL ABOUT HIM AT THE FESTIVAL TONIGHT.
CAN YOU COME ALONG TOO?
NO • WAY!
WHY NOT?! YOU SAID YOU'D HELP ME OUT!
Meanie!
I WAS TRYING TO MAKE FRIENDS WITH *YOU!* KAITO'S A HUMAN!
BUT HE REMEMBERED ME EVEN AFTER SEVEN WHOLE YEARS!

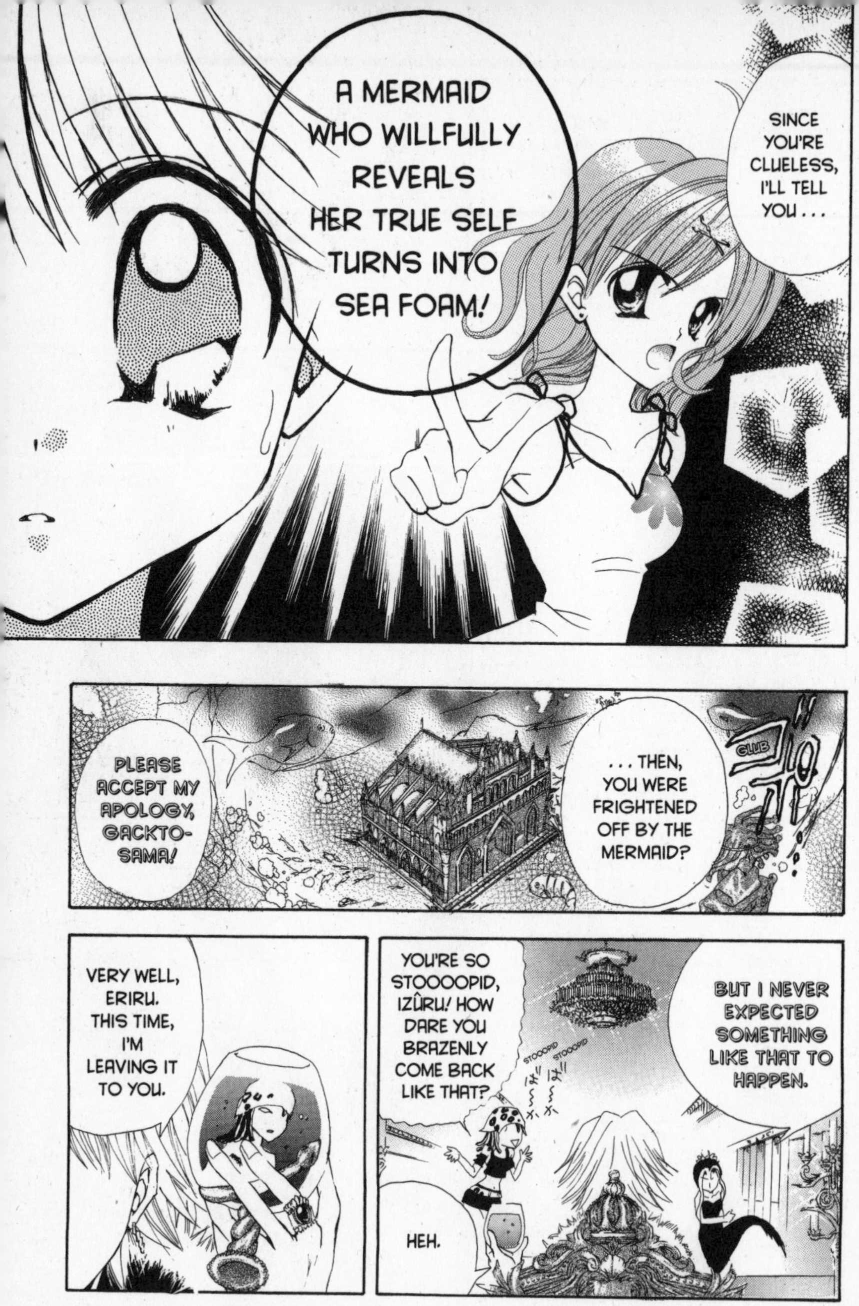
SINCE YOU'RE CLUELESS, I'LL TELL YOU . . .
A MERMAID WHO WILLFULLY REVEALS HER TRUE SELF TURNS INTO SEA FOAM!
. . . THEN, YOU WERE FRIGHTENED OFF BY THE MERMAID?
GLUB
PLEASE ACCEPT MY APOLOGY, GACKTO-SAMA!
BUT I NEVER EXPECTED SOMETHING LIKE THAT TO HAPPEN.
YOU'RE SO STOOOOPID, IZÛRU! HOW DARE YOU BRAZENLY COME BACK LIKE THAT?
STOOOPID
STOOOPID
HEH.
VERY WELL, ERIRU. THIS TIME, I'M LEAVING IT TO YOU.

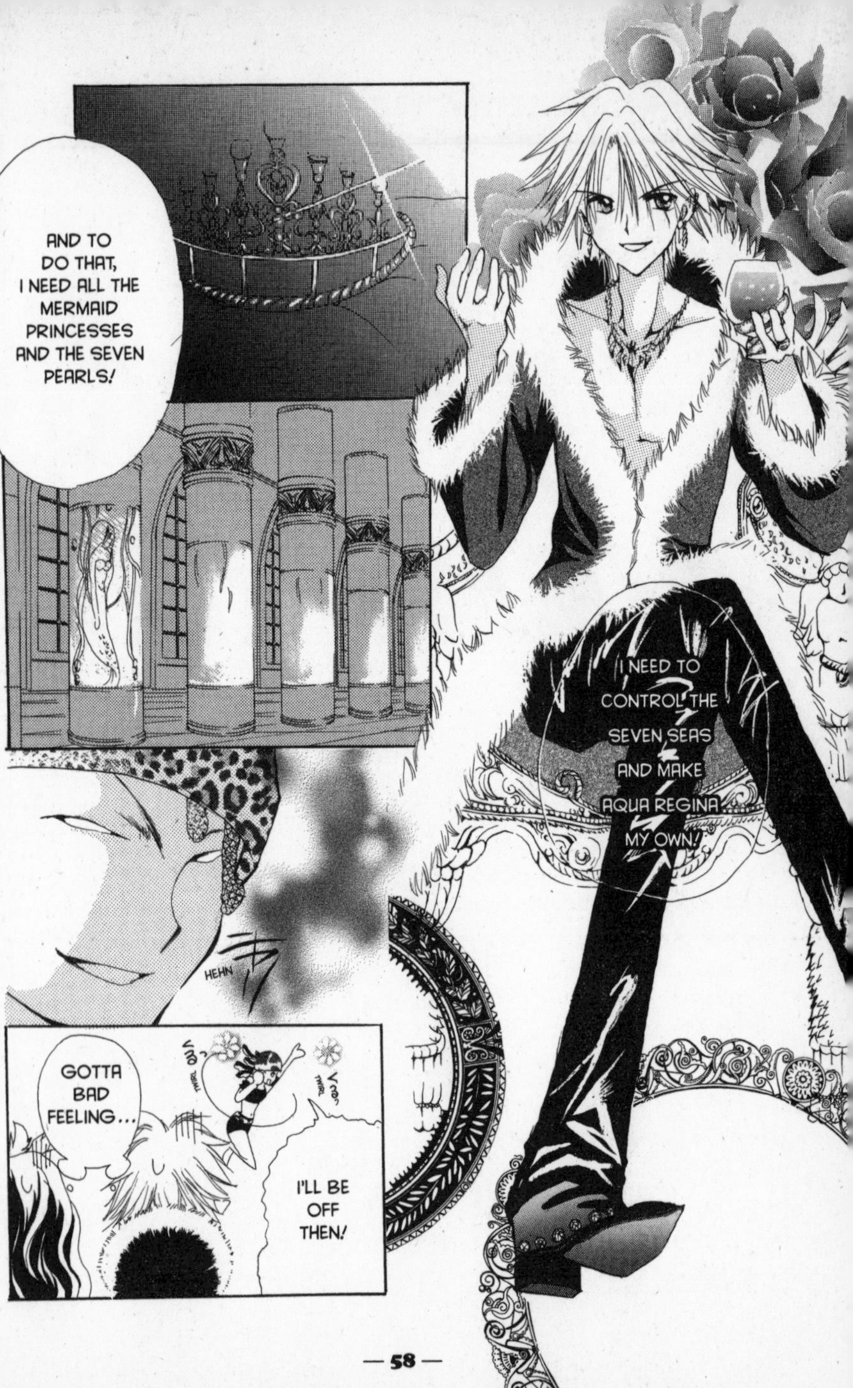
I NEED TO CONTROL THE SEVEN SEAS AND MAKE AQUA REGINA MY OWN!
AND TO DO THAT, I NEED ALL THE MERMAID PRINCESSES AND THE SEVEN PEARLS!
HEHN
TWIRL
TWIRL
I'LL BE OFF THEN!
GOTTA BAD FEELING...

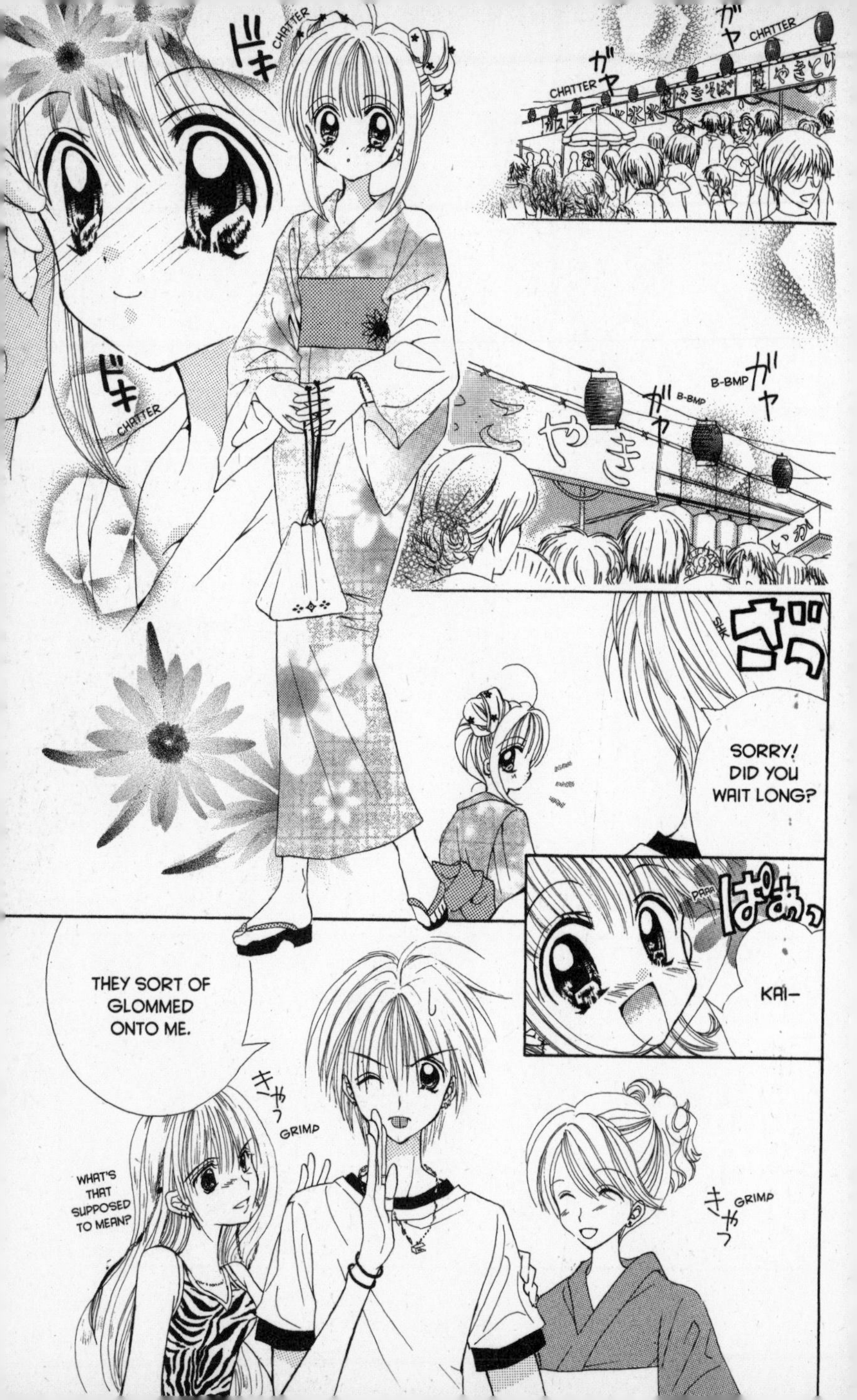
ガヤ
CHATTER
ガヤ
CHATTER
ガヤ
B-BMP
ガヤ
B-BMP
ドキ
CHATTER
ドキ
CHATTER
ざっ
SORRY! DID YOU WAIT LONG?
ぱぁっ
PAAA
KAI-
THEY SORT OF GLOMMED ONTO ME.
きゃっ
GRIMP
WHAT'S THAT SUPPOSED TO MEAN?
きゃっ
GRIMP

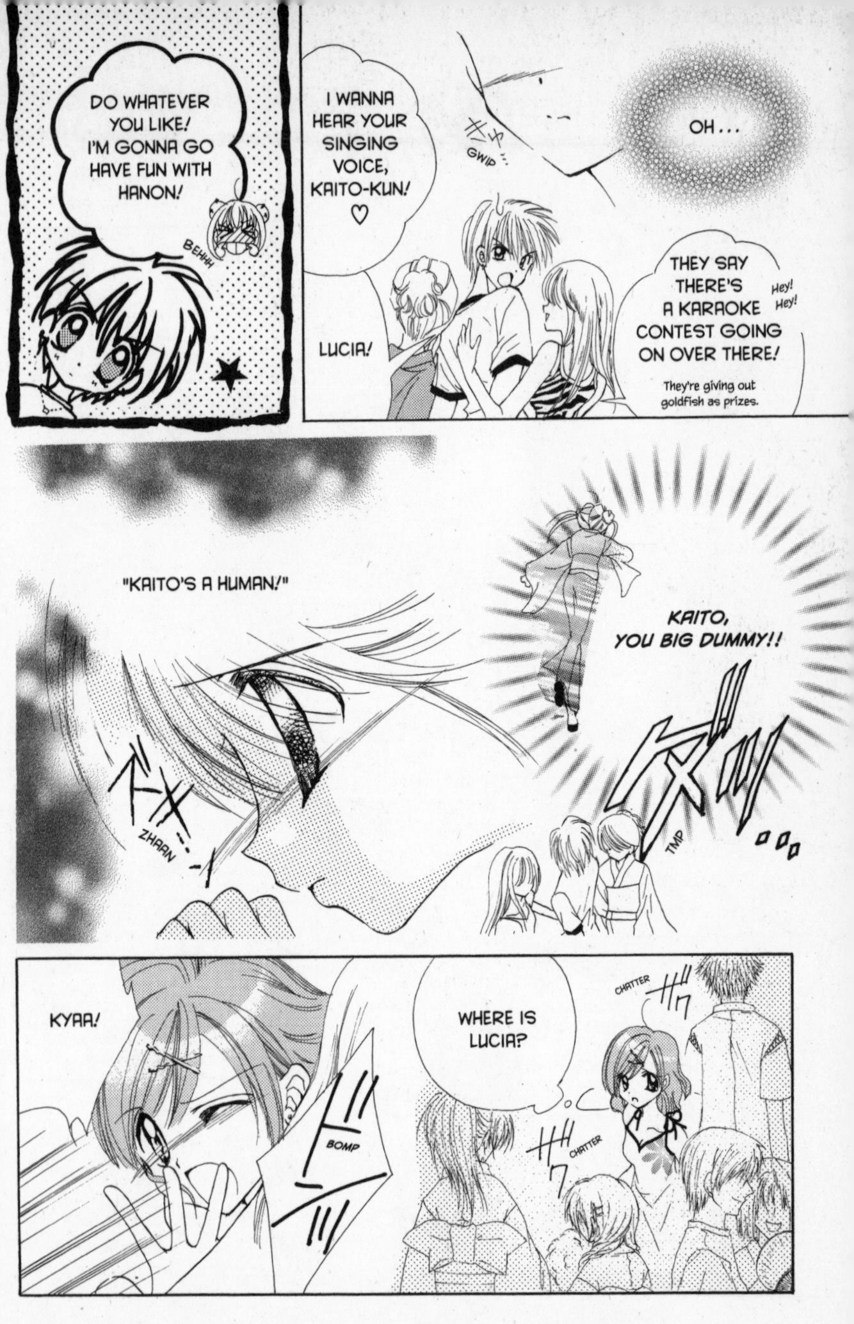
OH...
THEY SAY THERE'S A KARAOKE CONTEST GOING ON OVER THERE!
Hey! Hey!
They're giving out goldfish as prizes.
GWIP
I WANNA HEAR YOUR SINGING VOICE, KAITO-KUN! ♡
LUCIA!
DO WHATEVER YOU LIKE! I'M GONNA GO HAVE FUN WITH HANON!
BEHHH
KAITO, YOU BIG DUMMY!!
TMP
"KAITO'S A HUMAN!"
ZHAAN
CHATTER
WHERE IS LUCIA?
CHATTER
BOMP
KYAA!

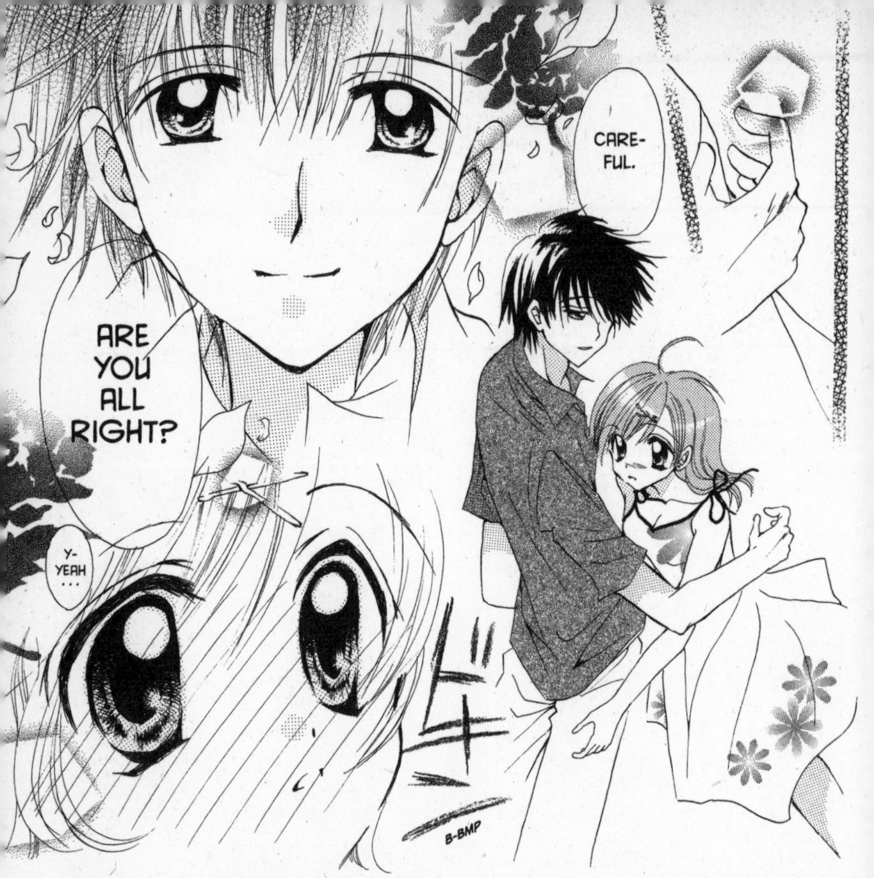
CARE-FUL.
ARE YOU ALL RIGHT?
Y-YEAH...
B-BMP
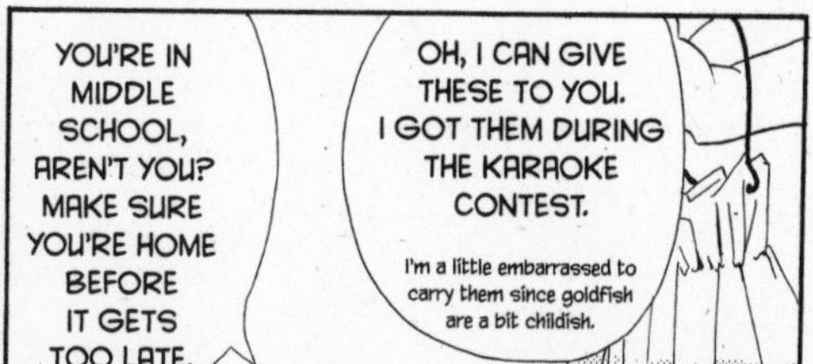
OH, I CAN GIVE THESE TO YOU. I GOT THEM DURING THE KARAOKE CONTEST.
I'm a little embarrassed to carry them since goldfish are a bit childish.
YOU'RE IN MIDDLE SCHOOL, AREN'T YOU? MAKE SURE YOU'RE HOME BEFORE IT GETS TOO LATE.
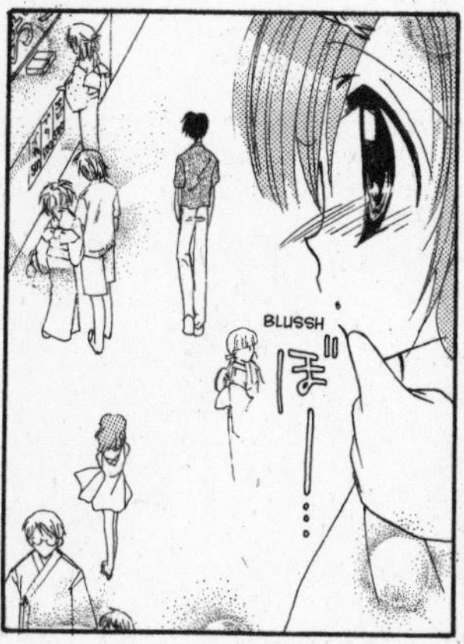
BLUSSH

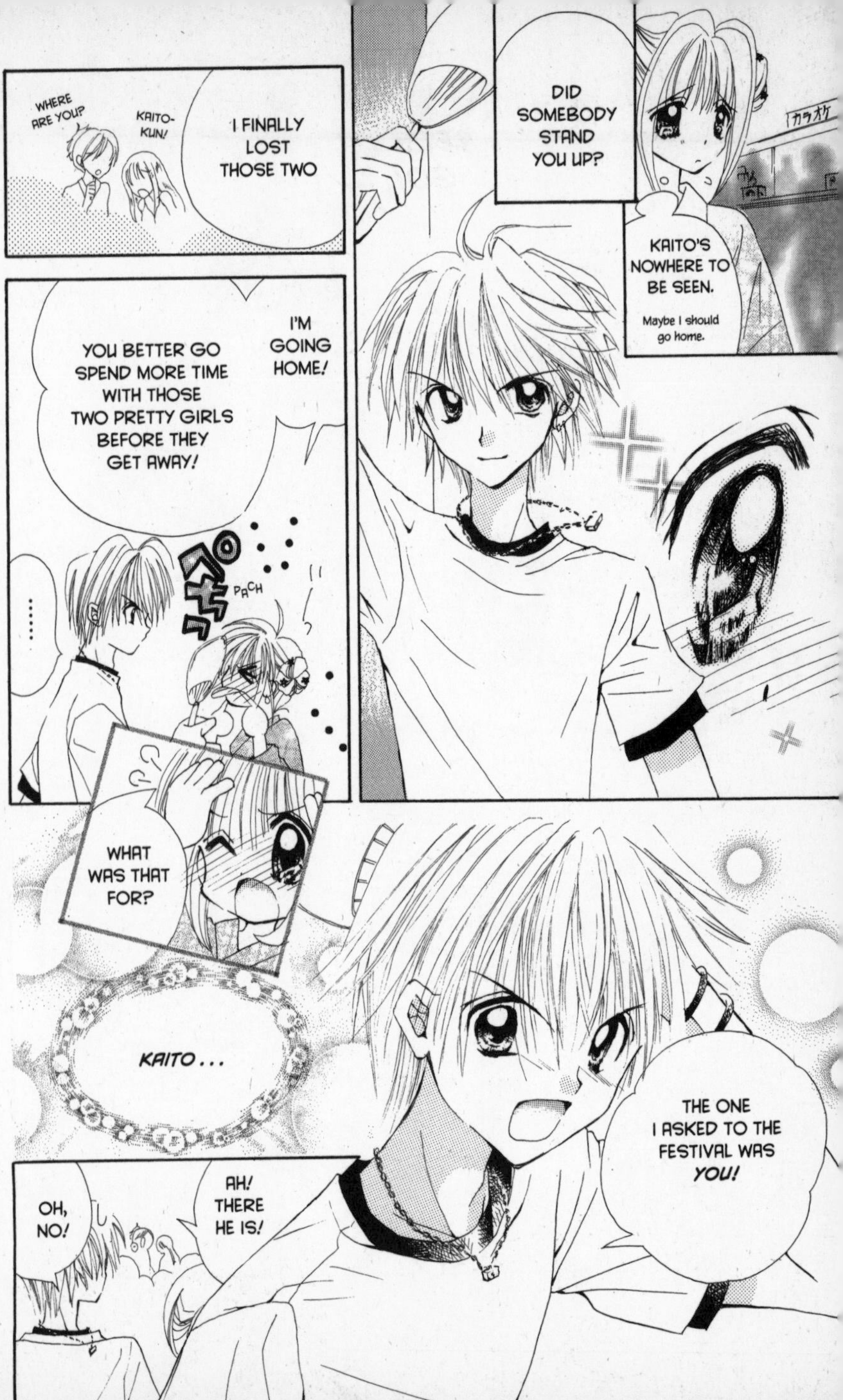
カラオケ
DID SOMEBODY STAND YOU UP?
KAITO'S NOWHERE TO BE SEEN.
Maybe I should go home.
I FINALLY LOST THOSE TWO
KAITO-KUN!
WHERE ARE YOU?
I'M GOING HOME!
YOU BETTER GO SPEND MORE TIME WITH THOSE TWO PRETTY GIRLS BEFORE THEY GET AWAY!
PACH
......
WHAT WAS THAT FOR?
THE ONE I ASKED TO THE FESTIVAL WAS *YOU!*
*KAITO . . .*
AH! THERE HE IS!
OH, NO!

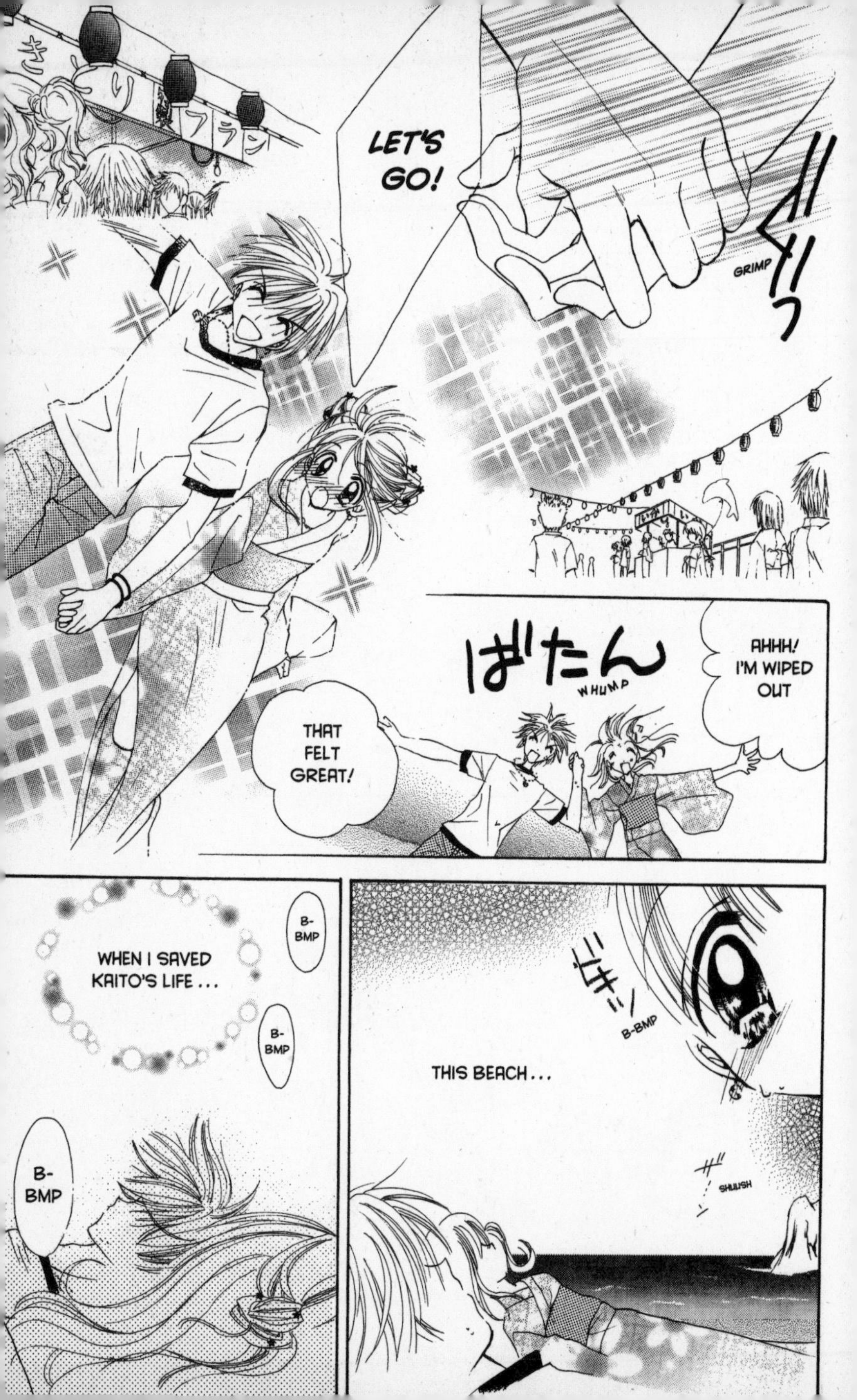

GRIMP
LET'S GO!
ばたん
WHUMP
AHHH! I'M WIPED OUT
THAT FELT GREAT!
B-BMP
THIS BEACH...
SHUUSH
B-BMP
WHEN I SAVED KAITO'S LIFE...
B-BMP
B-BMP

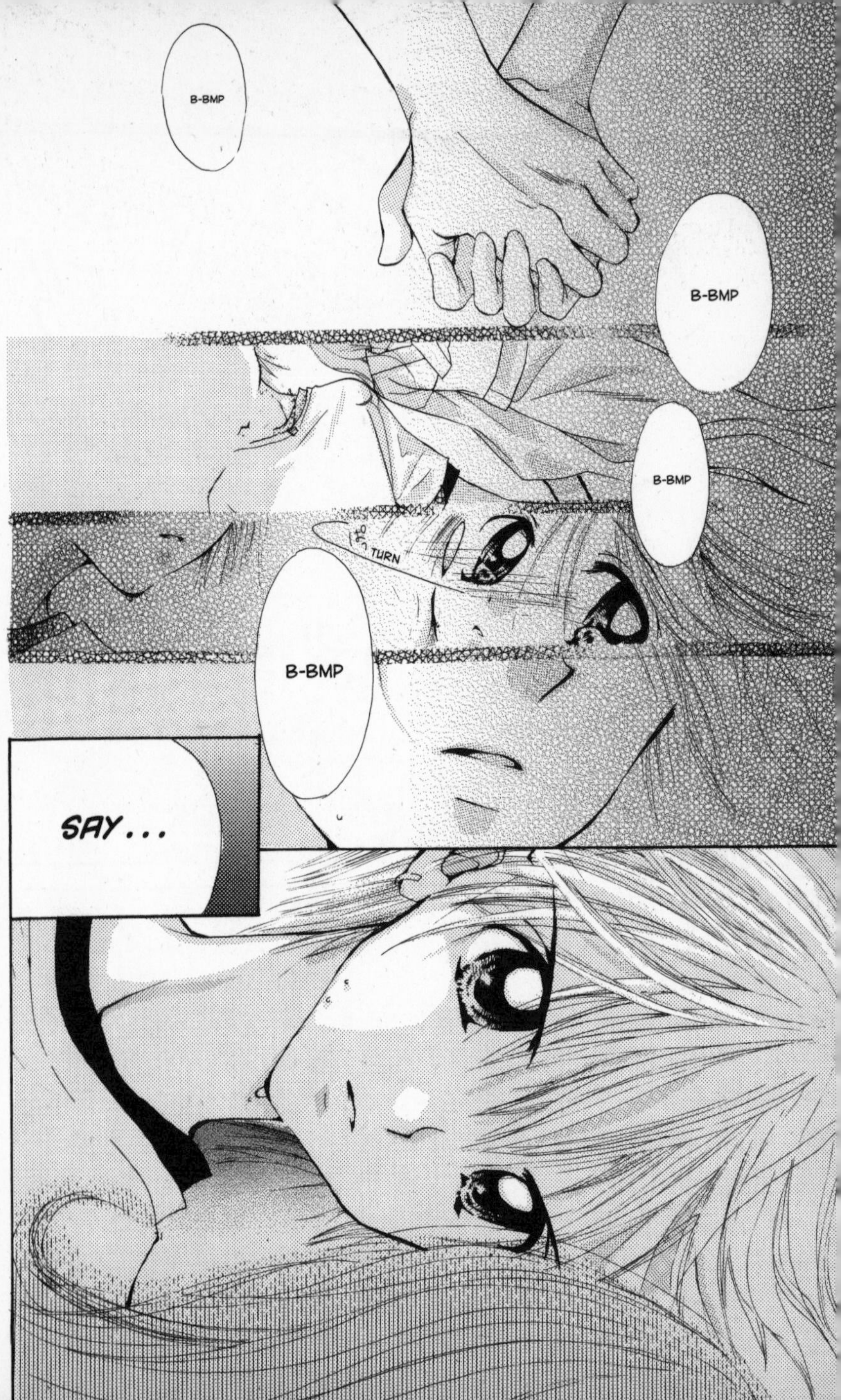
B-BMP
B-BMP
B-BMP
TURN
B-BMP
SAY...

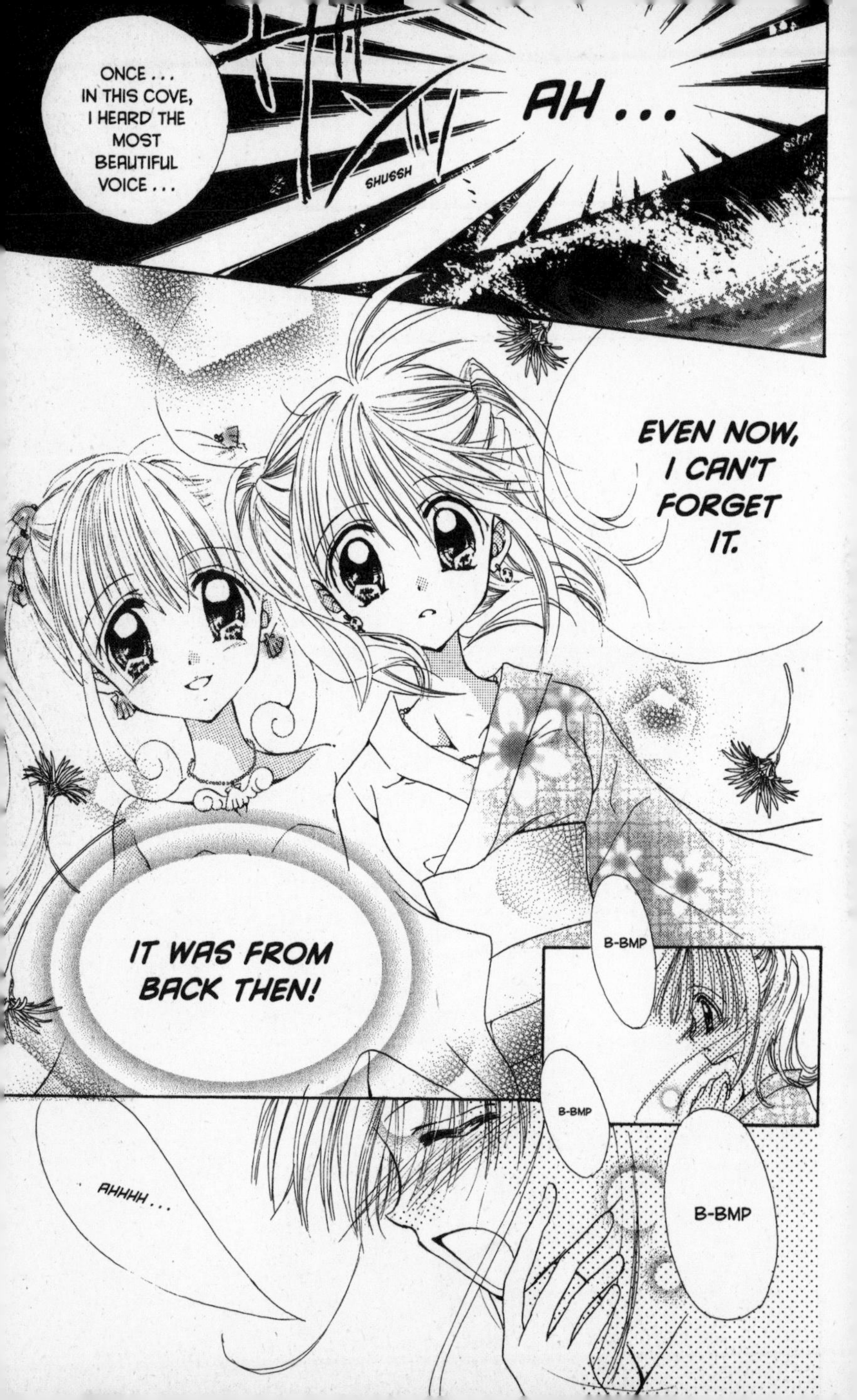
AH . . .
SHUSSH
ONCE . . . IN THIS COVE, I HEARD THE MOST BEAUTIFUL VOICE . . .
EVEN NOW, I CAN'T FORGET IT.
IT WAS FROM BACK THEN!
B-BMP
B-BMP
B-BMP
AHHHH . . .

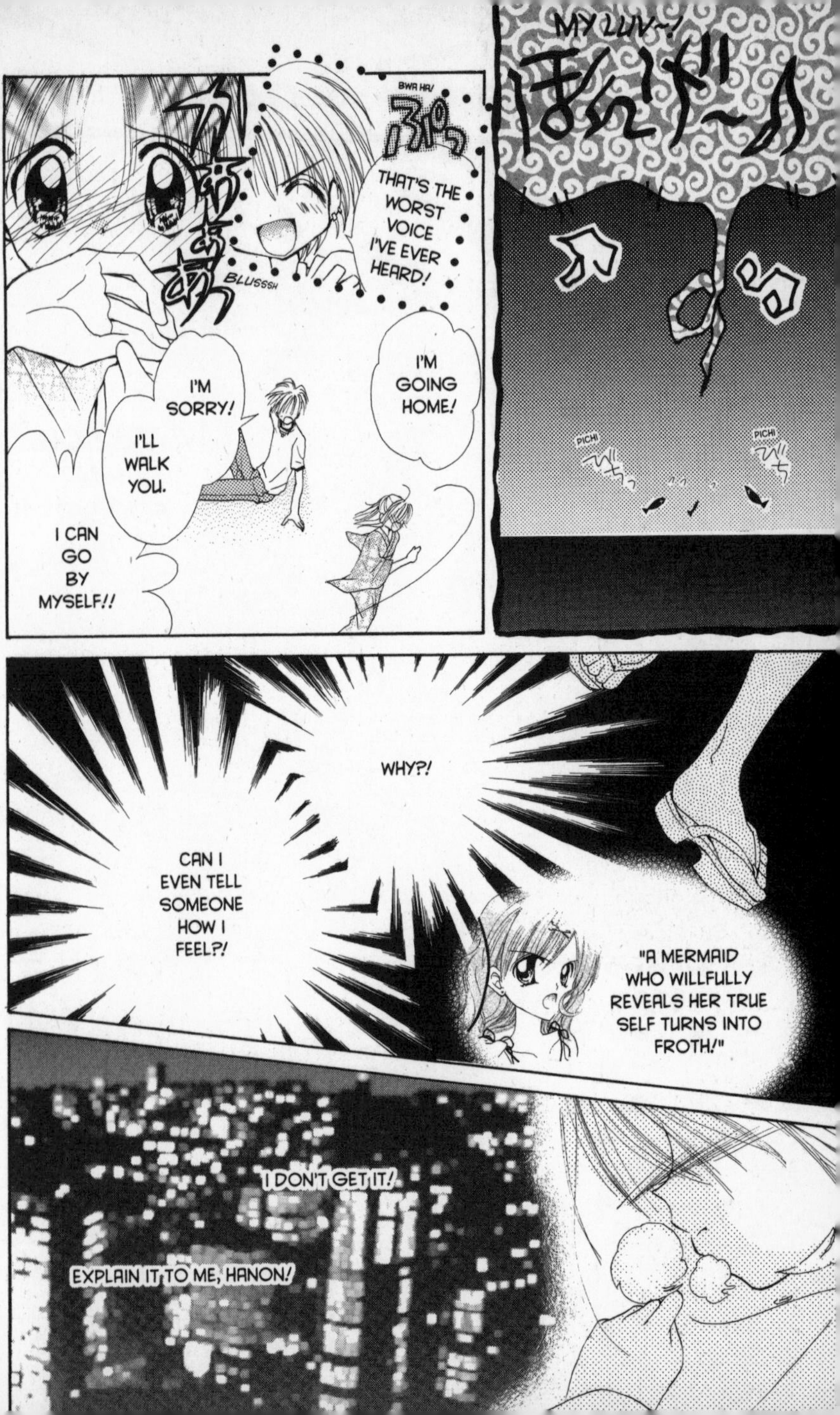
MY LUV~!
ほんにゃ~♪
PICHI
PICHI
BWA HA!
ぶはっ
THAT'S THE WORST VOICE I'VE EVER HEARD!
BLUSSSH
I'M GOING HOME!
I'M SORRY!
I'LL WALK YOU.
I CAN GO BY MYSELF!!
WHY?!
CAN I EVEN TELL SOMEONE HOW I FEEL?!
"A MERMAID WHO WILLFULLY REVEALS HER TRUE SELF TURNS INTO FROTH!"
I DON'T GET IT!
EXPLAIN IT TO ME, HANON!

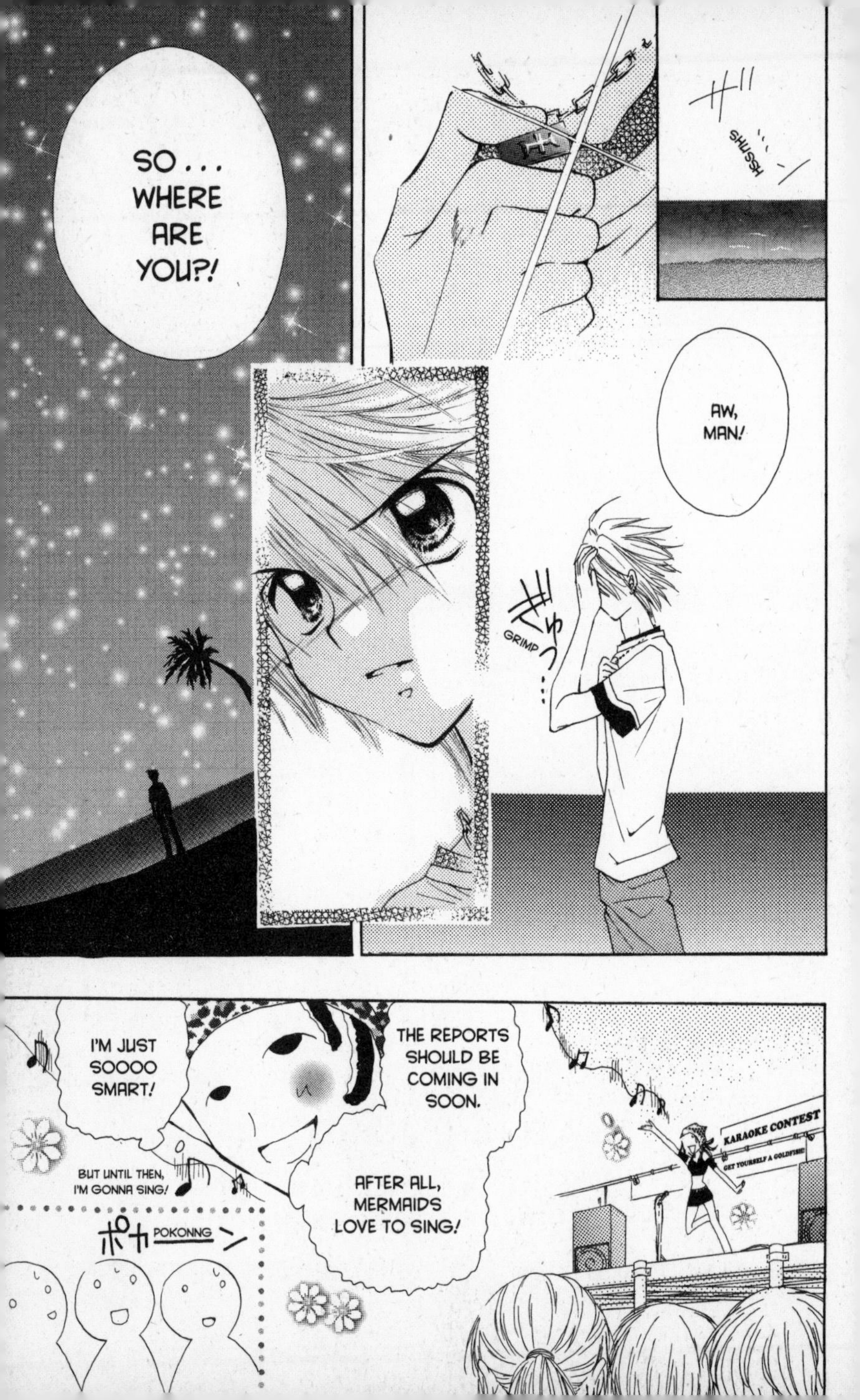
SHUSSH
AW, MAN!
ぎゅっ
GRIMP
SO... WHERE ARE YOU?!
KARAOKE CONTEST
GET YOURSELF A GOLDFISH!
THE REPORTS SHOULD BE COMING IN SOON.
AFTER ALL, MERMAIDS LOVE TO SING!
I'M JUST SOOOO SMART!
BUT UNTIL THEN, I'M GONNA SING!
ポカーン
POKONNG

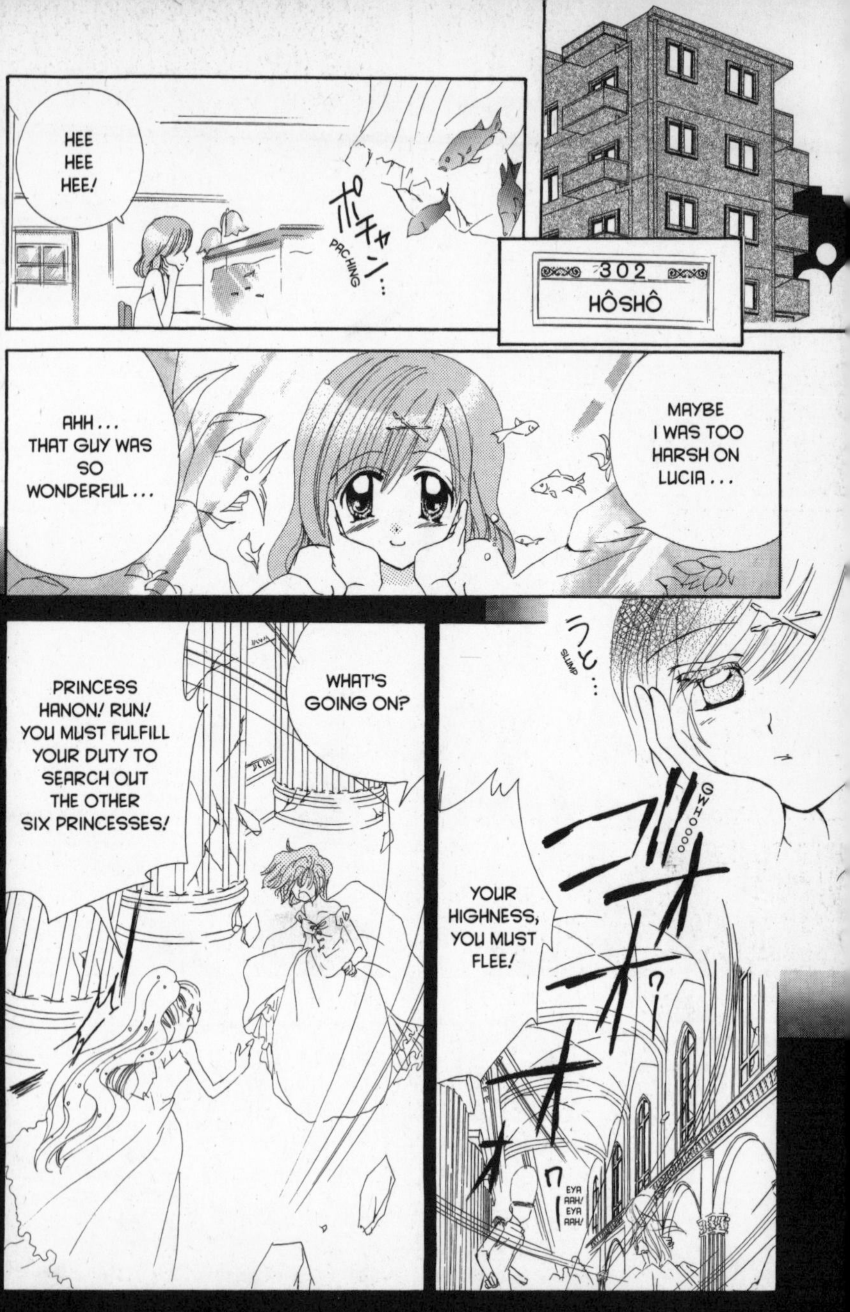
302
HÔSHÔ
HEE HEE HEE!
ポチャン…
PACHING
MAYBE I WAS TOO HARSH ON LUCIA...
AHH... THAT GUY WAS SO WONDERFUL...
うと…
SLUMP
ゴオオオ
GWHOOOO
YOUR HIGHNESS, YOU MUST FLEE!
EYA AAH! EYA AAH!
WHAT'S GOING ON?
PRINCESS HANON! RUN! YOU MUST FULFILL YOUR DUTY TO SEARCH OUT THE OTHER SIX PRINCESSES!

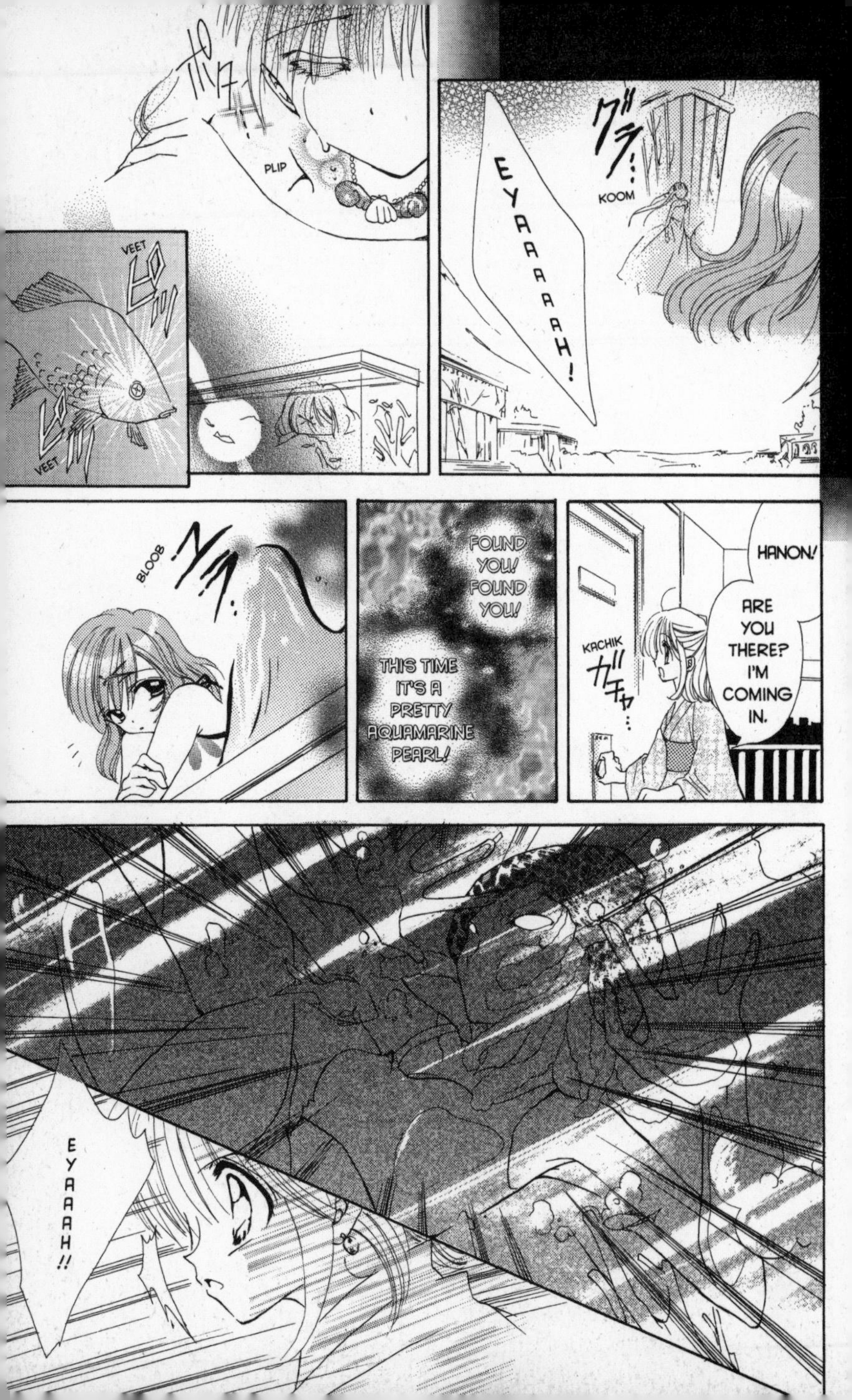

EYAAAAAAH!
KOOM
PLIP
VEET
VEET
HANON!
ARE YOU THERE? I'M COMING IN.
KACHIK
FOUND YOU! FOUND YOU!
THIS TIME IT'S A PRETTY AQUAMARINE PEARL!
BLOOB
EYAAAAH!!

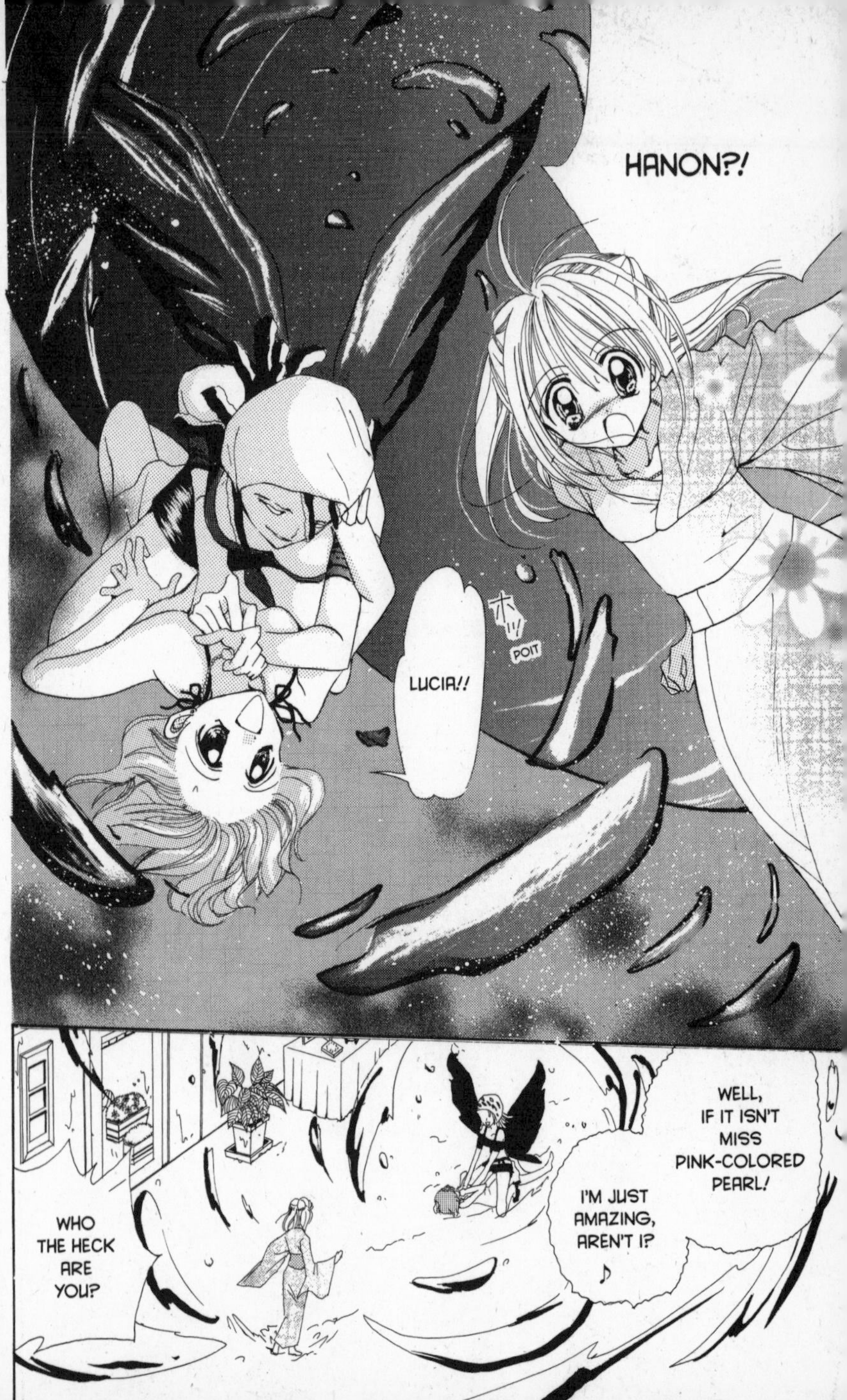
HANON?!
LUCIA!!
POIT
WELL, IF IT ISN'T MISS PINK-COLORED PEARL!
I'M JUST AMAZING, AREN'T I? ♪
WHO THE HECK ARE YOU?

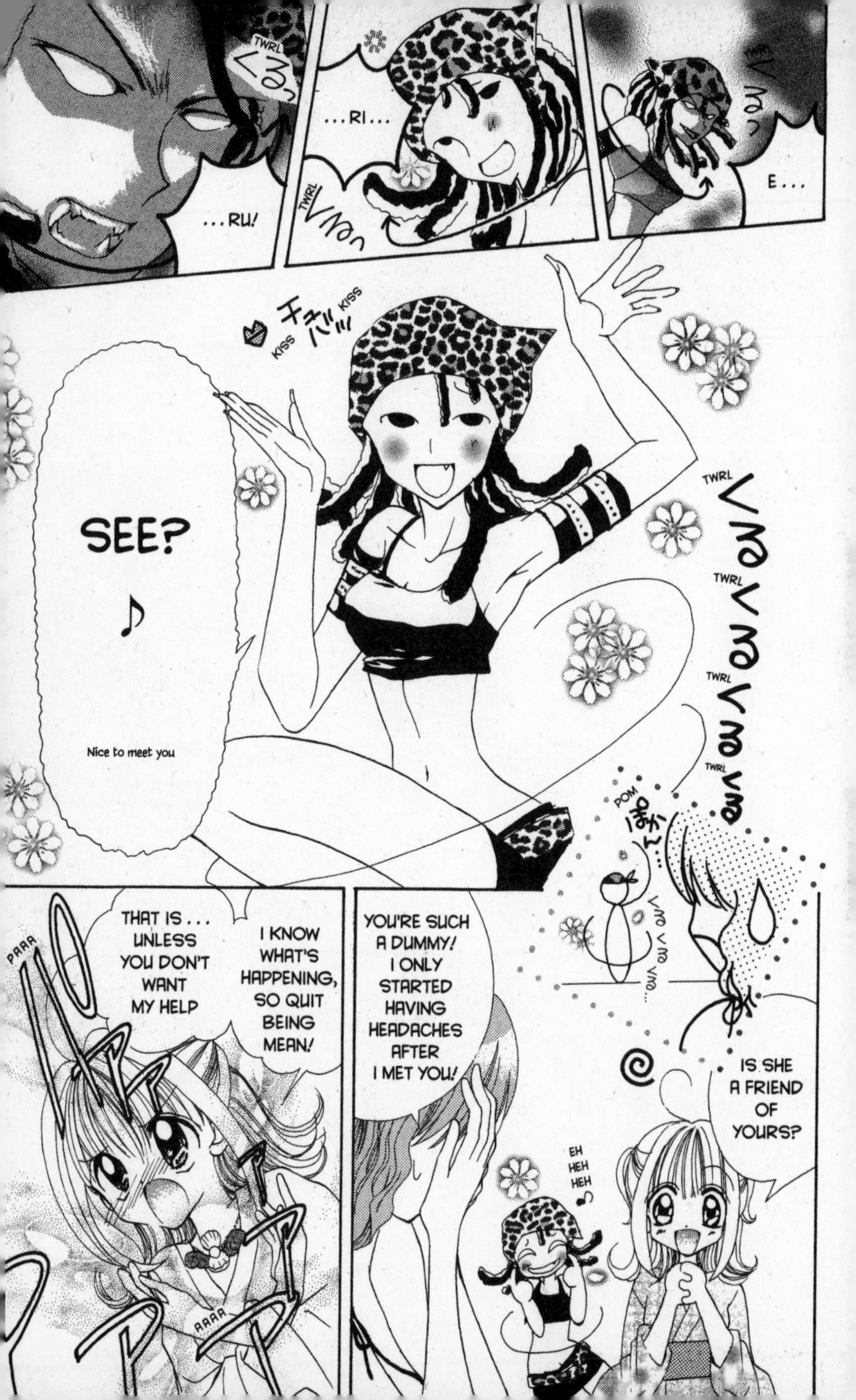

TWRL くるっ
E...
TWRL くるっ
...RI...
TWRL くるっ
...RU!
KISS チュバッ KISS
SEE? ♪
Nice to meet you
TWRL くる TWRL くる TWRL くる TWRL くる
POM ぽかん…
くるくるくる...
IS SHE A FRIEND OF YOURS?
EH HEH HEH ♪
YOU'RE SUCH A DUMMY! I ONLY STARTED HAVING HEADACHES AFTER I MET YOU!
I KNOW WHAT'S HAPPENING, SO QUIT BEING MEAN!
THAT IS... UNLESS YOU DON'T WANT MY HELP
PARRA
AAAA

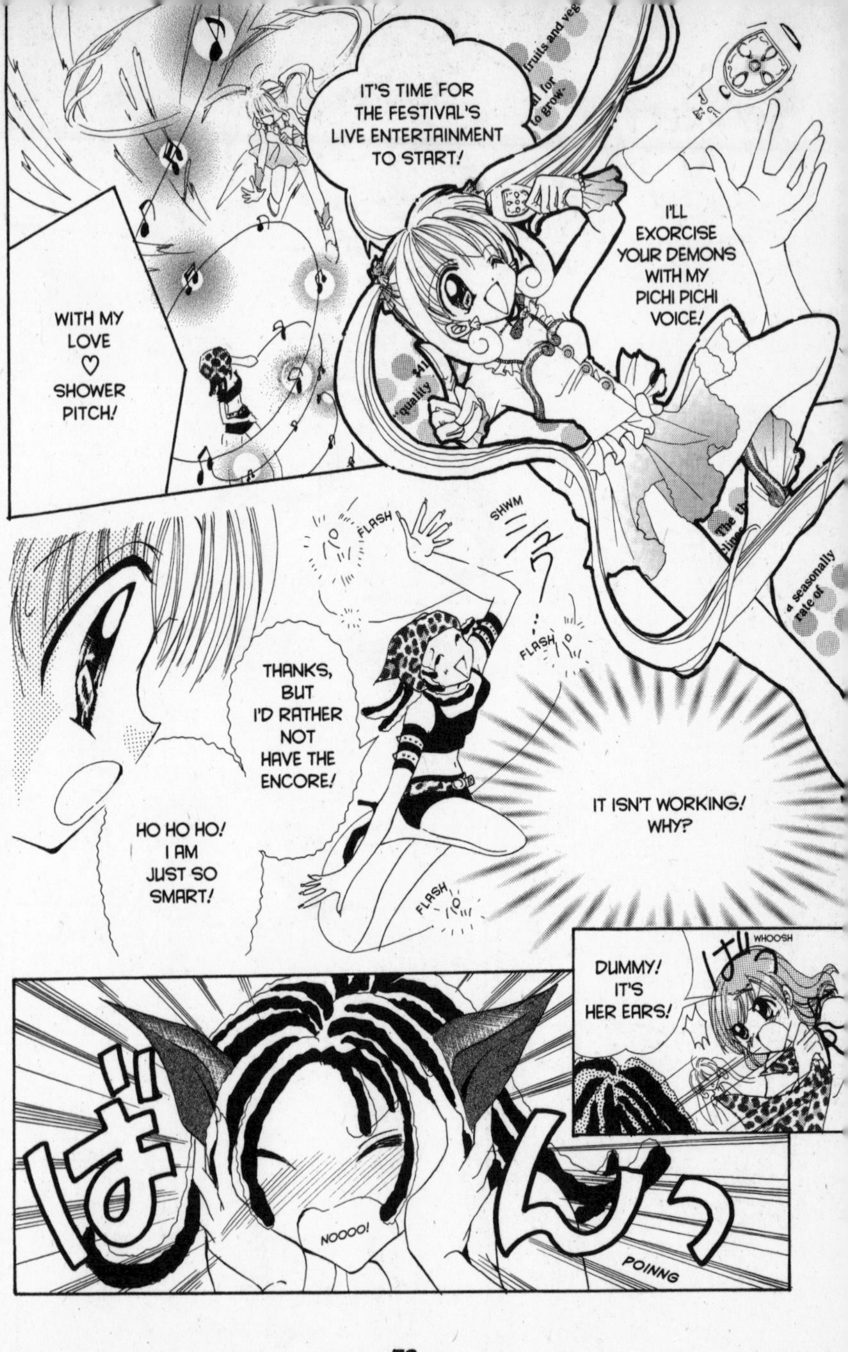
IT'S TIME FOR THE FESTIVAL'S LIVE ENTERTAINMENT TO START!
I'LL EXORCISE YOUR DEMONS WITH MY PICHI PICHI VOICE!
WITH MY LOVE ♡ SHOWER PITCH!
SHWM
FLASH
FLASH
IT ISN'T WORKING! WHY?
THANKS, BUT I'D RATHER NOT HAVE THE ENCORE!
HO HO HO! I AM JUST SO SMART!
FLASH
WHOOSH
DUMMY! IT'S HER EARS!
ばんっ
NOOOO!
POINNG

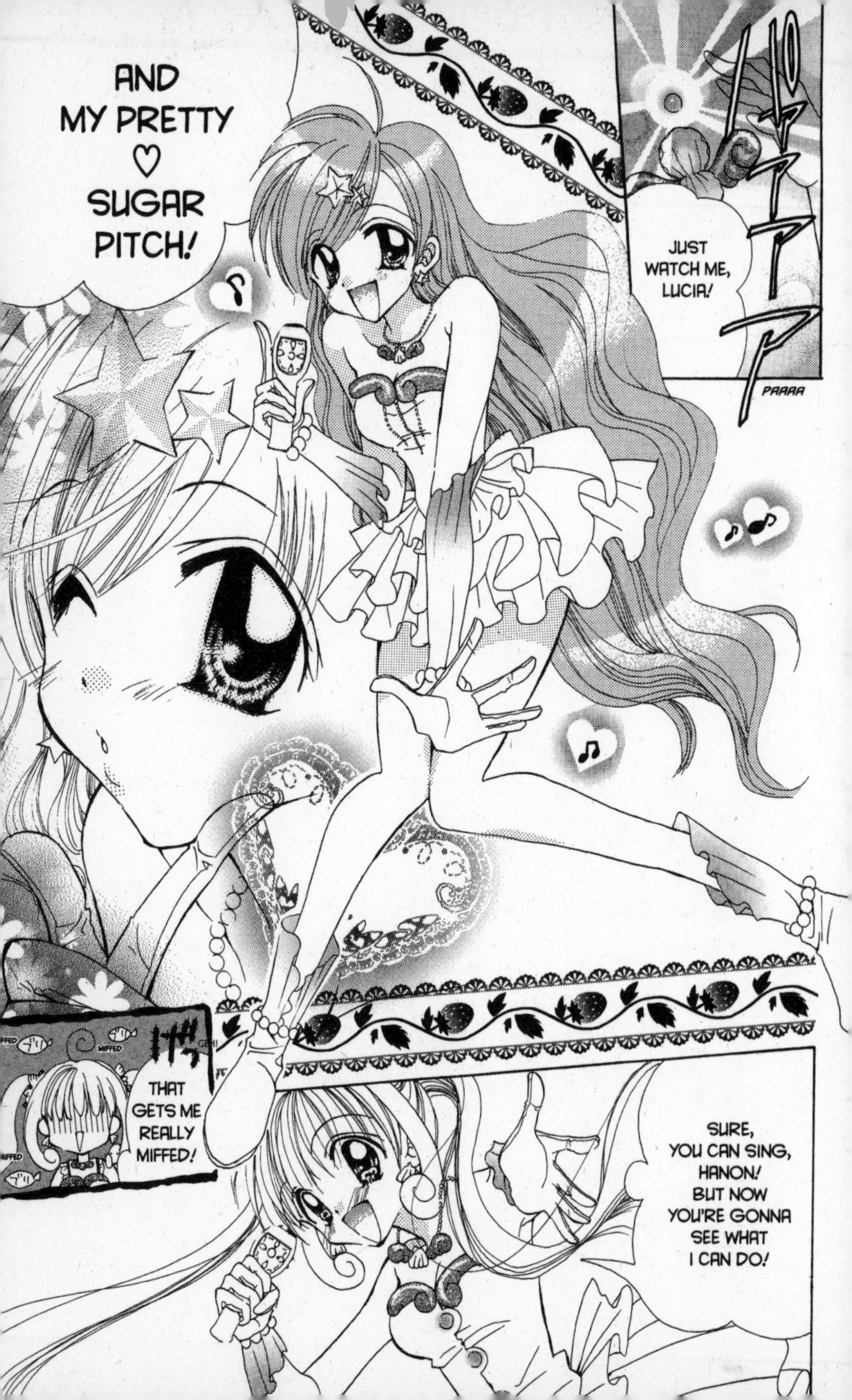
JUST WATCH ME, LUCIA!
PAAAA
AND MY PRETTY ♡ SUGAR PITCH!
SURE, YOU CAN SING, HANON! BUT NOW YOU'RE GONNA SEE WHAT I CAN DO!
MIFFED
MIFFED
THAT GETS ME REALLY MIFFED!
MIFFED

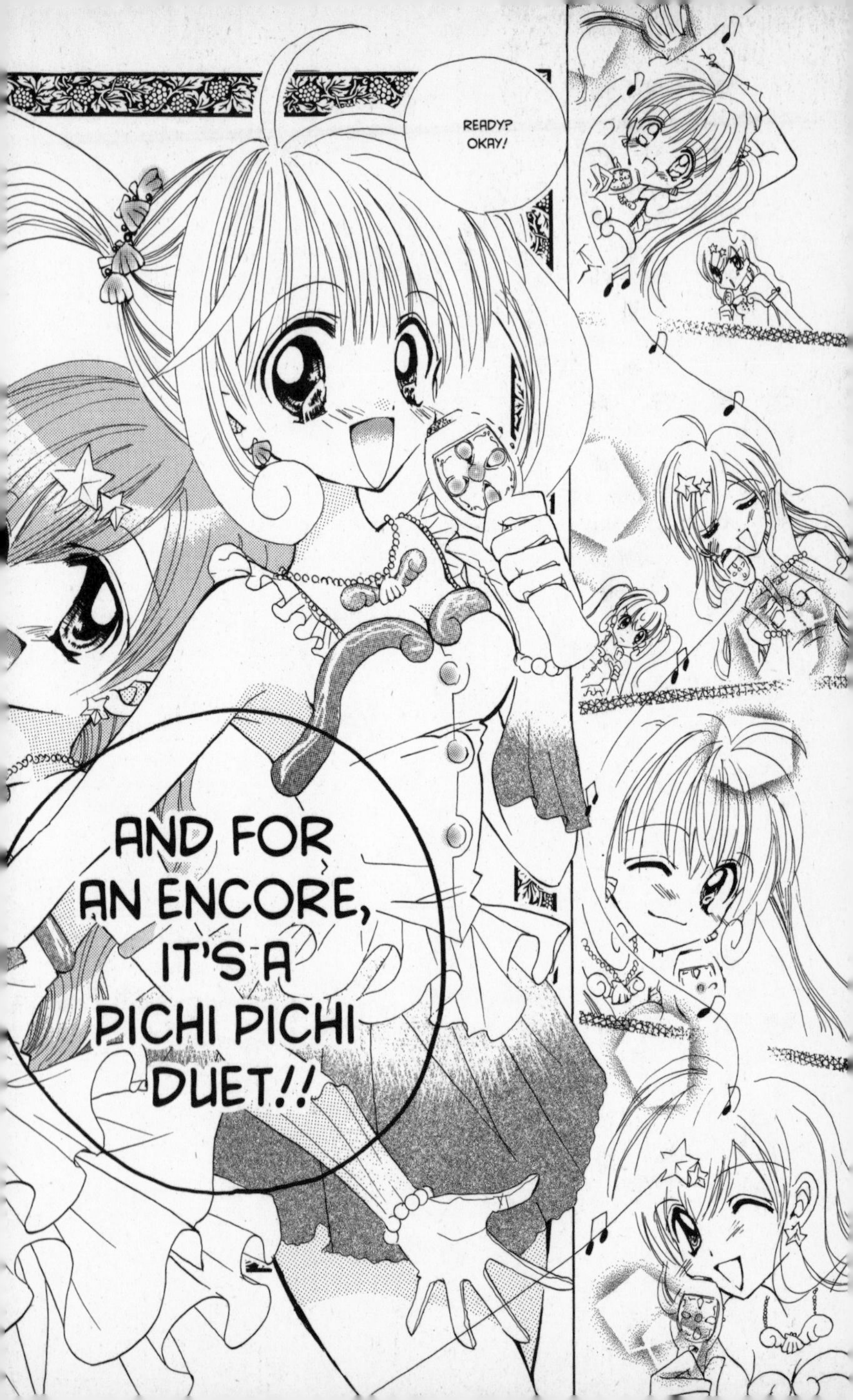
READY? OKAY!
AND FOR AN ENCORE, IT'S A PICHI PICHI DUET!!

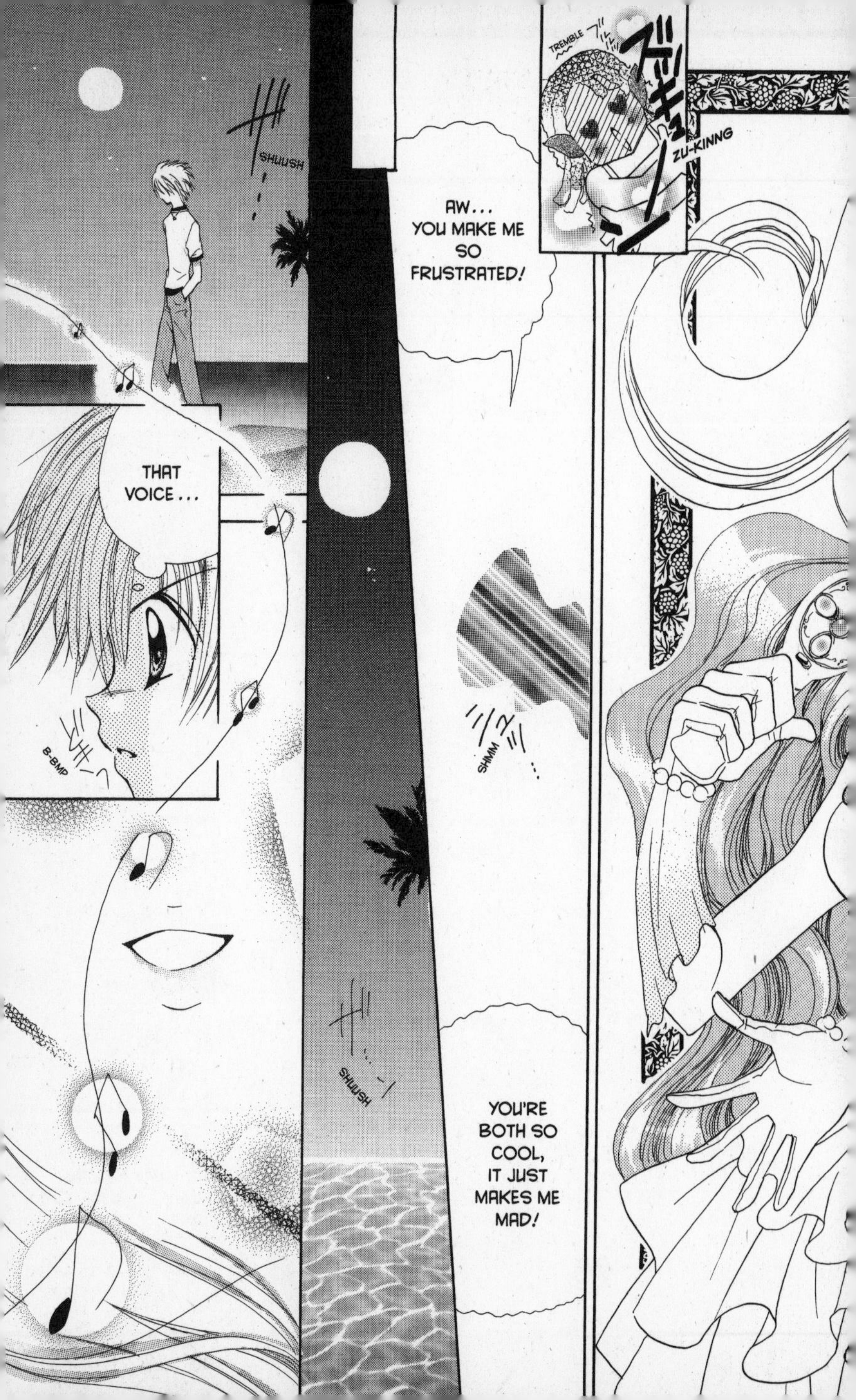
TREMBLE
ZU-KINNG
AW... YOU MAKE ME SO FRUSTRATED!
SHMM
SHUUSH
YOU'RE BOTH SO COOL, IT JUST MAKES ME MAD!
SHUUSH
THAT VOICE...
B-BMP

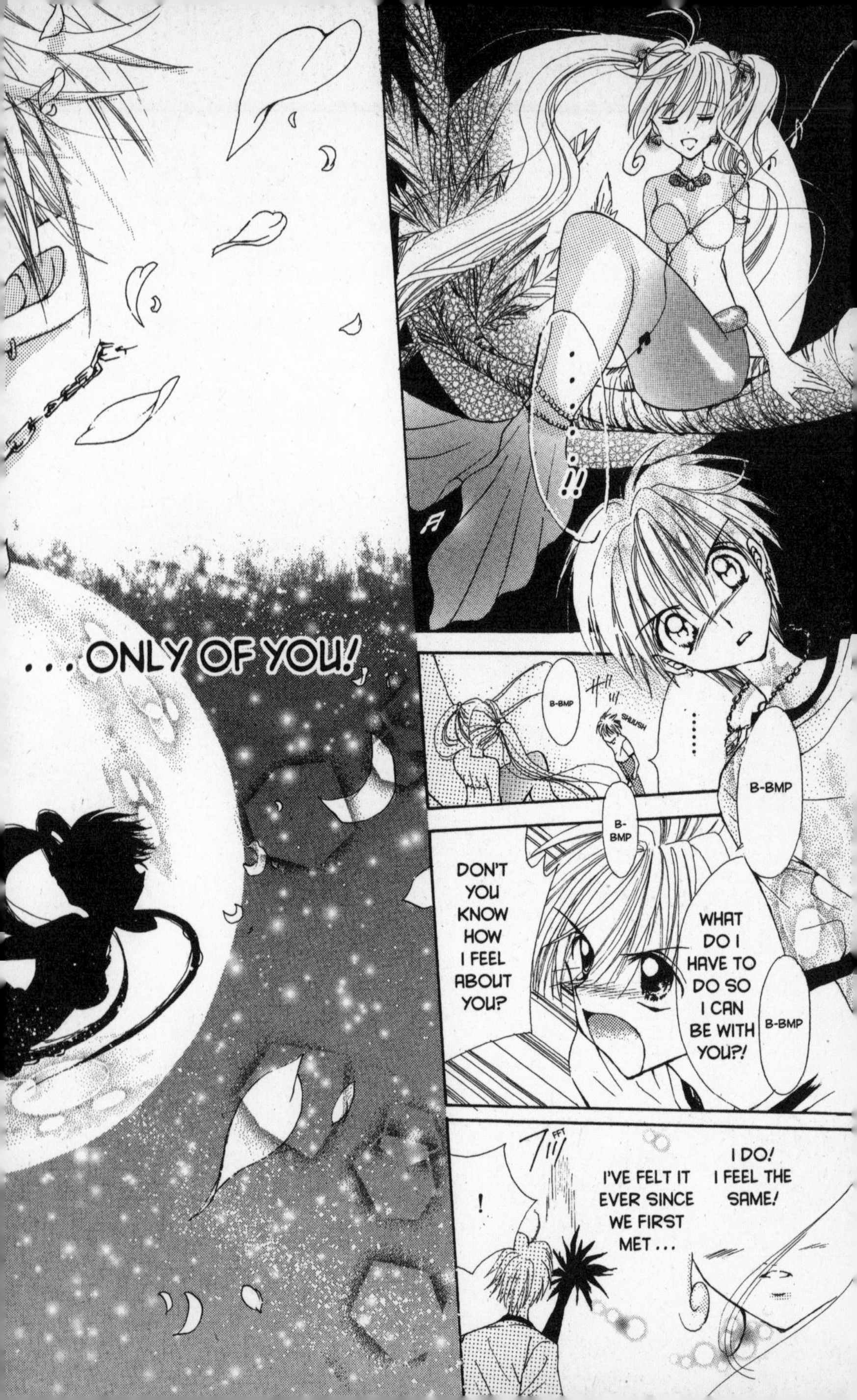
......!!
......
B-BMP
SHUSH
B-BMP
B-BMP
B-BMP
WHAT DO I HAVE TO DO SO I CAN BE WITH YOU?!
DON'T YOU KNOW HOW I FEEL ABOUT YOU?
I DO! I FEEL THE SAME!
I'VE FELT IT EVER SINCE WE FIRST MET...
FFT
!
...ONLY OF YOU!

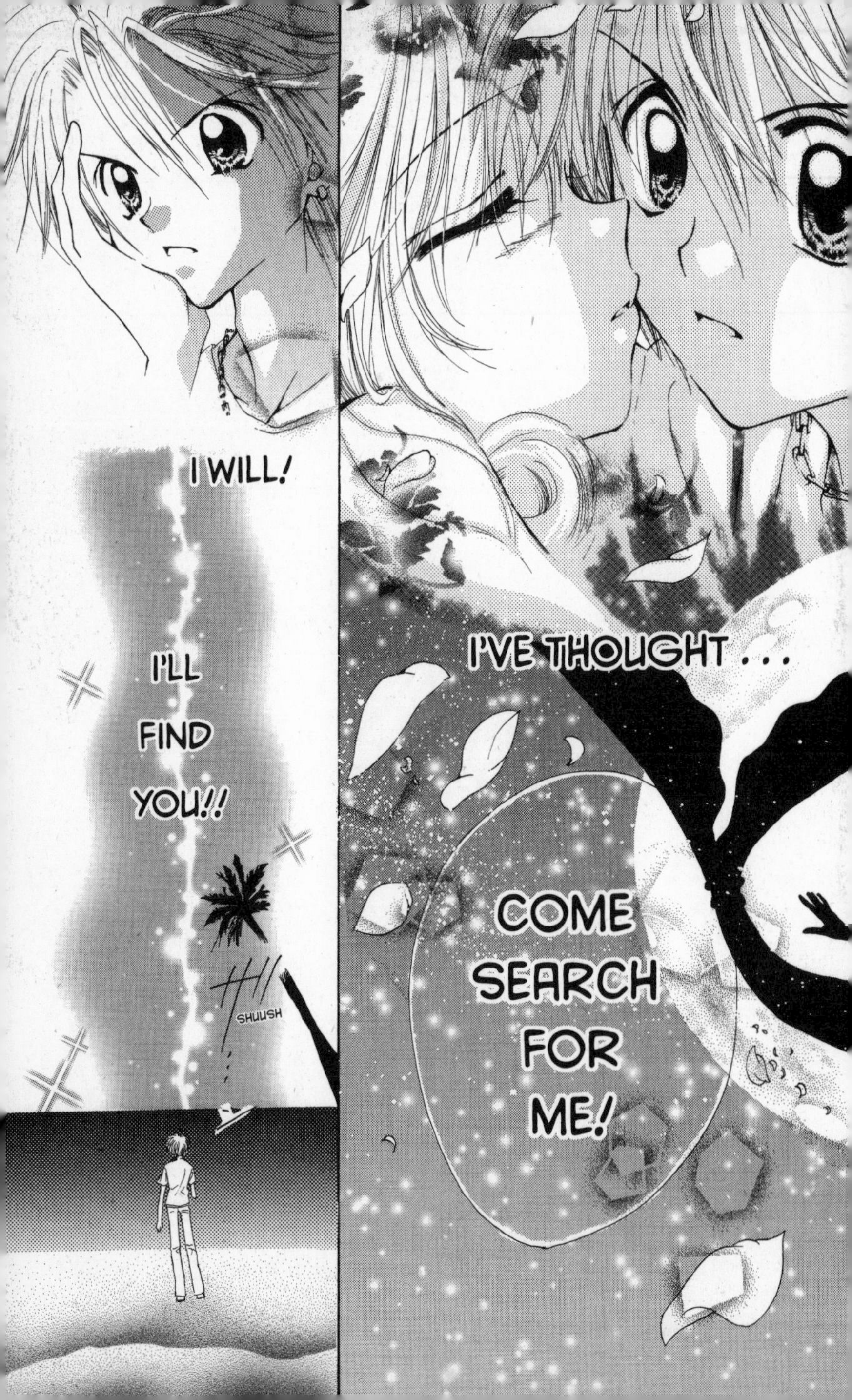
I'VE THOUGHT . . .
COME SEARCH FOR ME!
I WILL!
I'LL FIND YOU!!
SHUUSH

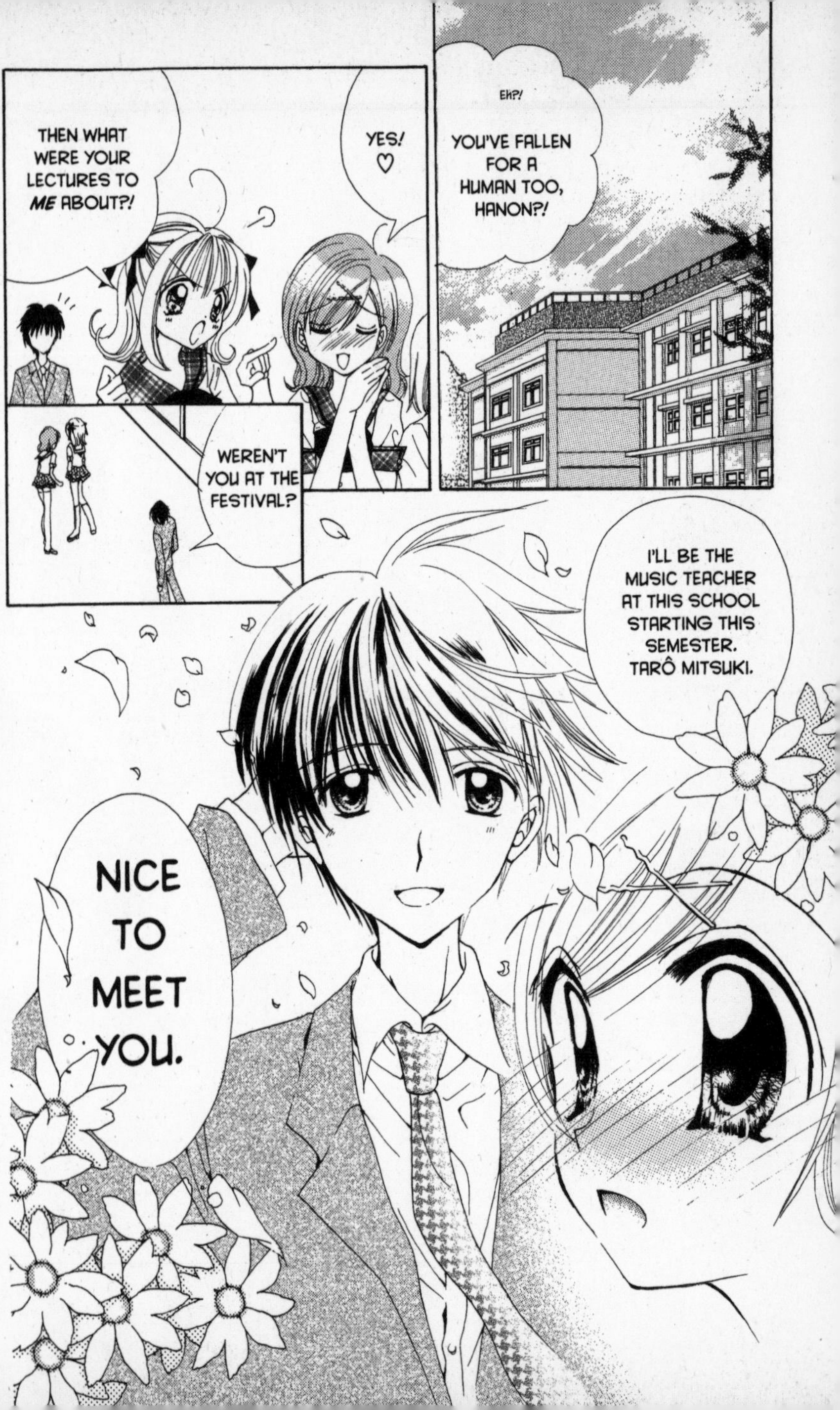
Eh?!
YOU'VE FALLEN FOR A HUMAN TOO, HANON?!
YES! ♡
THEN WHAT WERE YOUR LECTURES TO *ME* ABOUT?!
WEREN'T YOU AT THE FESTIVAL?
I'LL BE THE MUSIC TEACHER AT THIS SCHOOL STARTING THIS SEMESTER. TARÔ MITSUKI.
NICE TO MEET YOU.

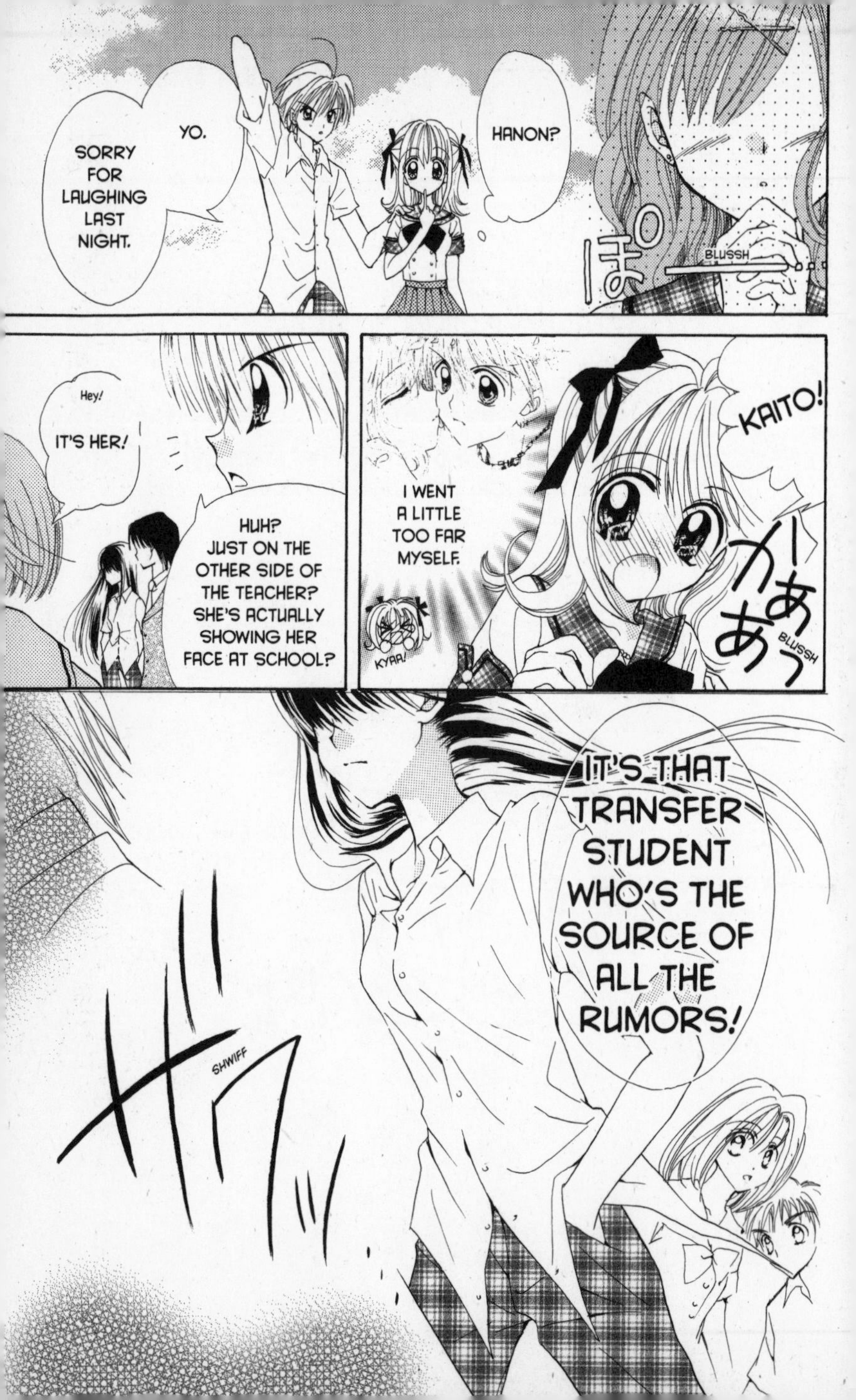
ぽー
BLUSSH
HANON?
YO.
SORRY FOR LAUGHING LAST NIGHT.
KAITO!
かあぁっ
BLUSSH
I WENT A LITTLE TOO FAR MYSELF.
KYAA!
Hey!
IT'S HER!
HUH? JUST ON THE OTHER SIDE OF THE TEACHER? SHE'S ACTUALLY SHOWING HER FACE AT SCHOOL?
IT'S THAT TRANSFER STUDENT WHO'S THE SOURCE OF ALL THE RUMORS!
SHWIFF

## THANK YOU SO MUCH FOR READING PICHI PICHI PITCH!!

NICE TO MEET YOU, EVERYONE. I AM YOKOTE, AND I'M IN CHARGE OF THE STORY.

IT FEELS LIKE A DREAM FOR THE STORY THAT I THOUGHT UP TO BECOME A MANGA! THANK YOU SO MUCH, HANAMORI-SENSEI!

BOW

礼！

PLEASE BE GOOD TO THE BOOK, OKAY?

FROM HERE ON OUT, I'M GOING TO TRY, TRY EVEN HARDER!!

2003.01

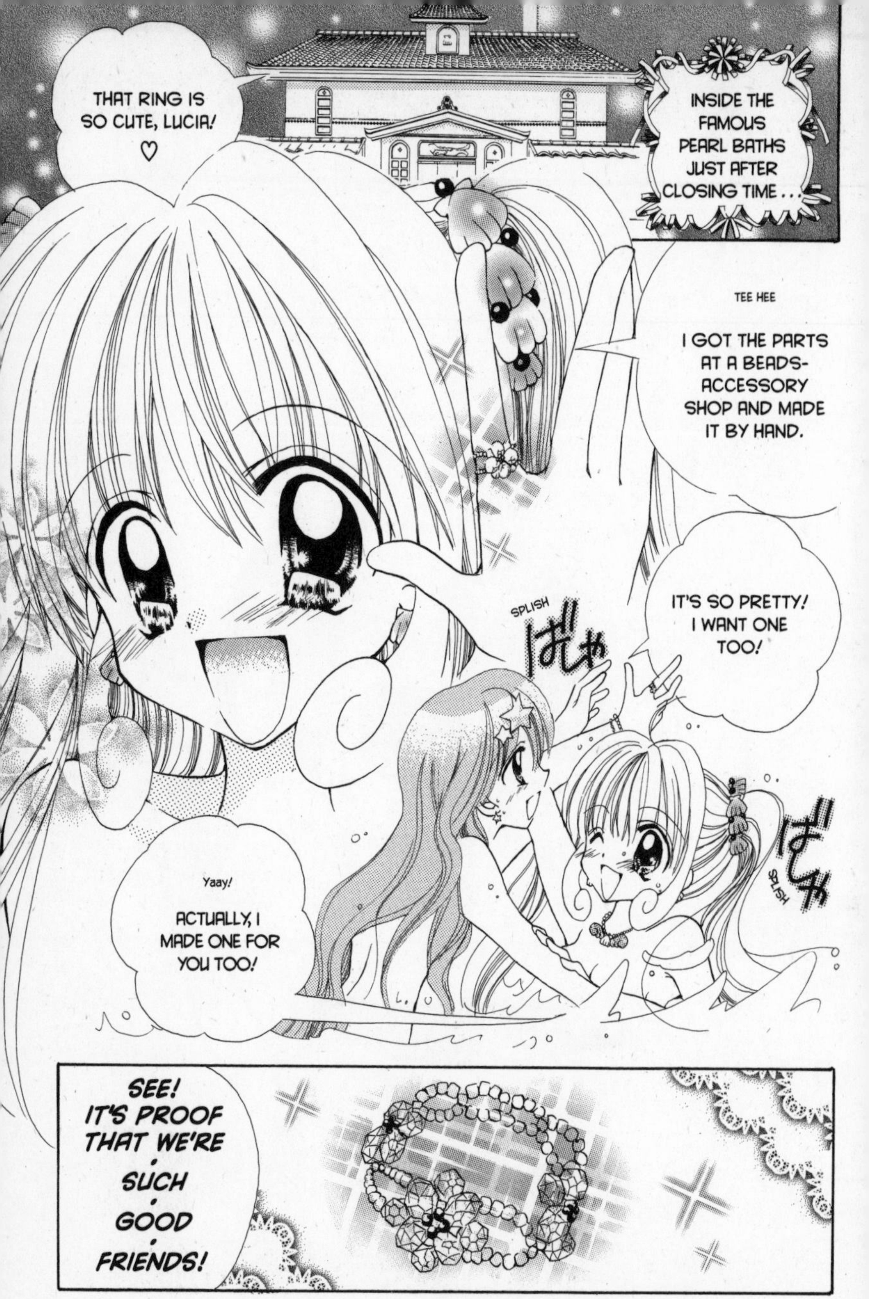
INSIDE THE FAMOUS PEARL BATHS JUST AFTER CLOSING TIME . . .
THAT RING IS SO CUTE, LUCIA! ♡
TEE HEE
I GOT THE PARTS AT A BEADS-ACCESSORY SHOP AND MADE IT BY HAND.
IT'S SO PRETTY! I WANT ONE TOO!
SPLISH
ばしゃ
SPLISH
ばしゃ
Yaay!
ACTUALLY, I MADE ONE FOR YOU TOO!
SEE! IT'S PROOF THAT WE'RE SUCH GOOD FRIENDS!

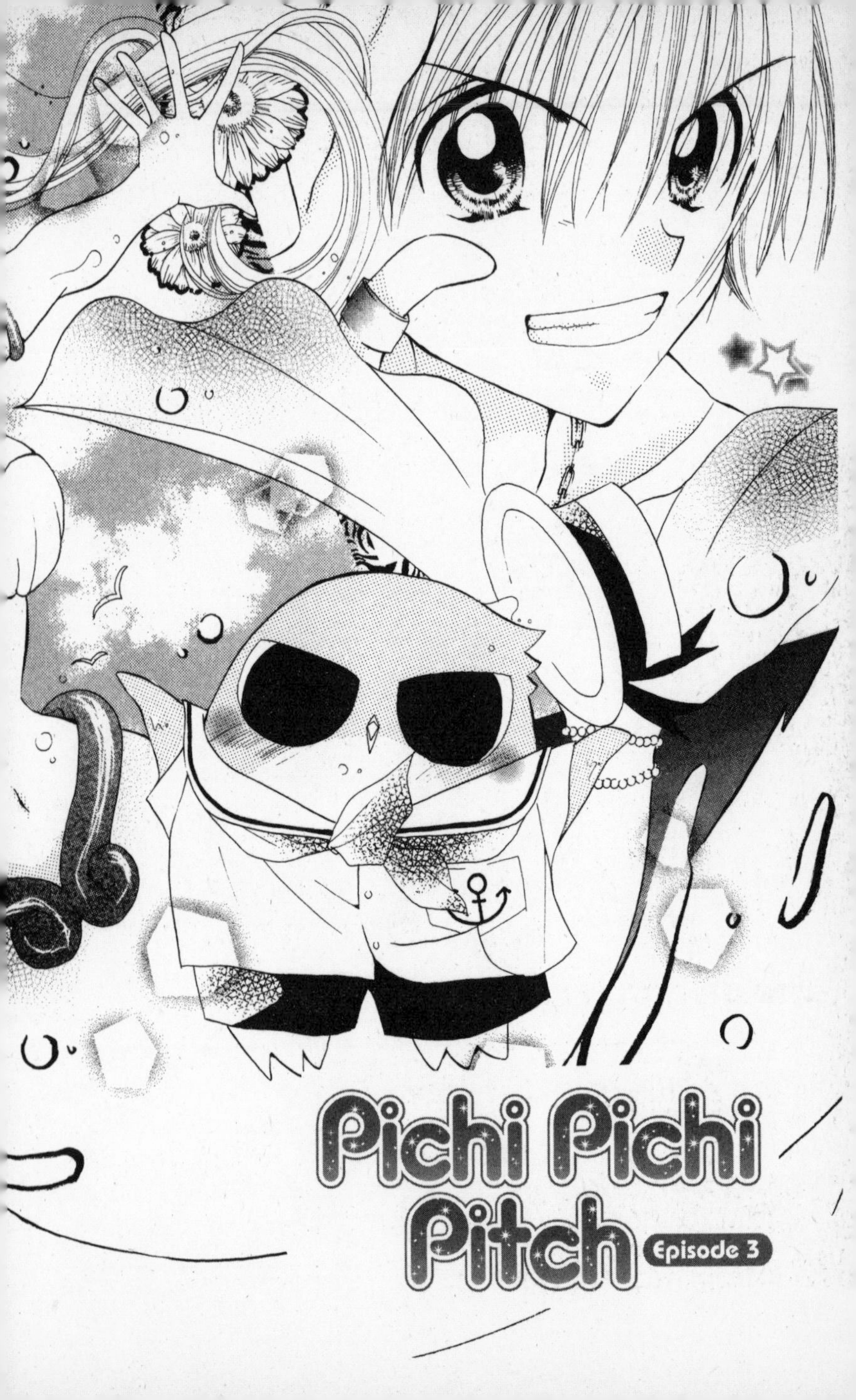
Pichi Pichi Pitch
Episode 3

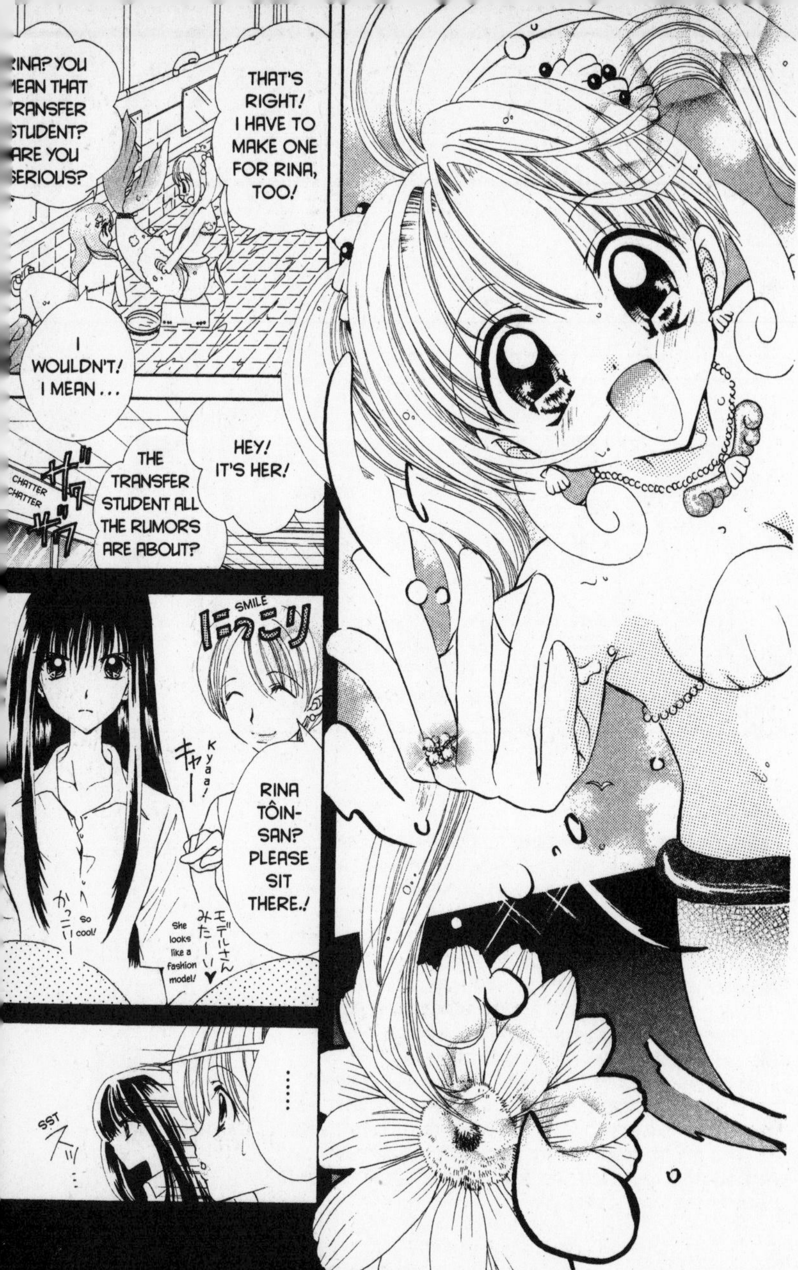
THAT'S RIGHT! I HAVE TO MAKE ONE FOR RINA, TOO!
RINA? YOU MEAN THAT TRANSFER STUDENT? ARE YOU SERIOUS?
I WOULDN'T! I MEAN...
HEY! IT'S HER!
THE TRANSFER STUDENT ALL THE RUMORS ARE ABOUT?
ザワザワ
CHATTER CHATTER
にっこり
SMILE
RINA TÔIN-SAN? PLEASE SIT THERE.!
キャー
Kyaa!
モデルさんみたーい♥
She looks like a fashion model!
かっこいー
So cool!
......
スッ...
SST

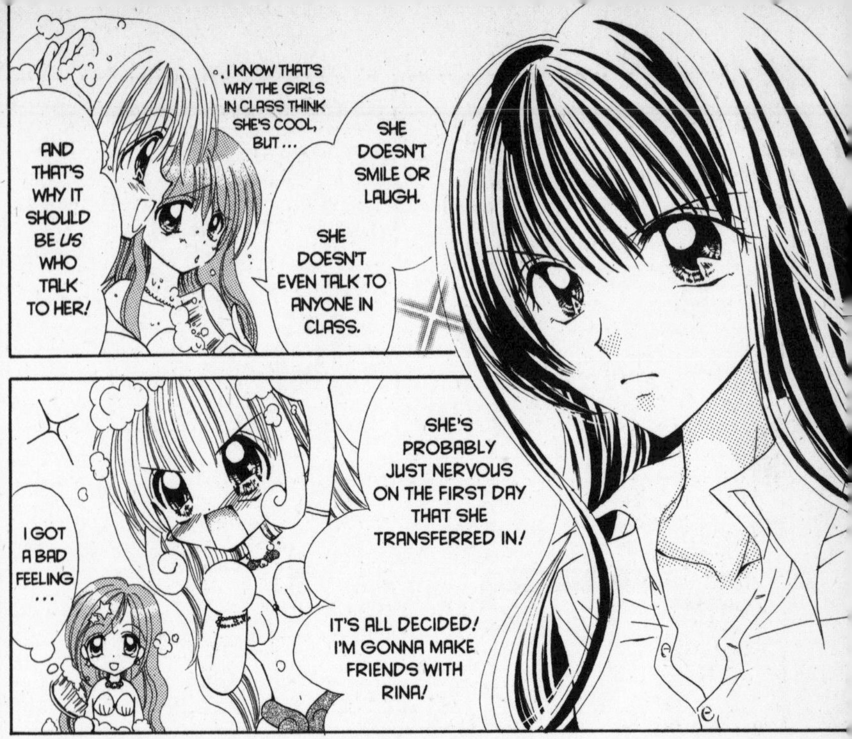
SHE DOESN'T SMILE OR LAUGH.
SHE DOESN'T EVEN TALK TO ANYONE IN CLASS.
I KNOW THAT'S WHY THE GIRLS IN CLASS THINK SHE'S COOL, BUT...
AND THAT'S WHY IT SHOULD BE *US* WHO TALK TO HER!
SHE'S PROBABLY JUST NERVOUS ON THE FIRST DAY THAT SHE TRANSFERRED IN!
IT'S ALL DECIDED! I'M GONNA MAKE FRIENDS WITH RINA!
I GOT A BAD FEELING...

(EPISODE 3)

I WAS TOLD THAT I REALLY TEND TO FOCUS ON LUCIA'S SISTER AND HIPPO IN THE TITLE PAGES. MAYBE BECAUSE THEIR EYES ARE SO BIG??? WHEN I DRAW HIPPO, THE WHITE PAPER TURNS DARKER AND I CAN RELAX A LITTLE MORE. ♥ RINA, THE THIRD MERMAID PRINCESS, AND THE ENEMY YÛRI BOTH APPEAR IN THIS EPISODE, BUT EVERYONE WORKING AROUND HANAMORI COULD ONLY TALK ABOUT KAITO'S SHOWER SCENE! THAT'S A HUGE REACTION FOR SOMETHING THAT TOOK UP ONLY HALF A PAGE.
OH! I REMEMBER NOW! WHILE I WAS DRAWING THIS EPISODE, MY WISDOM TEETH HURT SO MUCH I COULDN'T DO ANYTHING! I TOOK SOME MEDICINE, BUT IT DIDN'T HELP. THEY SEEM TO BE GROWING OUT WRONG. IT LOOKS LIKE I'LL HAVE TO BE ADMITTED TO THE HOSPITAL.
(IT HAPPENED ONCE BEFORE, BUT THESE WISDOM TEETH AREN'T SO SIMPLY CURED!)

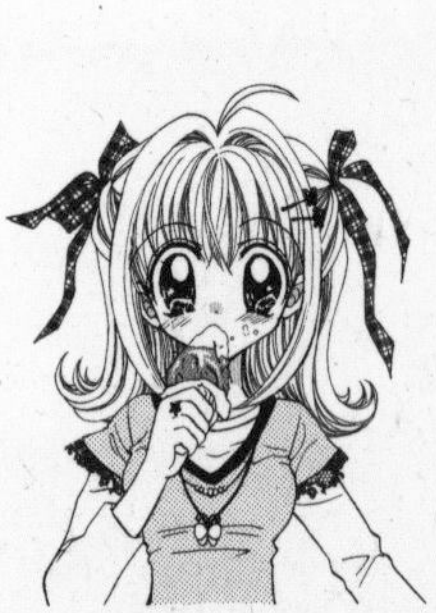

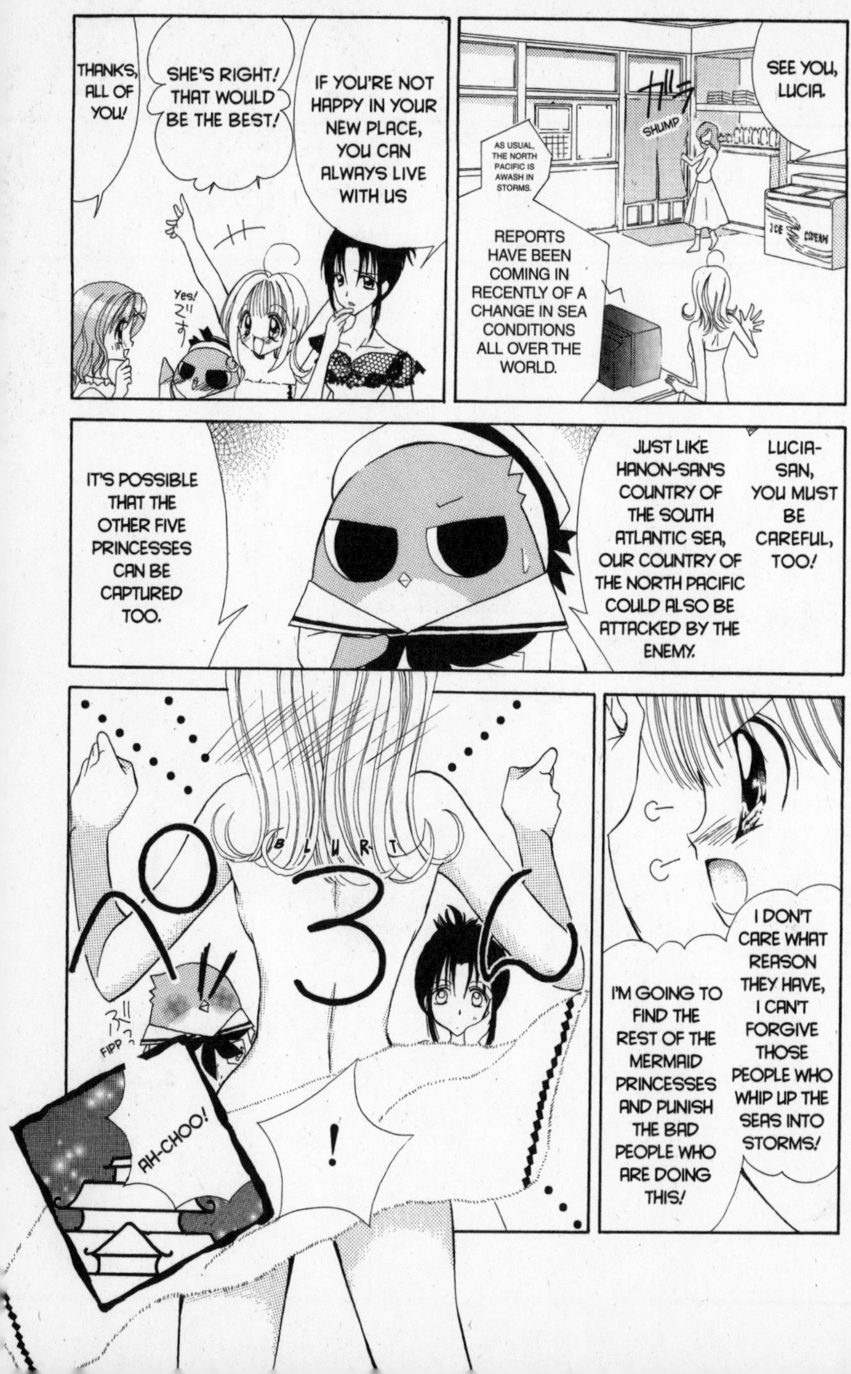
SEE YOU, LUCIA.
SHUMP
AS USUAL, THE NORTH PACIFIC IS AWASH IN STORMS.
REPORTS HAVE BEEN COMING IN RECENTLY OF A CHANGE IN SEA CONDITIONS ALL OVER THE WORLD.
ICE CREAM
IF YOU'RE NOT HAPPY IN YOUR NEW PLACE, YOU CAN ALWAYS LIVE WITH US
SHE'S RIGHT! THAT WOULD BE THE BEST!
THANKS, ALL OF YOU!
Yes!
LUCIA-SAN, YOU MUST BE CAREFUL, TOO!
JUST LIKE HANON-SAN'S COUNTRY OF THE SOUTH ATLANTIC SEA, OUR COUNTRY OF THE NORTH PACIFIC COULD ALSO BE ATTACKED BY THE ENEMY.
IT'S POSSIBLE THAT THE OTHER FIVE PRINCESSES CAN BE CAPTURED TOO.
I DON'T CARE WHAT REASON THEY HAVE, I CAN'T FORGIVE THOSE PEOPLE WHO WHIP UP THE SEAS INTO STORMS!
I'M GOING TO FIND THE REST OF THE MERMAID PRINCESSES AND PUNISH THE BAD PEOPLE WHO ARE DOING THIS!
BLURT
FIPP
AH-CHOO!
!

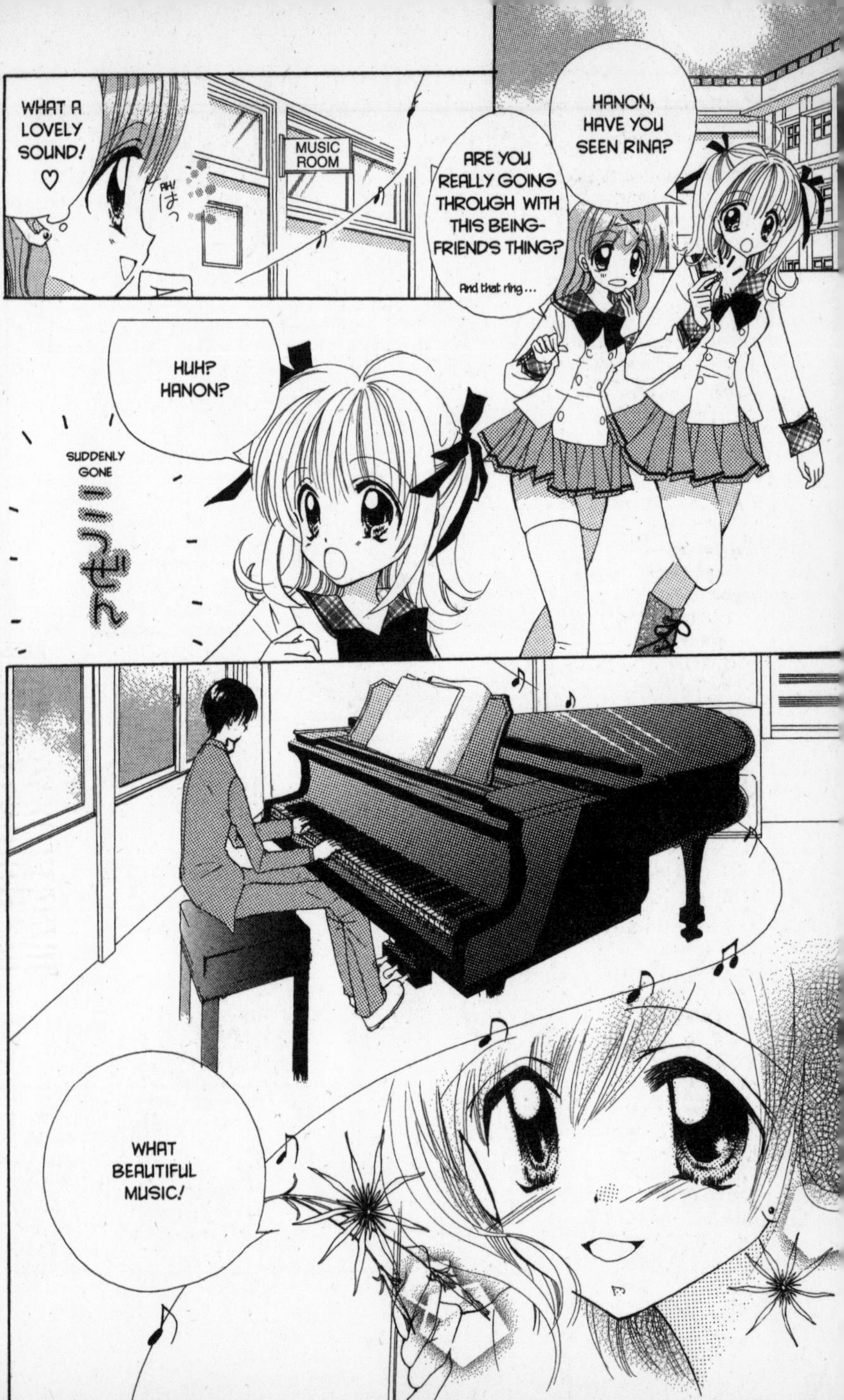
HANON, HAVE YOU SEEN RINA?
ARE YOU REALLY GOING THROUGH WITH THIS BEING-FRIENDS THING?
And that ring...
WHAT A LOVELY SOUND! ♡
AH! はっ
MUSIC ROOM
HUH? HANON?
SUDDENLY GONE
こつぜん
WHAT BEAUTIFUL MUSIC!

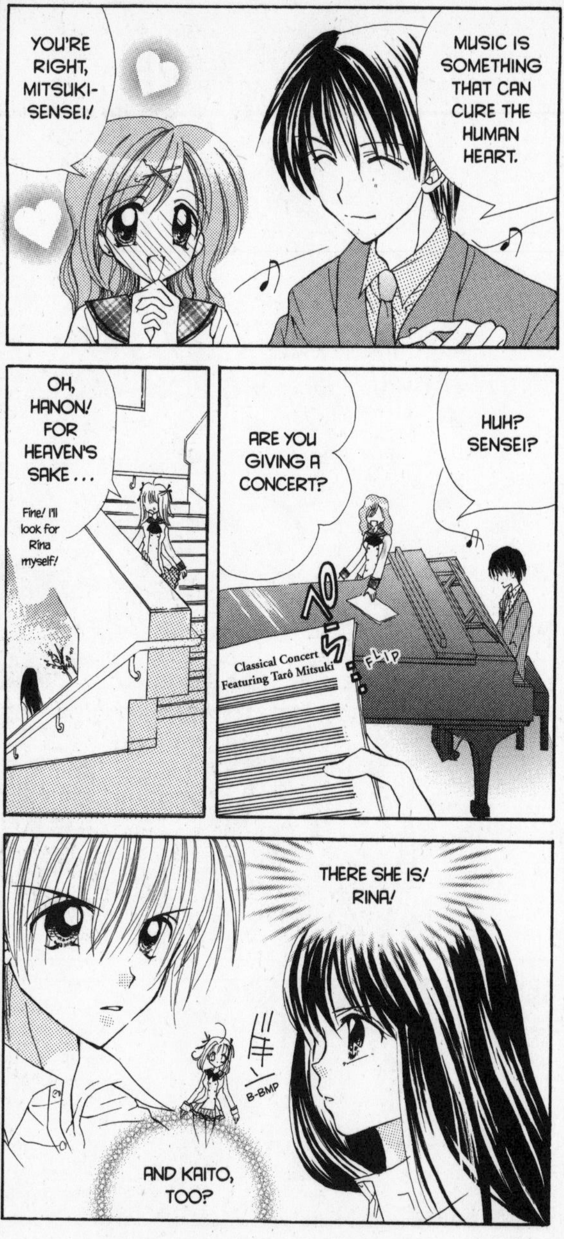
MUSIC IS SOMETHING THAT CAN CURE THE HUMAN HEART.
YOU'RE RIGHT, MITSUKI-SENSEI!
HUH? SENSEI?
ARE YOU GIVING A CONCERT?
Classical Concert Featuring Tarô Mitsuki
FLIP
OH, HANON! FOR HEAVEN'S SAKE . . .
Fine! I'll look for Rina myself!
THERE SHE IS! RINA!
B-BMP
AND KAITO, TOO?

ABOUT PICHI. (THE NAMES) ALL OF THE NAMES OF THE CHARACTERS WHO SHOW UP IN PICHI ARE DECIDED. ABOUT THE TITLE: PICHI PICHI PITCH, HERE'S EDITOR O.-SHI

A FISH'S FINS GO PICHI PICHI, AND UPBEAT PEOPLE ARE ALSO PICHI PICHI. AND WE ALSO COMBINED IT WITH THE MUSICAL PITCH. ♥

ISN'T THAT WONDERFUL?

LUCIA NANAMI→
YOKOTE-SHI
KAITO DÔMOTO
DÔMOTO→YOKOTE-SHI
KAITO→HANAMORI
RINA TÔIN→
EDITOR K.-SHI
TARÔ MITSUKI→
EDITOR K.-SHI

GACKTO→EVERYBODY

IZÛRU→HANAMORI
ERIRU→HANAMORI
YÛRI→HANAMORI
MARIA→HANAMORI

AND THAT'S ABOUT IT FOR THE FIRST 5 EPISODES.

THE ENEMY IZÛRU WAS MADE UP BY RE-ARRANGING THE PERSONAL NAMES OF EDITOR I.Z.-SHI AND EDITOR Y.O.-SHI. TOGETHER. THERE'S ONE OTHER PERSON'S NAME, K.K.-SHI, THAT I'D LIKE TO DO THE SAME WITH IN THE FUTURE. OH, KAITO'S NAME WAS ORIGINALLY RYUTO TSURUGI. HYA!

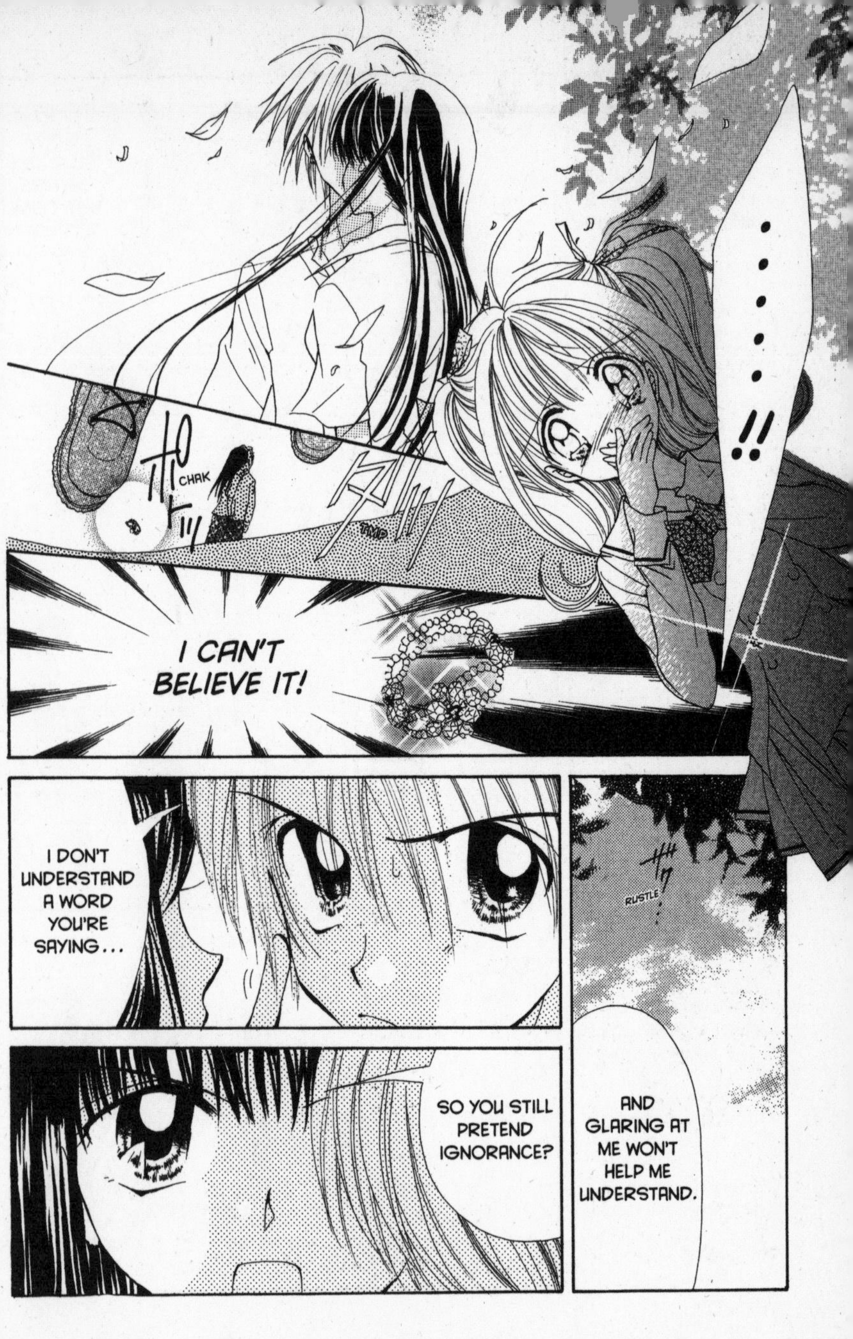
......!!
TMP
CHAK
I CAN'T BELIEVE IT!
RUSTLE
AND GLARING AT ME WON'T HELP ME UNDERSTAND.
I DON'T UNDERSTAND A WORD YOU'RE SAYING...
SO YOU STILL PRETEND IGNORANCE?

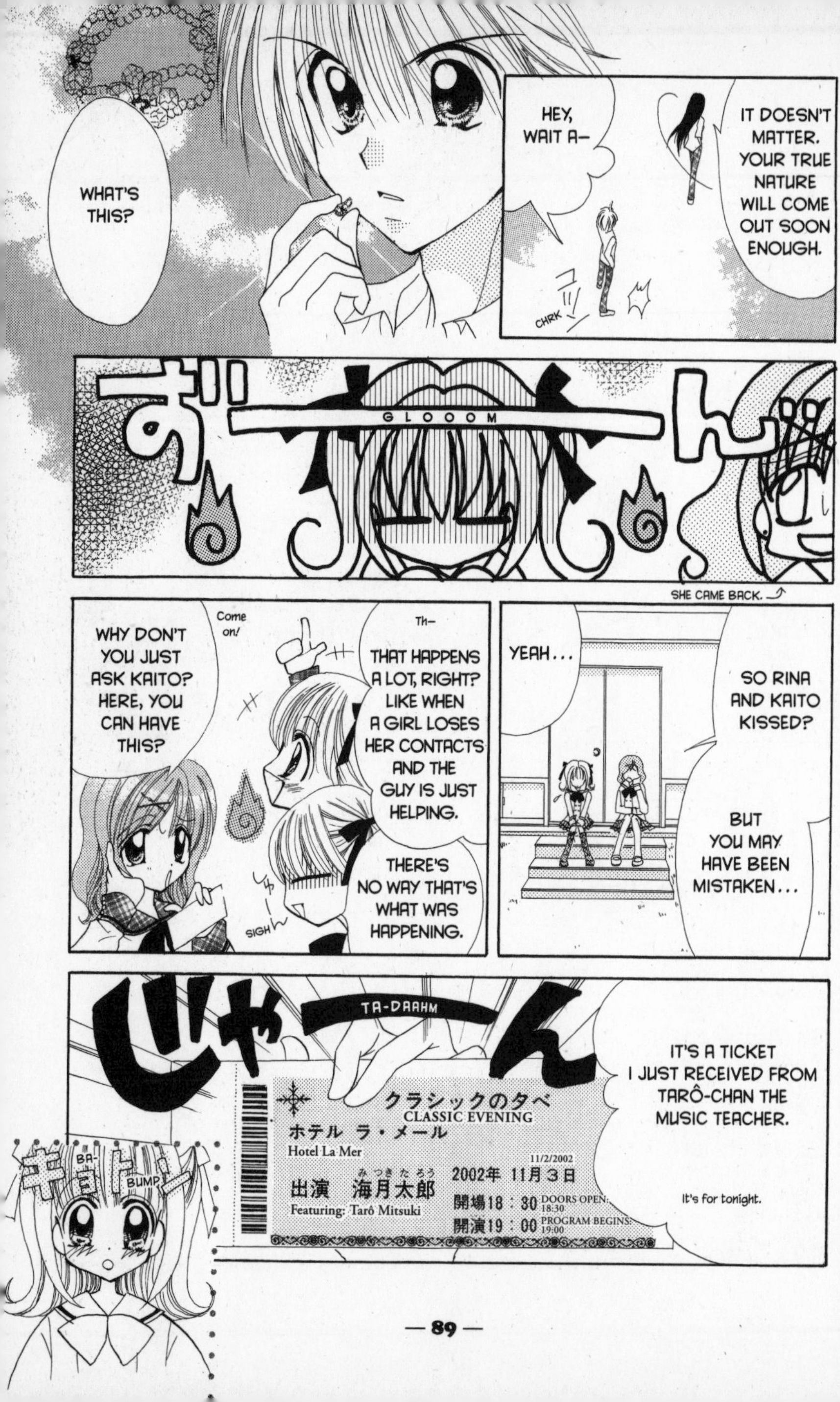

IT DOESN'T MATTER. YOUR TRUE NATURE WILL COME OUT SOON ENOUGH.
HEY, WAIT A—
CHRK
WHAT'S THIS?
GLOOOM
SHE CAME BACK.
SO RINA AND KAITO KISSED?
BUT YOU MAY HAVE BEEN MISTAKEN...
YEAH...
Th—
THAT HAPPENS A LOT, RIGHT? LIKE WHEN A GIRL LOSES HER CONTACTS AND THE GUY IS JUST HELPING.
THERE'S NO WAY THAT'S WHAT WAS HAPPENING.
SIGH
Come on!
WHY DON'T YOU JUST ASK KAITO? HERE, YOU CAN HAVE THIS?
TA-DAAHM
IT'S A TICKET I JUST RECEIVED FROM TARÔ-CHAN THE MUSIC TEACHER.
It's for tonight.
クラシックの夕べ
CLASSIC EVENING
ホテル ラ・メール
Hotel La Mer
2002年 11月3日
11/2/2002
出演 海月太郎
Featuring: Tarô Mitsuki
開場18：30 DOORS OPEN: 18:30
開演19：00 PROGRAM BEGINS: 19:00
BA-BUMP

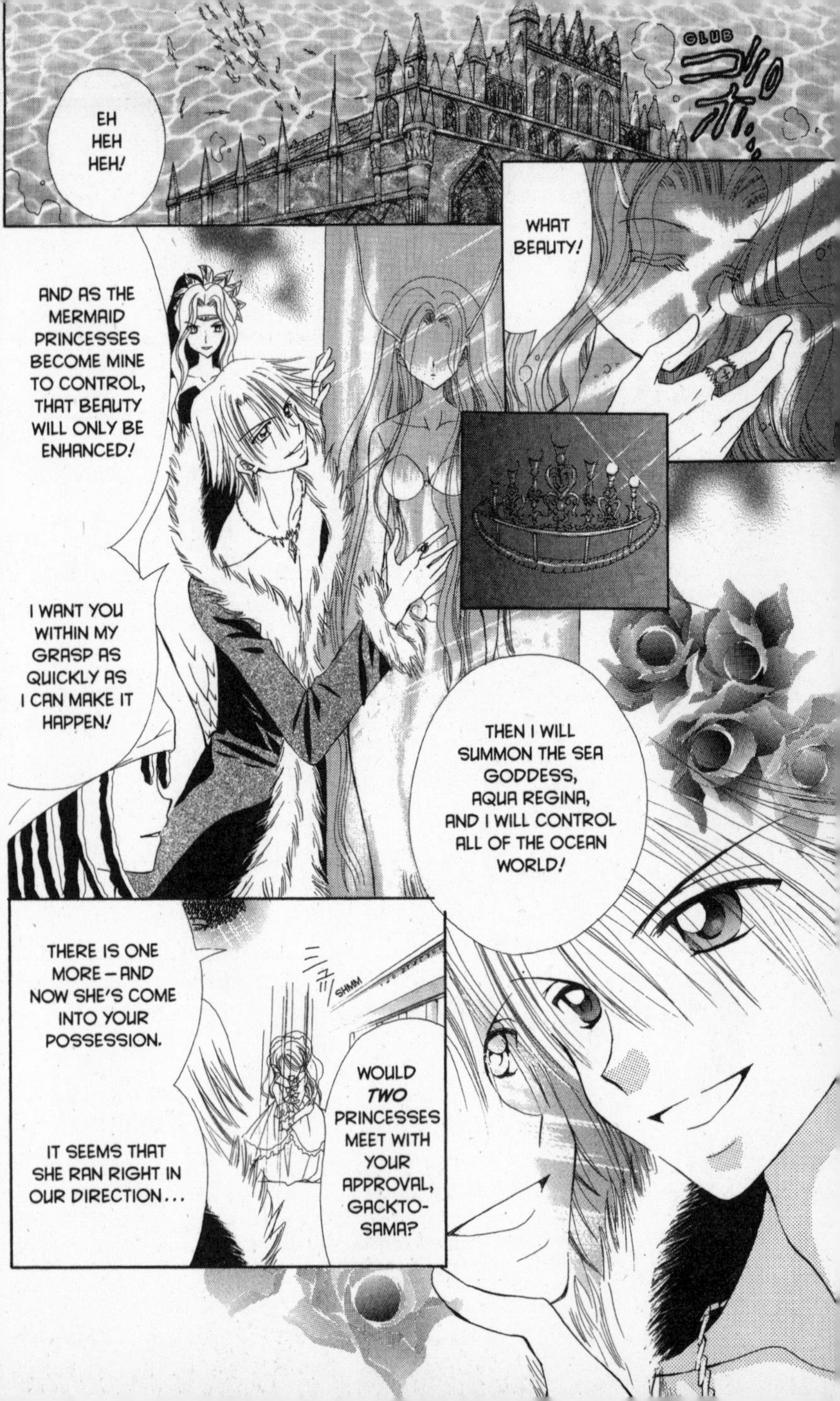
CLUB
EH HEH HEH!
WHAT BEAUTY!
AND AS THE MERMAID PRINCESSES BECOME MINE TO CONTROL, THAT BEAUTY WILL ONLY BE ENHANCED!
I WANT YOU WITHIN MY GRASP AS QUICKLY AS I CAN MAKE IT HAPPEN!
THEN I WILL SUMMON THE SEA GODDESS, AQUA REGINA, AND I WILL CONTROL ALL OF THE OCEAN WORLD!
THERE IS ONE MORE—AND NOW SHE'S COME INTO YOUR POSSESSION.
SHMM
IT SEEMS THAT SHE RAN RIGHT IN OUR DIRECTION...
WOULD *TWO* PRINCESSES MEET WITH YOUR APPROVAL, GACKTO-SAMA?

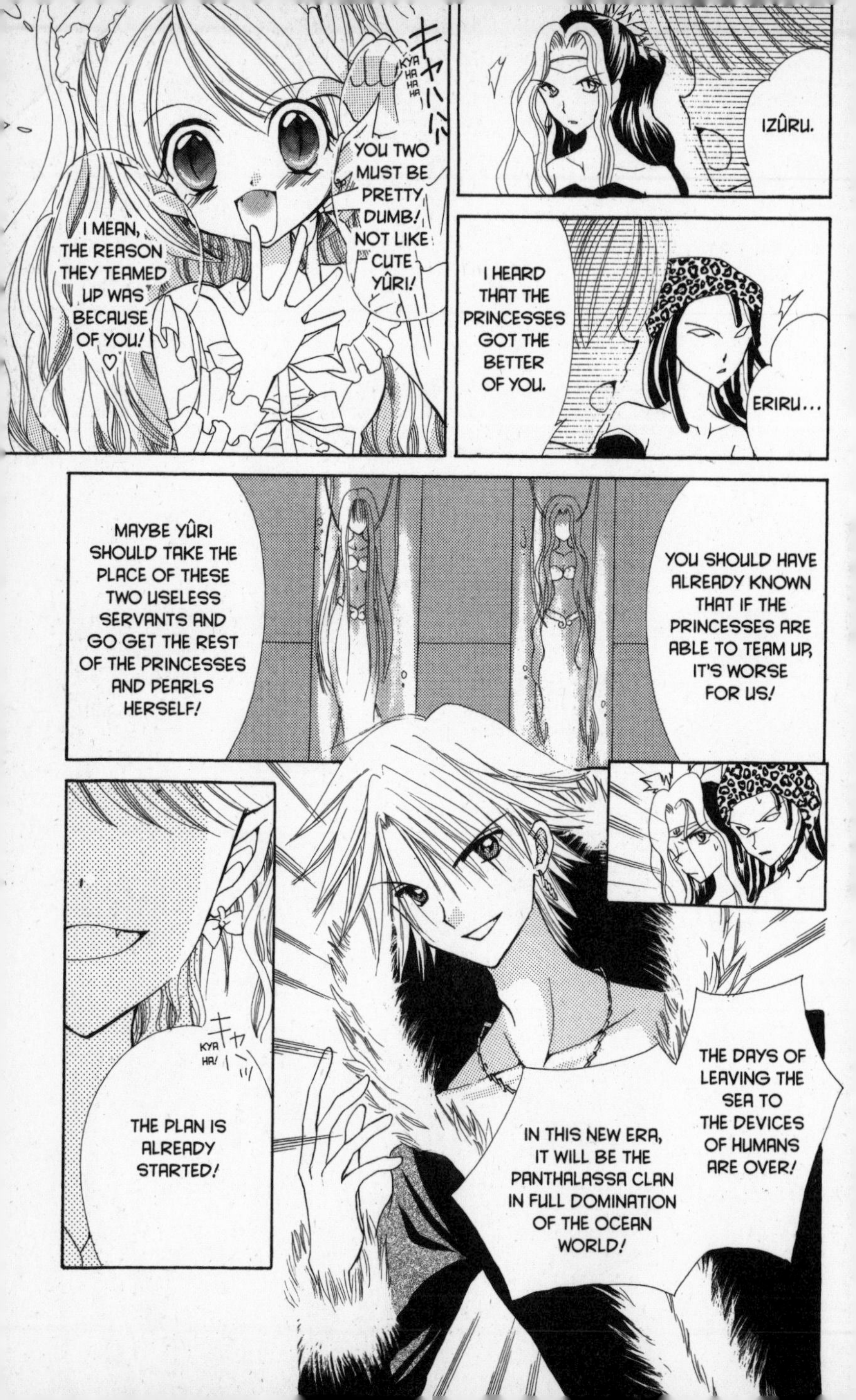
IZÛRU.
I HEARD THAT THE PRINCESSES GOT THE BETTER OF YOU.
ERIRU...
KYA HA HA HA
YOU TWO MUST BE PRETTY DUMB! NOT LIKE CUTE YÛRI!
I MEAN, THE REASON THEY TEAMED UP WAS BECAUSE OF YOU! ♡
YOU SHOULD HAVE ALREADY KNOWN THAT IF THE PRINCESSES ARE ABLE TO TEAM UP, IT'S WORSE FOR US!
MAYBE YÛRI SHOULD TAKE THE PLACE OF THESE TWO USELESS SERVANTS AND GO GET THE REST OF THE PRINCESSES AND PEARLS HERSELF!
THE DAYS OF LEAVING THE SEA TO THE DEVICES OF HUMANS ARE OVER!
IN THIS NEW ERA, IT WILL BE THE PANTHALASSA CLAN IN FULL DOMINATION OF THE OCEAN WORLD!
KYA HA!
THE PLAN IS ALREADY STARTED!

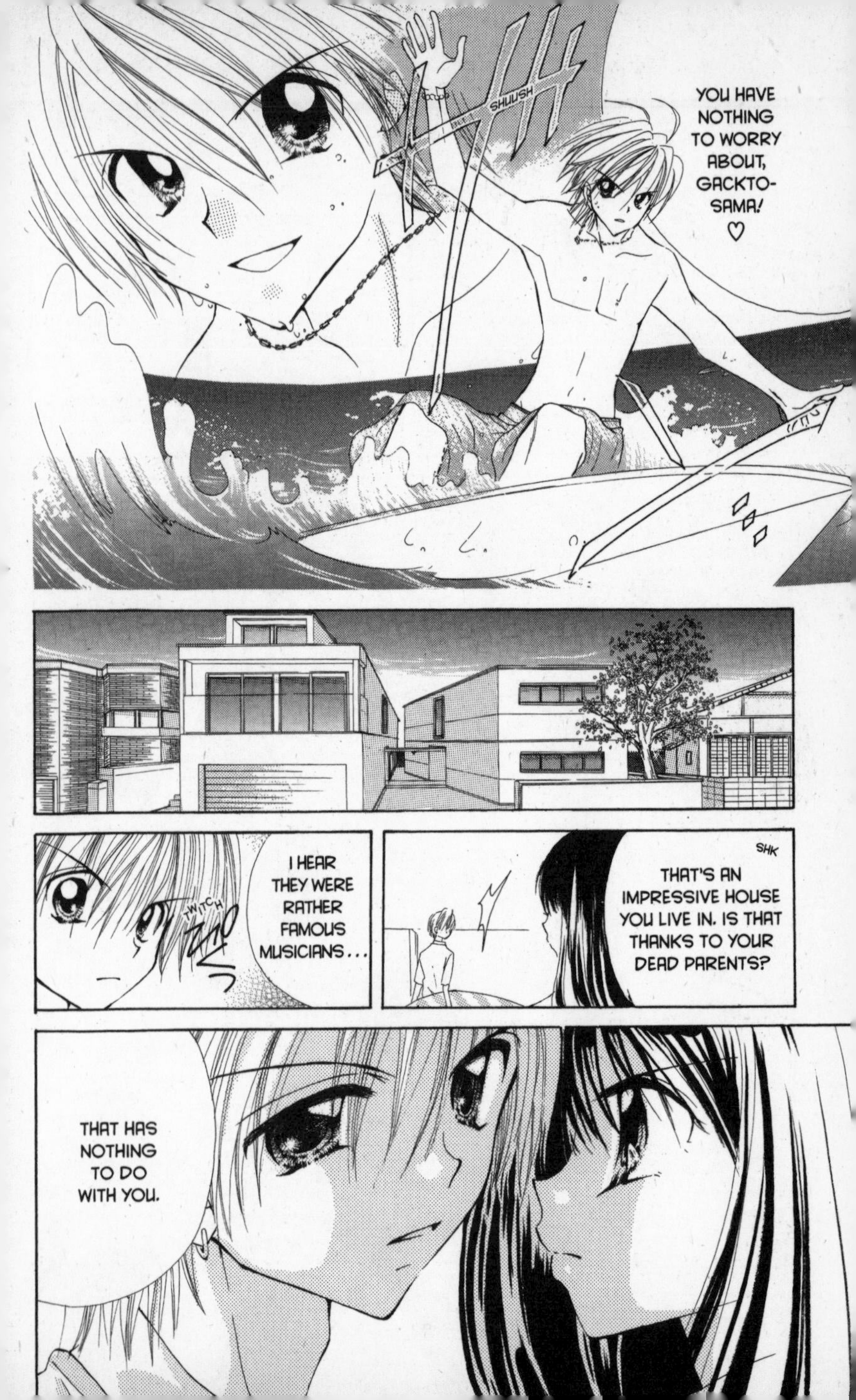
SHUUSH
YOU HAVE NOTHING TO WORRY ABOUT, GACKTO-SAMA! ♡
SHK
THAT'S AN IMPRESSIVE HOUSE YOU LIVE IN. IS THAT THANKS TO YOUR DEAD PARENTS?
I HEAR THEY WERE RATHER FAMOUS MUSICIANS...
TWITCH
THAT HAS NOTHING TO DO WITH YOU.

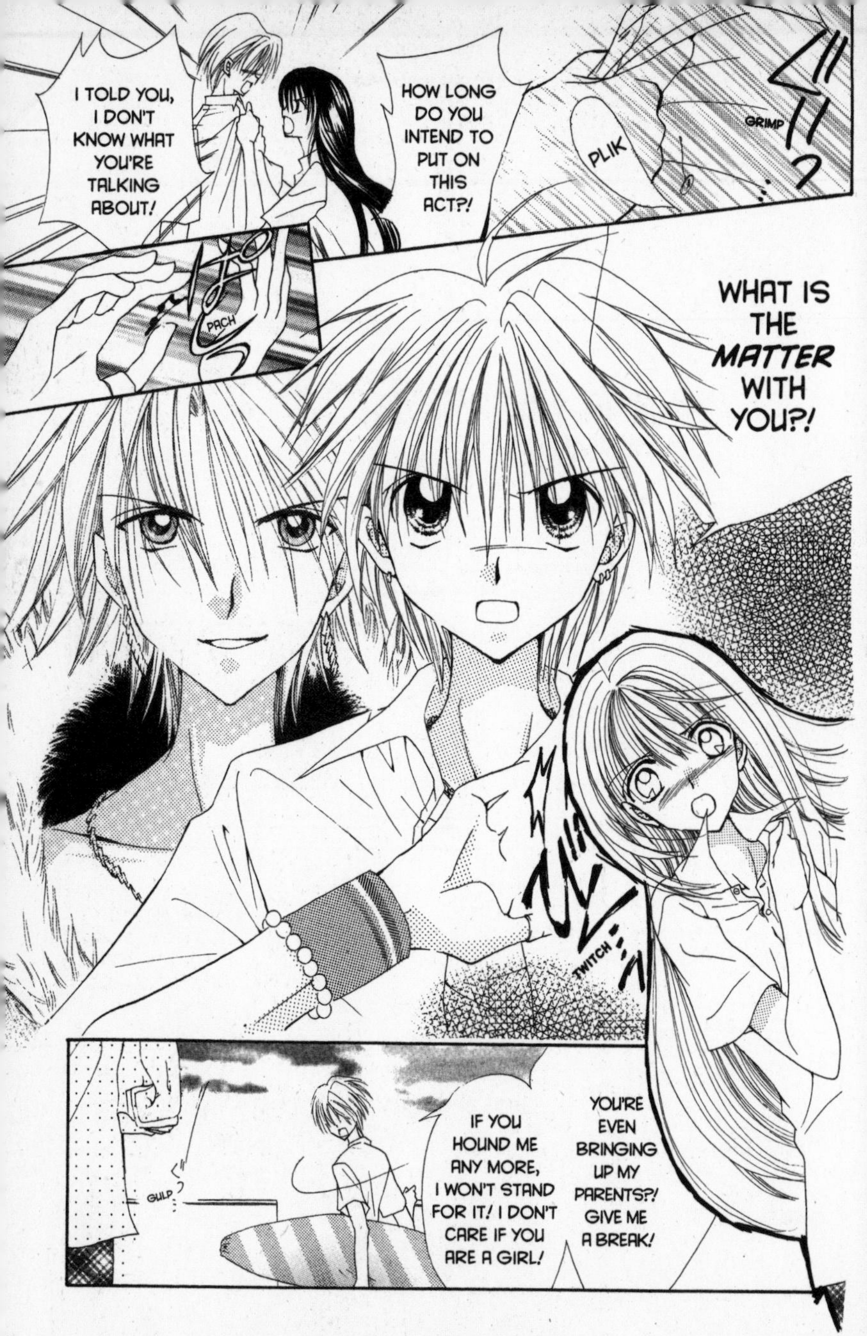
GRIMP
PLIK
HOW LONG DO YOU INTEND TO PUT ON THIS ACT?!
I TOLD YOU, I DON'T KNOW WHAT YOU'RE TALKING ABOUT!
WHAT IS THE MATTER WITH YOU?!
TWITCH
PACH
YOU'RE EVEN BRINGING UP MY PARENTS?! GIVE ME A BREAK!
IF YOU HOUND ME ANY MORE, I WON'T STAND FOR IT! I DON'T CARE IF YOU ARE A GIRL!
GULP

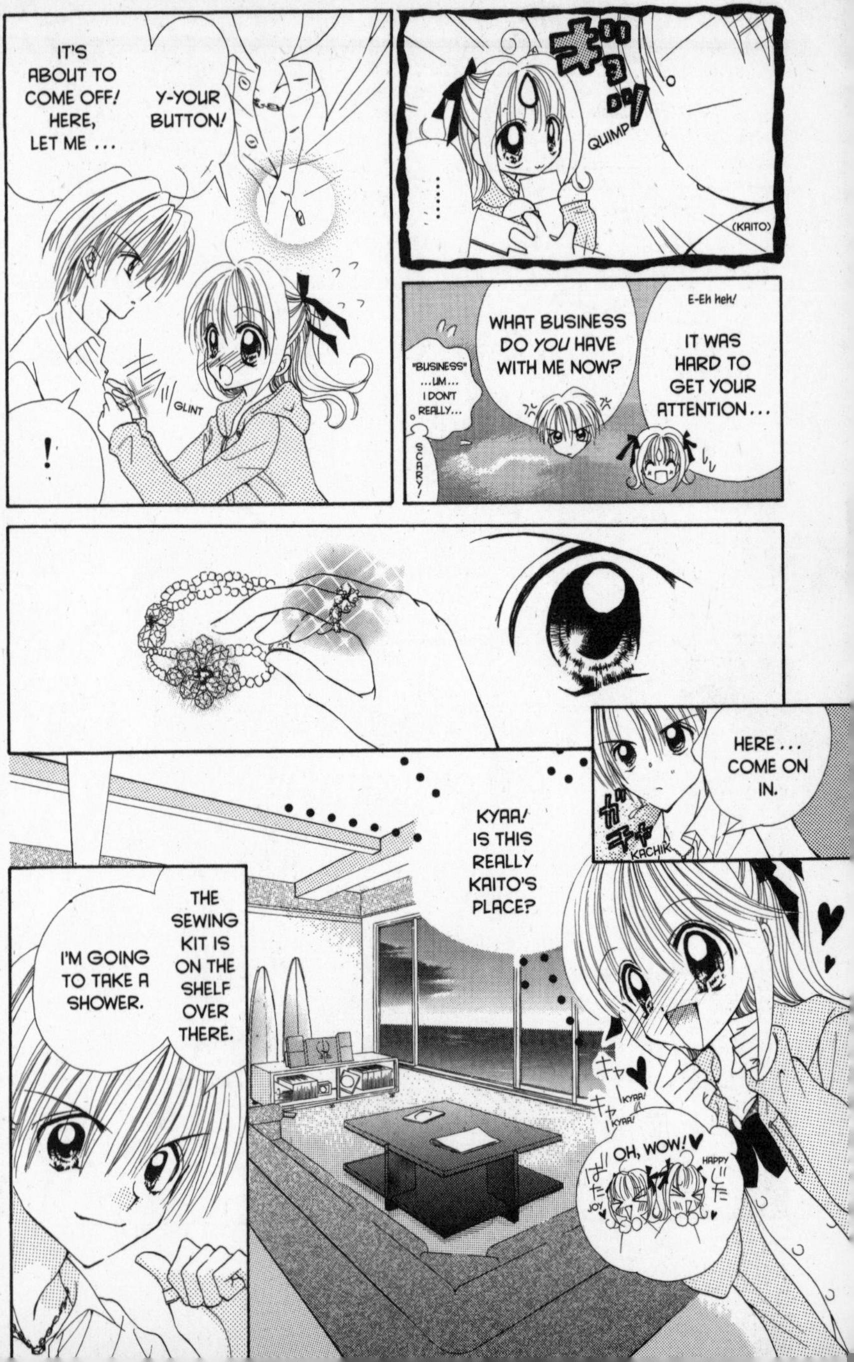
QUIMP
......
(KAITO)
E-Eh heh!
IT WAS HARD TO GET YOUR ATTENTION...
WHAT BUSINESS DO YOU HAVE WITH ME NOW?
"BUSINESS" ...UM... I DON'T REALLY...
SCARY!
Y-YOUR BUTTON!
IT'S ABOUT TO COME OFF! HERE, LET ME ...
GLINT
!
HERE... COME ON IN.
KACHIK
KYAA! IS THIS REALLY KAITO'S PLACE?
KYAA! KYAA!
OH, WOW!
HAPPY
JOY
THE SEWING KIT IS ON THE SHELF OVER THERE.
I'M GOING TO TAKE A SHOWER.

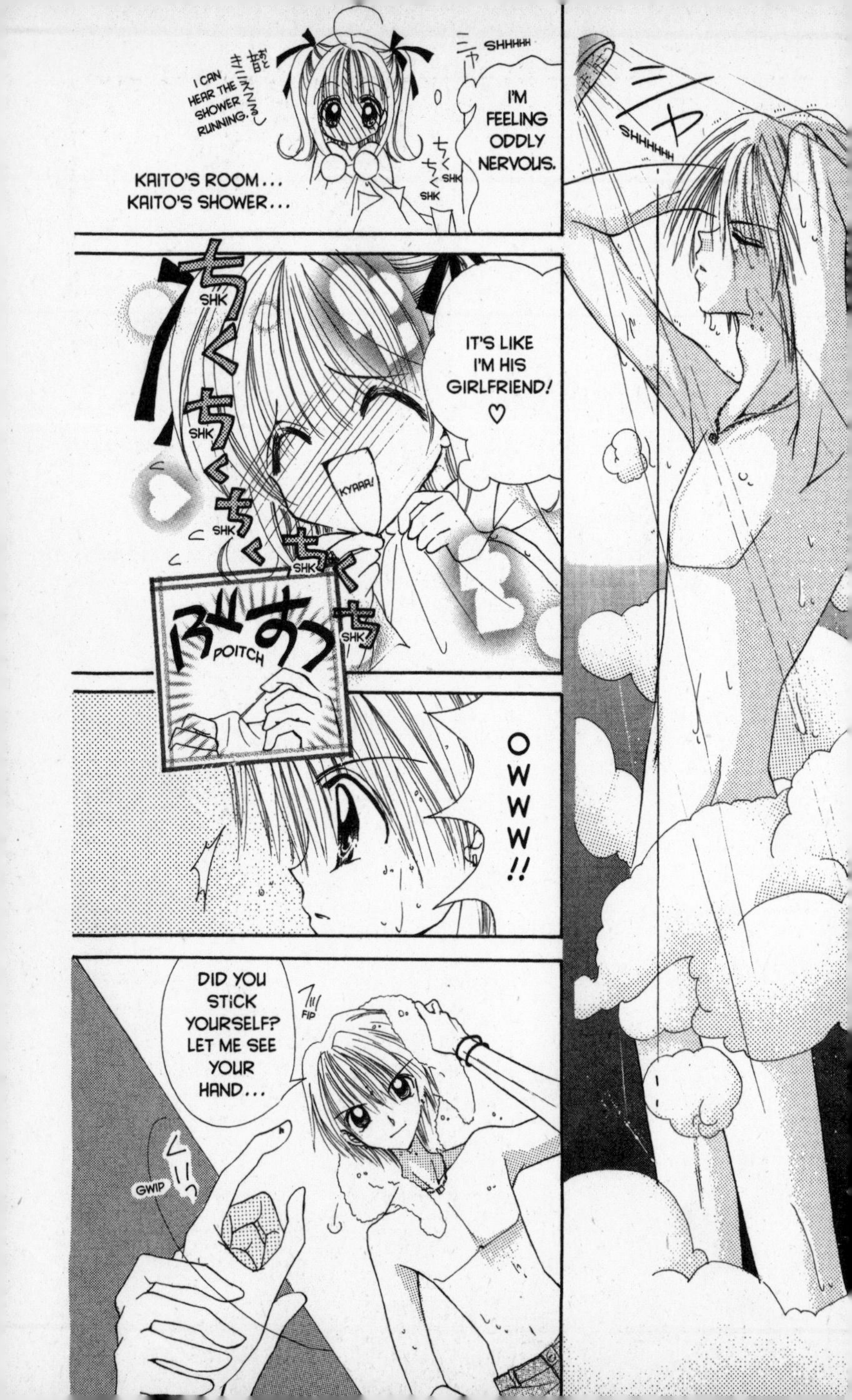

SHHHHHH
SHHHHH
I'M FEELING ODDLY NERVOUS.
SHK
SHK
I CAN HEAR THE SHOWER RUNNING.
KAITO'S ROOM... KAITO'S SHOWER...
IT'S LIKE I'M HIS GIRLFRIEND! ♡
KYAAA!
SHK
SHK
SHK
SHK
SHK
POITCH
OWWW!!
FIP
DID YOU STICK YOURSELF? LET ME SEE YOUR HAND...
GWIP

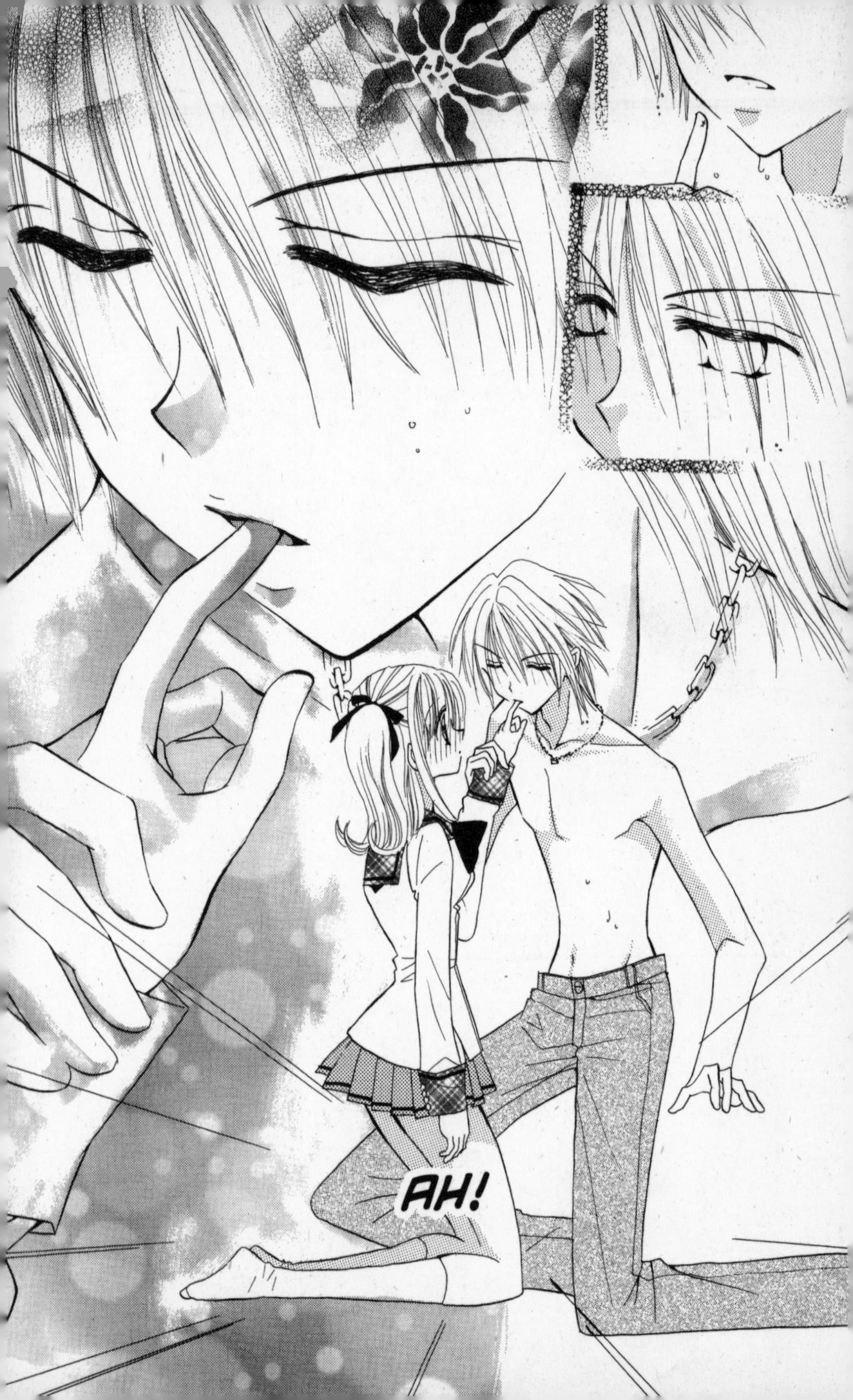
AH!

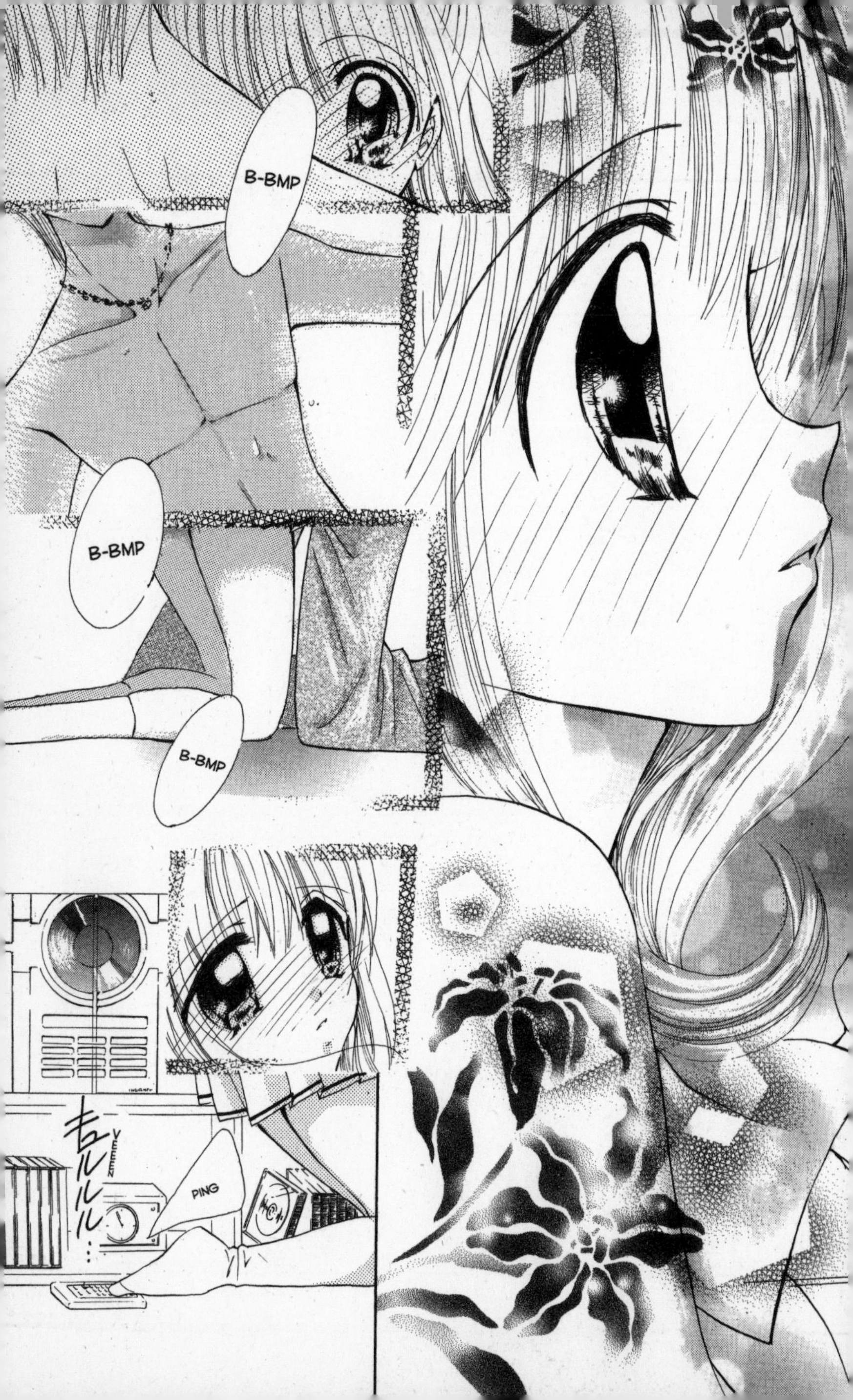
B-BMP
B-BMP
B-BMP
PING
VEEN
キュルルル…

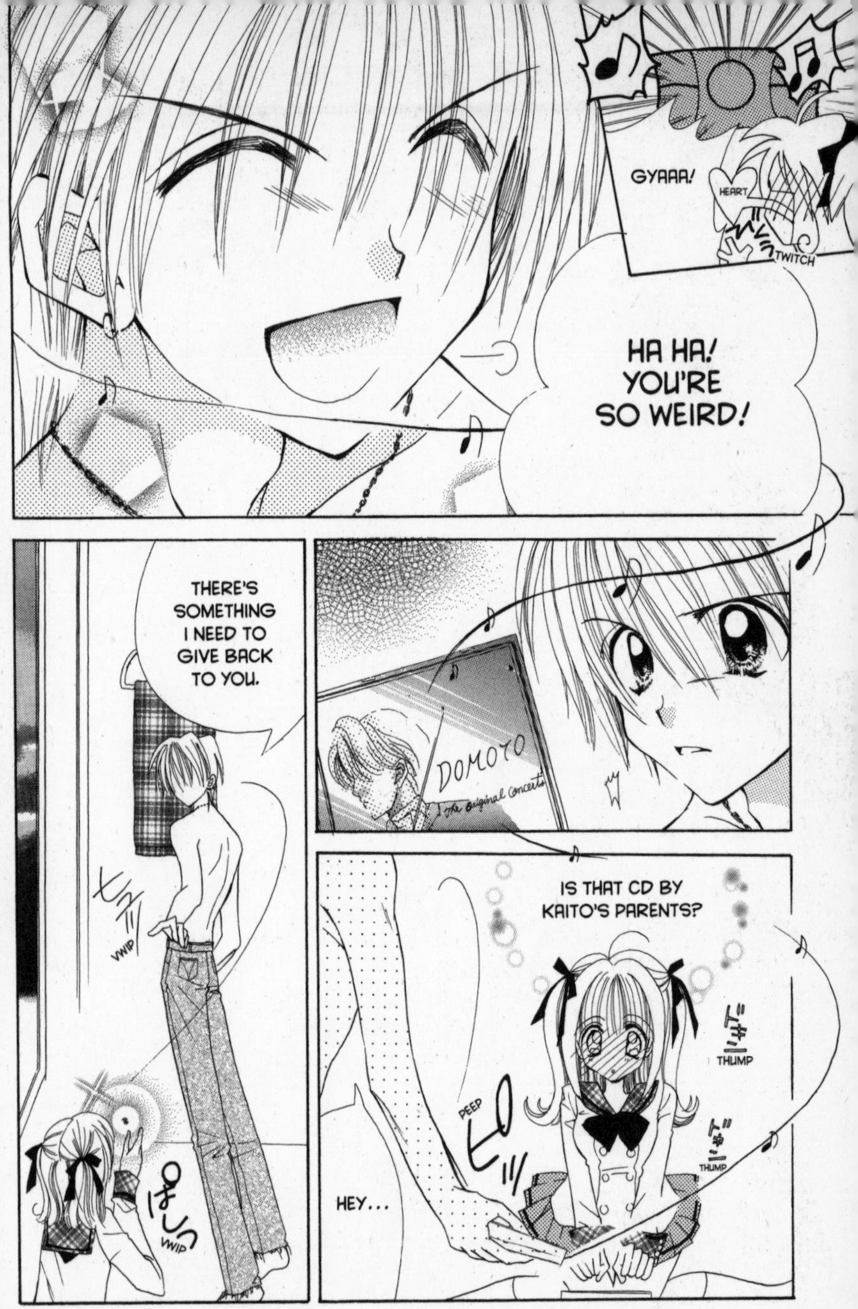
GYAAA!
HEART
TWITCH
HA HA! YOU'RE SO WEIRD!
DOMOTO
The Original Concerto
IS THAT CD BY KAITO'S PARENTS?
THUMP
THUMP
PEEP
HEY...
THERE'S SOMETHING I NEED TO GIVE BACK TO YOU.
VWIP
VWIP

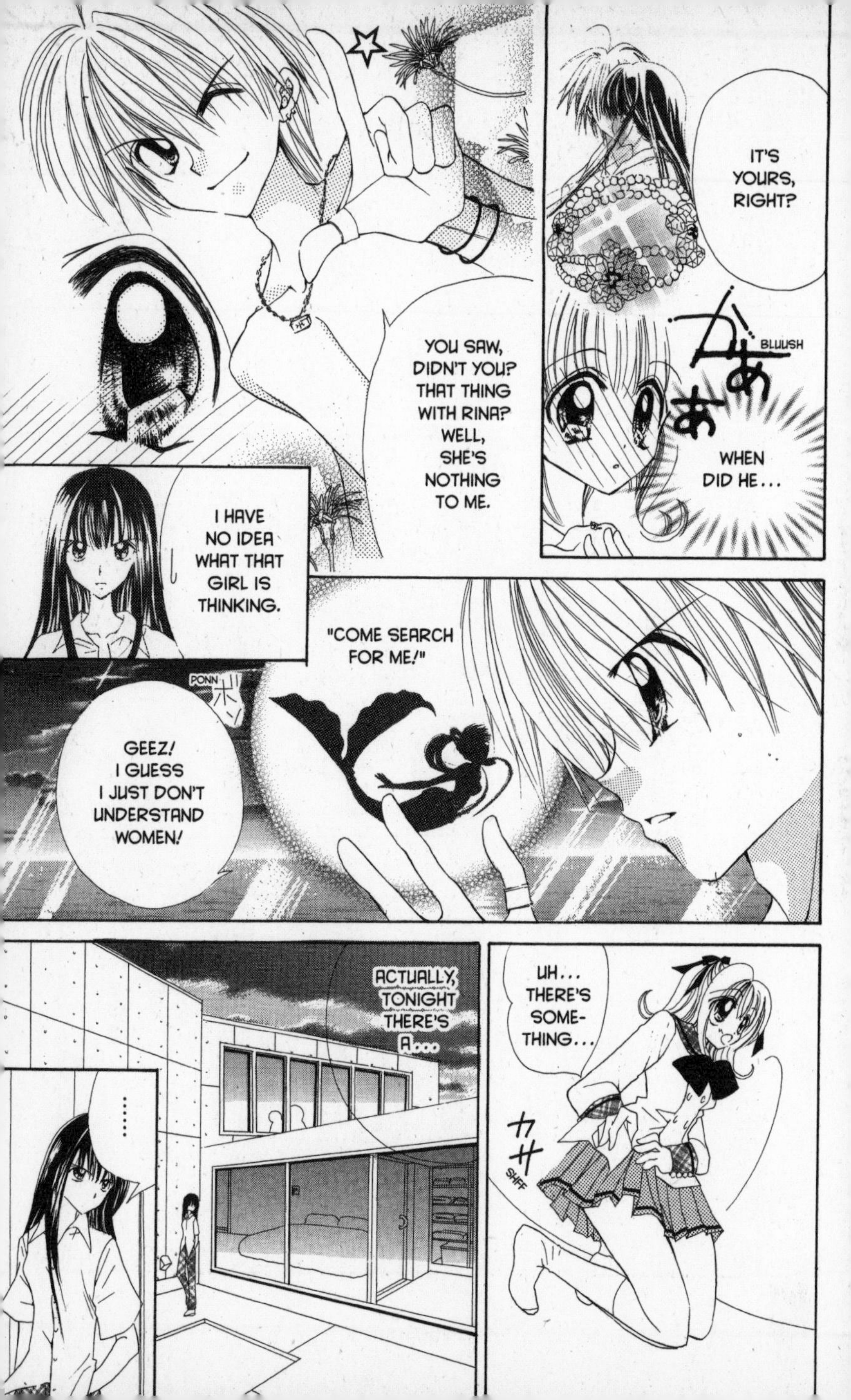
IT'S YOURS, RIGHT?
BLUUSH
WHEN DID HE...
YOU SAW, DIDN'T YOU? THAT THING WITH RINA? WELL, SHE'S NOTHING TO ME.
I HAVE NO IDEA WHAT THAT GIRL IS THINKING.
"COME SEARCH FOR ME!"
PONN
GEEZ! I GUESS I JUST DON'T UNDERSTAND WOMEN!
UH... THERE'S SOME-THING...
SHFF
ACTUALLY, TONIGHT THERE'S A...
......

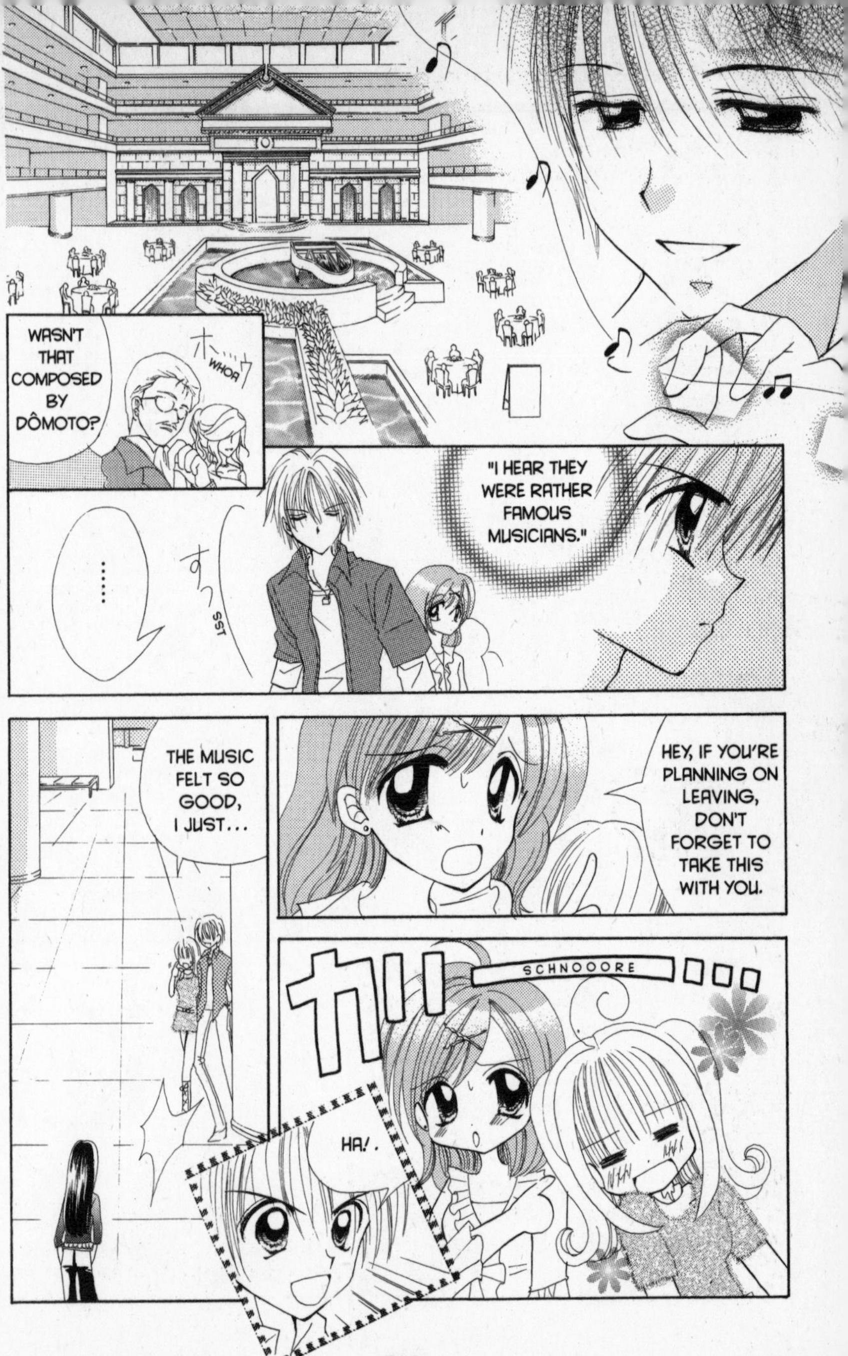
WHOA
WASN'T THAT COMPOSED BY DÔMOTO?
"I HEAR THEY WERE RATHER FAMOUS MUSICIANS."
SST
……
HEY, IF YOU'RE PLANNING ON LEAVING, DON'T FORGET TO TAKE THIS WITH YOU.
SCHNOOORE
HA!.
THE MUSIC FELT SO GOOD, I JUST...

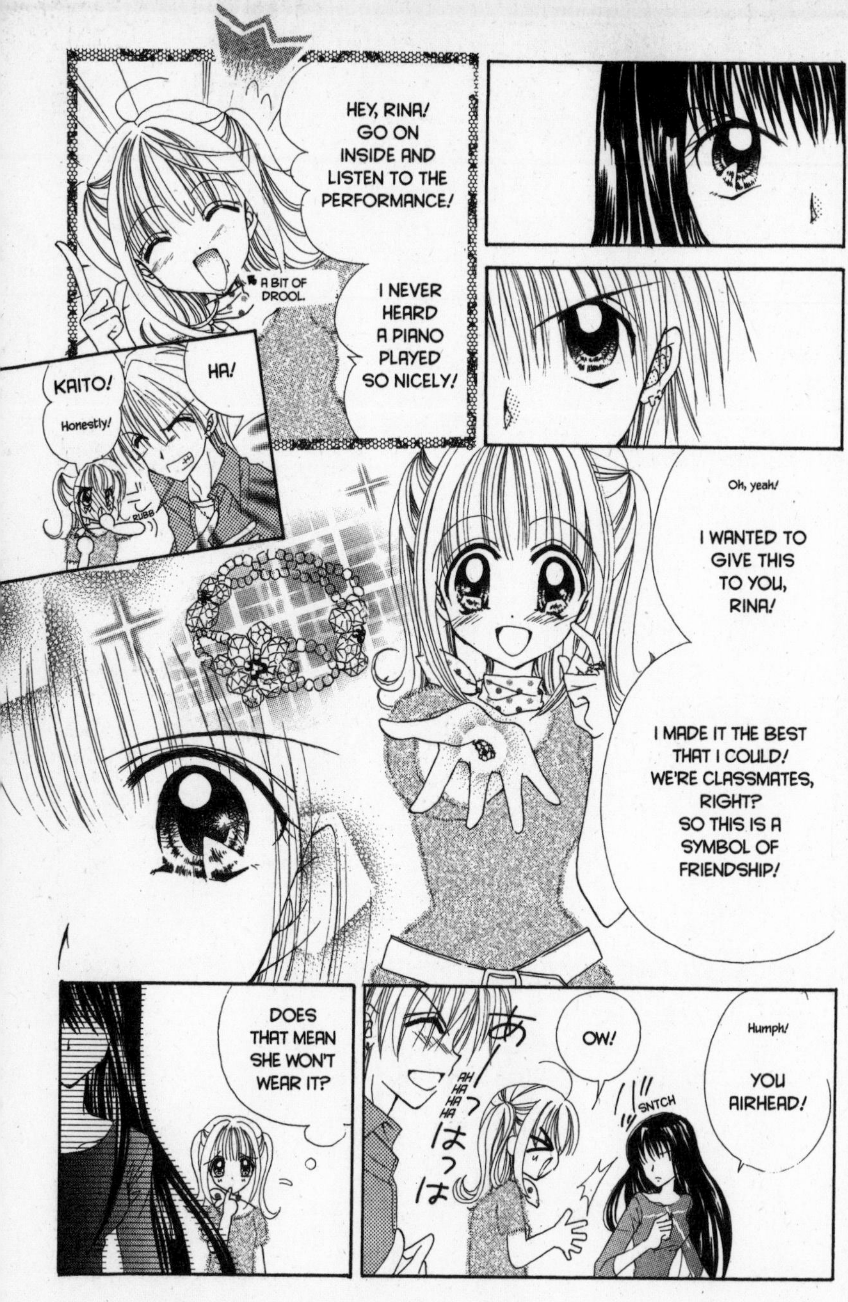
HEY, RINA! GO ON INSIDE AND LISTEN TO THE PERFORMANCE!
A BIT OF DROOL.
I NEVER HEARD A PIANO PLAYED SO NICELY!
HA!
KAITO!
Honestly!
RUBB
Oh, yeah!
I WANTED TO GIVE THIS TO YOU, RINA!
I MADE IT THE BEST THAT I COULD! WE'RE CLASSMATES, RIGHT? SO THIS IS A SYMBOL OF FRIENDSHIP!
Humph!
YOU AIRHEAD!
SNTCH
OW!
AH HA HA HA
あっはっは
DOES THAT MEAN SHE WON'T WEAR IT?

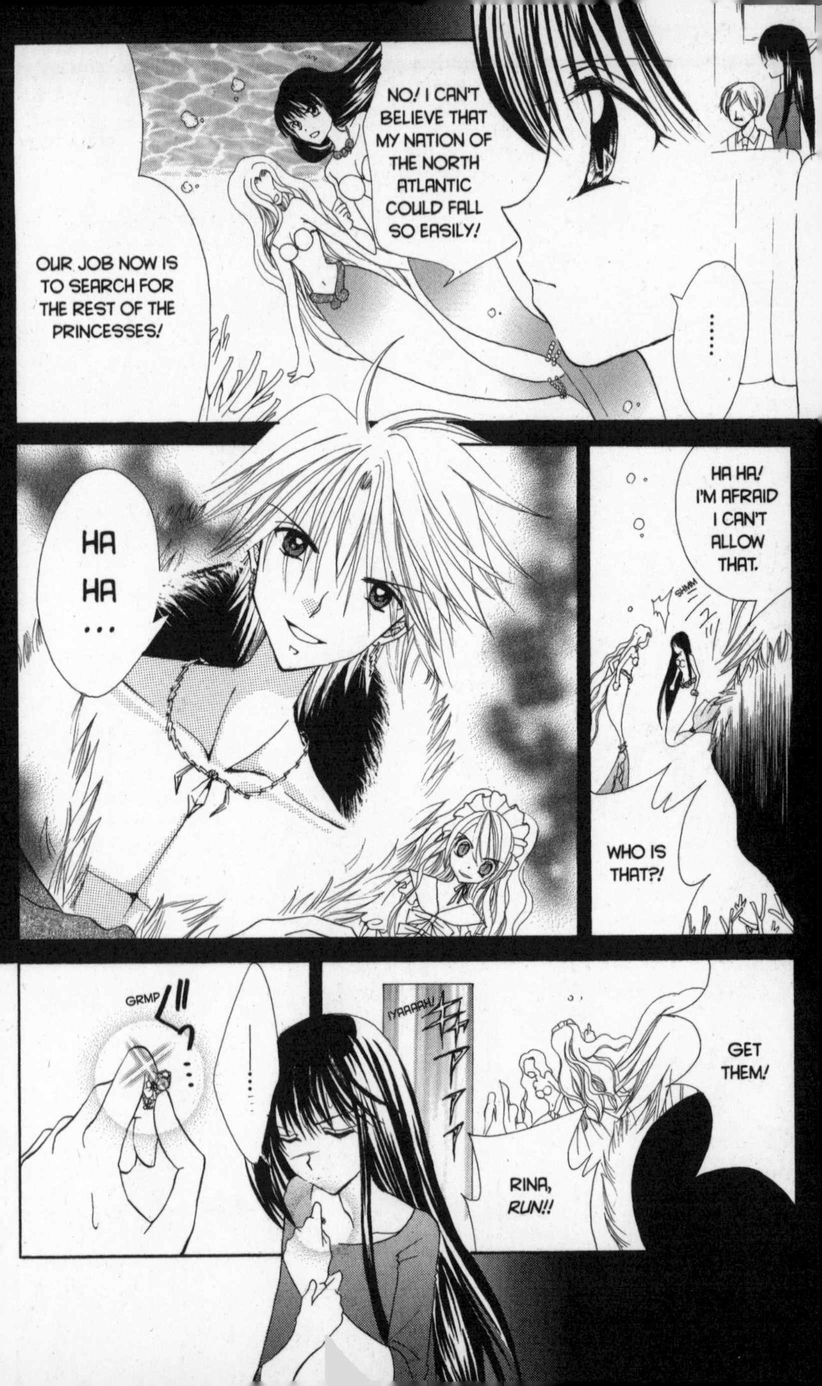
......
NO! I CAN'T BELIEVE THAT MY NATION OF THE NORTH ATLANTIC COULD FALL SO EASILY!
OUR JOB NOW IS TO SEARCH FOR THE REST OF THE PRINCESSES!
HA HA! I'M AFRAID I CAN'T ALLOW THAT.
SHMM
WHO IS THAT?!
HA HA ...
GET THEM!
IYAAAAH!
RINA, RUN!!
......
GRMP
...

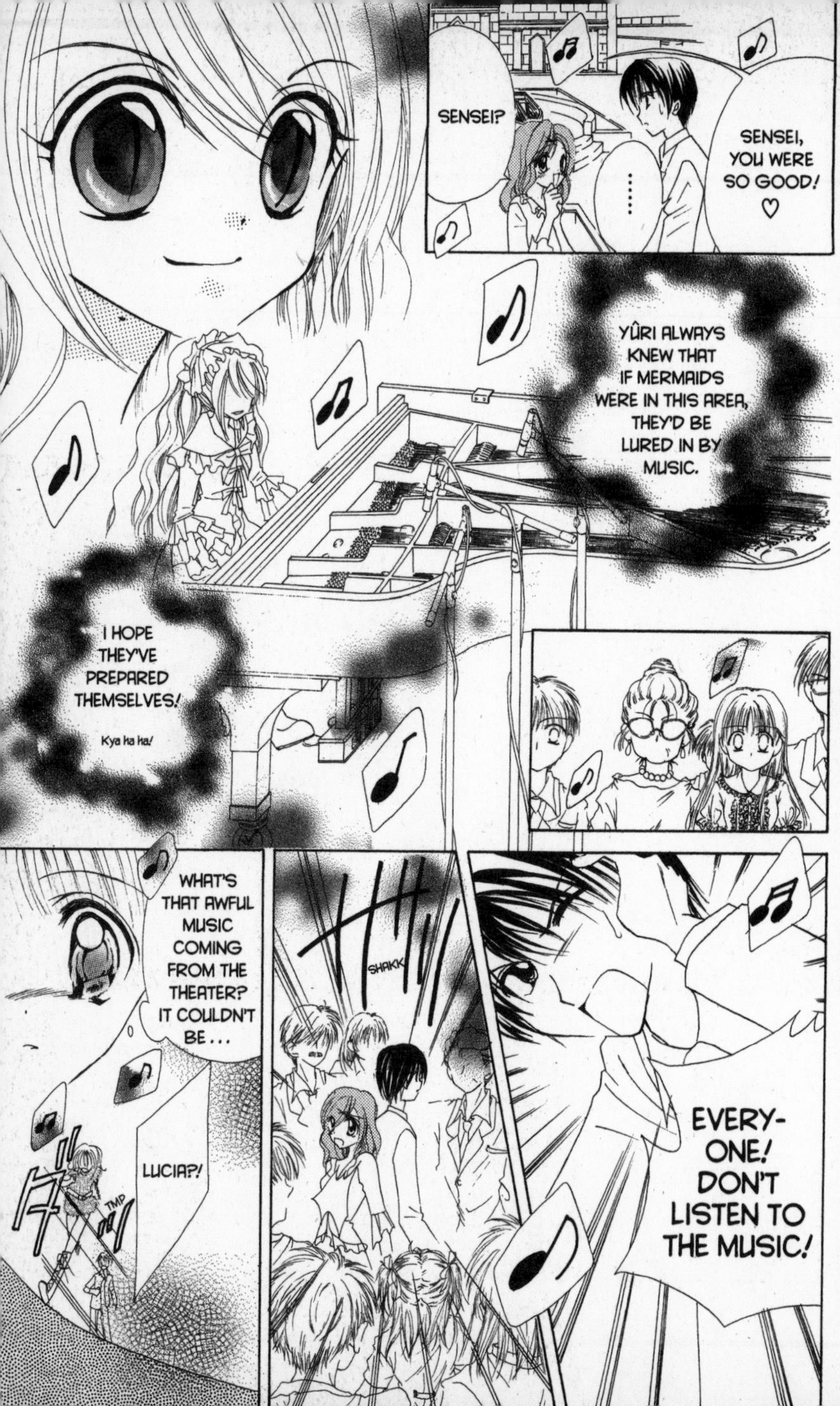
SENSEI, YOU WERE SO GOOD! ♡
......
SENSEI?
YÛRI ALWAYS KNEW THAT IF MERMAIDS WERE IN THIS AREA, THEY'D BE LURED IN BY MUSIC.
I HOPE THEY'VE PREPARED THEMSELVES!
Kya ha ha!
EVERY-ONE! DON'T LISTEN TO THE MUSIC!
SHAKK
WHAT'S THAT AWFUL MUSIC COMING FROM THE THEATER? IT COULDN'T BE . . .
LUCIA?!
TMP

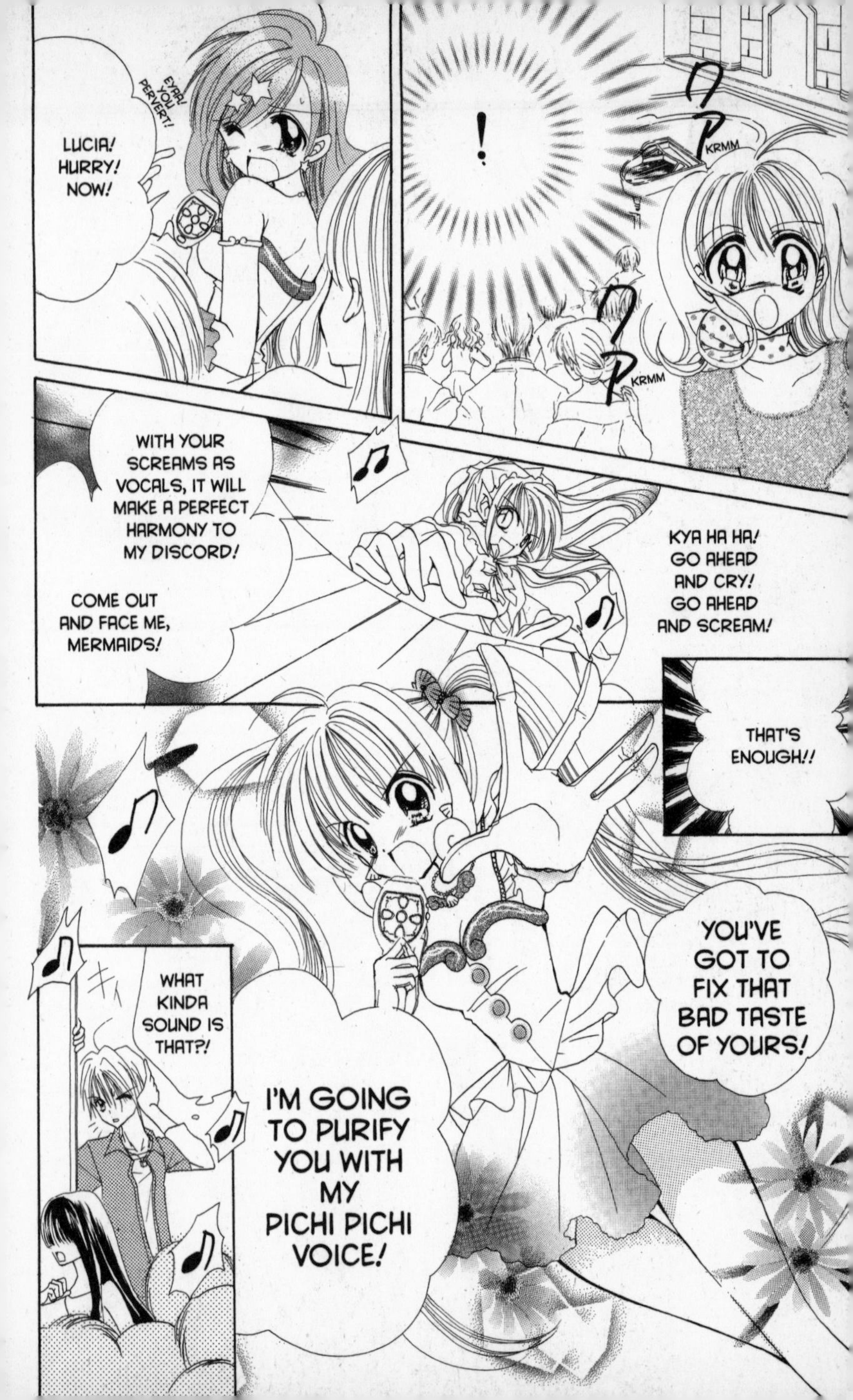
!
KRMM
KRMM
EYAA! YOU PERVERT!
LUCIA! HURRY! NOW!
KYA HA HA! GO AHEAD AND CRY! GO AHEAD AND SCREAM!
WITH YOUR SCREAMS AS VOCALS, IT WILL MAKE A PERFECT HARMONY TO MY DISCORD!
COME OUT AND FACE ME, MERMAIDS!
THAT'S ENOUGH!!
YOU'VE GOT TO FIX THAT BAD TASTE OF YOURS!
I'M GOING TO PURIFY YOU WITH MY PICHI PICHI VOICE!
WHAT KINDA SOUND IS THAT?!

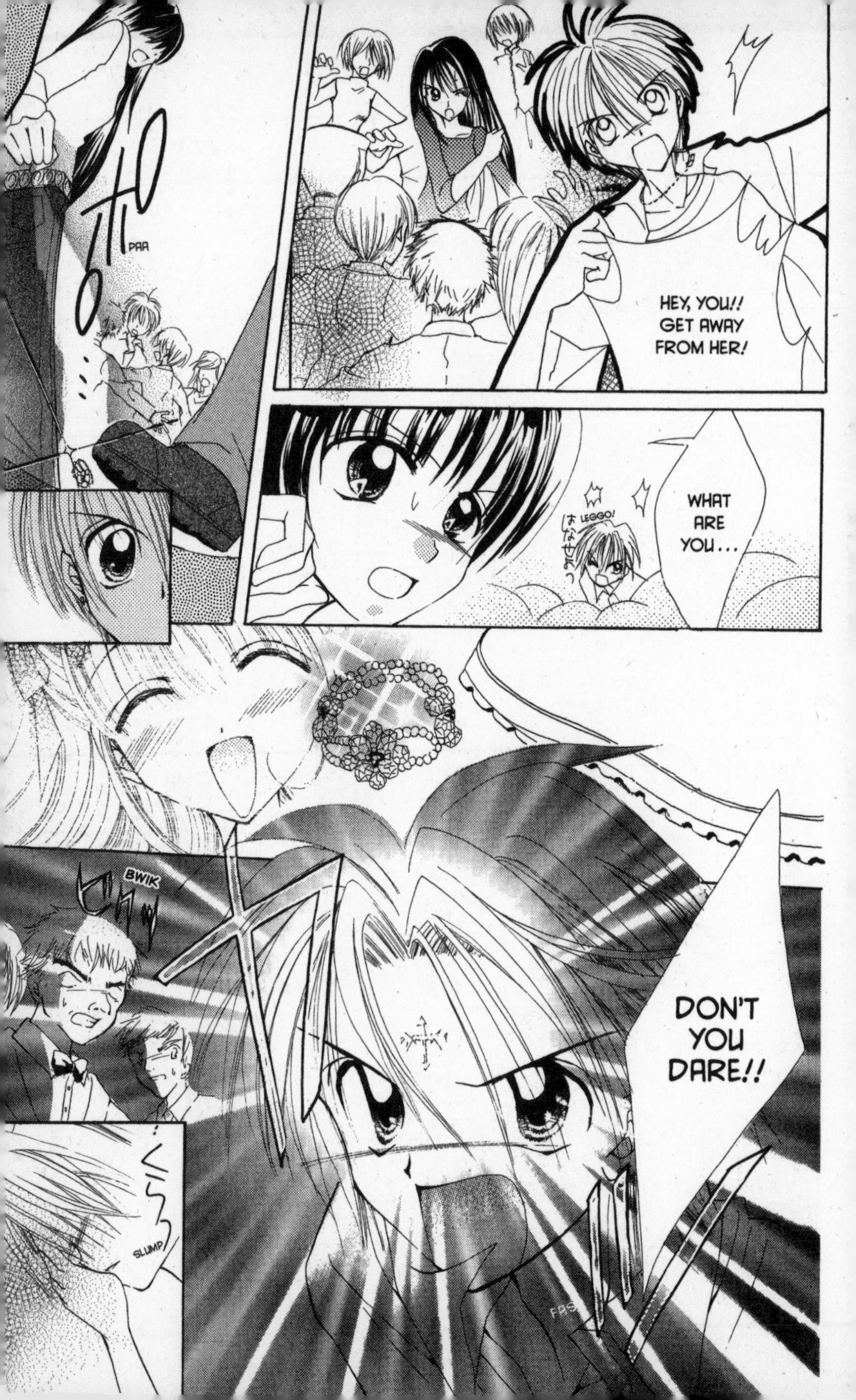
HEY, YOU!! GET AWAY FROM HER!
PAA
WHAT ARE YOU...
はなせぇっ
LEGGO!
DON'T YOU DARE!!
BWIK
SLUMP
FAS

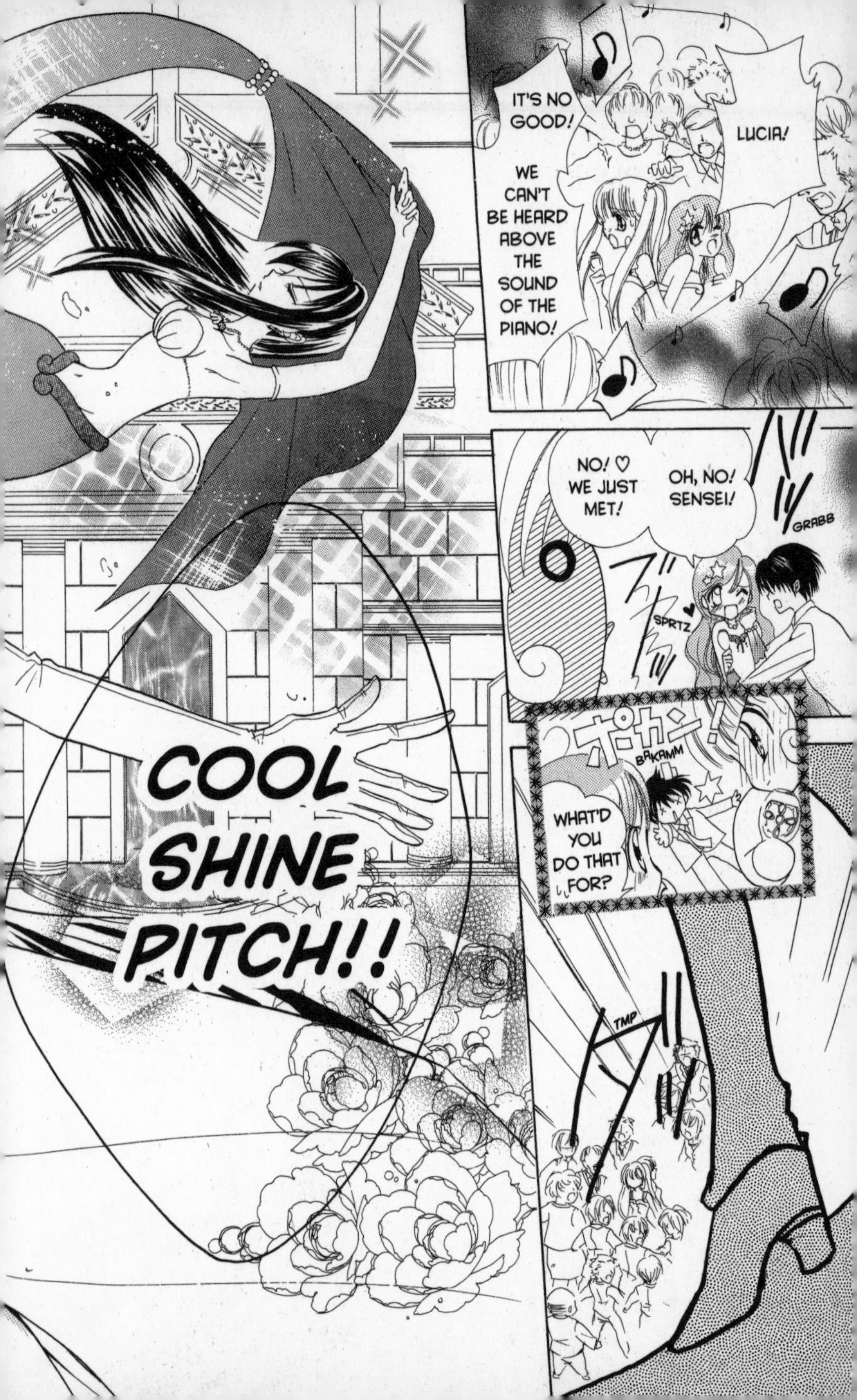
LUCIA!
IT'S NO GOOD!
WE CAN'T BE HEARD ABOVE THE SOUND OF THE PIANO!
GRABB
OH, NO! SENSEI!
NO! ♡ WE JUST MET!
SPRTZ
ポカン!
BAKAMM
WHAT'D YOU DO THAT FOR?
TMP
COOL SHINE PITCH!!

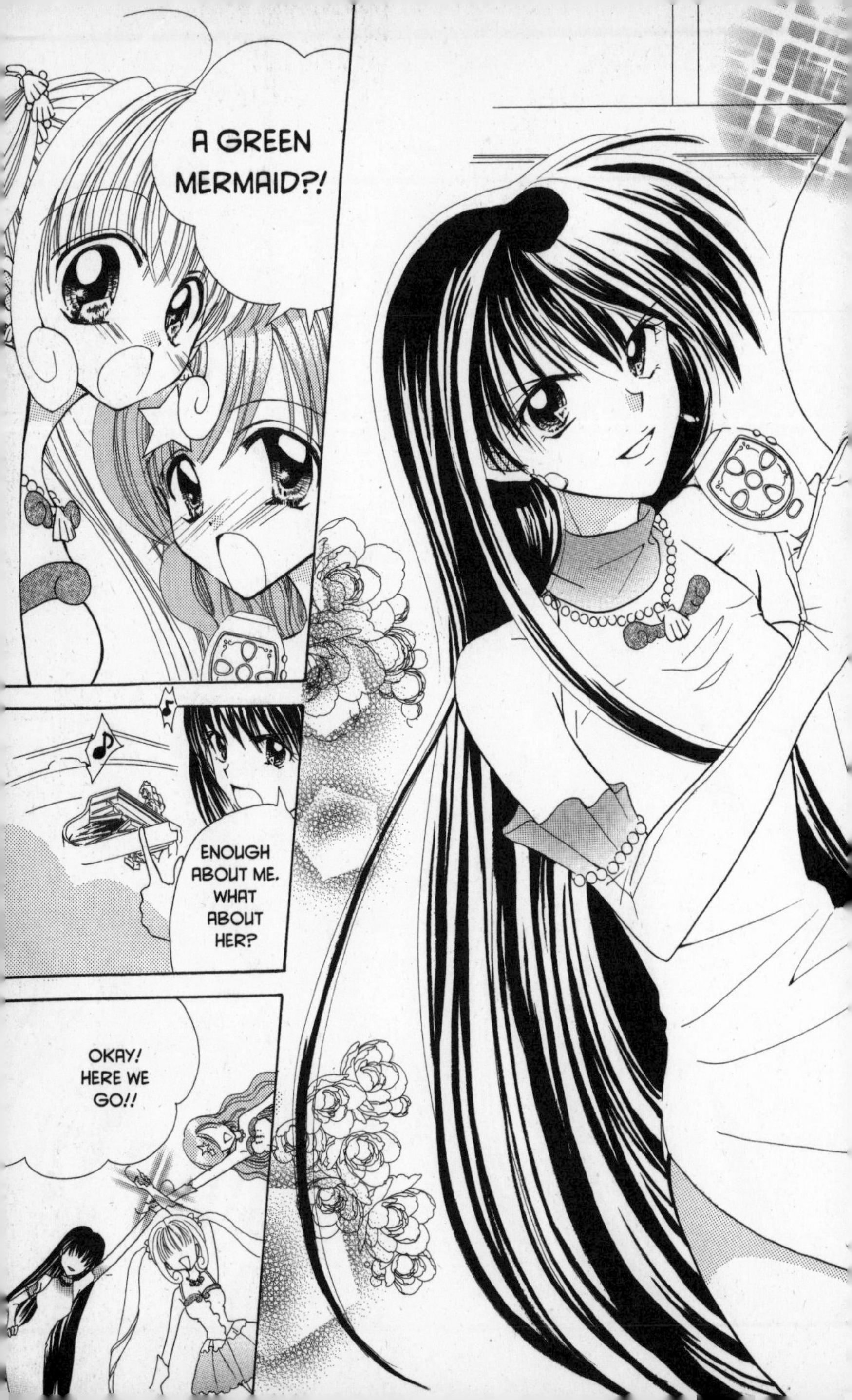
A GREEN MERMAID?!
ENOUGH ABOUT ME. WHAT ABOUT HER?
OKAY! HERE WE GO!!

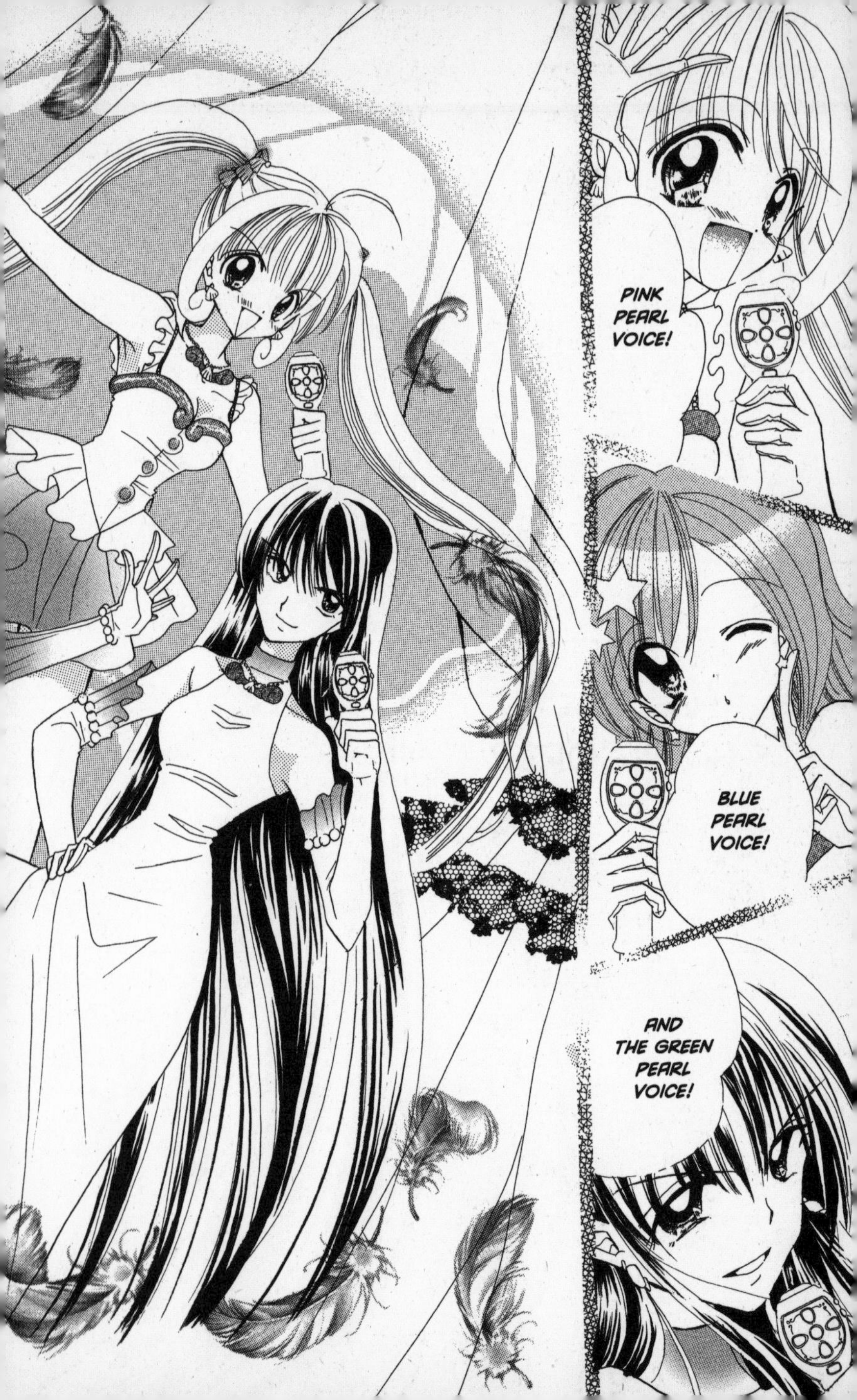
PINK PEARL VOICE!
BLUE PEARL VOICE!
AND THE GREEN PEARL VOICE!

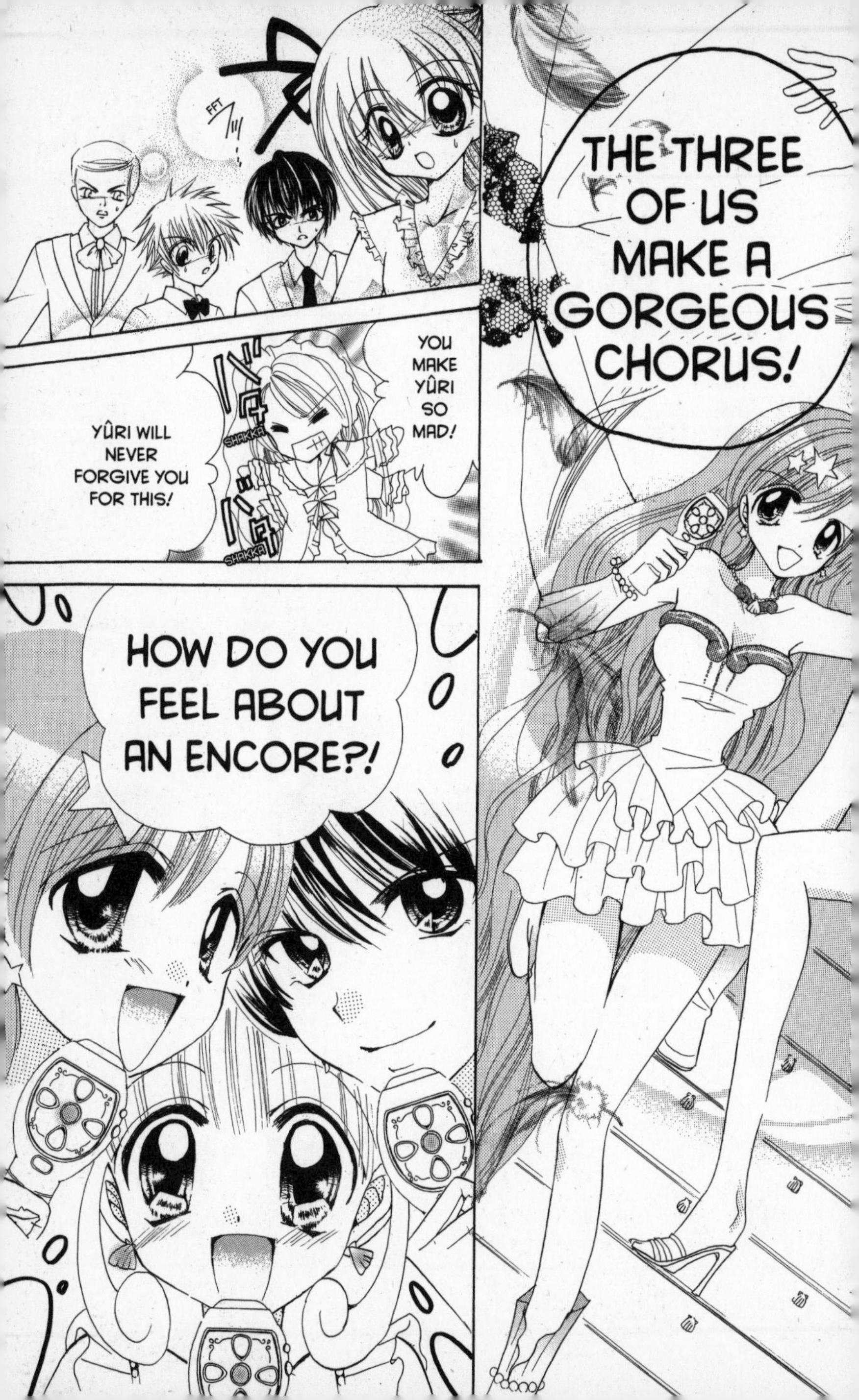
THE THREE OF US MAKE A GORGEOUS CHORUS!
FFT
YOU MAKE YÛRI SO MAD!
SHAKKA
SHAKKA
YÛRI WILL NEVER FORGIVE YOU FOR THIS!
HOW DO YOU FEEL ABOUT AN ENCORE?!

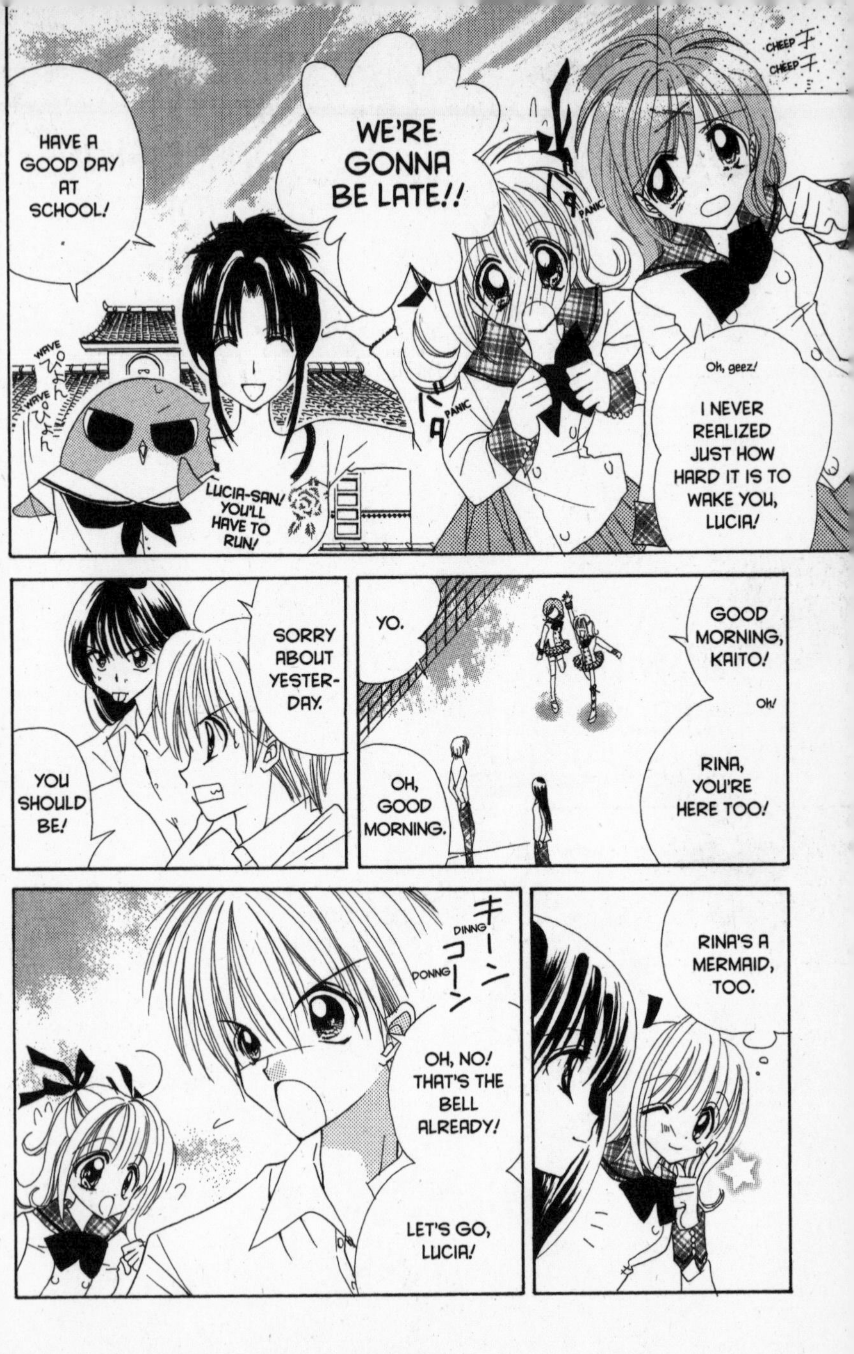
CHEEP
CHEEP
Oh, geez!
I NEVER REALIZED JUST HOW HARD IT IS TO WAKE YOU, LUCIA!
PANIC
PANIC
WE'RE GONNA BE LATE!!
LUCIA-SAN! YOU'LL HAVE TO RUN!
HAVE A GOOD DAY AT SCHOOL!
WAVE
WAVE
GOOD MORNING, KAITO!
Oh!
RINA, YOU'RE HERE TOO!
YO.
OH, GOOD MORNING.
SORRY ABOUT YESTER-DAY.
YOU SHOULD BE!
RINA'S A MERMAID, TOO.
DINNG
DONNG
OH, NO! THAT'S THE BELL ALREADY!
LET'S GO, LUCIA!

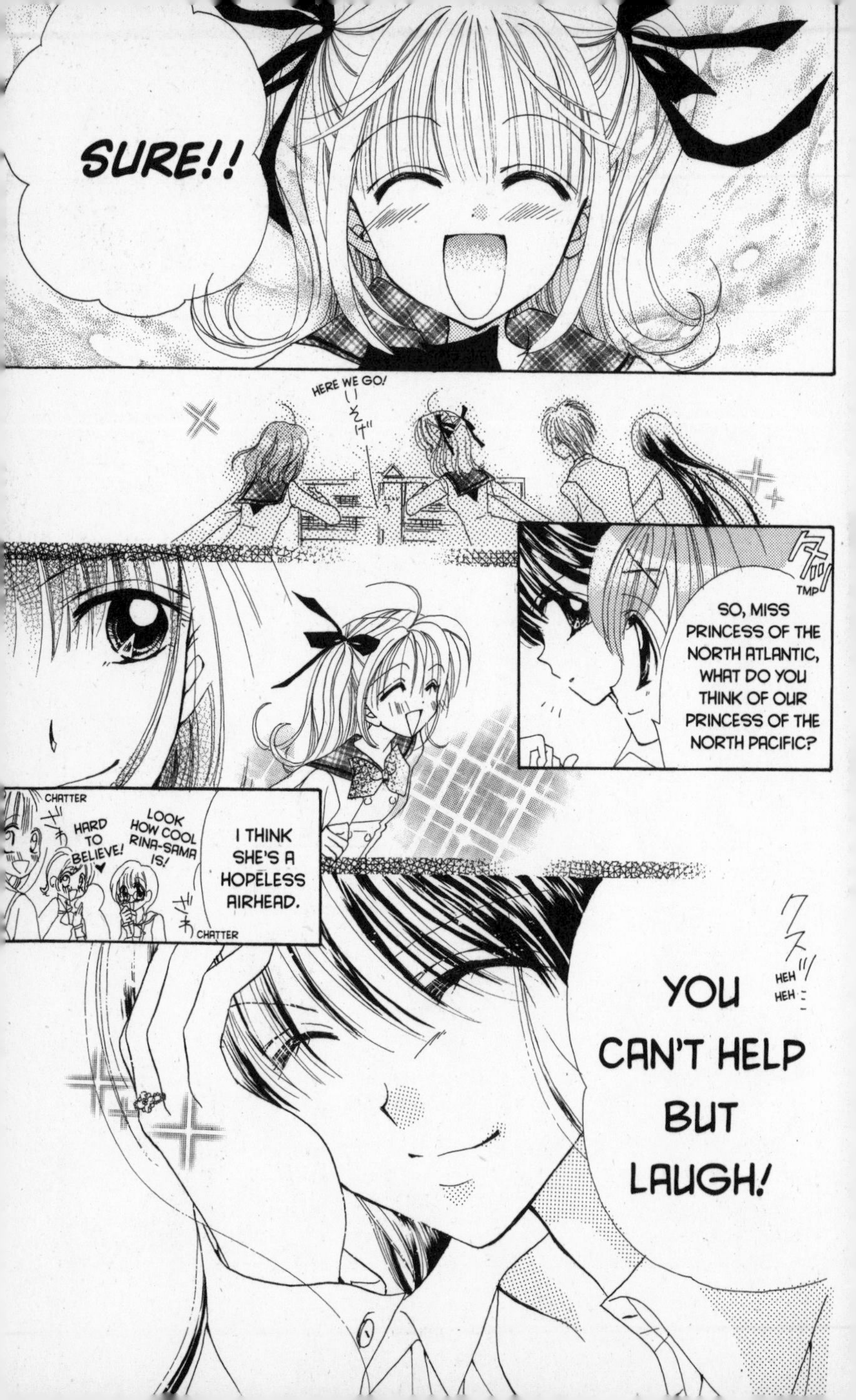
SURE!!
HERE WE GO!
TMP
SO, MISS PRINCESS OF THE NORTH ATLANTIC, WHAT DO YOU THINK OF OUR PRINCESS OF THE NORTH PACIFIC?
I THINK SHE'S A HOPELESS AIRHEAD.
LOOK HOW COOL RINA-SAMA IS!
HARD TO BELIEVE! ♥
CHATTER
CHATTER
YOU CAN'T HELP BUT LAUGH!
HEH HEH

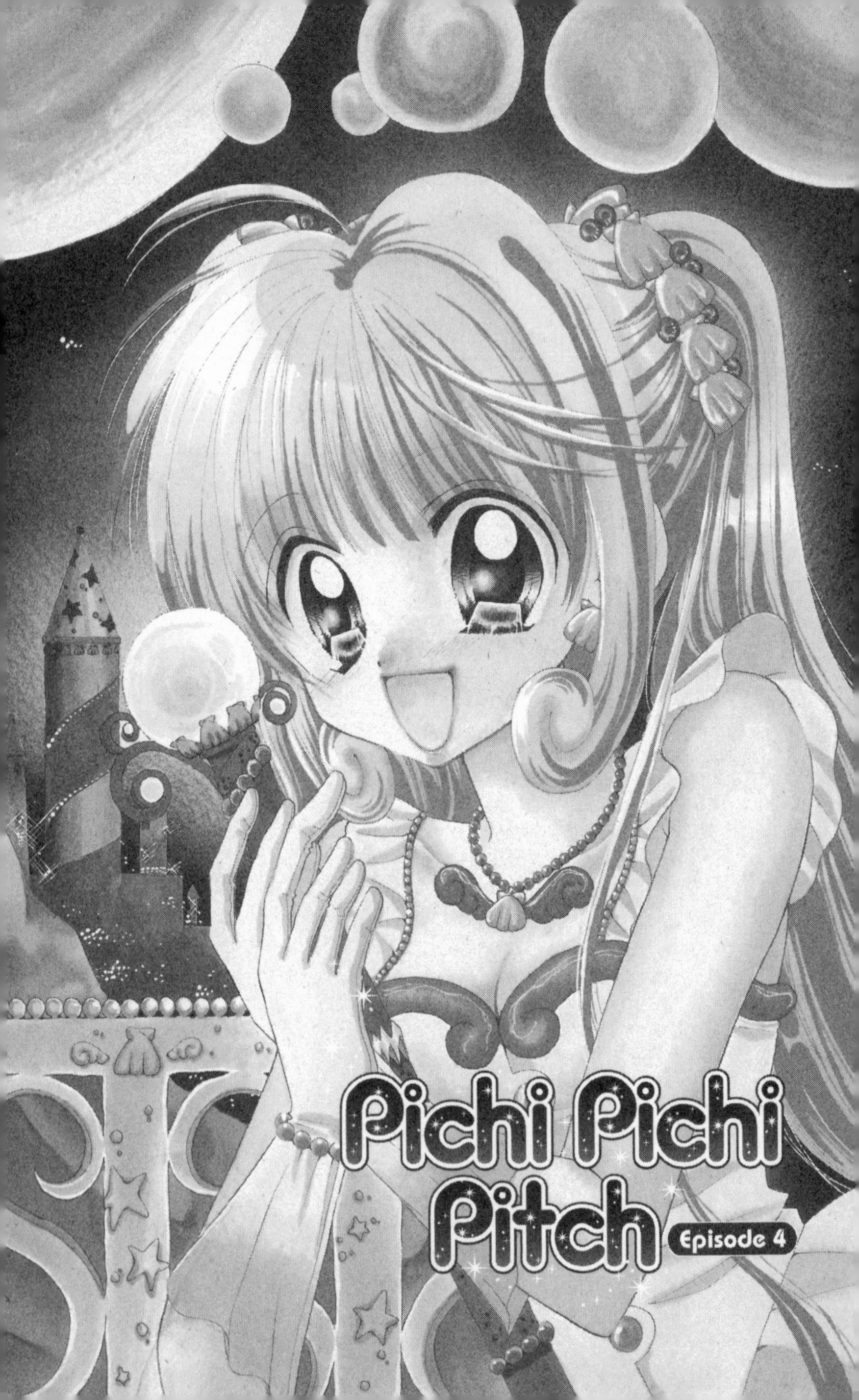
Pichi Pichi Pitch
Episode 4

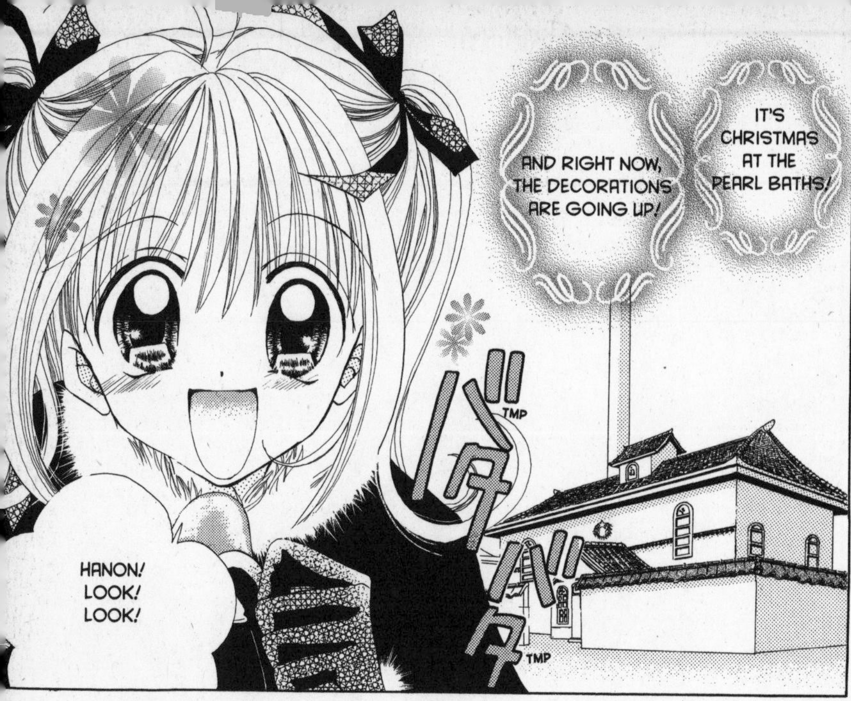
IT'S CHRISTMAS AT THE PEARL BATHS!
AND RIGHT NOW, THE DECORATIONS ARE GOING UP!
TMP
TMP
HANON! LOOK! LOOK!

(EPISODE 4)

AS RESEARCH I WENT TO AN AQUARIUM. I REALLY LIKE RESEARCH! I CAN TAKE PICTURES OF BACKGROUNDS I WANT BEFOREHAND, THEN WHEN IT COMES TIME TO PUT IT ON PAPER, THE DRAWING GOES SO FAST! ♥ (BUT IT ALWAYS HAS TO BE AT THE ANGLE OF THE PHOTO.) FOR ME, DRAWING HIPPO IS REALLY FUN! BUT IN THE END, HE DIDN'T GET HIMSELF A GIRLFRIEND. SORRY HIPPO! THEY WERE ABLE TO INCLUDE A LOT OF HANAMORI'S OPINIONS IN THE SCENARIO THIS TIME! I REALLY HAVE TO THANK THE EDITORS AND YOKOTE-SAMA FOR ACTUALLY TAKING SERIOUSLY THE OPINIONS OF A FLEDGLING MANGA-KA LIKE ME. !! BUT A FLEDGLING HAS TO TRY ONE'S FLEDGLING BEST! FLEDGLING

NOW THAT I THINK OF IT, WHEN SEEING IZÛRU IN LOVE, SOMEONE SENT MAIL TO MY WEB SITE HOME PAGE SAYING, "GACKTO-SAMA IS . . . A MAN WHO DOES WRONG. HE'S ALSO TOO MUCH OF A PRETTY BOY."

AH HA HA!

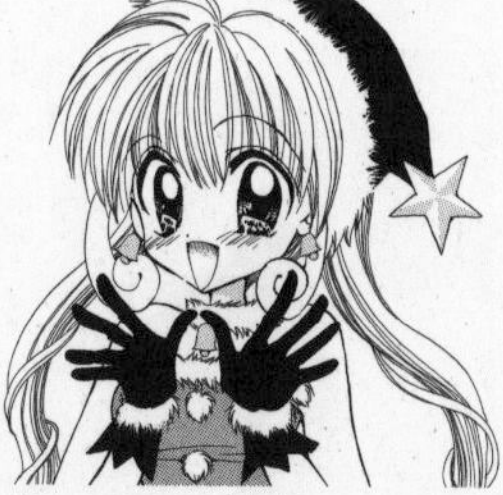

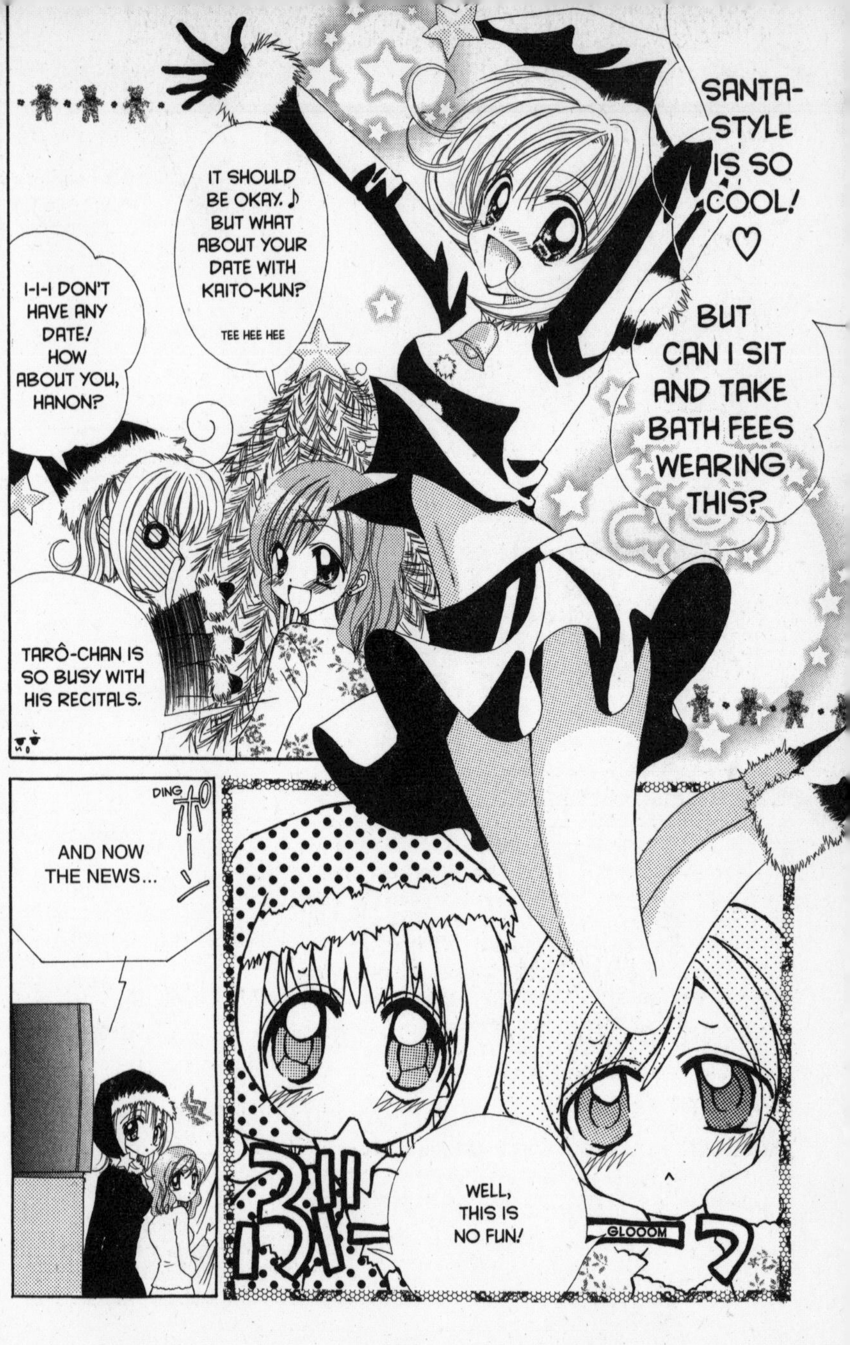
SANTA-STYLE IS SO COOL! ♡
BUT CAN I SIT AND TAKE BATH FEES WEARING THIS?
IT SHOULD BE OKAY. ♪ BUT WHAT ABOUT YOUR DATE WITH KAITO-KUN?
TEE HEE HEE
I-I-I DON'T HAVE ANY DATE! HOW ABOUT YOU, HANON?
TARÔ-CHAN IS SO BUSY WITH HIS RECITALS.
GLOOOM
WELL, THIS IS NO FUN!
DING
AND NOW THE NEWS...

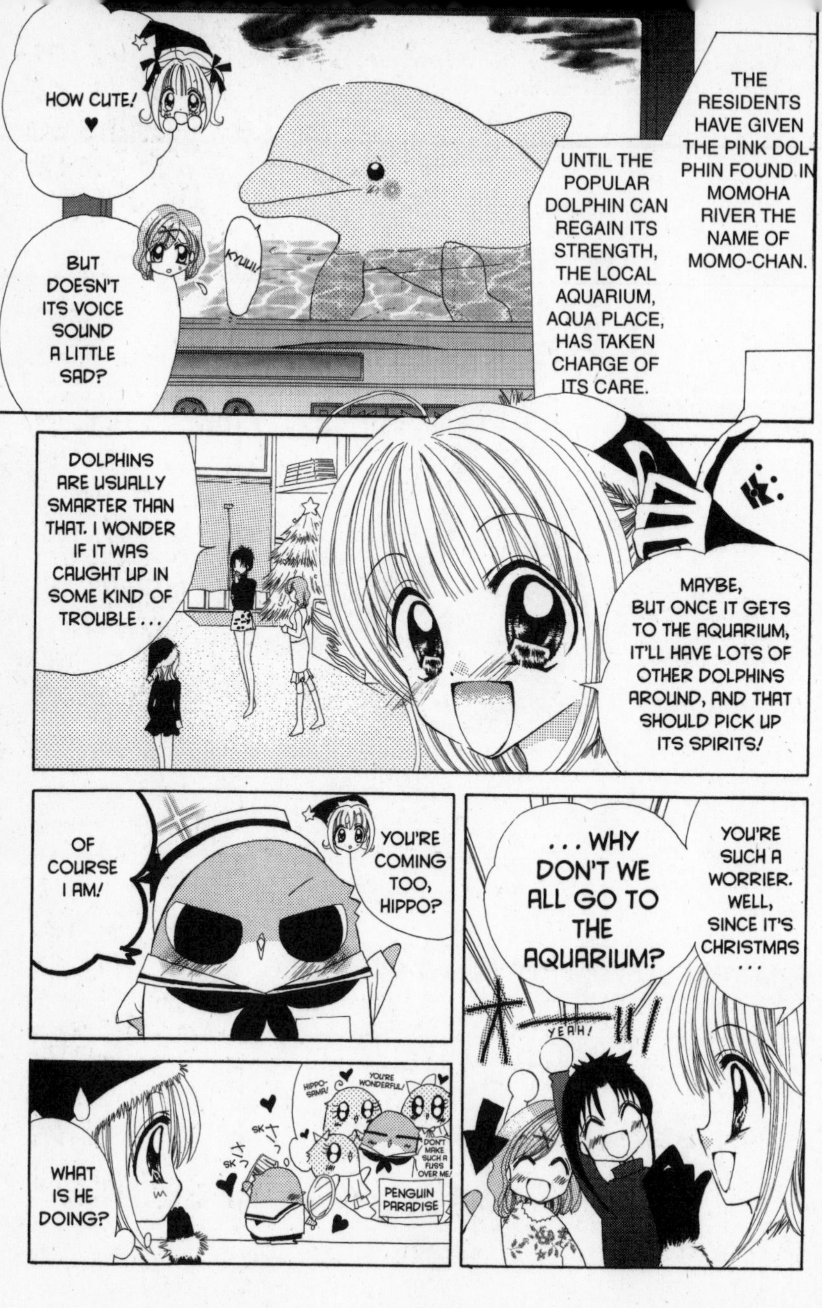
THE RESIDENTS HAVE GIVEN THE PINK DOLPHIN FOUND IN MOMOHA RIVER THE NAME OF MOMO-CHAN.
UNTIL THE POPULAR DOLPHIN CAN REGAIN ITS STRENGTH, THE LOCAL AQUARIUM, AQUA PLACE, HAS TAKEN CHARGE OF ITS CARE.
HOW CUTE! ♥
KYUUI!
BUT DOESN'T ITS VOICE SOUND A LITTLE SAD?
MAYBE, BUT ONCE IT GETS TO THE AQUARIUM, IT'LL HAVE LOTS OF OTHER DOLPHINS AROUND, AND THAT SHOULD PICK UP ITS SPIRITS!
DOLPHINS ARE USUALLY SMARTER THAN THAT. I WONDER IF IT WAS CAUGHT UP IN SOME KIND OF TROUBLE...
YOU'RE SUCH A WORRIER. WELL, SINCE IT'S CHRISTMAS...
...WHY DON'T WE ALL GO TO THE AQUARIUM?
YEAH!
YOU'RE COMING TOO, HIPPO?
OF COURSE I AM!
YOU'RE WONDERFUL!
HIPPO-SAMA!
DON'T MAKE SUCH A FUSS OVER ME!
SK
SK
PENGUIN PARADISE
WHAT IS HE DOING?

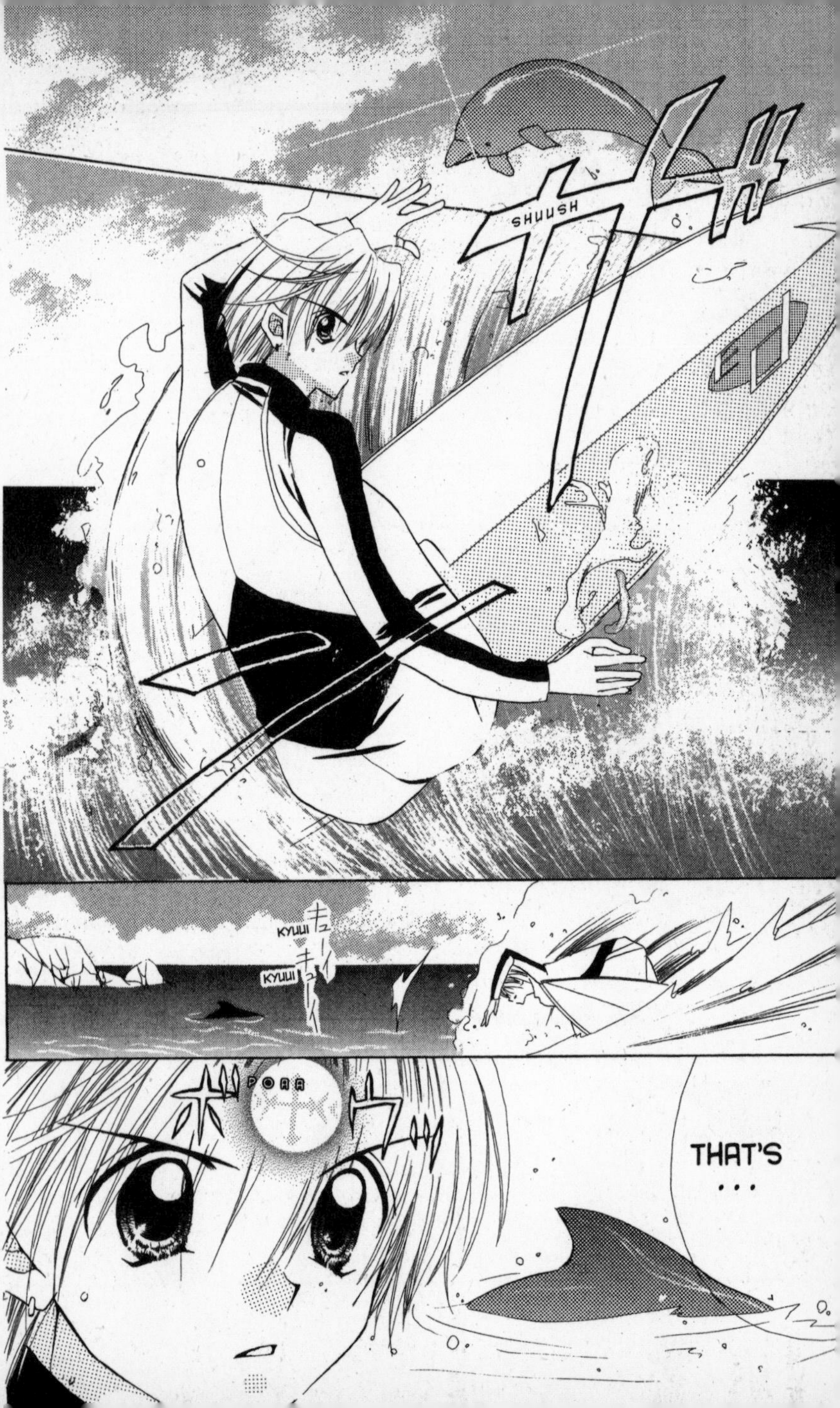
SHUUSH
KYUUI
KYUUI
PORA
THAT'S
...

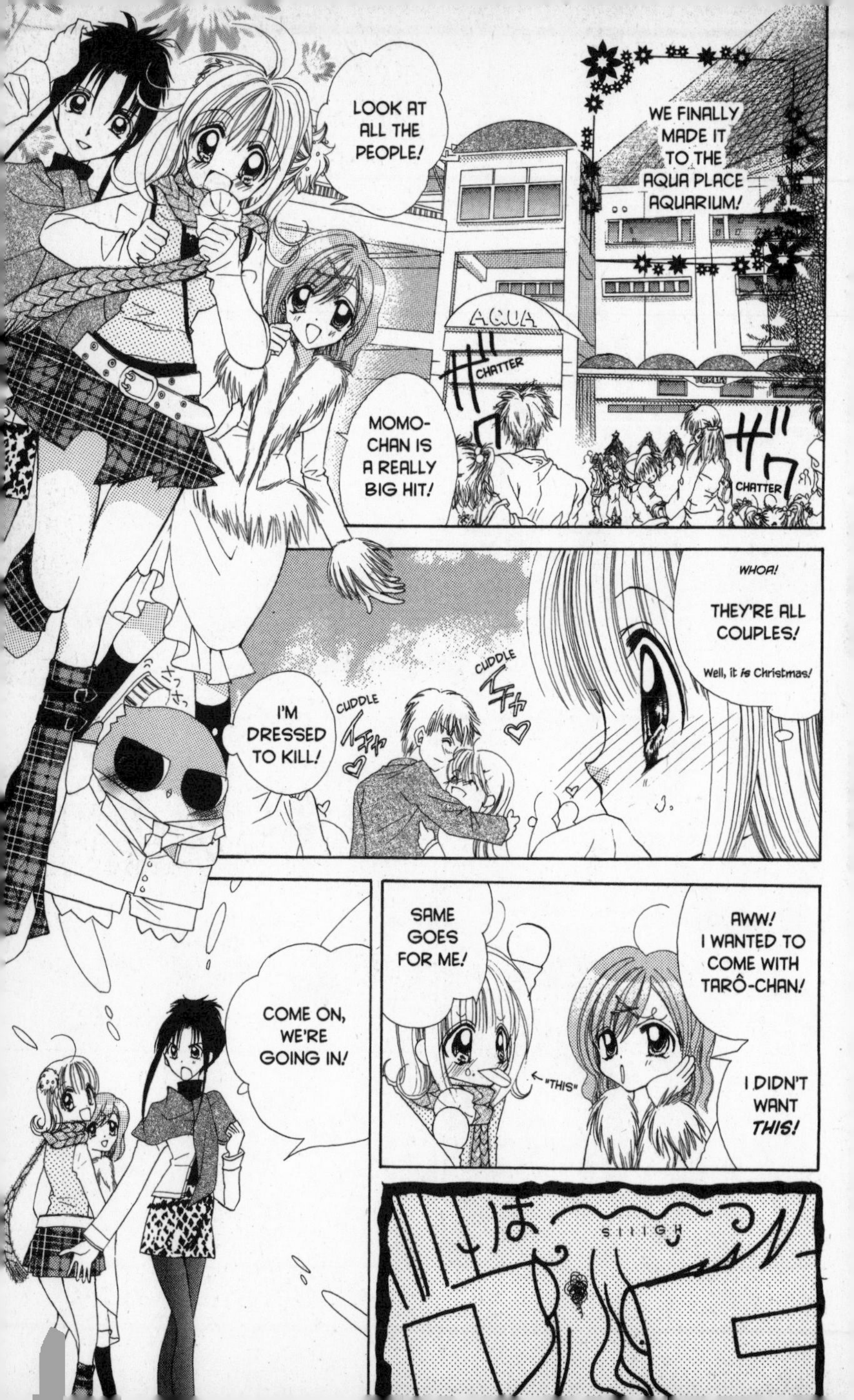
WE FINALLY MADE IT TO THE AQUA PLACE AQUARIUM!
AQUA
CHATTER
CHATTER
LOOK AT ALL THE PEOPLE!
MOMO-CHAN IS A REALLY BIG HIT!
WHOA!
THEY'RE ALL COUPLES!
Well, it *is* Christmas!
CUDDLE
CUDDLE
I'M DRESSED TO KILL!
AWW! I WANTED TO COME WITH TARÔ-CHAN!
I DIDN'T WANT *THIS!*
"THIS"
SAME GOES FOR ME!
SIIIGH
COME ON, WE'RE GOING IN!

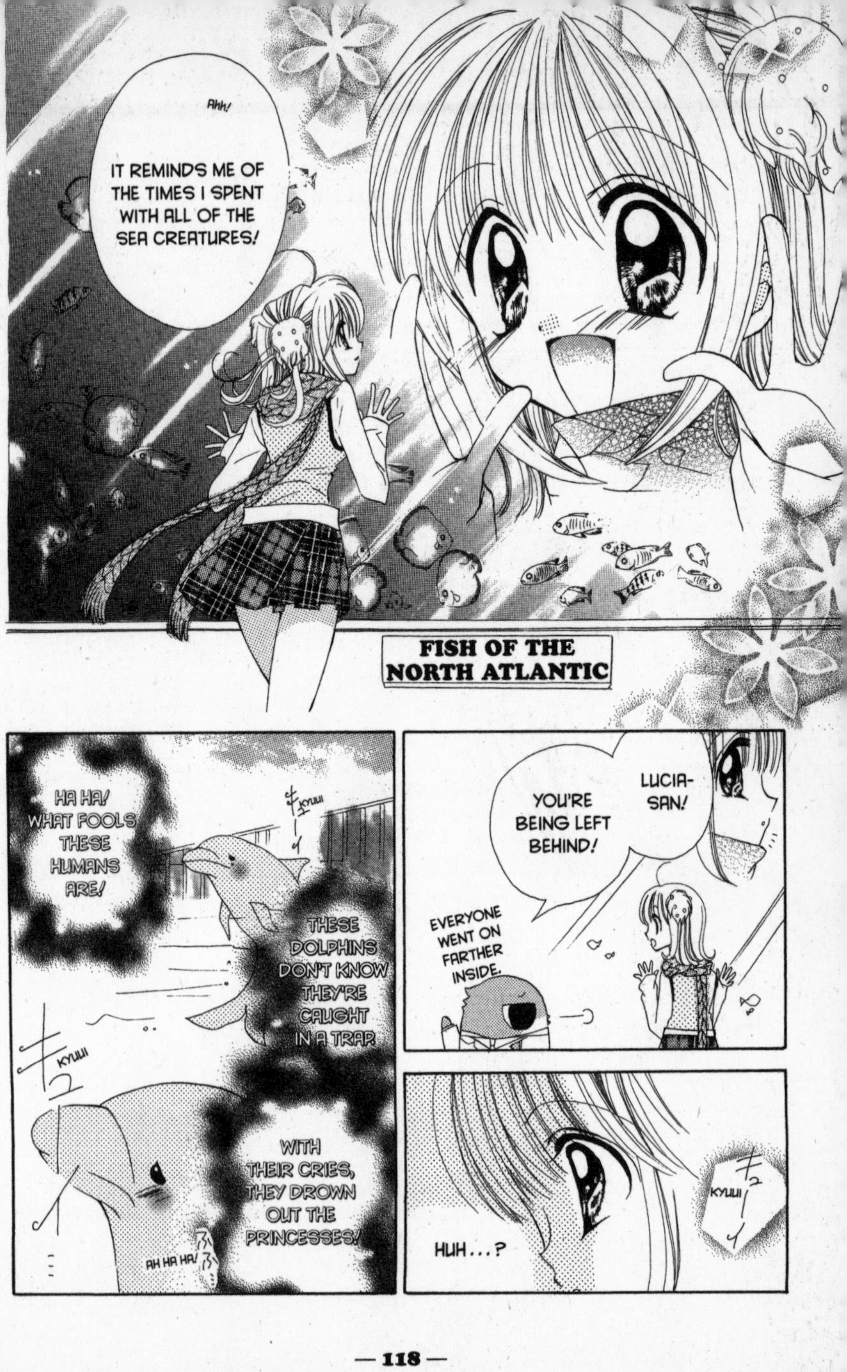
Ahh!
IT REMINDS ME OF THE TIMES I SPENT WITH ALL OF THE SEA CREATURES!
FISH OF THE NORTH ATLANTIC
LUCIA-SAN!
YOU'RE BEING LEFT BEHIND!
EVERYONE WENT ON FARTHER INSIDE.
KYUUI
HUH...?
HA HA! WHAT FOOLS THESE HUMANS ARE!
KYUUI
THESE DOLPHINS DON'T KNOW THEY'RE CAUGHT IN A TRAP.
KYUUI
WITH THEIR CRIES, THEY DROWN OUT THE PRINCESSES!
AH HA HA!

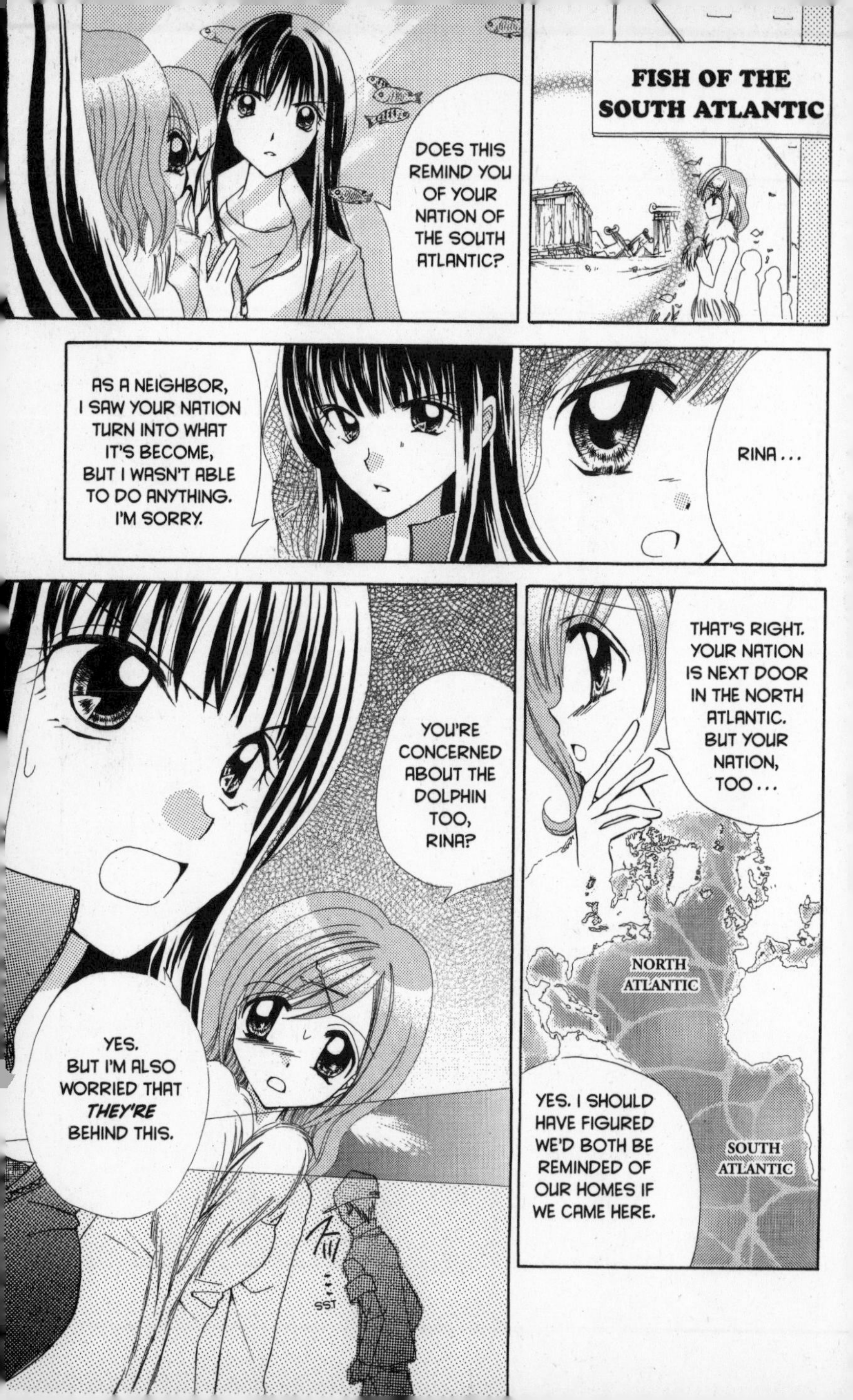
FISH OF THE SOUTH ATLANTIC
DOES THIS REMIND YOU OF YOUR NATION OF THE SOUTH ATLANTIC?
RINA...
AS A NEIGHBOR, I SAW YOUR NATION TURN INTO WHAT IT'S BECOME, BUT I WASN'T ABLE TO DO ANYTHING. I'M SORRY.
THAT'S RIGHT. YOUR NATION IS NEXT DOOR IN THE NORTH ATLANTIC. BUT YOUR NATION, TOO...
NORTH ATLANTIC
SOUTH ATLANTIC
YES. I SHOULD HAVE FIGURED WE'D BOTH BE REMINDED OF OUR HOMES IF WE CAME HERE.
YOU'RE CONCERNED ABOUT THE DOLPHIN TOO, RINA?
YES. BUT I'M ALSO WORRIED THAT *THEY'RE* BEHIND THIS.
SST

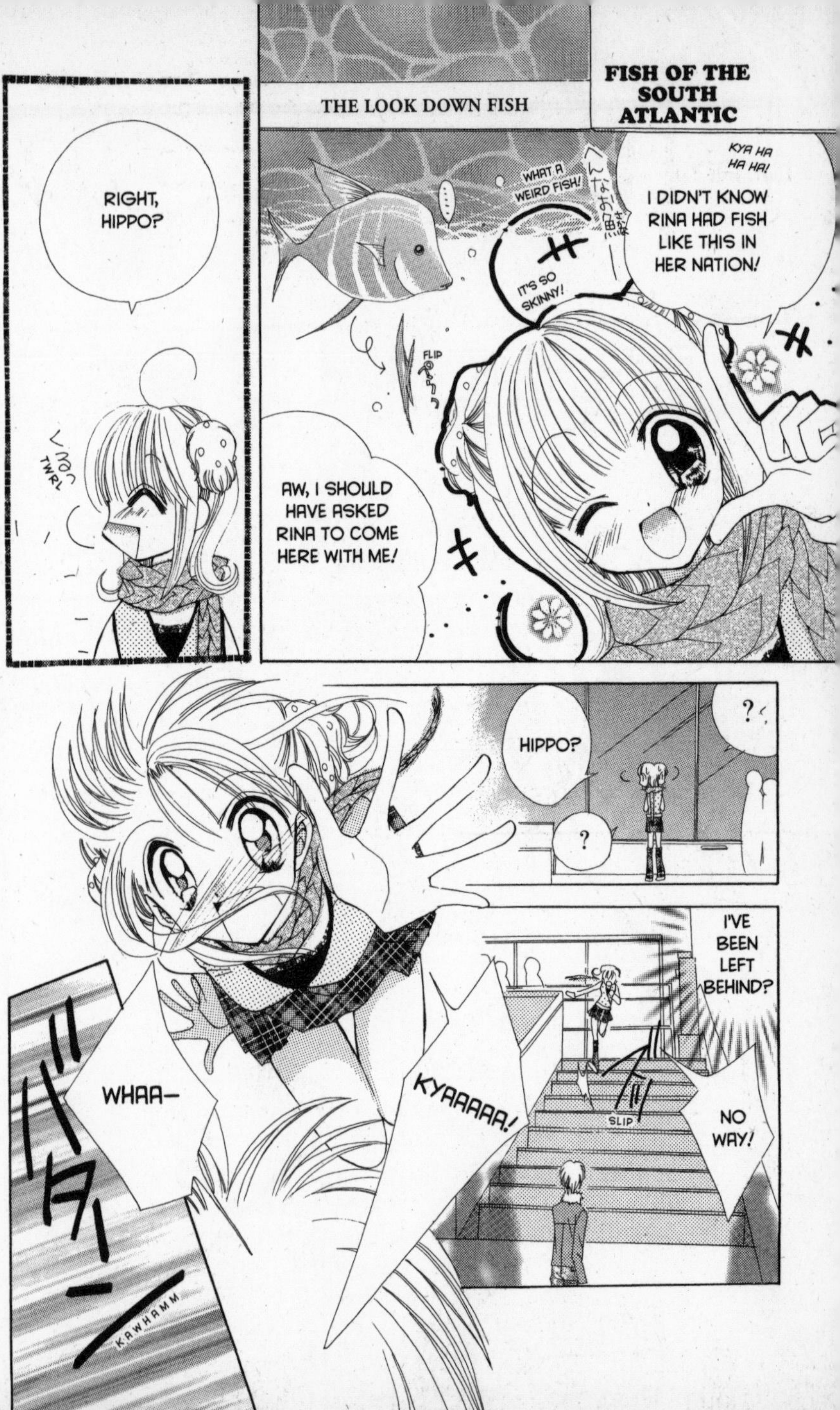

FISH OF THE SOUTH ATLANTIC
THE LOOK DOWN FISH
KYA HA HA HA!
I DIDN'T KNOW RINA HAD FISH LIKE THIS IN HER NATION!
WHAT A WEIRD FISH!
IT'S SO SKINNY!
FLIP
AW, I SHOULD HAVE ASKED RINA TO COME HERE WITH ME!
RIGHT, HIPPO?
TWRL
HIPPO?
?
?
I'VE BEEN LEFT BEHIND?
SLIP
NO WAY!
KYAAAAA!
WHAA-
KAWHAMM

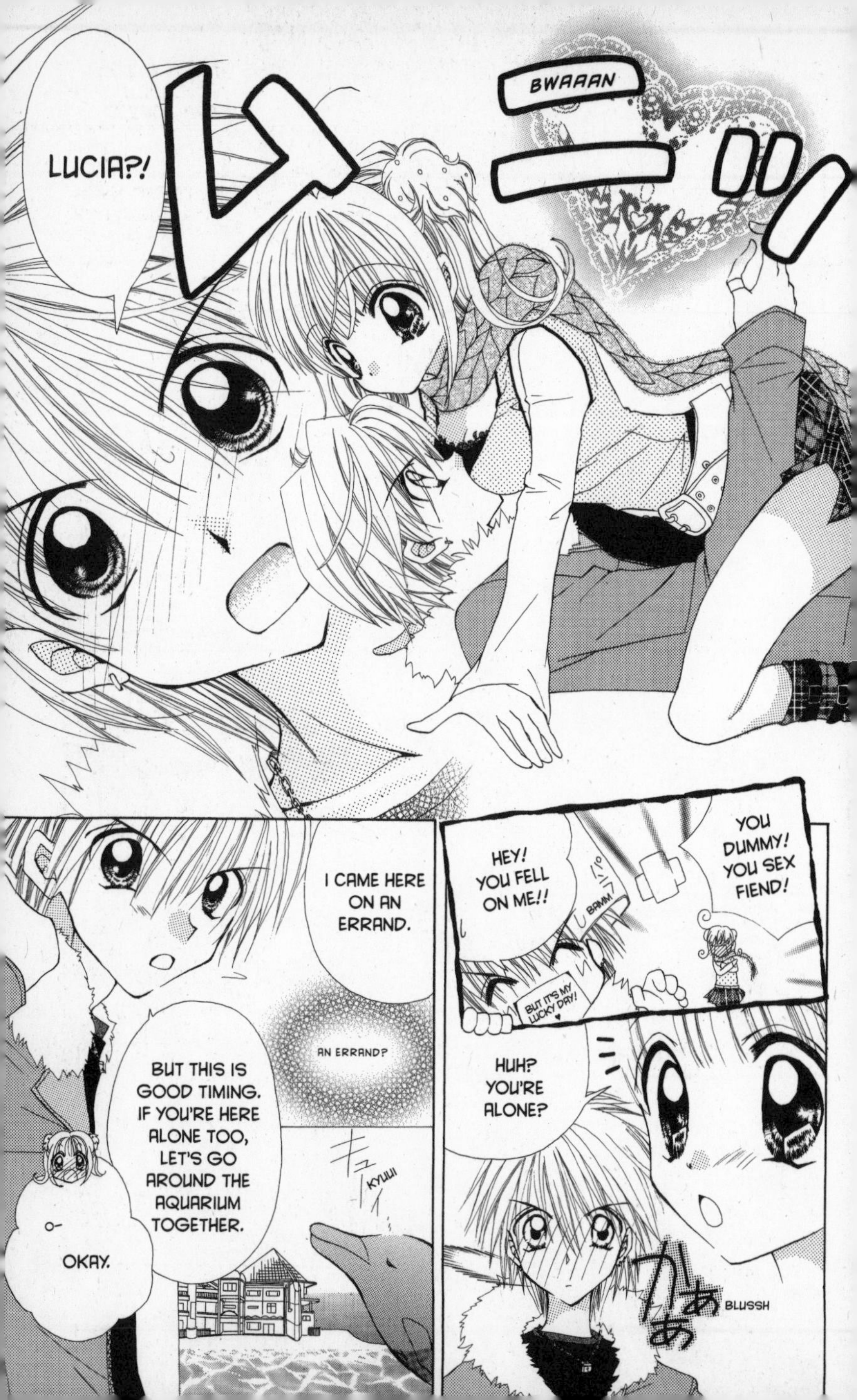
BWAAAN
LUCIA?!
YOU DUMMY! YOU SEX FIEND!
HEY! YOU FELL ON ME!!
BAMM
BUT IT'S MY LUCKY DAY!
I CAME HERE ON AN ERRAND.
AN ERRAND?
HUH? YOU'RE ALONE?
BLUSSH
BUT THIS IS GOOD TIMING. IF YOU'RE HERE ALONE TOO, LET'S GO AROUND THE AQUARIUM TOGETHER.
KYUUI
O- OKAY.

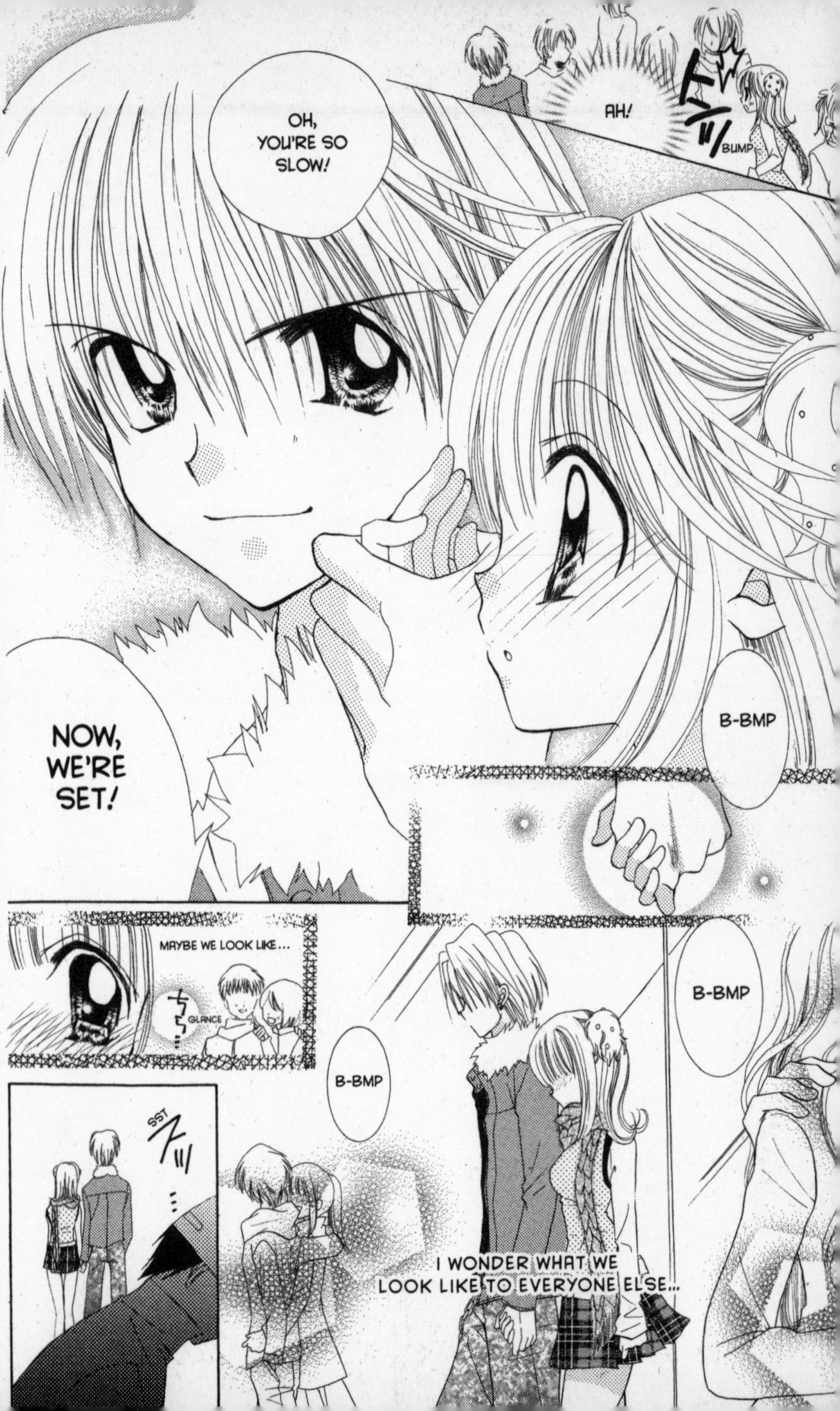
AH!
BUMP
OH, YOU'RE SO SLOW!
B-BMP
NOW, WE'RE SET!
B-BMP
B-BMP
I WONDER WHAT WE LOOK LIKE TO EVERYONE ELSE...
MAYBE WE LOOK LIKE...
GLANCE
SST

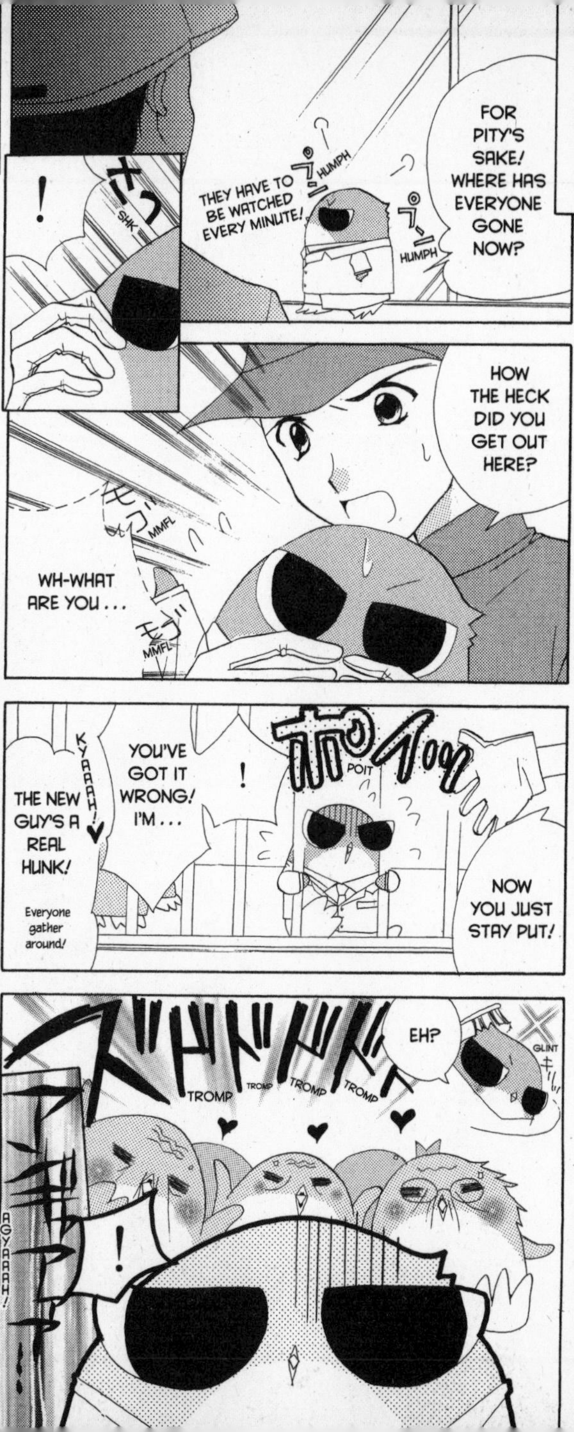
FOR PITY'S SAKE! WHERE HAS EVERYONE GONE NOW?
HUMPH
HUMPH
THEY HAVE TO BE WATCHED EVERY MINUTE!
!
SHK
HOW THE HECK DID YOU GET OUT HERE?
MMFL
WH-WHAT ARE YOU . . .
MMFL
NOW YOU JUST STAY PUT!
POIT
!
YOU'VE GOT IT WRONG! I'M . . .
KYAAAAH!
THE NEW GUY'S A REAL HUNK!
Everyone gather around!
GLINT
EH?
TROMP
TROMP
TROMP
TROMP
!
AGYAAAAH!

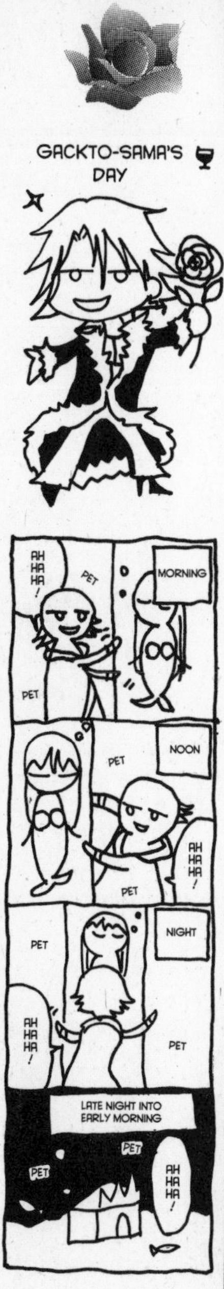
GACKTO-SAMA'S DAY
MORNING
AH HA HA!
PET
PET
NOON
PET
AH HA HA!
PET
NIGHT
PET
AH HA HA!
PET
LATE NIGHT INTO EARLY MORNING
PET
PET
AH HA HA!

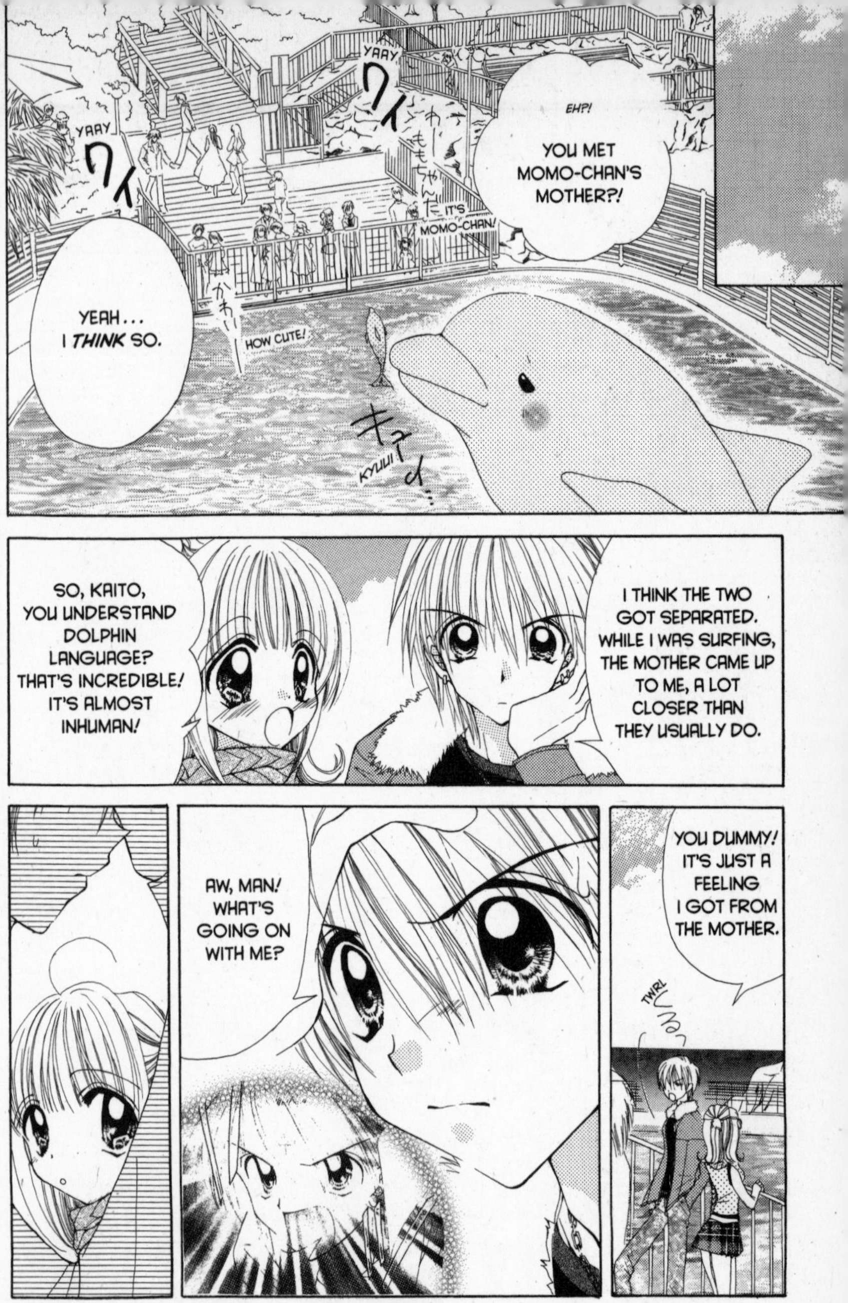
YAAY
YAAY
IT'S MOMO-CHAN!
EH?!
YOU MET MOMO-CHAN'S MOTHER?!
YEAH... I *THINK* SO.
HOW CUTE!
KYUUI
I THINK THE TWO GOT SEPARATED. WHILE I WAS SURFING, THE MOTHER CAME UP TO ME, A LOT CLOSER THAN THEY USUALLY DO.
SO, KAITO, YOU UNDERSTAND DOLPHIN LANGUAGE? THAT'S INCREDIBLE! IT'S ALMOST INHUMAN!
YOU DUMMY! IT'S JUST A FEELING I GOT FROM THE MOTHER.
TWRL
AW, MAN! WHAT'S GOING ON WITH ME?

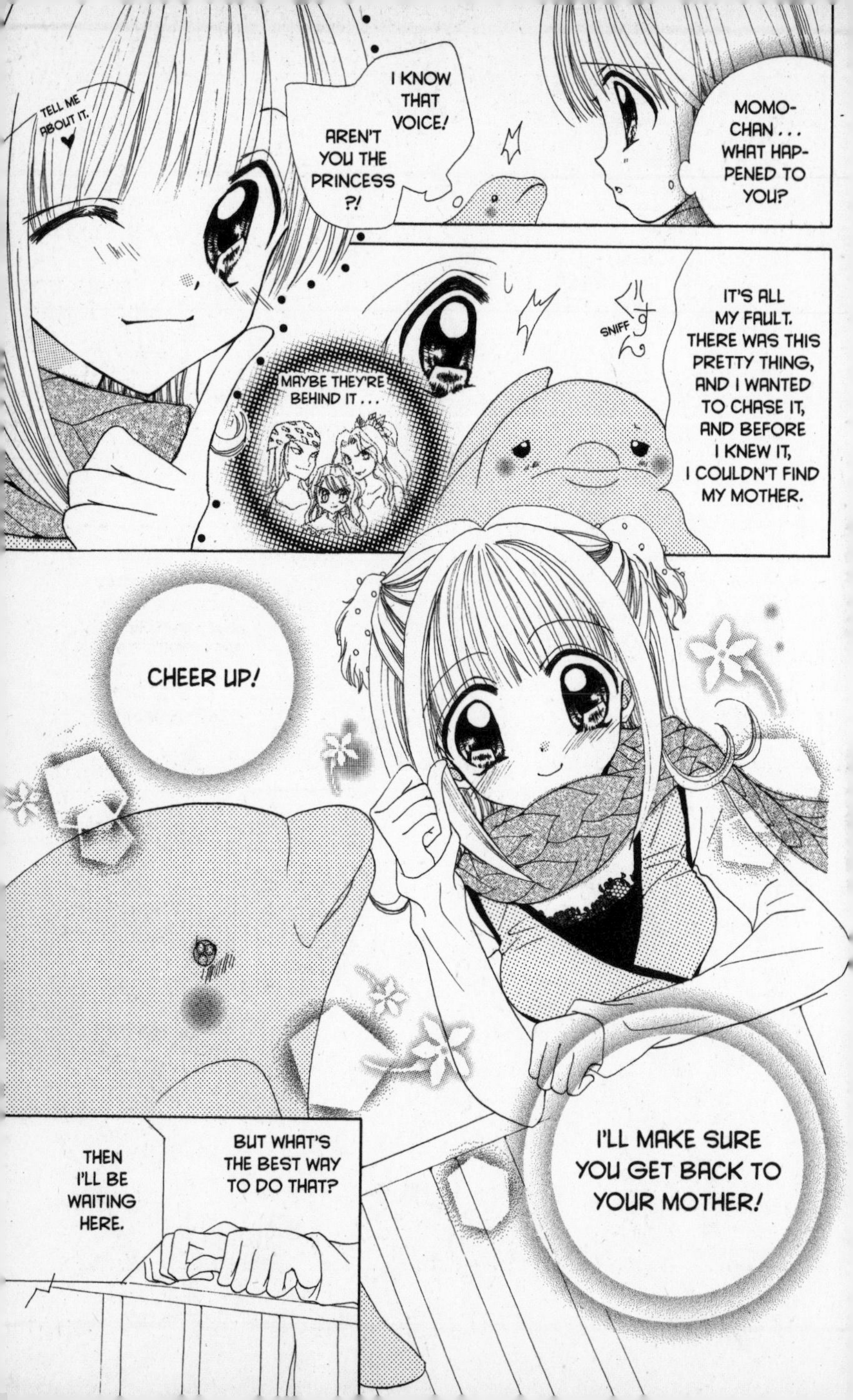
MOMO-CHAN . . . WHAT HAPPENED TO YOU?
IT'S ALL MY FAULT. THERE WAS THIS PRETTY THING, AND I WANTED TO CHASE IT, AND BEFORE I KNEW IT, I COULDN'T FIND MY MOTHER.
ぐすん
SNIFF
I KNOW THAT VOICE!
AREN'T YOU THE PRINCESS?!
TELL ME ABOUT IT. ♥
MAYBE THEY'RE BEHIND IT . . .
CHEER UP!
I'LL MAKE SURE YOU GET BACK TO YOUR MOTHER!
BUT WHAT'S THE BEST WAY TO DO THAT?
THEN I'LL BE WAITING HERE.

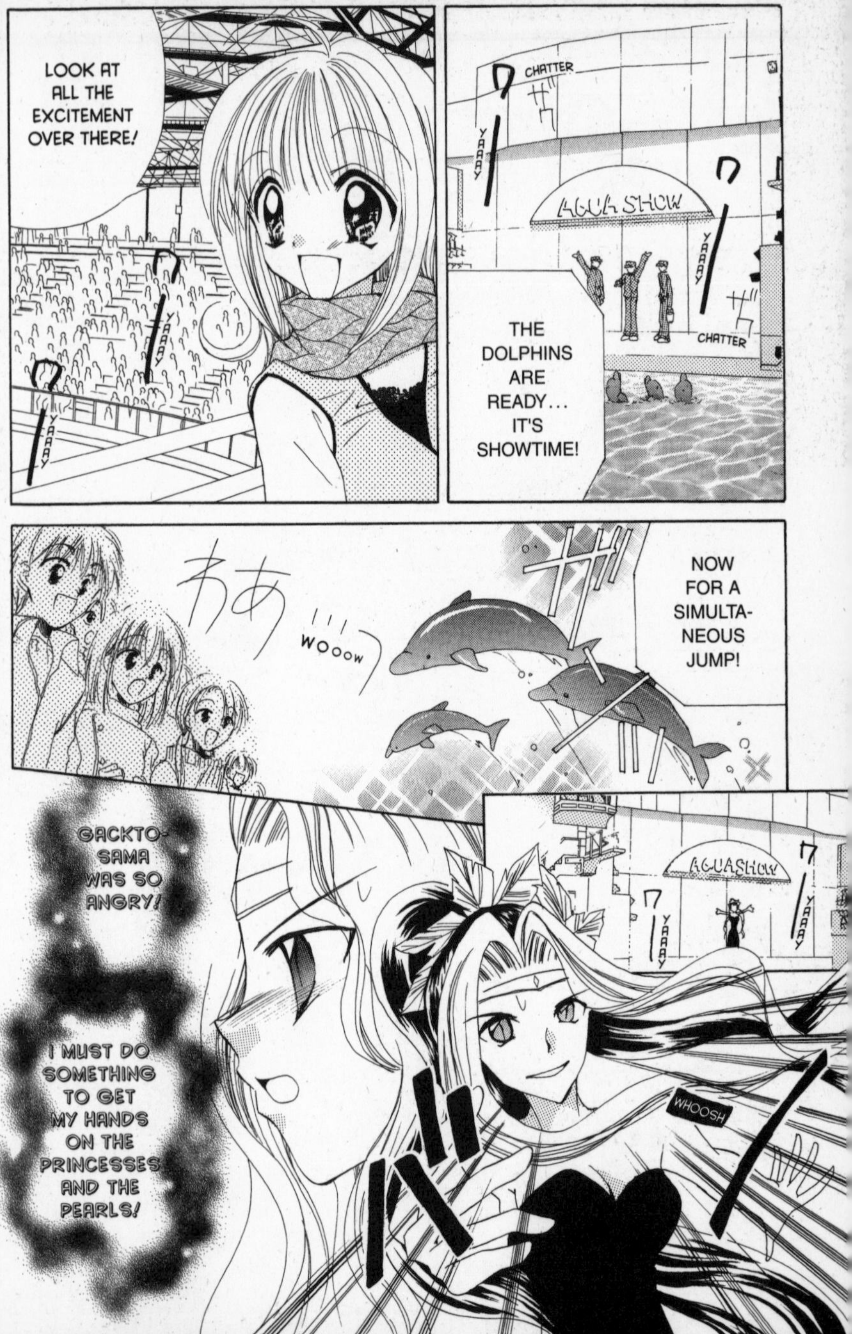
CHATTER
YAAAY
AQUA SHOW
THE DOLPHINS ARE READY… IT'S SHOWTIME!
CHATTER
YAAAY
LOOK AT ALL THE EXCITEMENT OVER THERE!
YAAAY
YAAAY
NOW FOR A SIMULTA-NEOUS JUMP!
WOOOW
AQUASHOW
YAAAY
YAAAY
GACKTO-SAMA WAS SO ANGRY!
I MUST DO SOMETHING TO GET MY HANDS ON THE PRINCESSES AND THE PEARLS!
WHOOSH

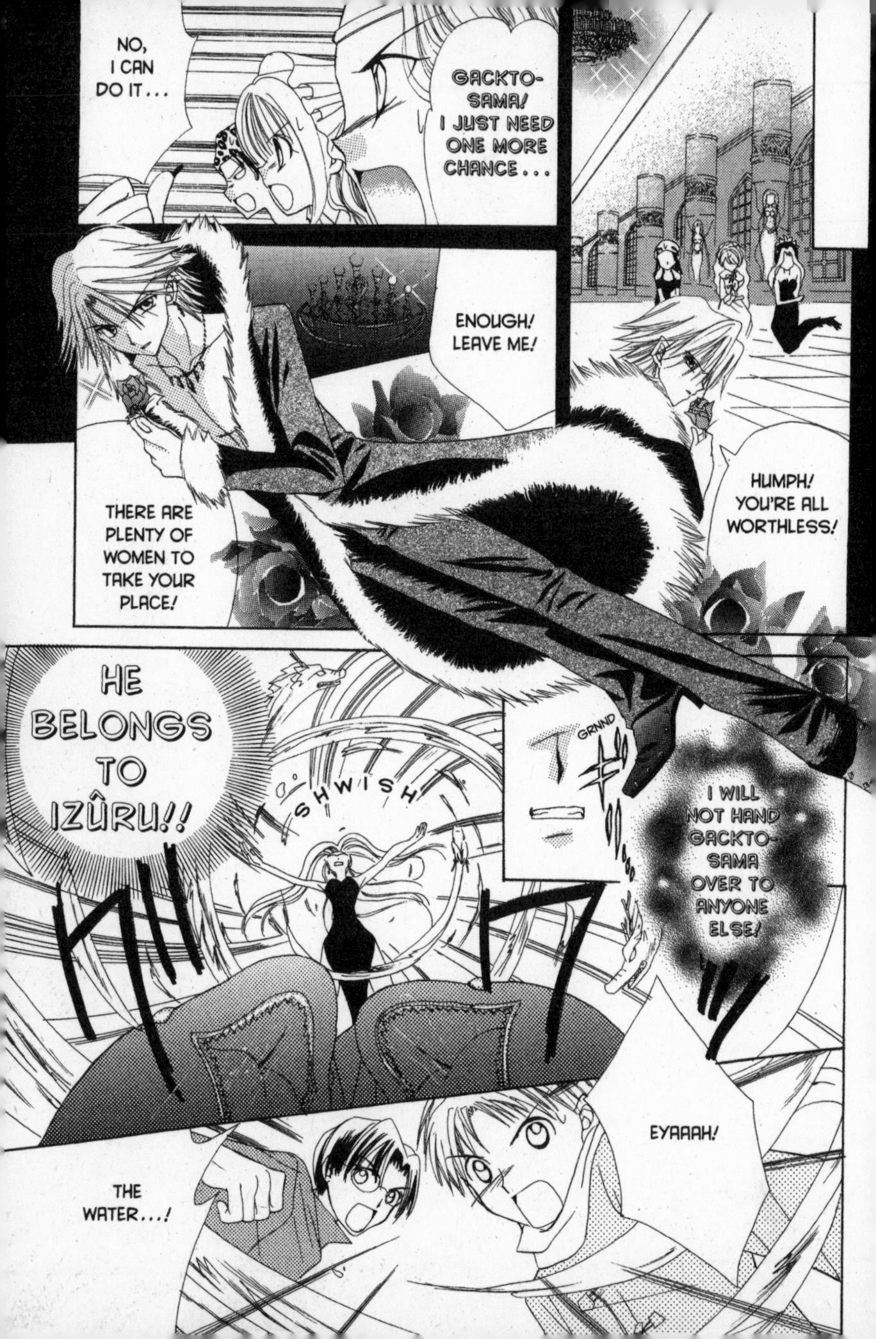
HUMPH! YOU'RE ALL WORTHLESS!
GACKTO-SAMA! I JUST NEED ONE MORE CHANCE...
NO, I CAN DO IT...
ENOUGH! LEAVE ME!
THERE ARE PLENTY OF WOMEN TO TAKE YOUR PLACE!
GRNND
I WILL NOT HAND GACKTO-SAMA OVER TO ANYONE ELSE!
HE BELONGS TO IZÛRU!!
SHWISH
EYAAAH!
THE WATER...!

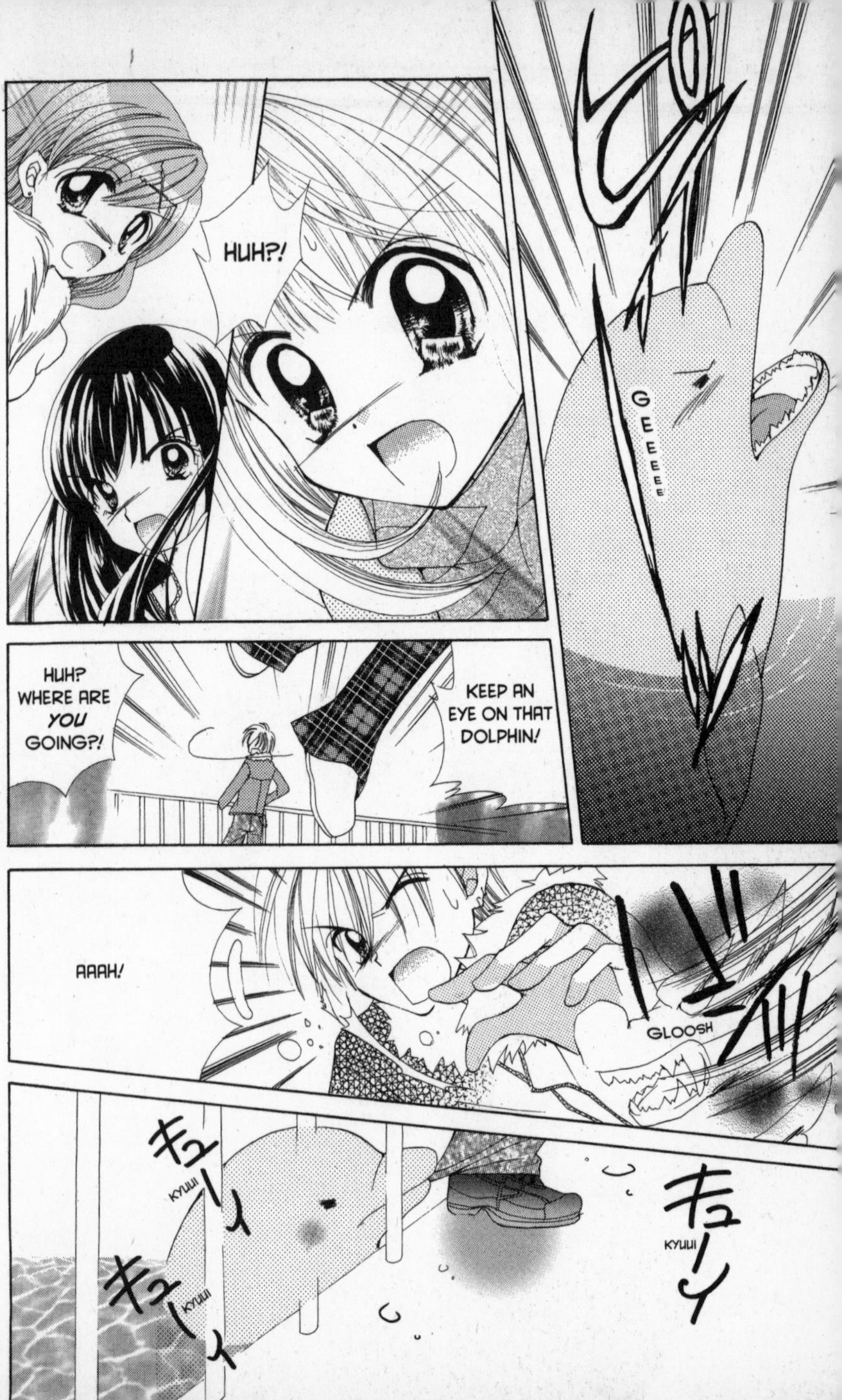
GEEEEEE
HUH?!
KEEP AN EYE ON THAT DOLPHIN!
HUH? WHERE ARE YOU GOING?!
GLOOSH
AAAH!
キューイ
KYUUI
キューイ
KYUUI
キューイ
KYUUI

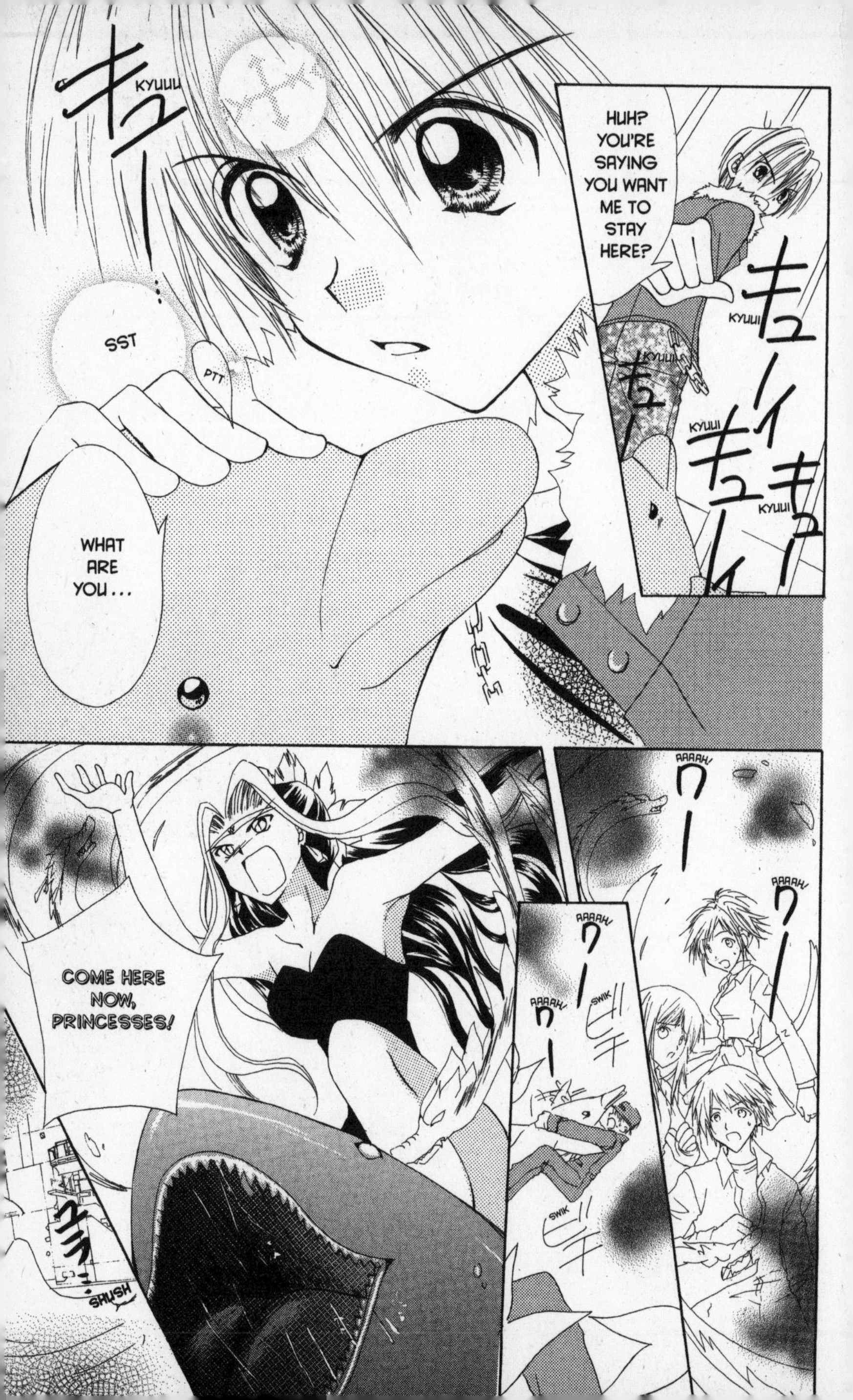
HUH? YOU'RE SAYING YOU WANT ME TO STAY HERE?
KYUUI
KYUUI
KYUUI
KYUUI
KYUUU
SST
PTT
WHAT ARE YOU...
AAAAH!
AAAAH!
AAAAH!
AAAAH!
SWIK
SWIK
COME HERE NOW, PRINCESSES!
SPLISH

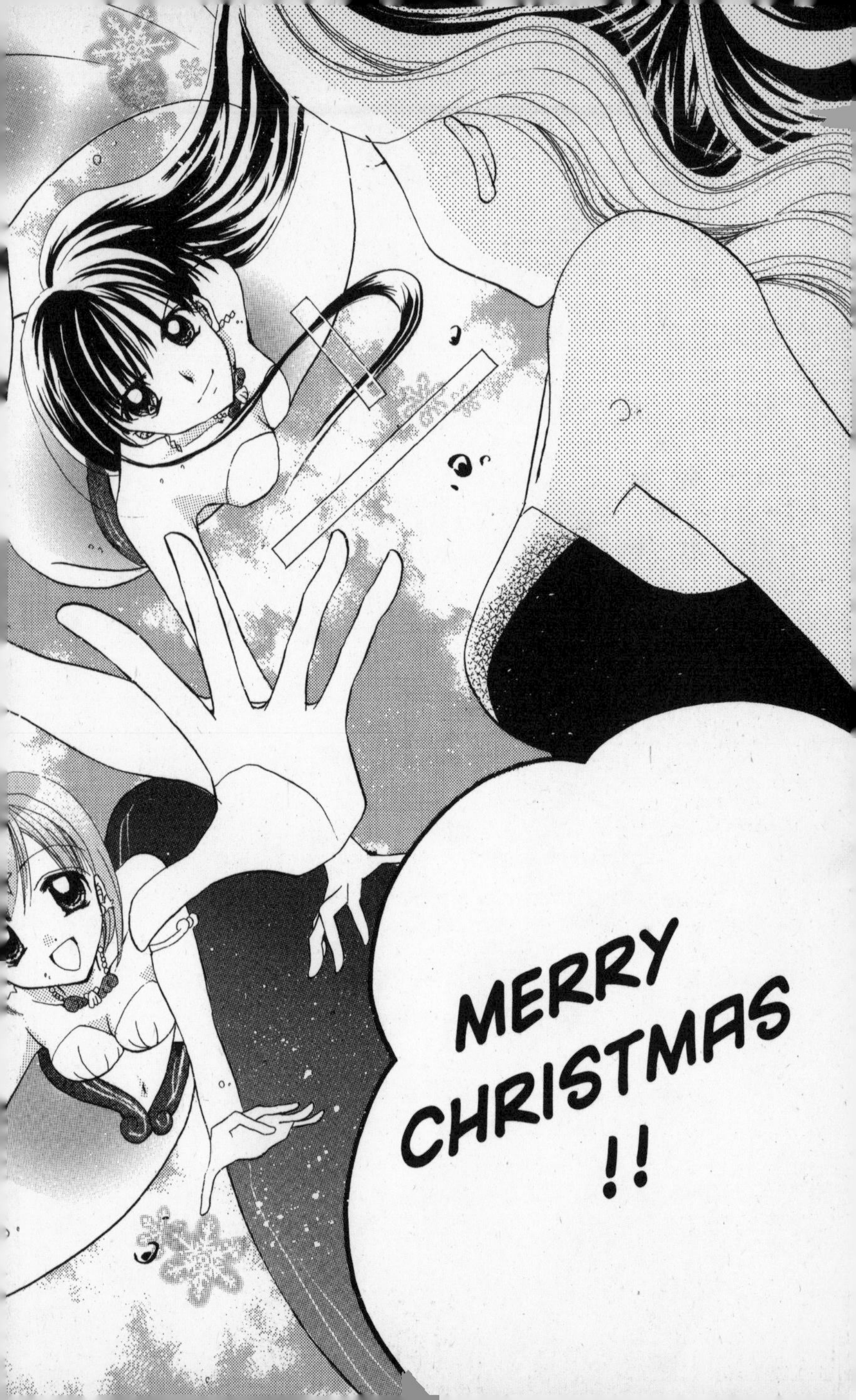
MERRY CHRISTMAS !!

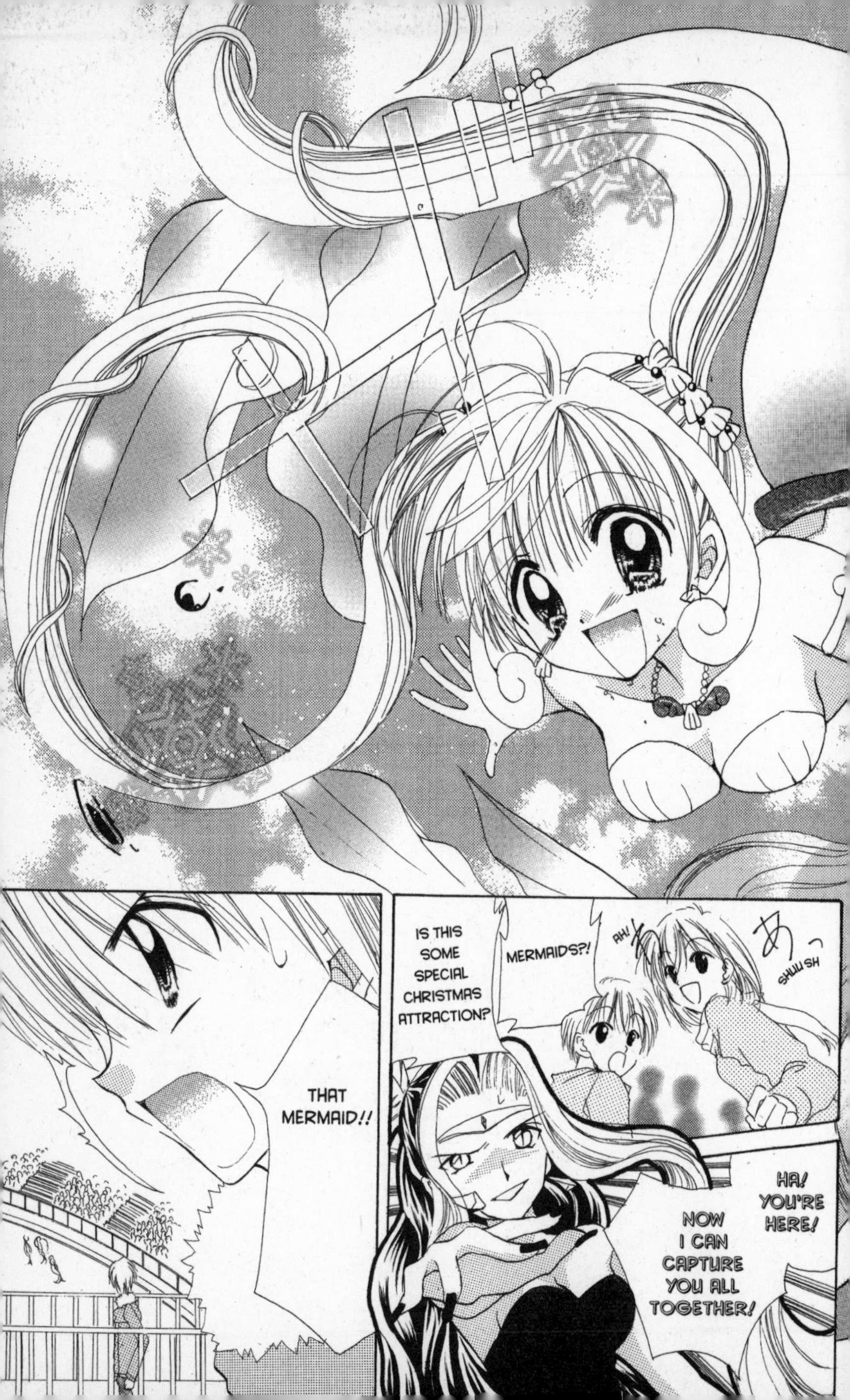
あっ
SHUU SH
AH!
MERMAIDS?!
IS THIS SOME SPECIAL CHRISTMAS ATTRACTION?
HA! YOU'RE HERE!
NOW I CAN CAPTURE YOU ALL TOGETHER!
THAT MERMAID!!

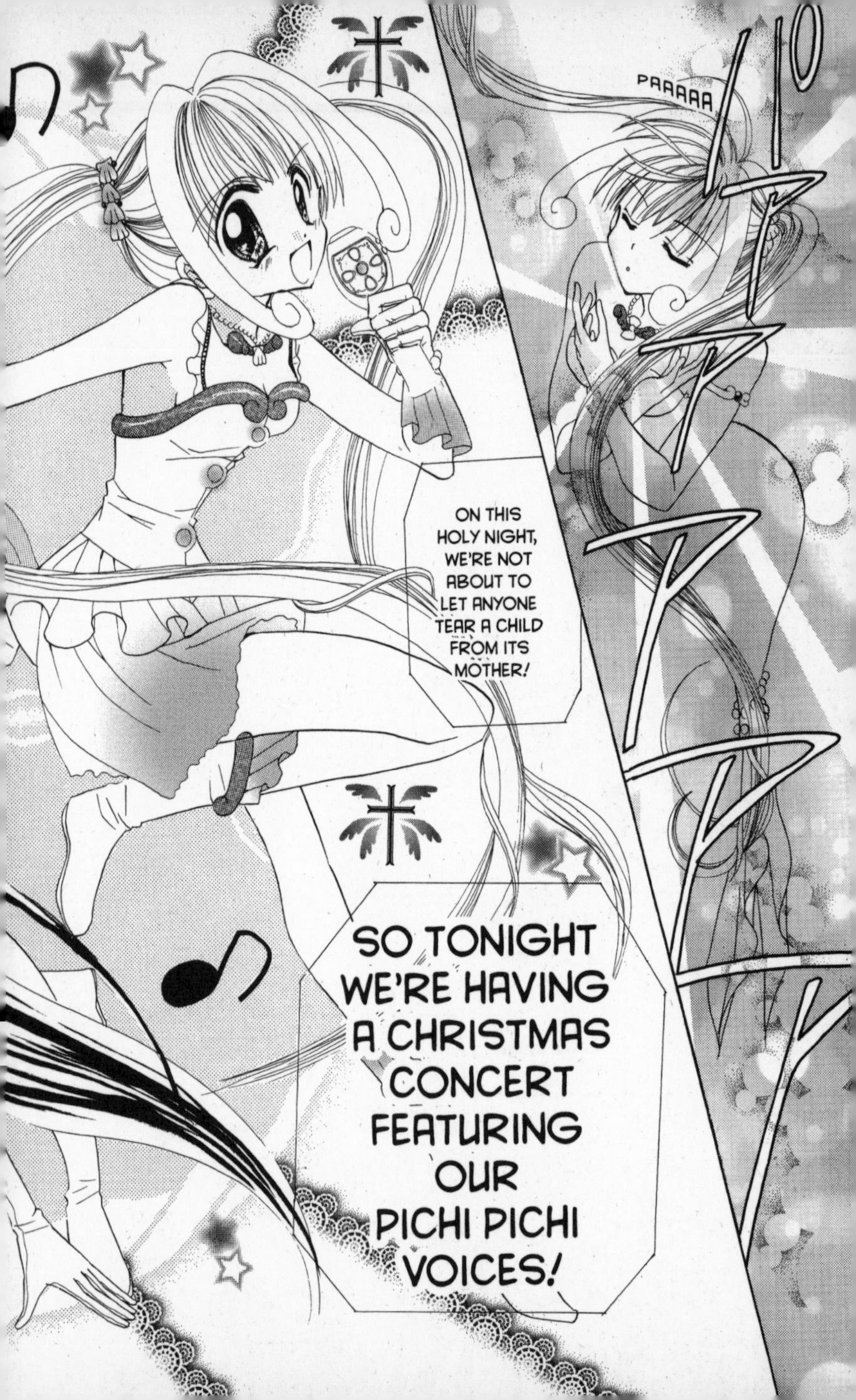
PAAAAA
ON THIS HOLY NIGHT, WE'RE NOT ABOUT TO LET ANYONE TEAR A CHILD FROM ITS MOTHER!
SO TONIGHT WE'RE HAVING A CHRISTMAS CONCERT FEATURING OUR PICHI PICHI VOICES!

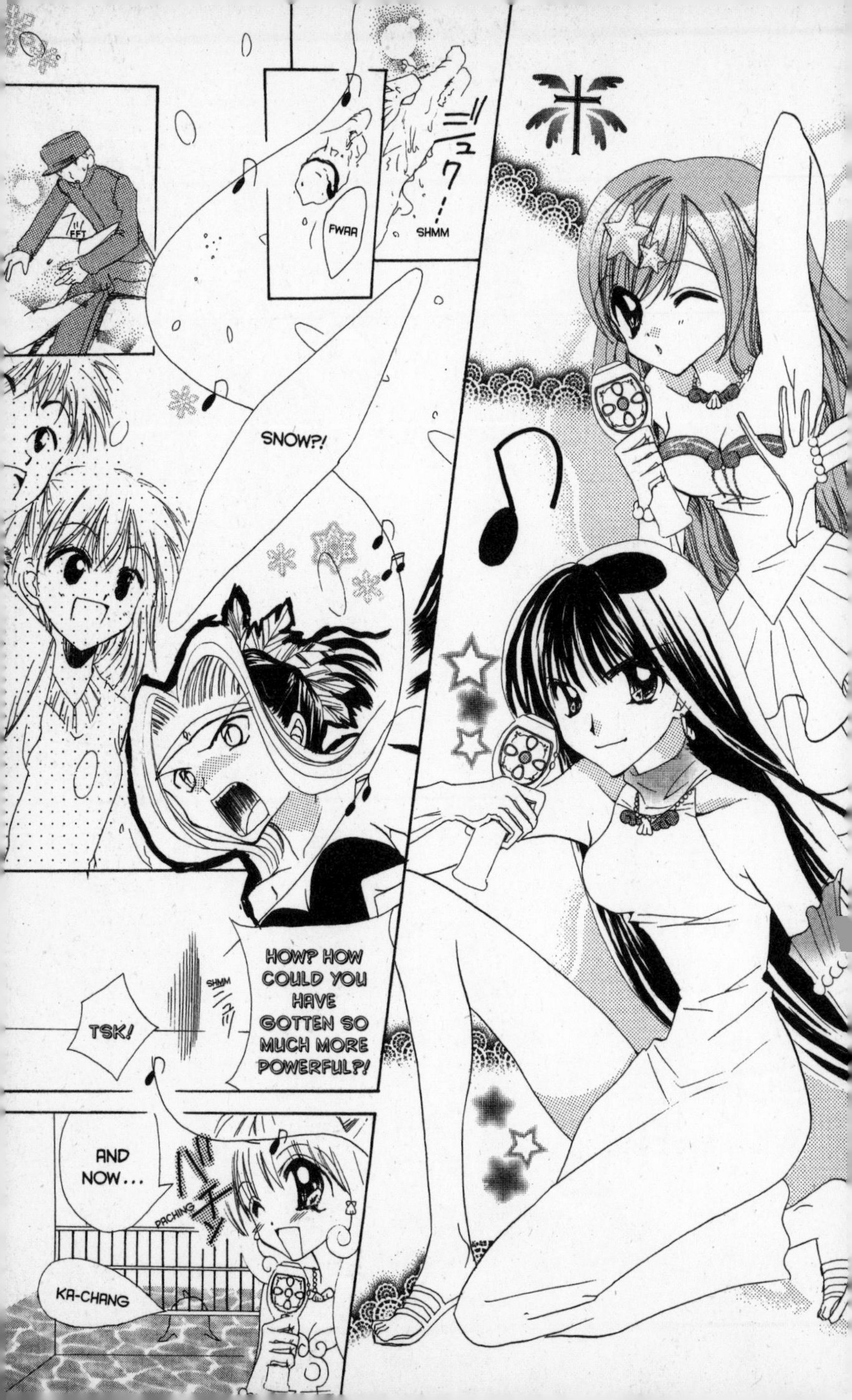
FWAA
SHMM
FFT
SNOW?!
HOW? HOW COULD YOU HAVE GOTTEN SO MUCH MORE POWERFUL?!
SHMM
TSK!
AND NOW...
PACHING
KA-CHANG

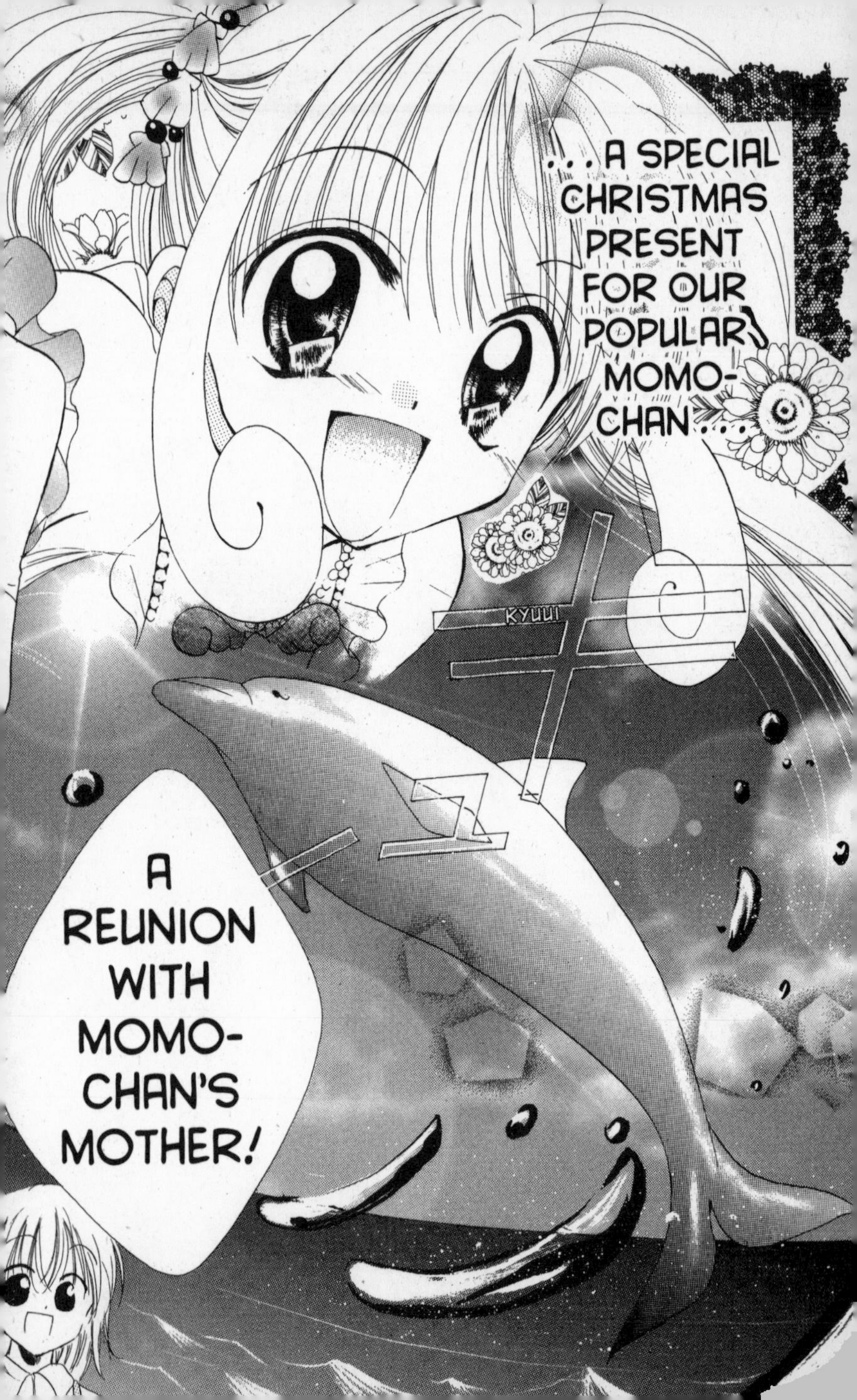
...A SPECIAL CHRISTMAS PRESENT FOR OUR POPULAR MOMO-CHAN...
KYUUI
A REUNION WITH MOMO-CHAN'S MOTHER!

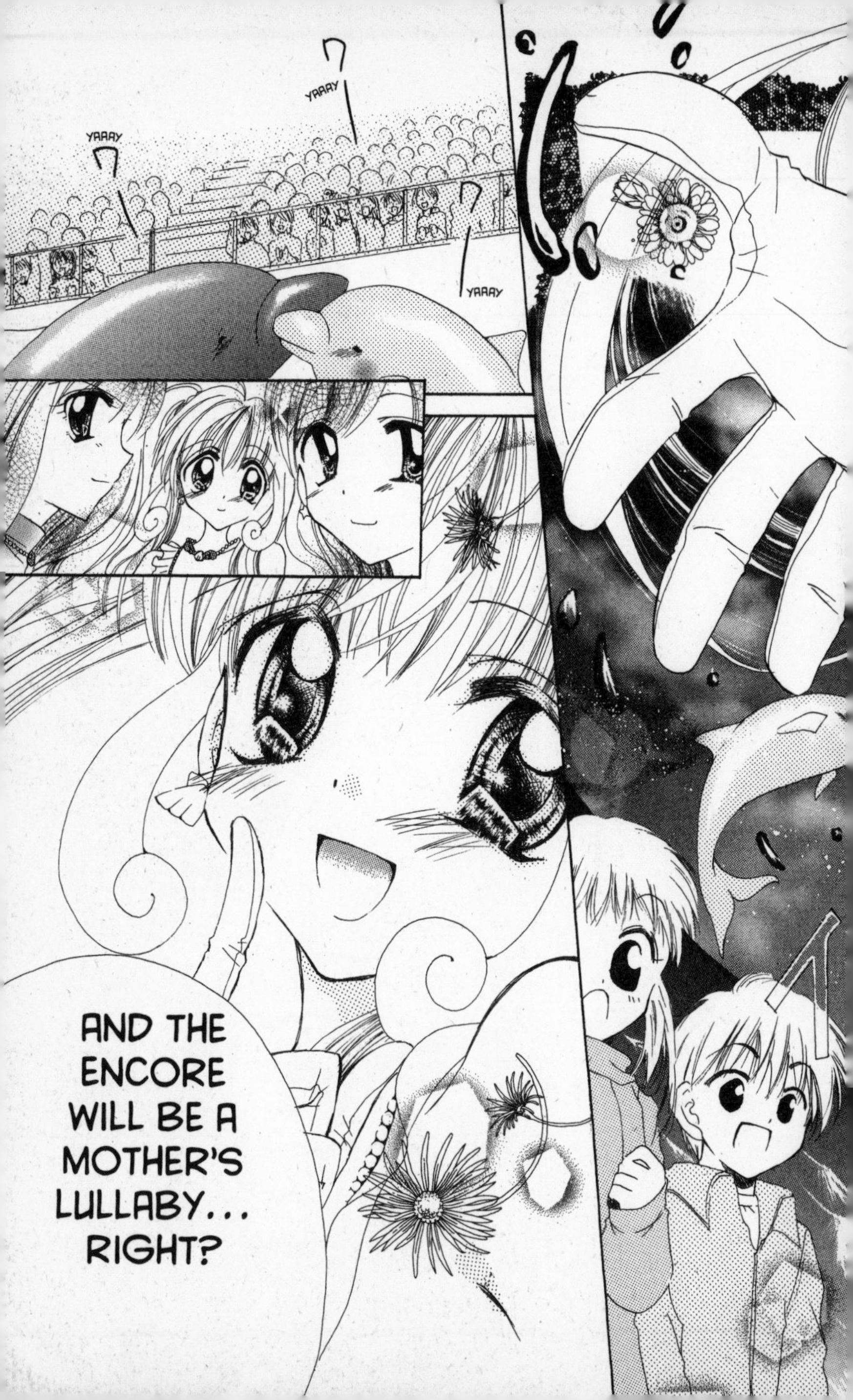
YAAAY
YAAAY
YAAAY
AND THE ENCORE WILL BE A MOTHER'S LULLABY... RIGHT?

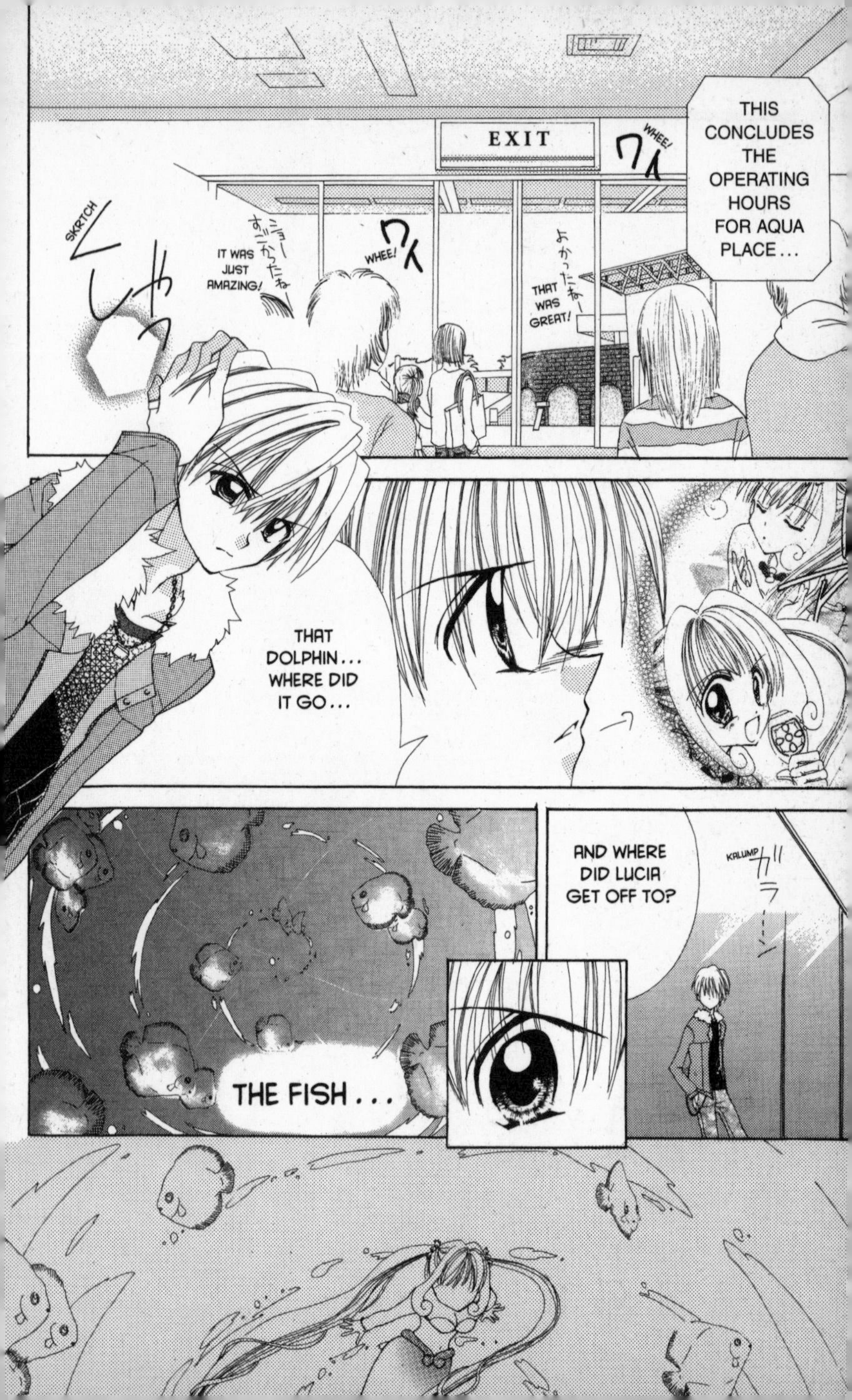
THIS CONCLUDES THE OPERATING HOURS FOR AQUA PLACE...
ワイ
WHEE!
よかったねー
THAT WAS GREAT!
ワイ
WHEE!
IT WAS JUST AMAZING!
SKRTCH
THAT DOLPHIN... WHERE DID IT GO...
AND WHERE DID LUCIA GET OFF TO?
ガラ
KALUMP
THE FISH...

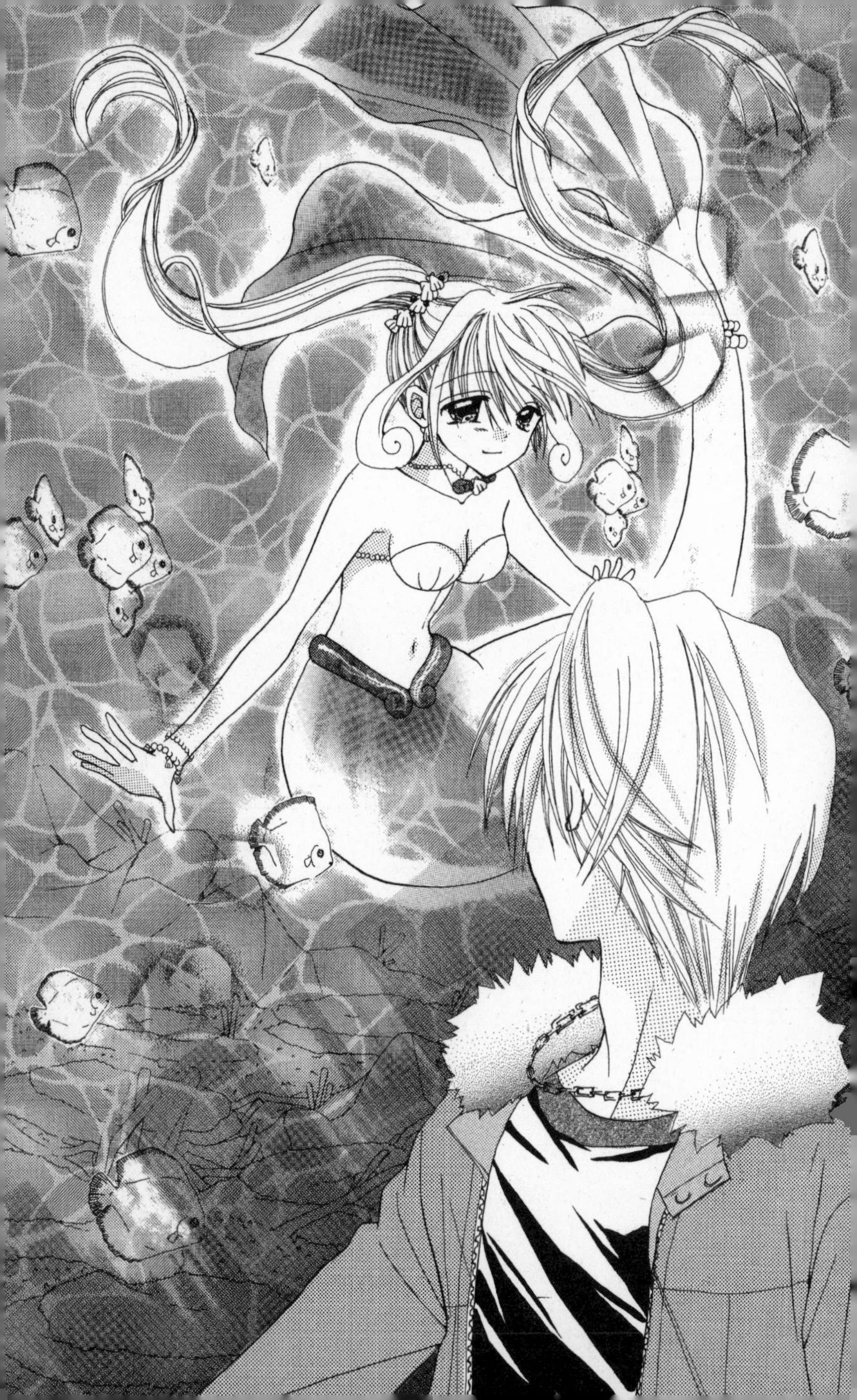

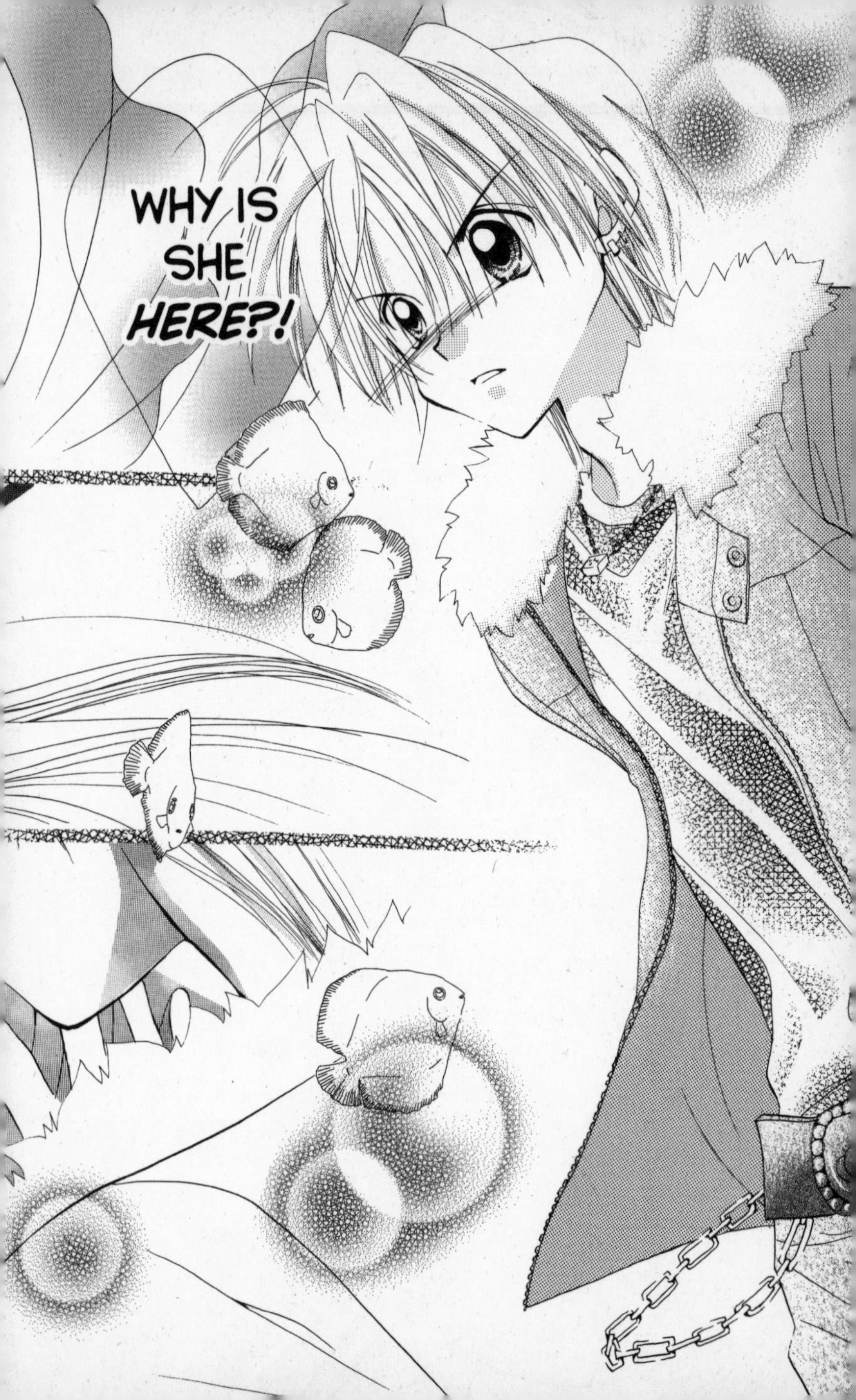
WHY IS SHE HERE?!

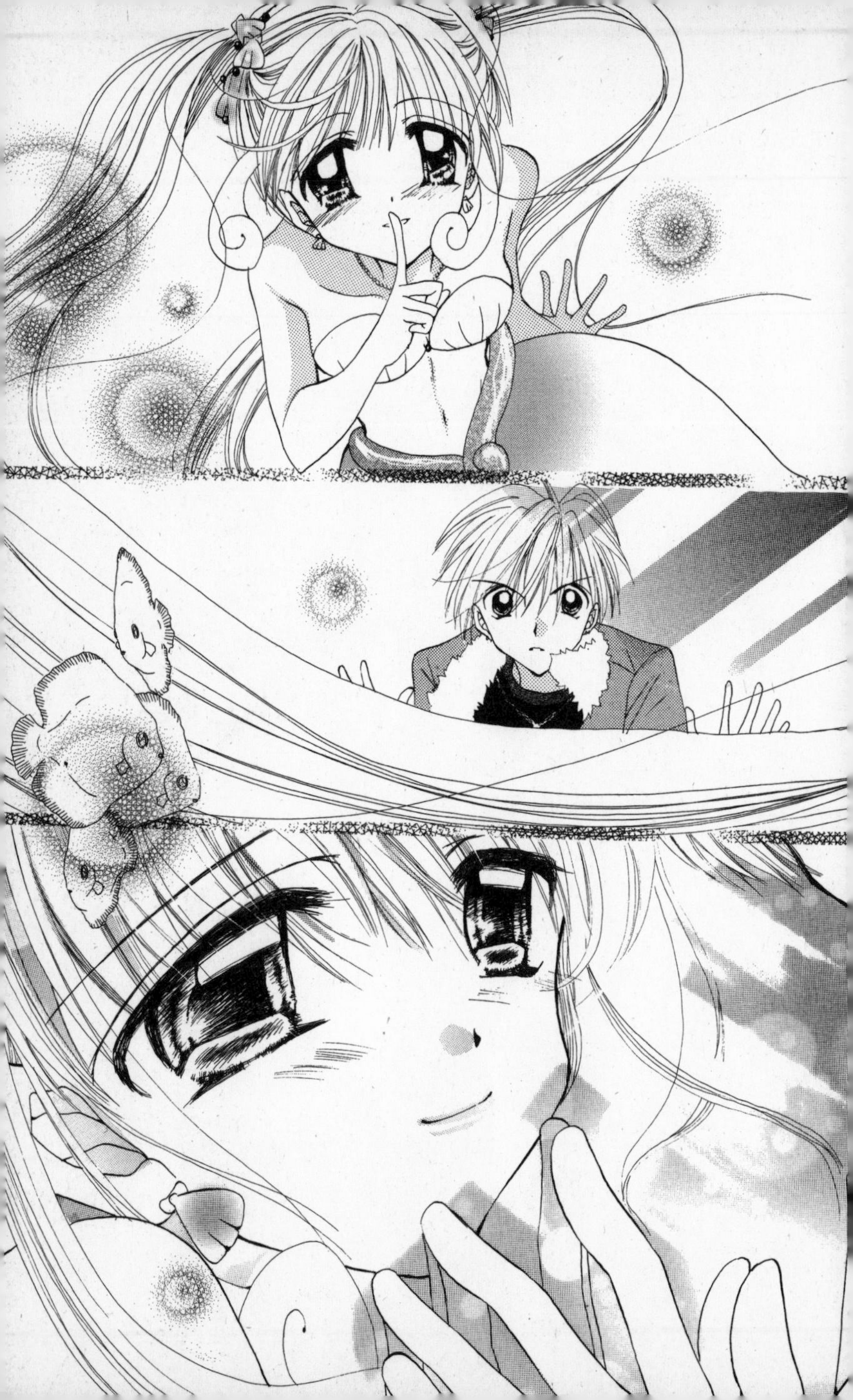

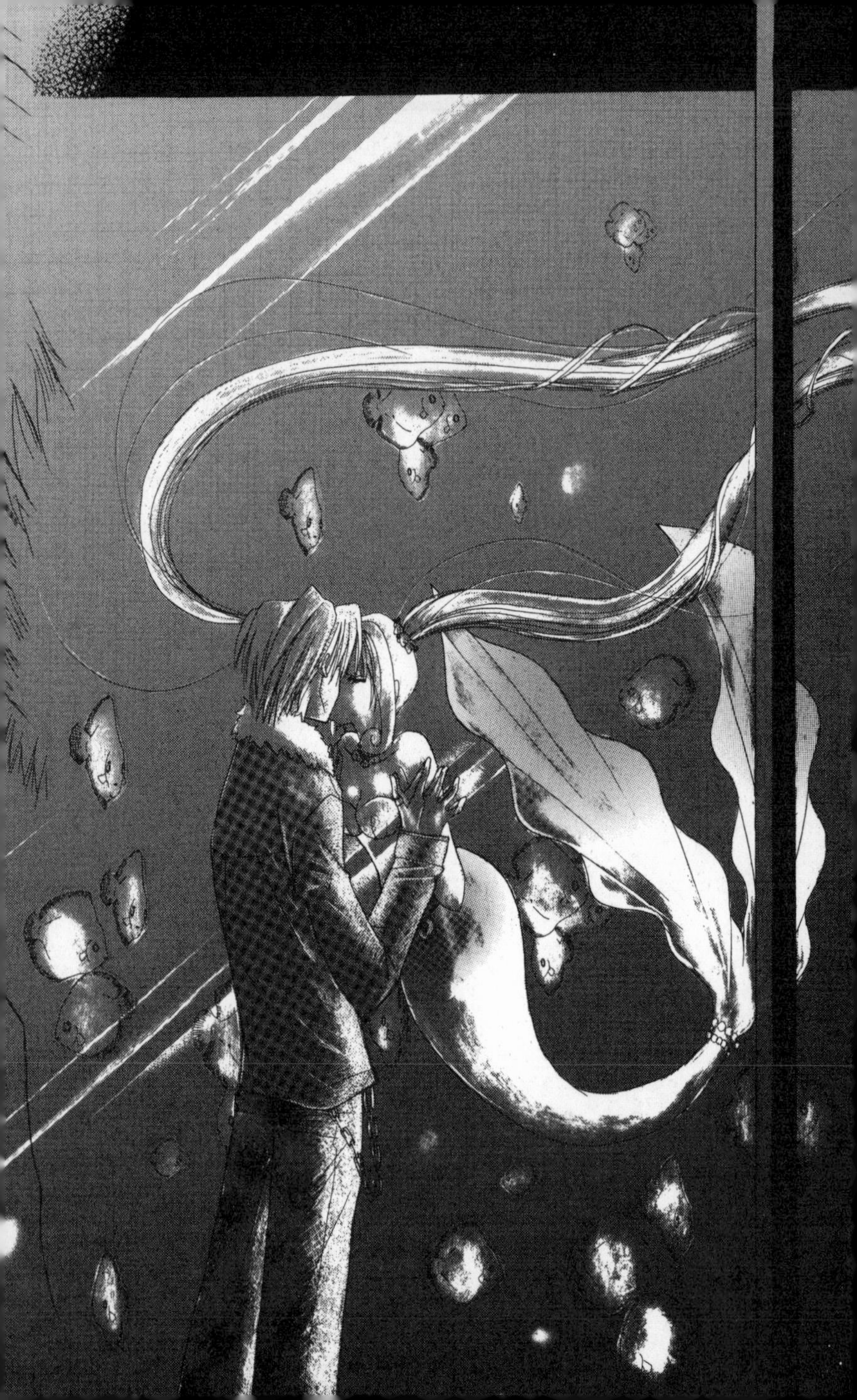

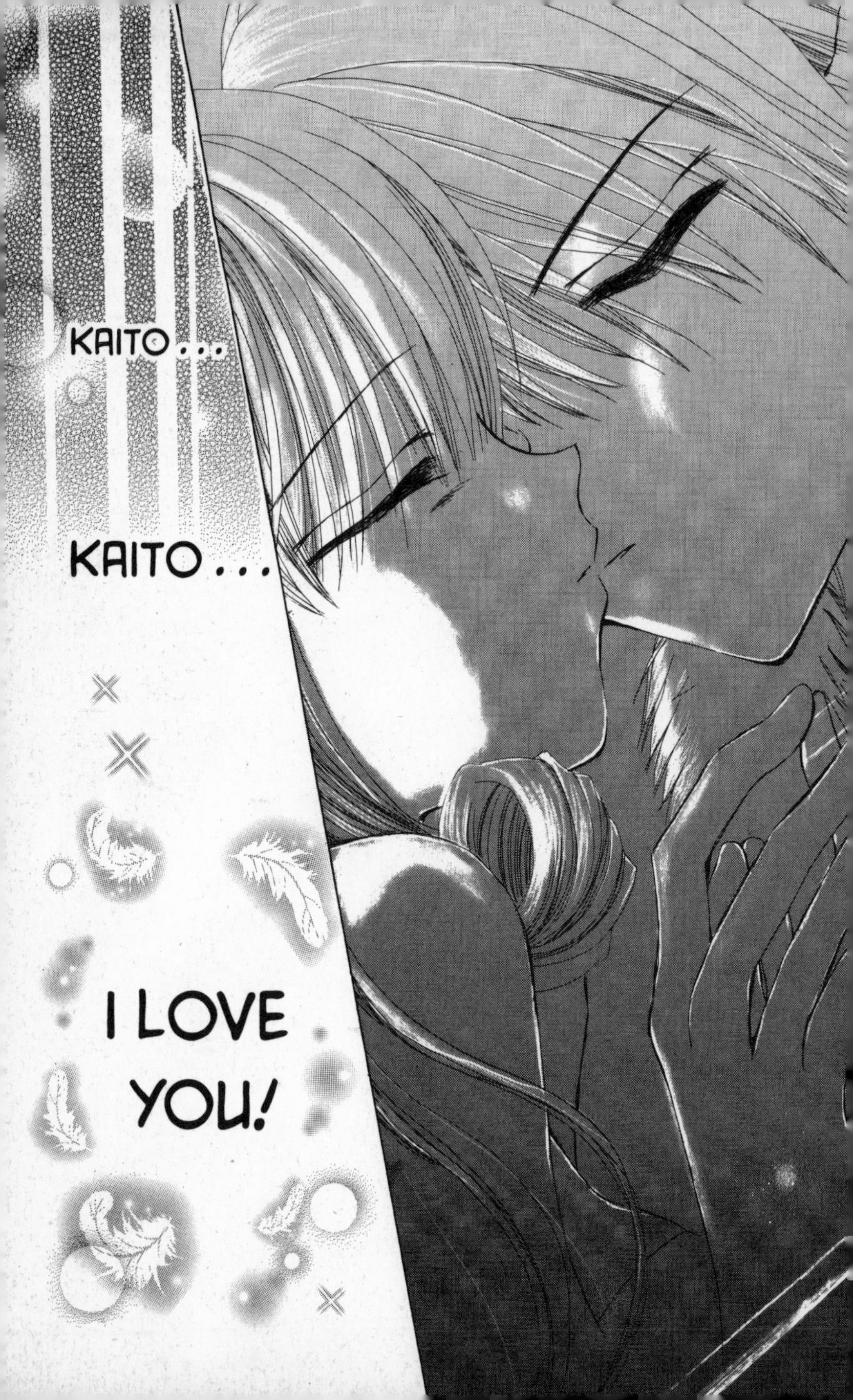
KAITO...
KAITO...
I LOVE YOU!

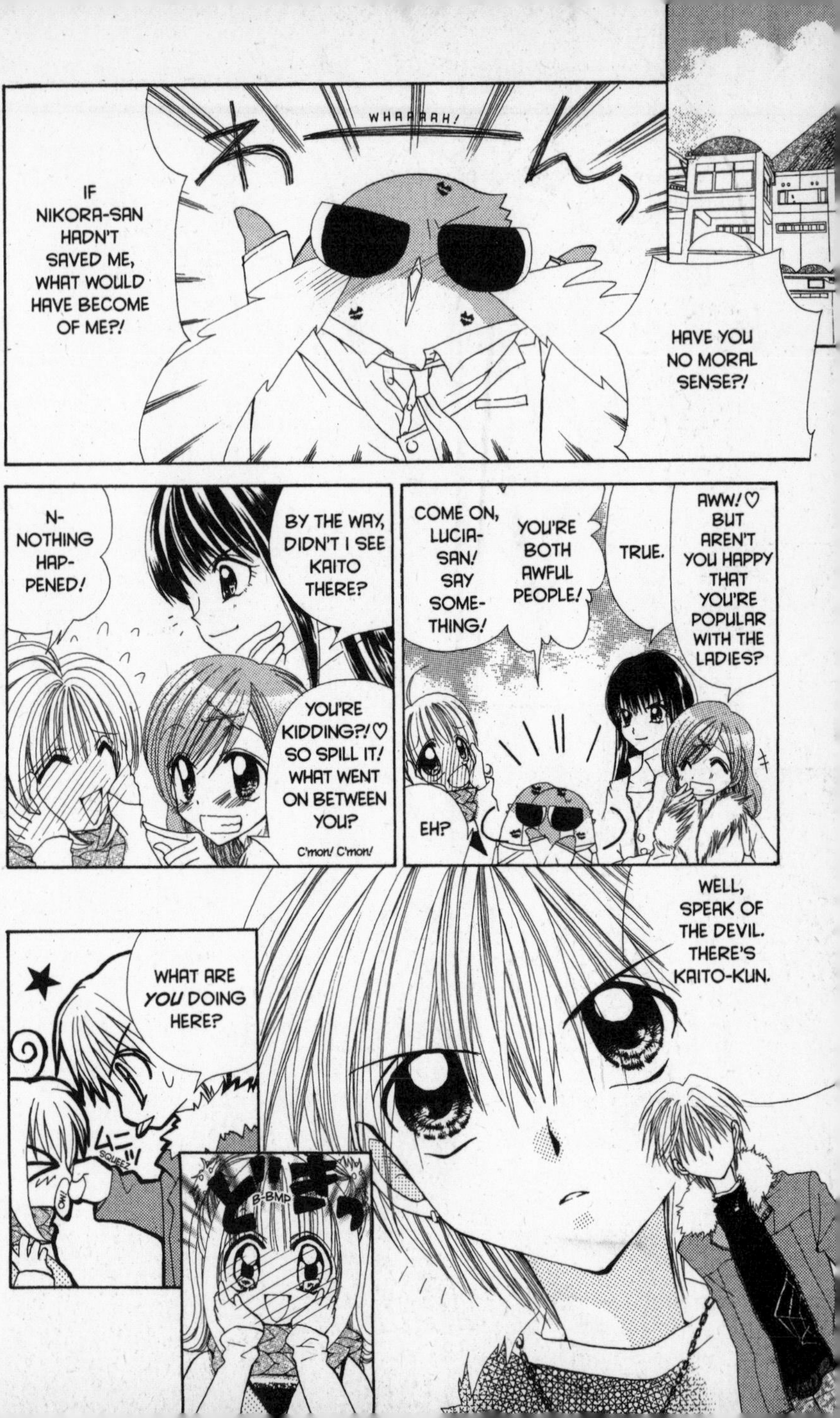
WHAAAAH!
IF NIKORA-SAN HADN'T SAVED ME, WHAT WOULD HAVE BECOME OF ME?!
HAVE YOU NO MORAL SENSE?!
AWW! ♡ BUT AREN'T YOU HAPPY THAT YOU'RE POPULAR WITH THE LADIES?
TRUE.
YOU'RE BOTH AWFUL PEOPLE!
COME ON, LUCIA-SAN! SAY SOMETHING!
EH?
BY THE WAY, DIDN'T I SEE KAITO THERE?
YOU'RE KIDDING?! ♡ SO SPILL IT! WHAT WENT ON BETWEEN YOU?
C'mon! C'mon!
N-NOTHING HAPPENED!
WELL, SPEAK OF THE DEVIL. THERE'S KAITO-KUN.
WHAT ARE YOU DOING HERE?
SQUEEZ
OW!
B-BMP

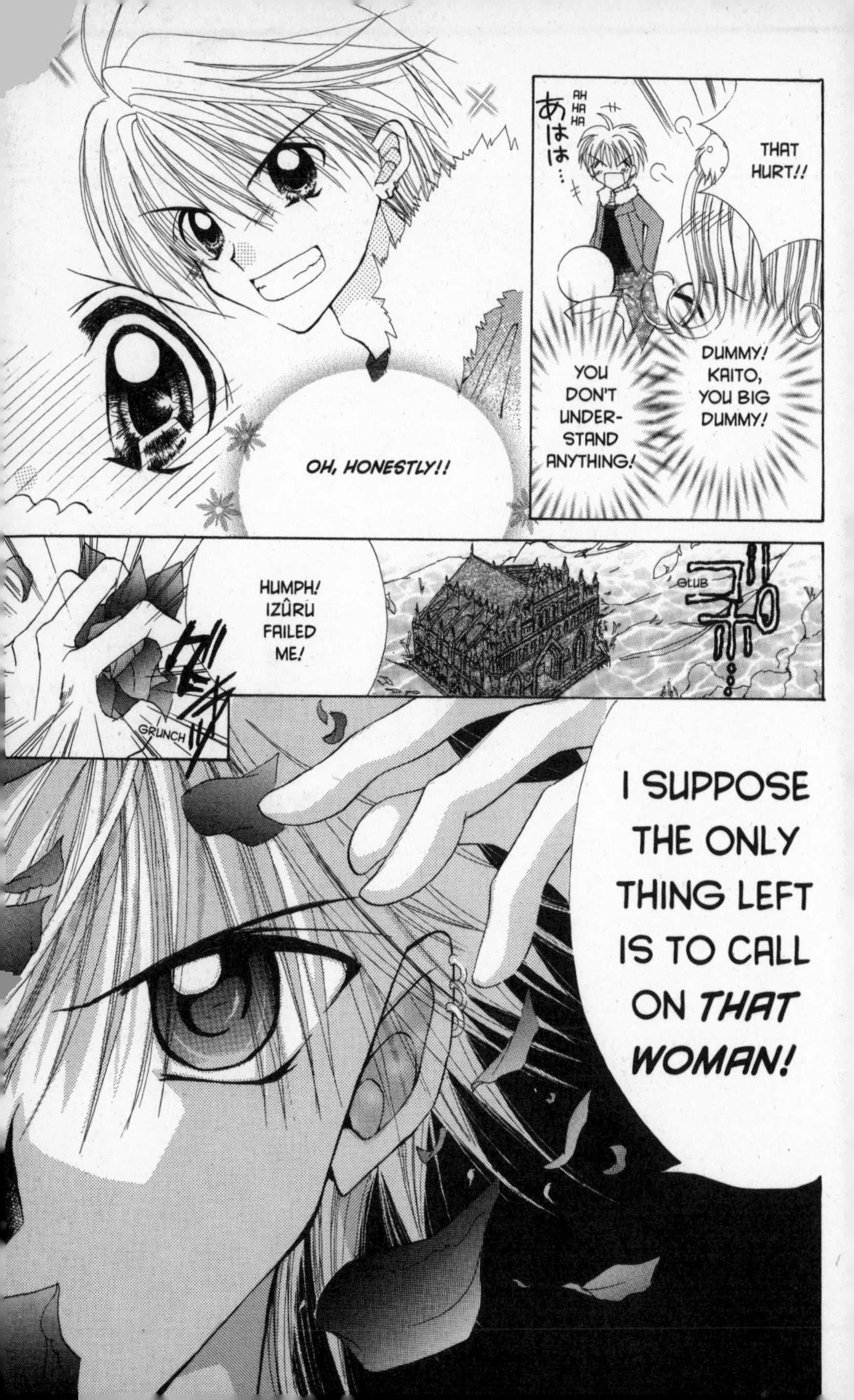
THAT HURT!!
AH HA HA
DUMMY! KAITO, YOU BIG DUMMY!
YOU DON'T UNDER-STAND ANYTHING!
OH, HONESTLY!!
GLUB
HUMPH! IZÛRU FAILED ME!
GRUNCH
I SUPPOSE THE ONLY THING LEFT IS TO CALL ON *THAT WOMAN!*

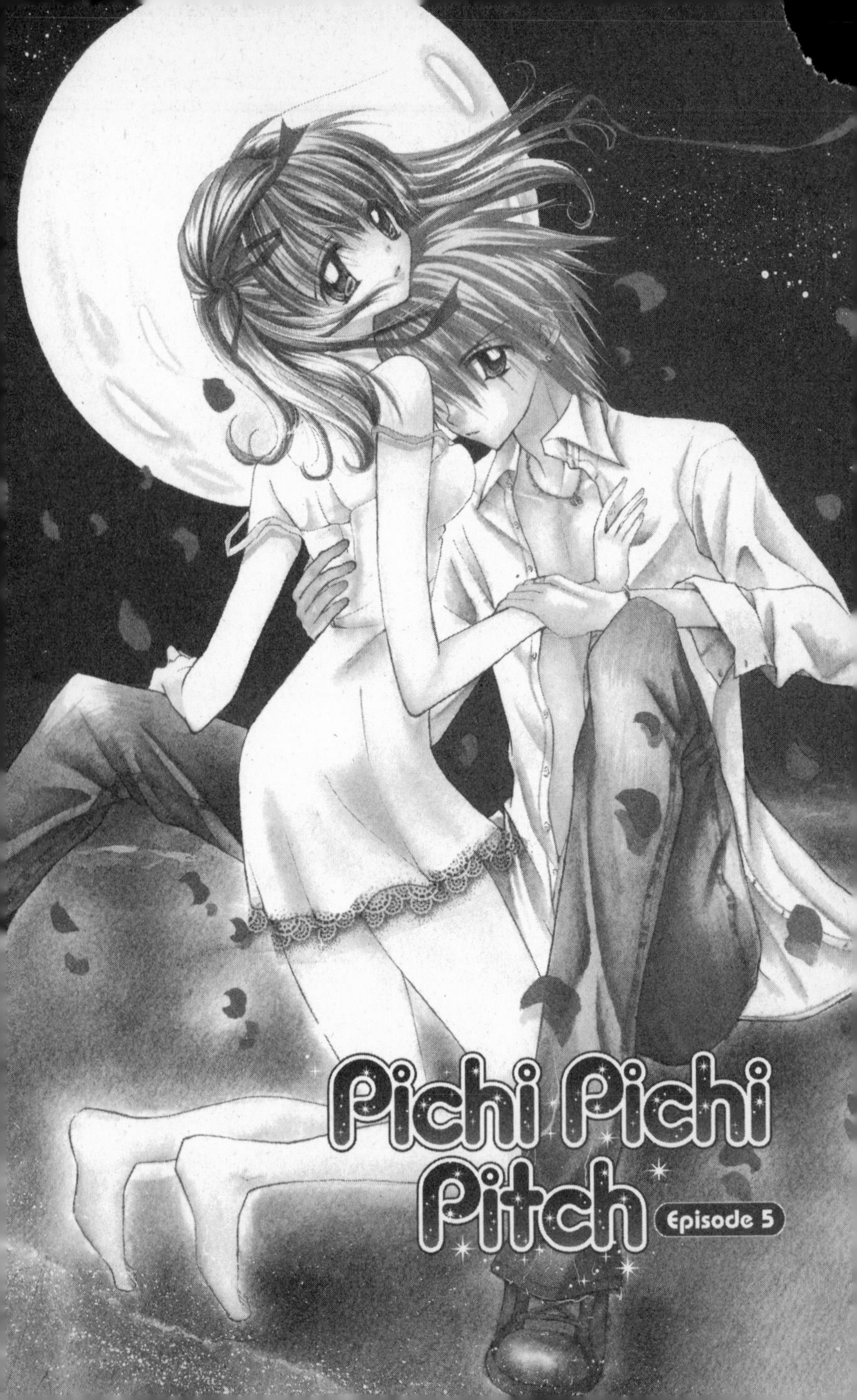
Pichi Pichi Pitch
Episode 5

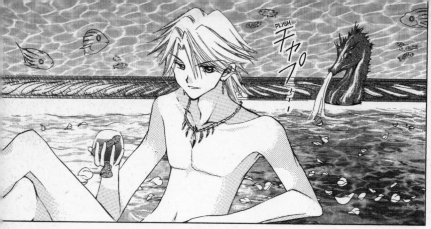

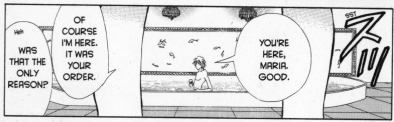

PLISH
SST
YOU'RE HERE, MARIA. GOOD.
OF COURSE I'M HERE. IT WAS YOUR ORDER.
Heh
WAS THAT THE ONLY REASON?

(EPISODE 5)

I'LL NEVER FORGET THIS SPLASH PAGE. I DIDN'T KNOW WHAT WAS BEST SO I SHOWED TWO DIFFERENT ROUGH DRAWN OPTIONS TO EDITOR K. (ONE IS THE ONE YOU SEE, AND THE OTHER HAD KAITO AS THE FOCUS CHARACTER).

EDITOR: YOU WANT ME TO CHOOSE THIS TWO-SHOT, RIGHT?

HANAMORI: I COULD GO WITH EITHER. I DON'T KNOW WHICH TO PICK.

EDITOR: THERE YOU GO AGAIN! JUST ACCEPT IT! YOU WANT TO DRAW THIS ONE, RIGHT?

. . . AND SO I DREW THIS ONE. BUT REALLY, I FELT THE SAME ABOUT BOTH OF THEM. BUT IT WAS FUN TO DRAW!

THE REACTION TO THIS EPISODE WAS VERRRRRY INTENSE! I MEAN . . . I MEAN . . . THINK ABOUT IT! KYAAA!

THE OPINIONS OF WHAT KAITO DID WAS SPLIT STRAIGHT DOWN THE MIDDLE. THEY WERE FRIENDS, RIGHT? WELL . . . HE IS A MAN. BUT WHEN I STARTED DRAWING THE SCENE, I THOUGHT, "WHOA! THIS IS REALLY ADULT!" BLUSSH!

WHEN I DREW THEIR EYES, THE OUTLINES, EVERYTHING WAS DONE WITH A MARU-PEN (QUILL-TIP PEN). (I DIDN'T EVEN PAINT IN THE EYES OR ANYTHING.) I THOUGHT IT WOULD COME OUT TOO DELICATE. (IT WAS SOMETHING OF A PAIN, THOUGH . . . ) BUT IN THE END, NOBODY REALLY NOTICED! I'M STILL LEARNING.

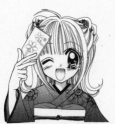

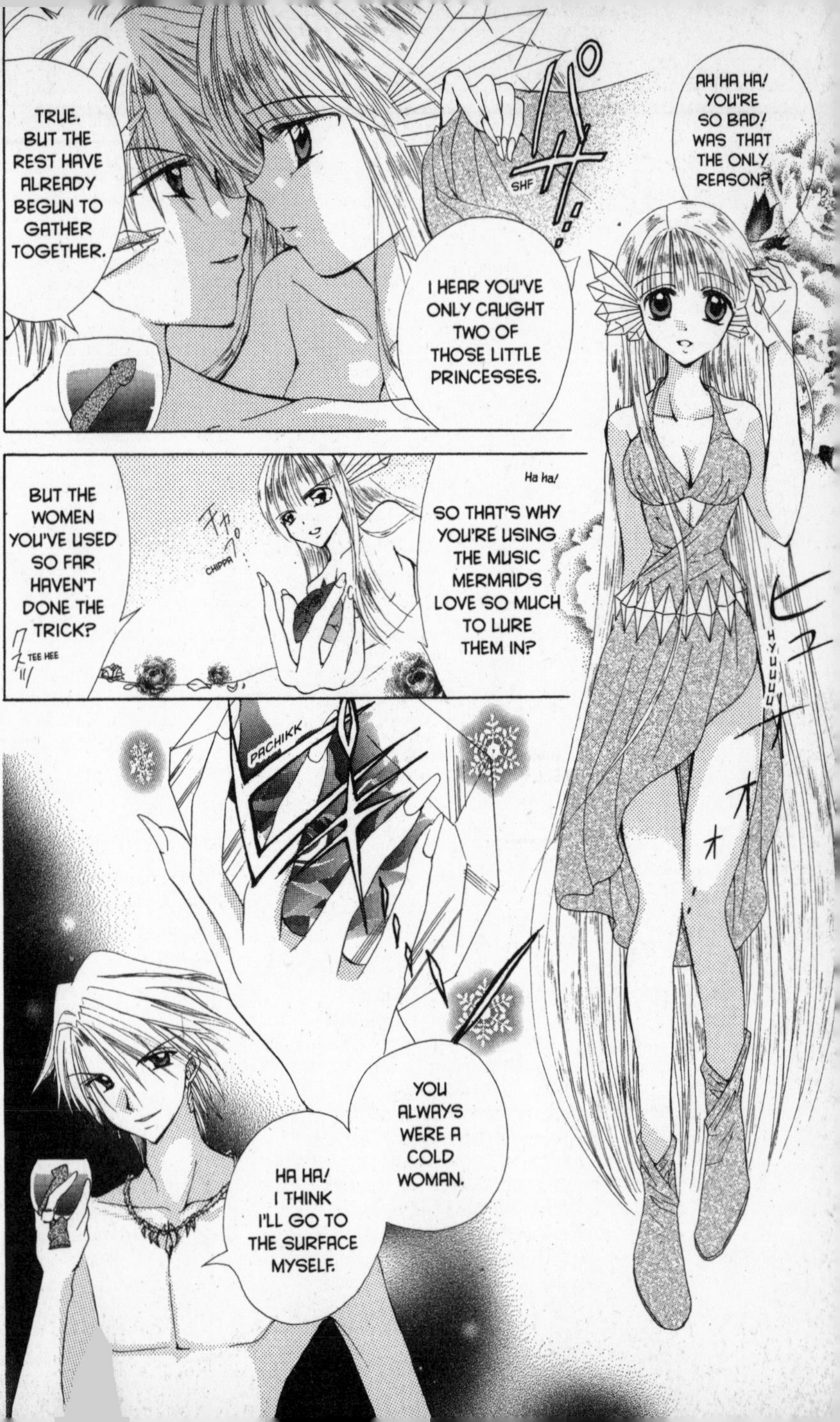
AH HA HA! YOU'RE SO BAD! WAS THAT THE ONLY REASON?
HYUUUU
SHF
I HEAR YOU'VE ONLY CAUGHT TWO OF THOSE LITTLE PRINCESSES.
TRUE. BUT THE REST HAVE ALREADY BEGUN TO GATHER TOGETHER.
Ha ha!
SO THAT'S WHY YOU'RE USING THE MUSIC MERMAIDS LOVE SO MUCH TO LURE THEM IN?
CHIPPA
BUT THE WOMEN YOU'VE USED SO FAR HAVEN'T DONE THE TRICK?
TEE HEE
PACHIKK
YOU ALWAYS WERE A COLD WOMAN.
HA HA! I THINK I'LL GO TO THE SURFACE MYSELF.

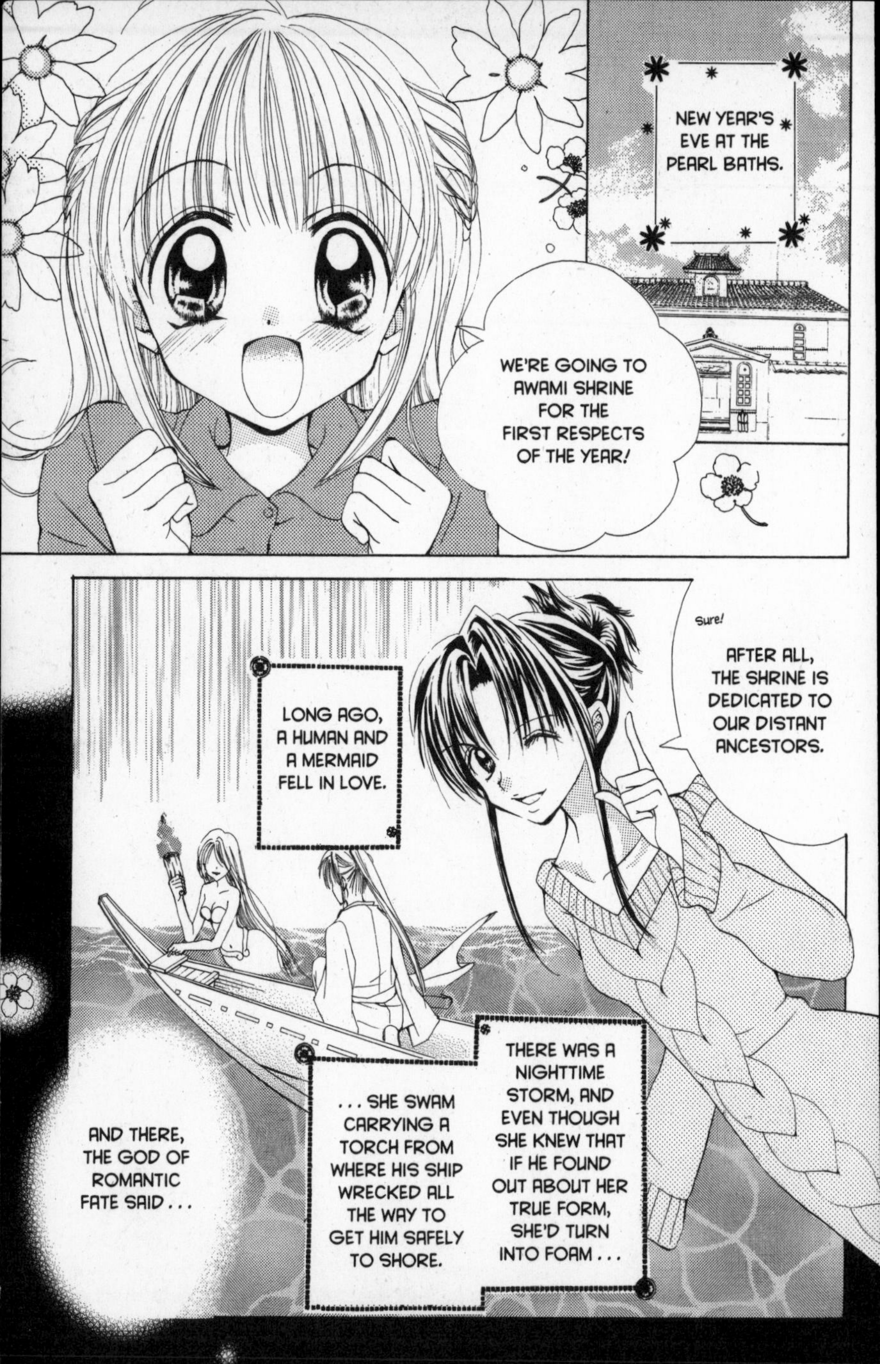
NEW YEAR'S EVE AT THE PEARL BATHS.
WE'RE GOING TO AWAMI SHRINE FOR THE FIRST RESPECTS OF THE YEAR!
Sure!
AFTER ALL, THE SHRINE IS DEDICATED TO OUR DISTANT ANCESTORS.
LONG AGO, A HUMAN AND A MERMAID FELL IN LOVE.
THERE WAS A NIGHTTIME STORM, AND EVEN THOUGH SHE KNEW THAT IF HE FOUND OUT ABOUT HER TRUE FORM, SHE'D TURN INTO FOAM . . .
. . . SHE SWAM CARRYING A TORCH FROM WHERE HIS SHIP WRECKED ALL THE WAY TO GET HIM SAFELY TO SHORE.
AND THERE, THE GOD OF ROMANTIC FATE SAID . . .

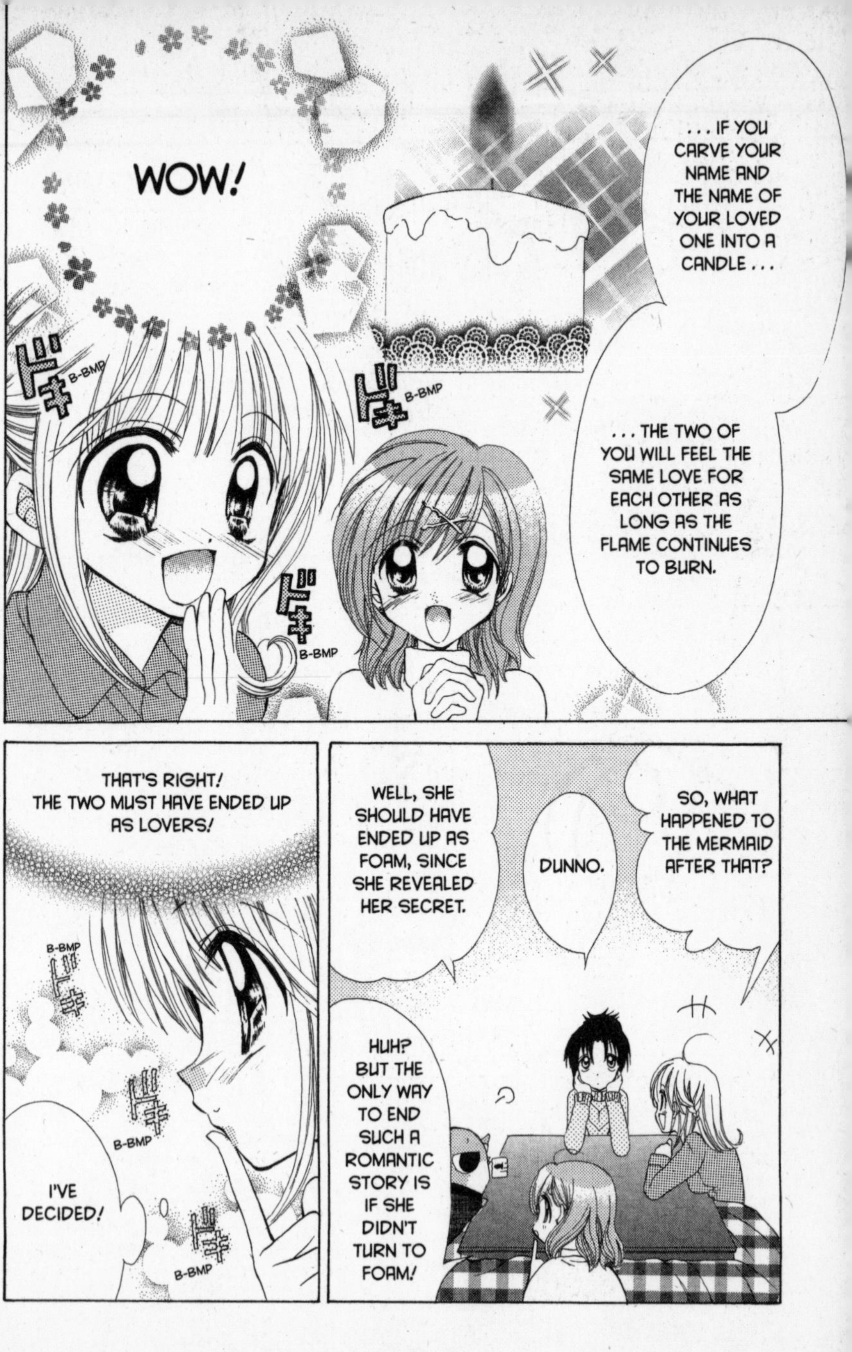
. . . IF YOU CARVE YOUR NAME AND THE NAME OF YOUR LOVED ONE INTO A CANDLE . . .
. . . THE TWO OF YOU WILL FEEL THE SAME LOVE FOR EACH OTHER AS LONG AS THE FLAME CONTINUES TO BURN.
B-BMP
WOW!
B-BMP
B-BMP
SO, WHAT HAPPENED TO THE MERMAID AFTER THAT?
DUNNO.
WELL, SHE SHOULD HAVE ENDED UP AS FOAM, SINCE SHE REVEALED HER SECRET.
HUH? BUT THE ONLY WAY TO END SUCH A ROMANTIC STORY IS IF SHE DIDN'T TURN TO FOAM!
THAT'S RIGHT! THE TWO MUST HAVE ENDED UP AS LOVERS!
B-BMP
B-BMP
B-BMP
I'VE DECIDED!

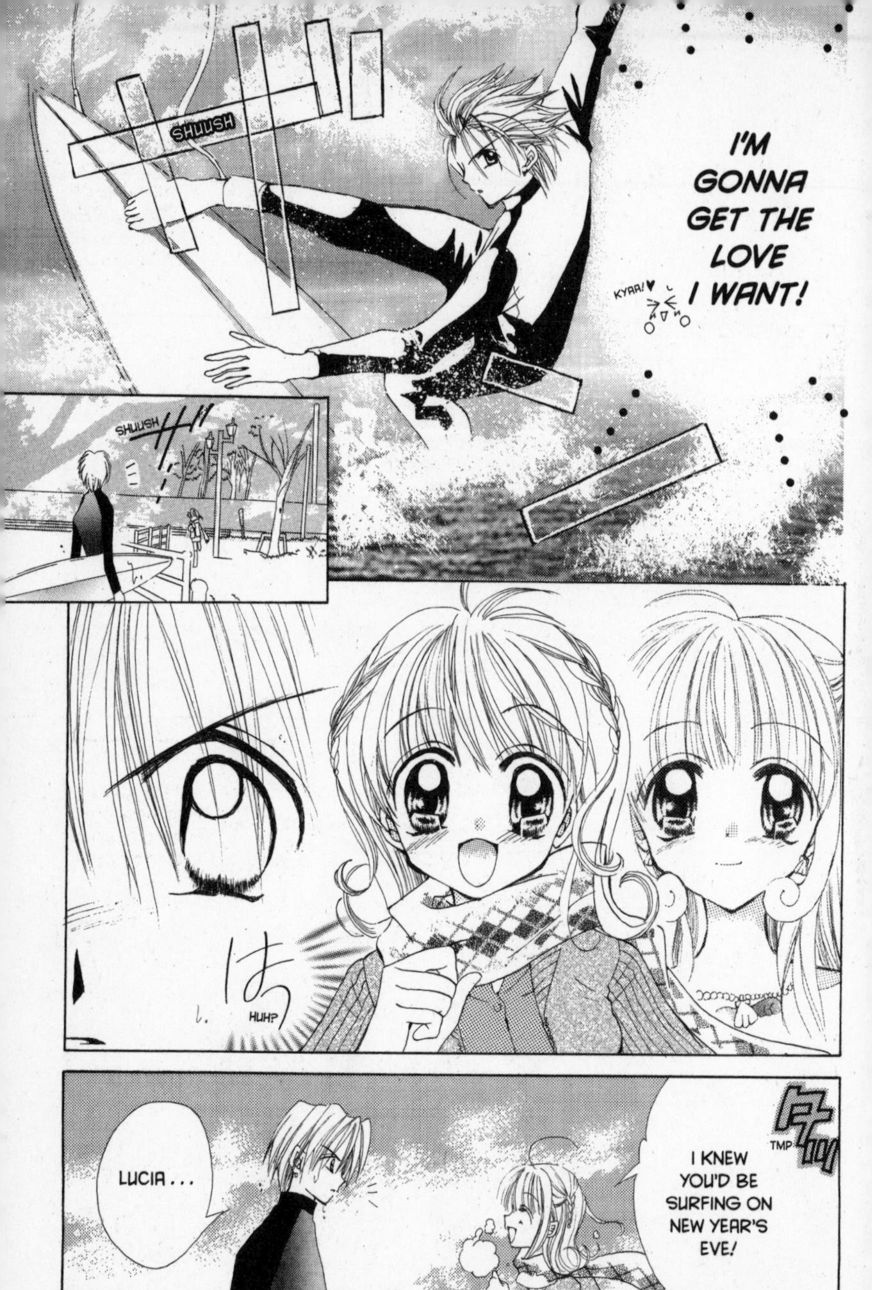
I'M GONNA GET THE LOVE I WANT!
KYAA! ♥
SHUUSH
SHUUSH
HUH?
TMP
I KNEW YOU'D BE SURFING ON NEW YEAR'S EVE!
LUCIA . . .

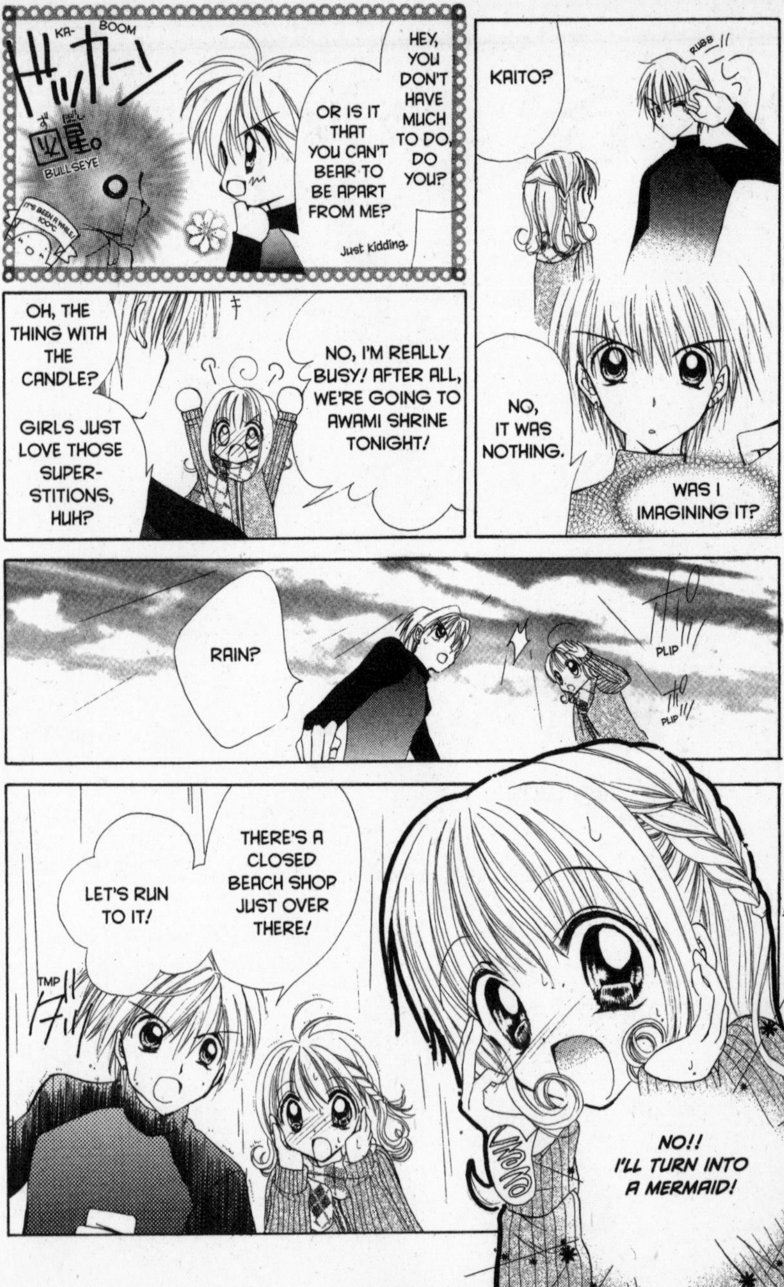
KAITO?
RUBB
NO, IT WAS NOTHING.
WAS I IMAGINING IT?
HEY, YOU DON'T HAVE MUCH TO DO, DO YOU?
OR IS IT THAT YOU CAN'T BEAR TO BE APART FROM ME?
Just kidding.
KA-BOOM
BULLSEYE
IT'S BEEN A WHILE! 100°C
NO, I'M REALLY BUSY! AFTER ALL, WE'RE GOING TO AWAMI SHRINE TONIGHT!
OH, THE THING WITH THE CANDLE?
GIRLS JUST LOVE THOSE SUPER-STITIONS, HUH?
PLIP
PLIP
RAIN?
NO!! I'LL TURN INTO A MERMAID!
THERE'S A CLOSED BEACH SHOP JUST OVER THERE!
LET'S RUN TO IT!
TMP

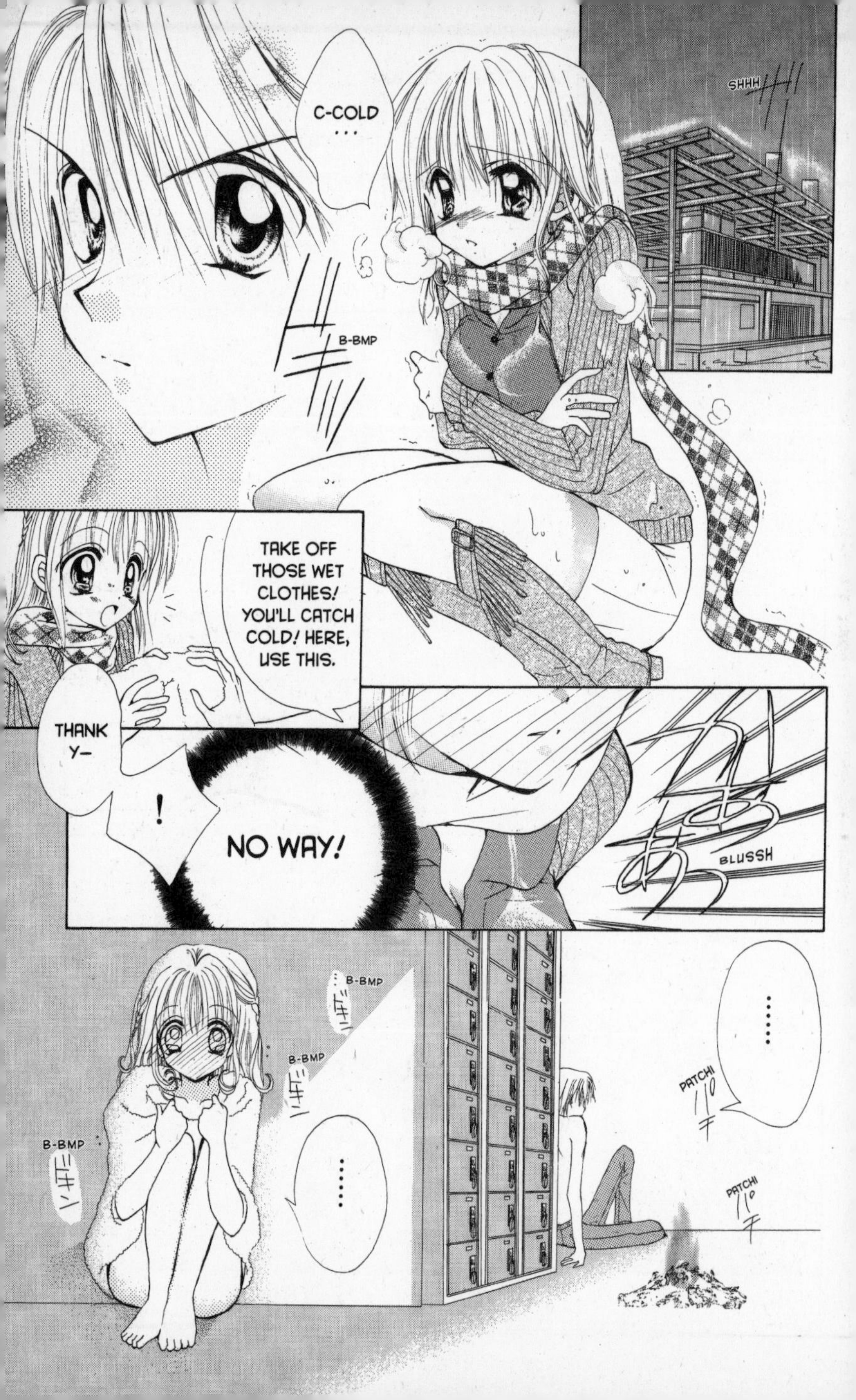
SHHH
C-COLD . . .
B-BMP
TAKE OFF THOSE WET CLOTHES! YOU'LL CATCH COLD! HERE, USE THIS.
THANK Y—
!
NO WAY!
BLUSSH
......
PATCHI
PATCHI
......
B-BMP
B-BMP
B-BMP

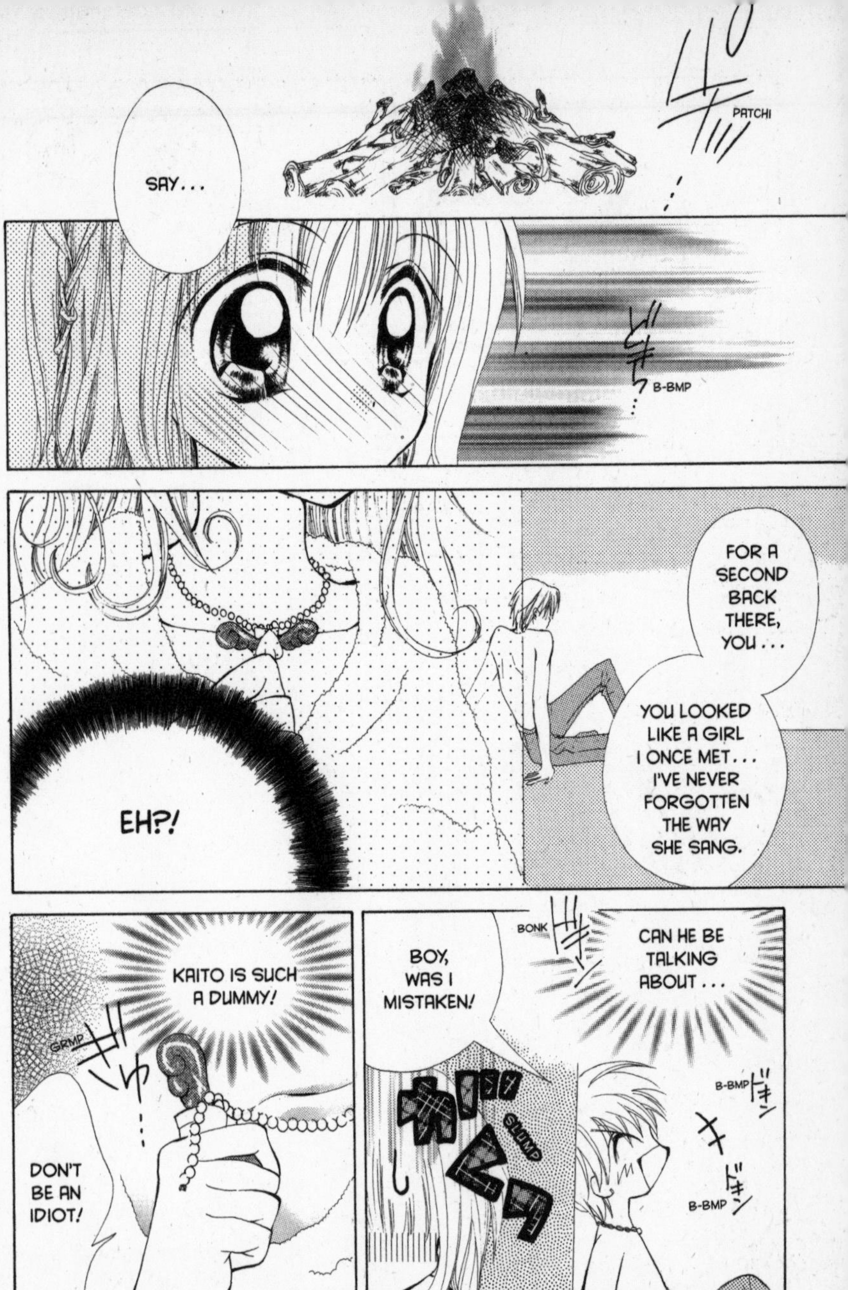
PATCHI
SAY...
B-BMP
FOR A SECOND BACK THERE, YOU...
YOU LOOKED LIKE A GIRL I ONCE MET... I'VE NEVER FORGOTTEN THE WAY SHE SANG.
EH?!
CAN HE BE TALKING ABOUT...
BONK
BOY, WAS I MISTAKEN!
B-BMP
SLUMP
B-BMP
KAITO IS SUCH A DUMMY!
GRMP
DON'T BE AN IDIOT!

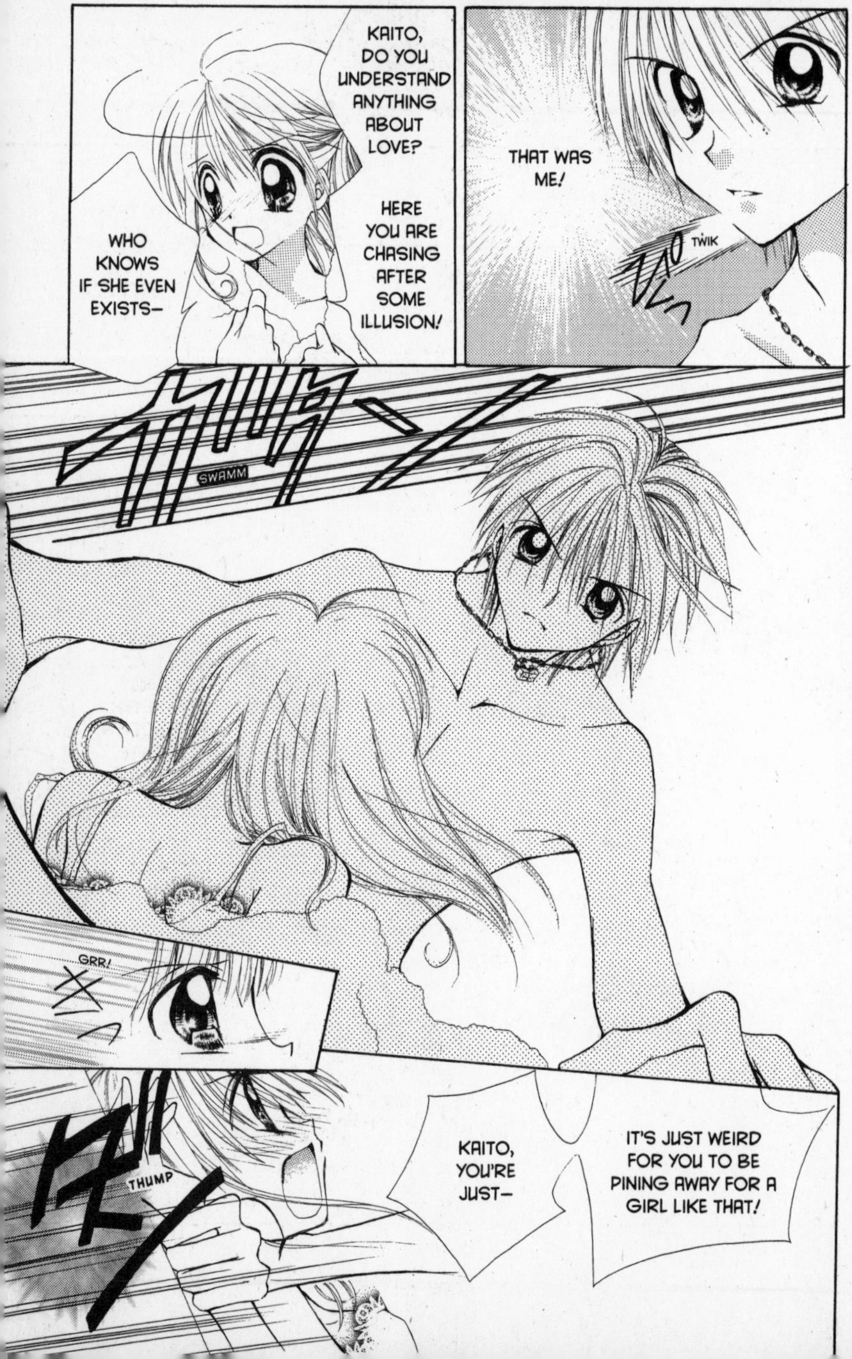
THAT WAS ME!
TWIK
KAITO, DO YOU UNDERSTAND ANYTHING ABOUT LOVE?
HERE YOU ARE CHASING AFTER SOME ILLUSION!
WHO KNOWS IF SHE EVEN EXISTS—
SWAMM
GRR!
IT'S JUST WEIRD FOR YOU TO BE PINING AWAY FOR A GIRL LIKE THAT!
KAITO, YOU'RE JUST—
THUMP

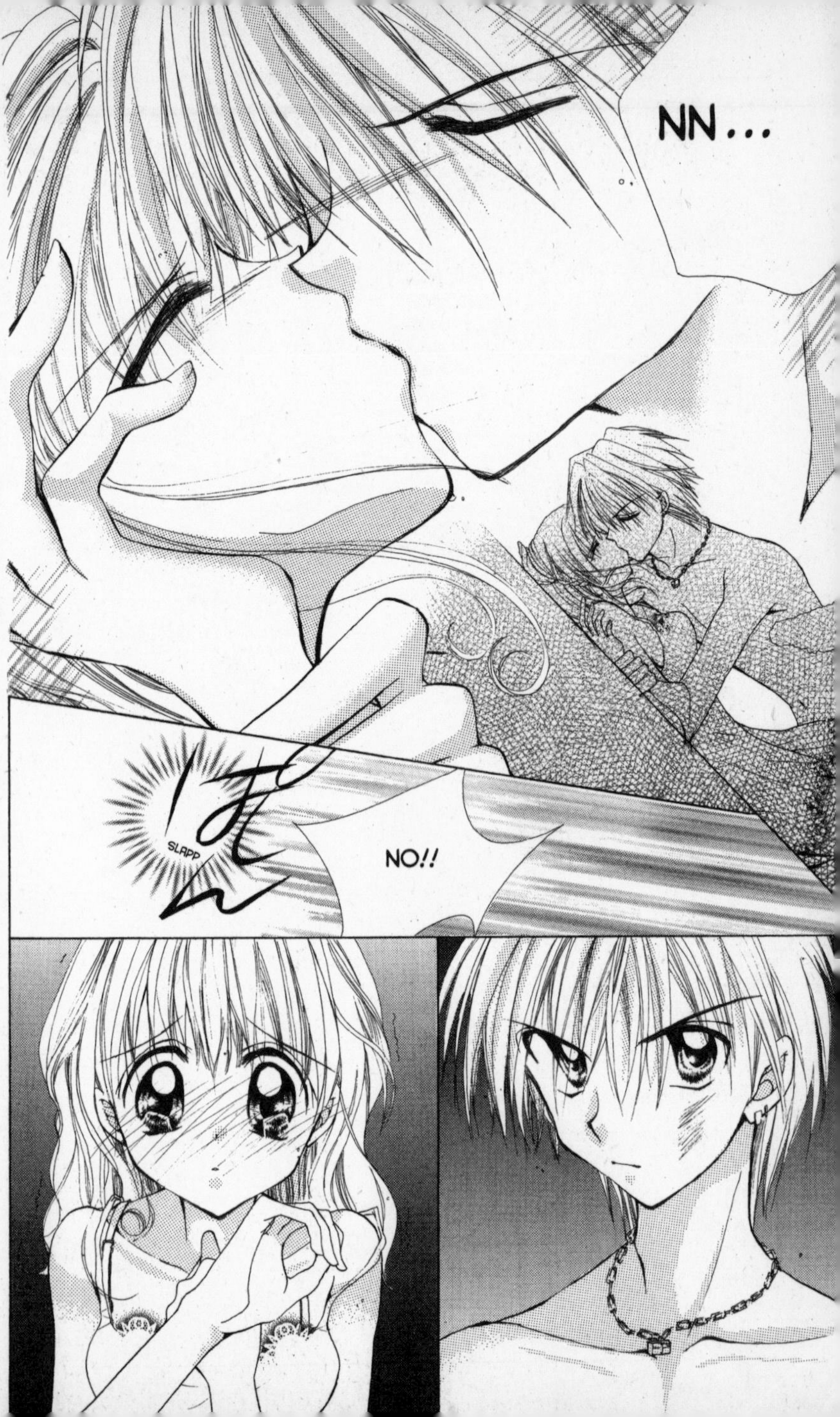
NN...
SLAPP
NO!!

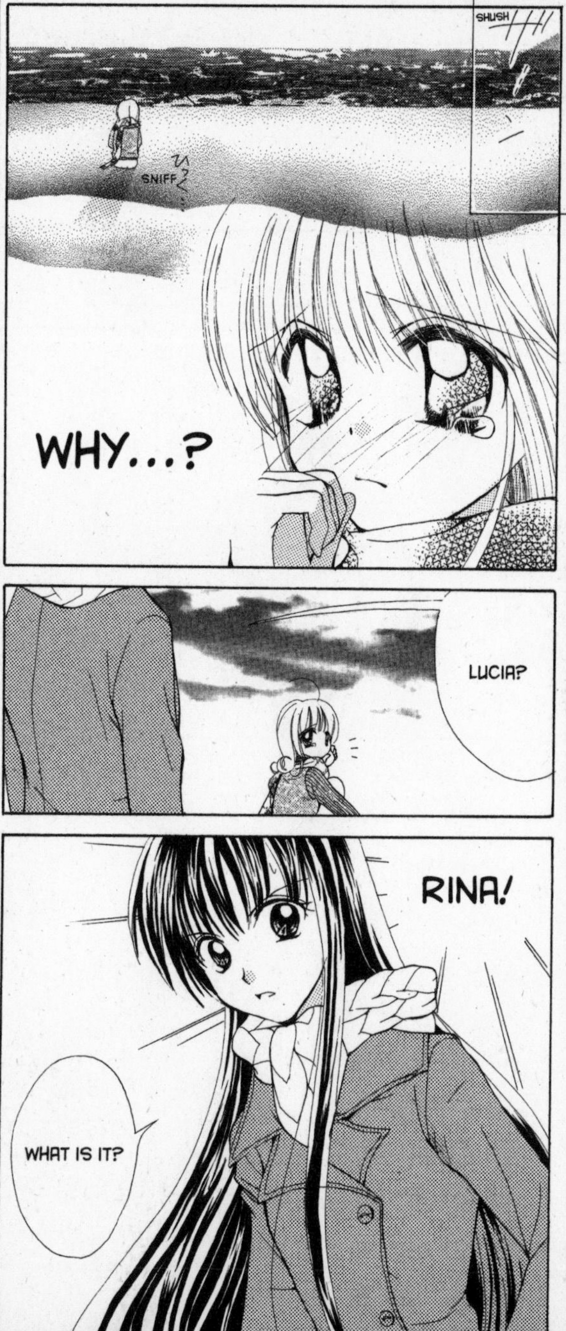
SHUSH
SNIFF
WHY...?
LUCIA?
RINA!
WHAT IS IT?

AFTERWORD.
THANK YOU SO MUCH FOR READING ALL THE WAY TO THE END!! I GET THE FEELING THAT I'VE ONLY WRITTEN ABOUT ONE THIRD OF THE THINGS I WAS THINKING TO WRITE. BUT THE COMIC IS OVER A LOT QUICKER THAN I THOUGHT! SO THAT'S HOW IT IS?
I'LL BE WAITING FOR YOU TO SEND YOUR COMMENTS AND FEELINGS ABOUT PICHI TO KC COMICS! ♥

HANAMORI PINK
C/O DEL REY BOOKS
1745 BROADWAY, 18-3
NEW YORK, NY 10019

♥ Special Thanks ♥

- MOMO SORAKI-SAMA
- MICHIYO KIKUTA-SAMA
- RUMIKO NAGANO-SAMA
- MINORI HIKAWA-SAMA
- MEI HIROUMI-SAMA
- MASAKO YOKOYAMA-SAMA
- EDITORS:
  KAWAMOTO-SAMA
  ZUSHI-SAMA
  OZAWA-SAMA

AND YOU!

~ 2003・1・15 ~

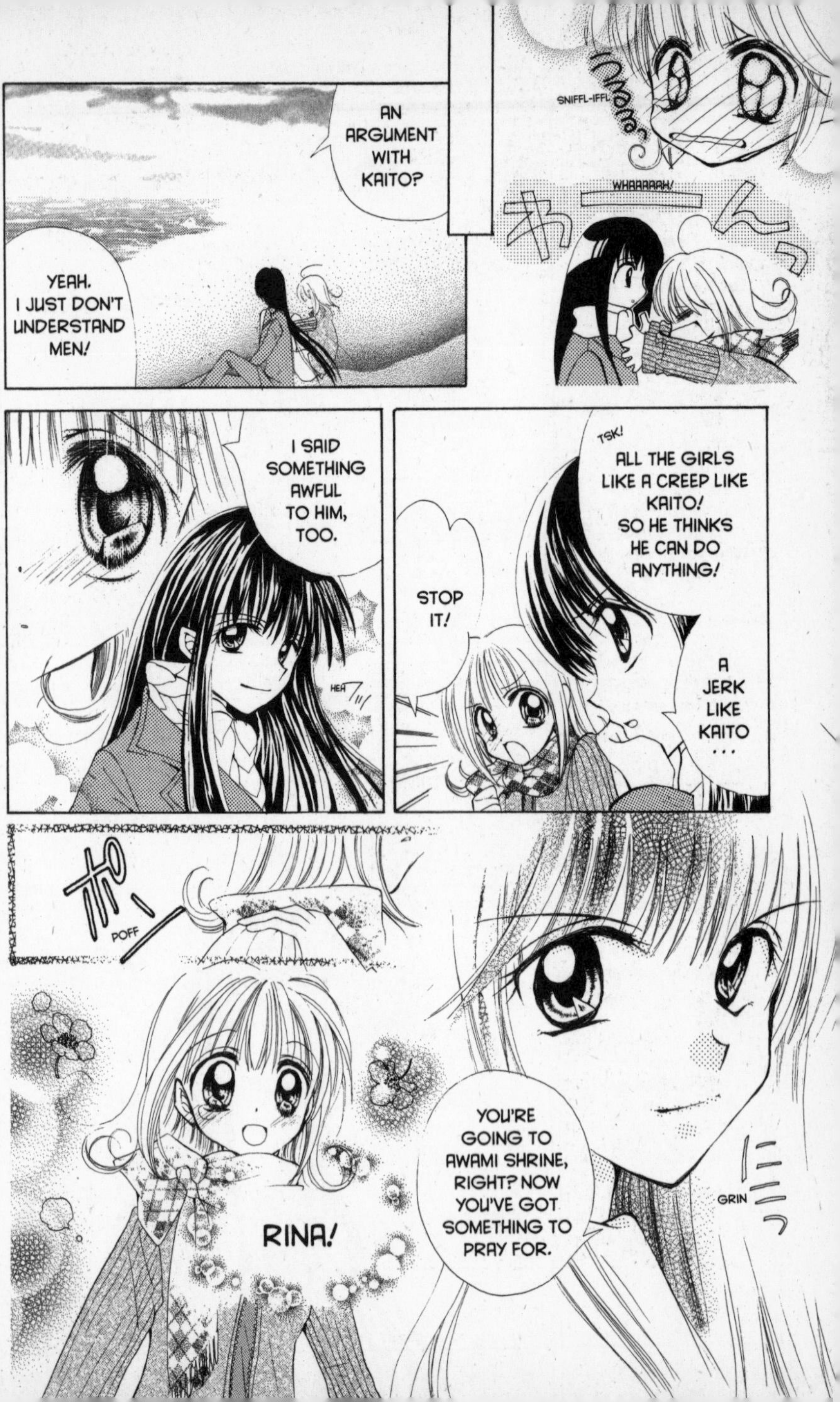
SNIFFL-IFFL
WHAAAAAH!
AN ARGUMENT WITH KAITO?
YEAH. I JUST DON'T UNDERSTAND MEN!
TSK!
ALL THE GIRLS LIKE A CREEP LIKE KAITO! SO HE THINKS HE CAN DO ANYTHING!
A JERK LIKE KAITO...
STOP IT!
I SAID SOMETHING AWFUL TO HIM, TOO.
HEH
GRIN
YOU'RE GOING TO AWAMI SHRINE, RIGHT? NOW YOU'VE GOT SOMETHING TO PRAY FOR.
POFF
RINA!

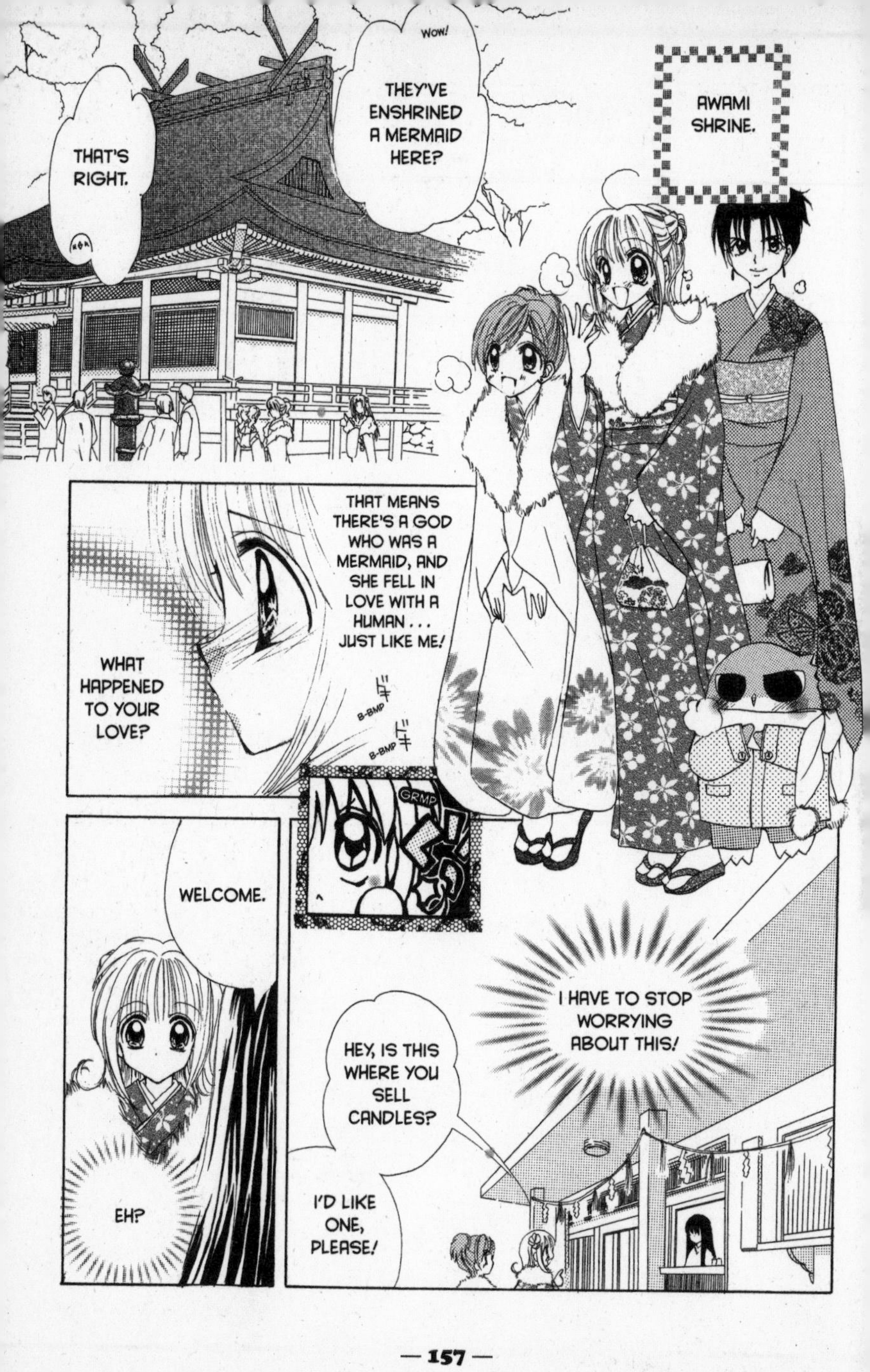
AWAMI SHRINE.
WOW!
THEY'VE ENSHRINED A MERMAID HERE?
THAT'S RIGHT.
THAT MEANS THERE'S A GOD WHO WAS A MERMAID, AND SHE FELL IN LOVE WITH A HUMAN . . . JUST LIKE ME!
B-BMP
B-BMP
WHAT HAPPENED TO YOUR LOVE?
GRMP
I HAVE TO STOP WORRYING ABOUT THIS!
HEY, IS THIS WHERE YOU SELL CANDLES?
I'D LIKE ONE, PLEASE!
WELCOME.
EH?

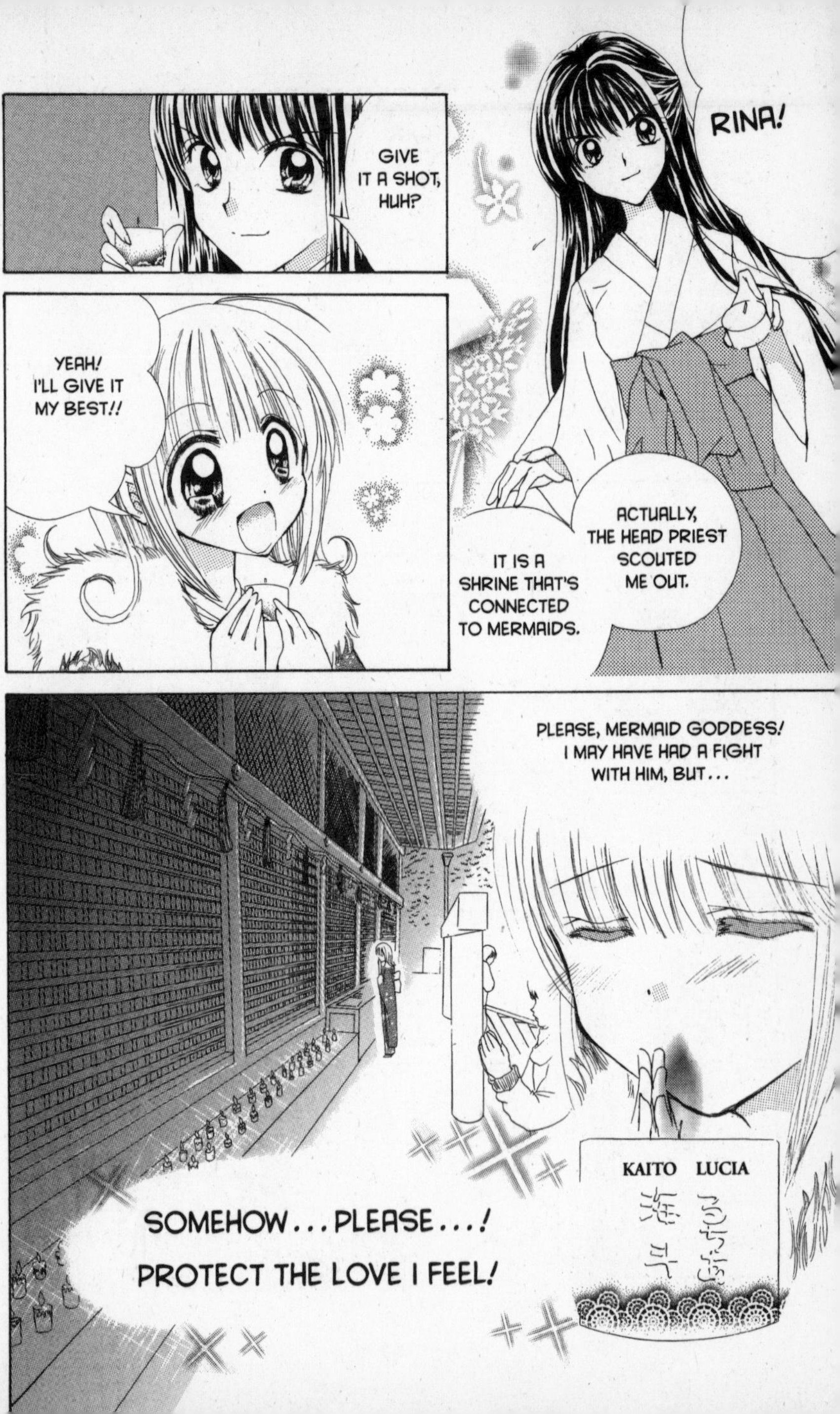
RINA!
ACTUALLY, THE HEAD PRIEST SCOUTED ME OUT.
IT IS A SHRINE THAT'S CONNECTED TO MERMAIDS.
GIVE IT A SHOT, HUH?
YEAH! I'LL GIVE IT MY BEST!!
PLEASE, MERMAID GODDESS! I MAY HAVE HAD A FIGHT WITH HIM, BUT...
KAITO LUCIA
SOMEHOW... PLEASE...!
PROTECT THE LOVE I FEEL!

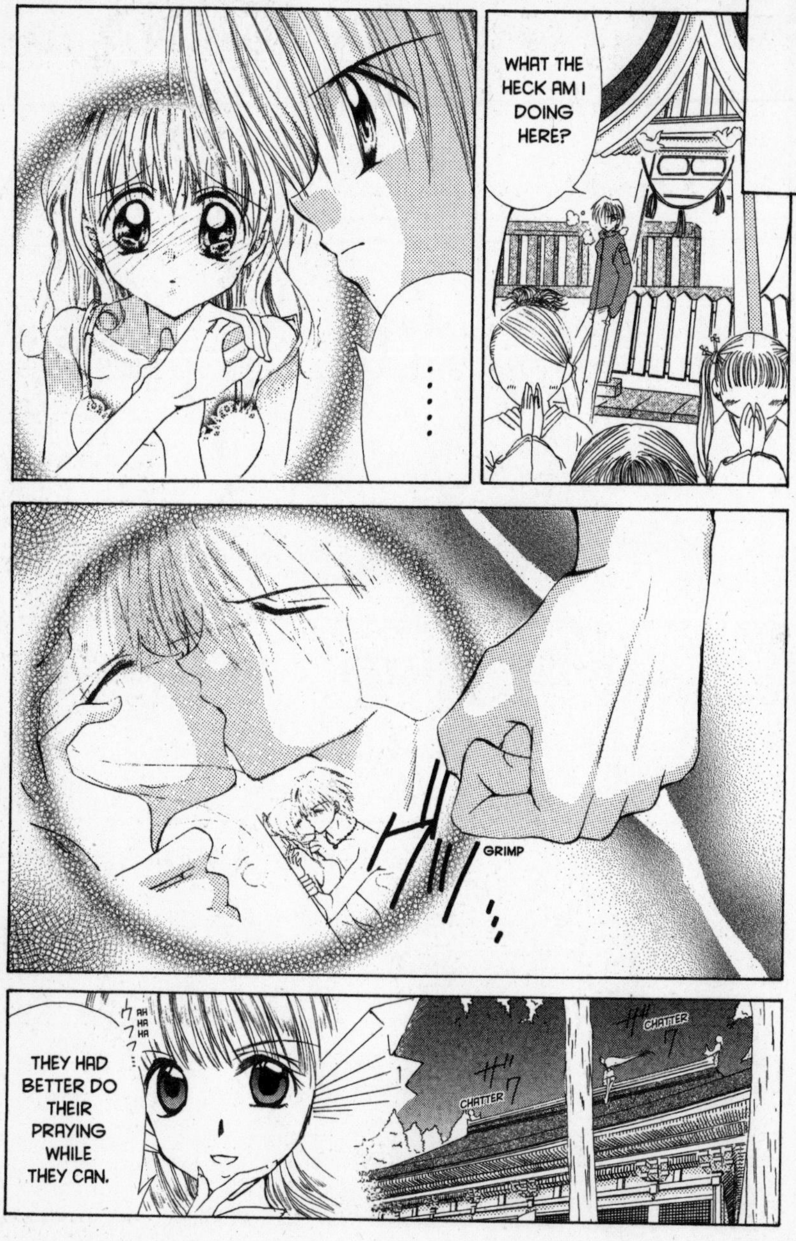
WHAT THE HECK AM I DOING HERE?
.....
GRIMP
CHATTER
CHATTER
AH HA HA
THEY HAD BETTER DO THEIR PRAYING WHILE THEY CAN.

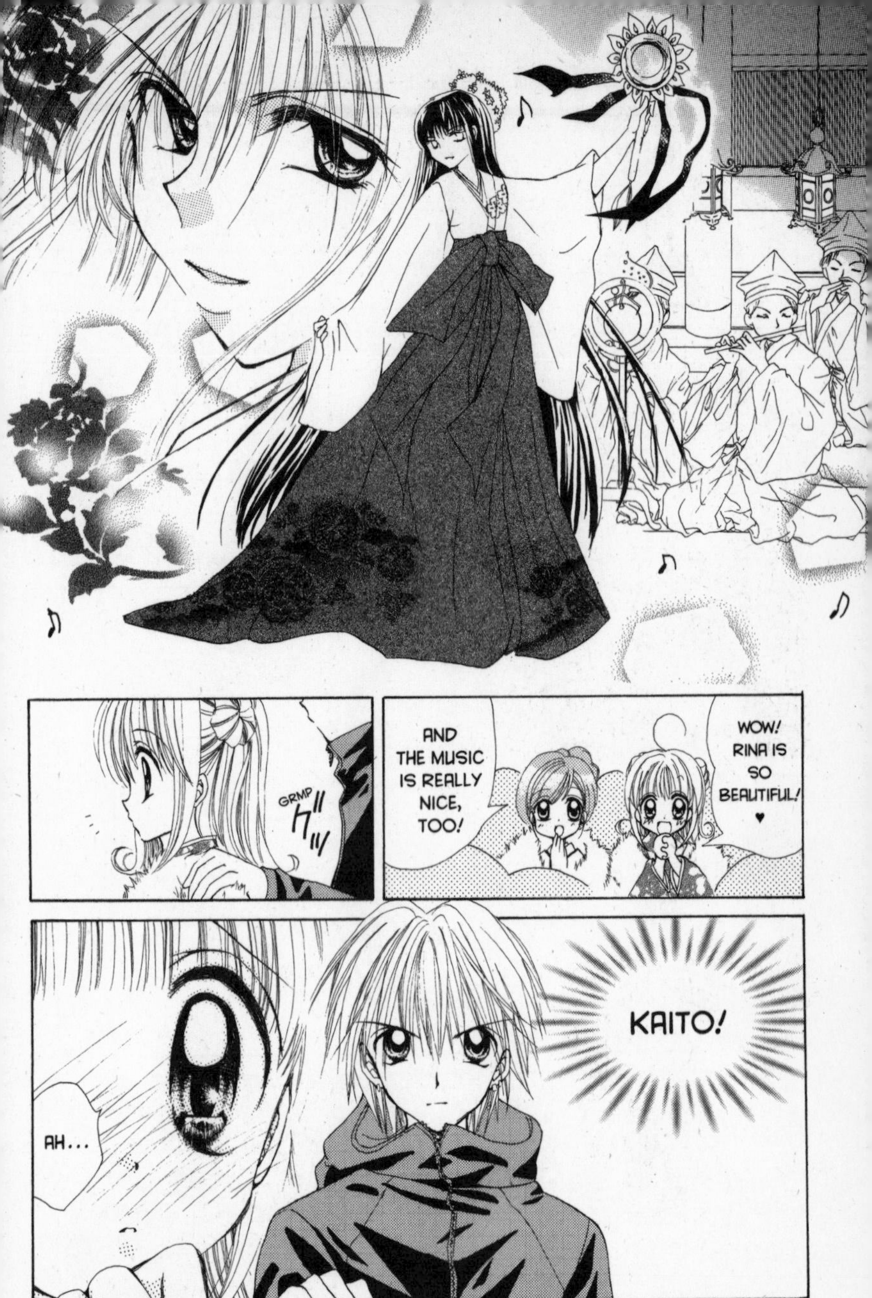
WOW! RINA IS SO BEAUTIFUL! ♥
AND THE MUSIC IS REALLY NICE, TOO!
GRMP
KAITO!
AH...

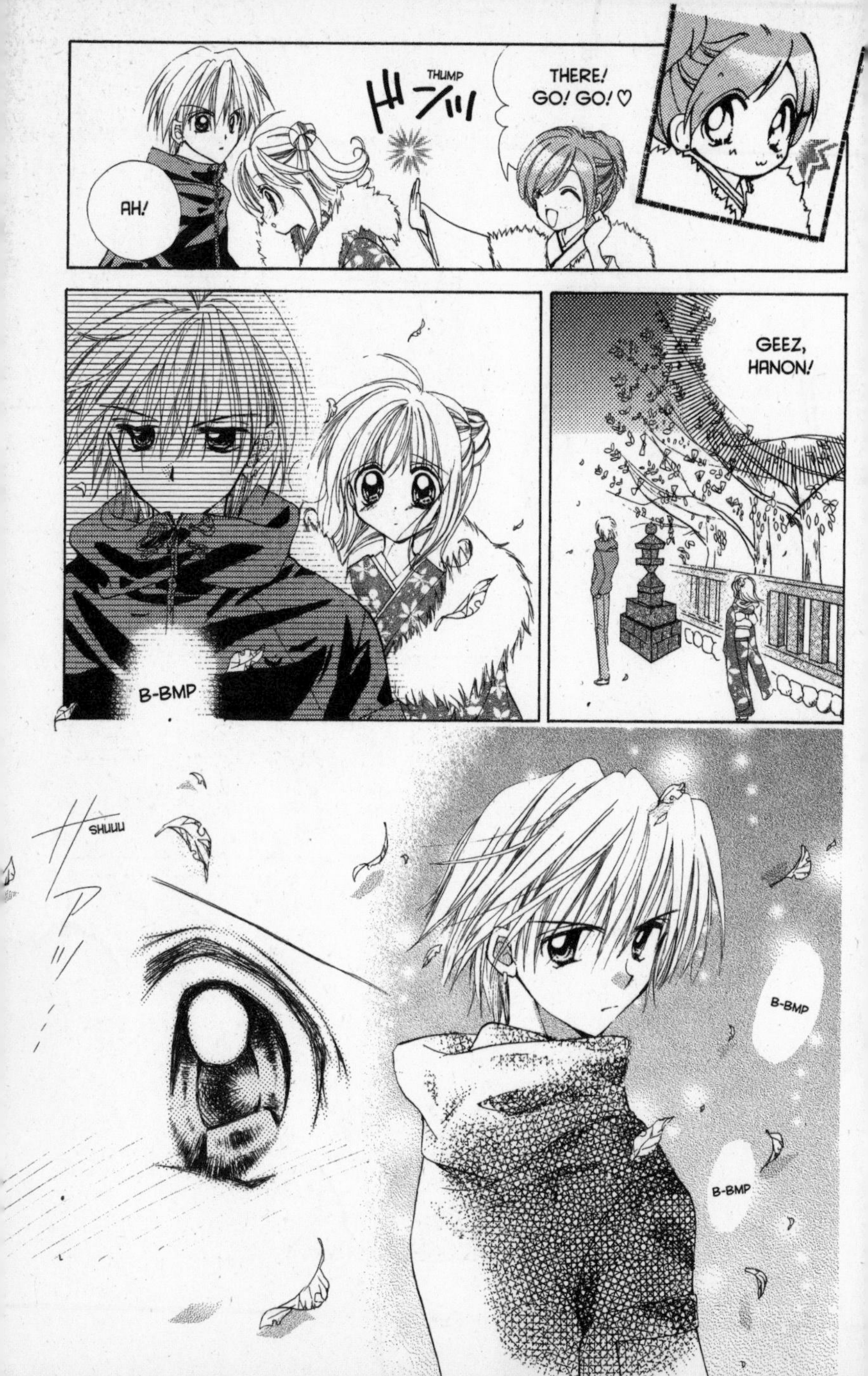
THERE!
GO! GO! ♡
THUMP
AH!
GEEZ, HANON!
B-BMP
B-BMP
B-BMP
SHUUU

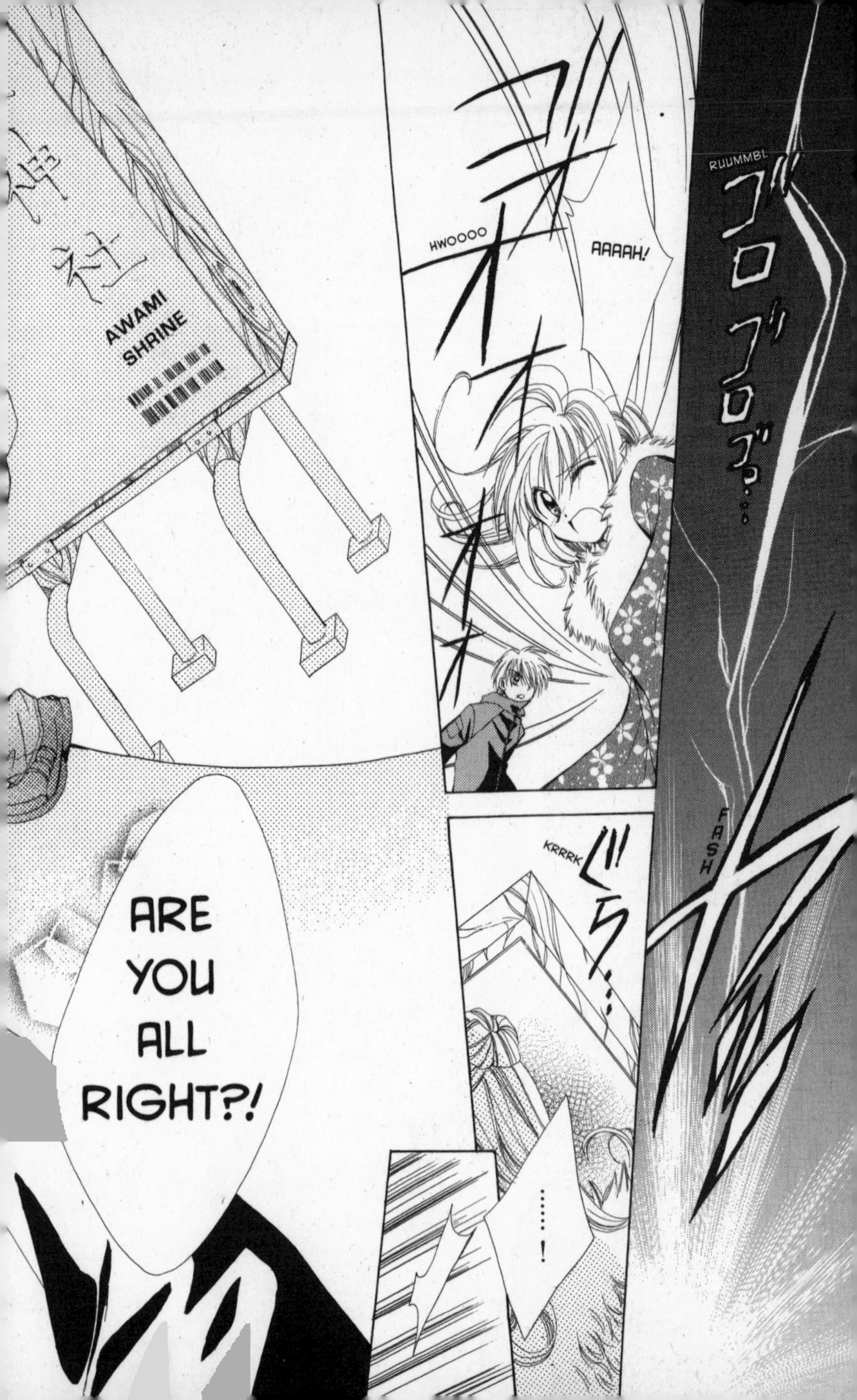
RUUMMBL
FASH
AAAAH!
HWOOOO
KRRRK
......!
神社
AWAMI SHRINE
ARE YOU ALL RIGHT?!

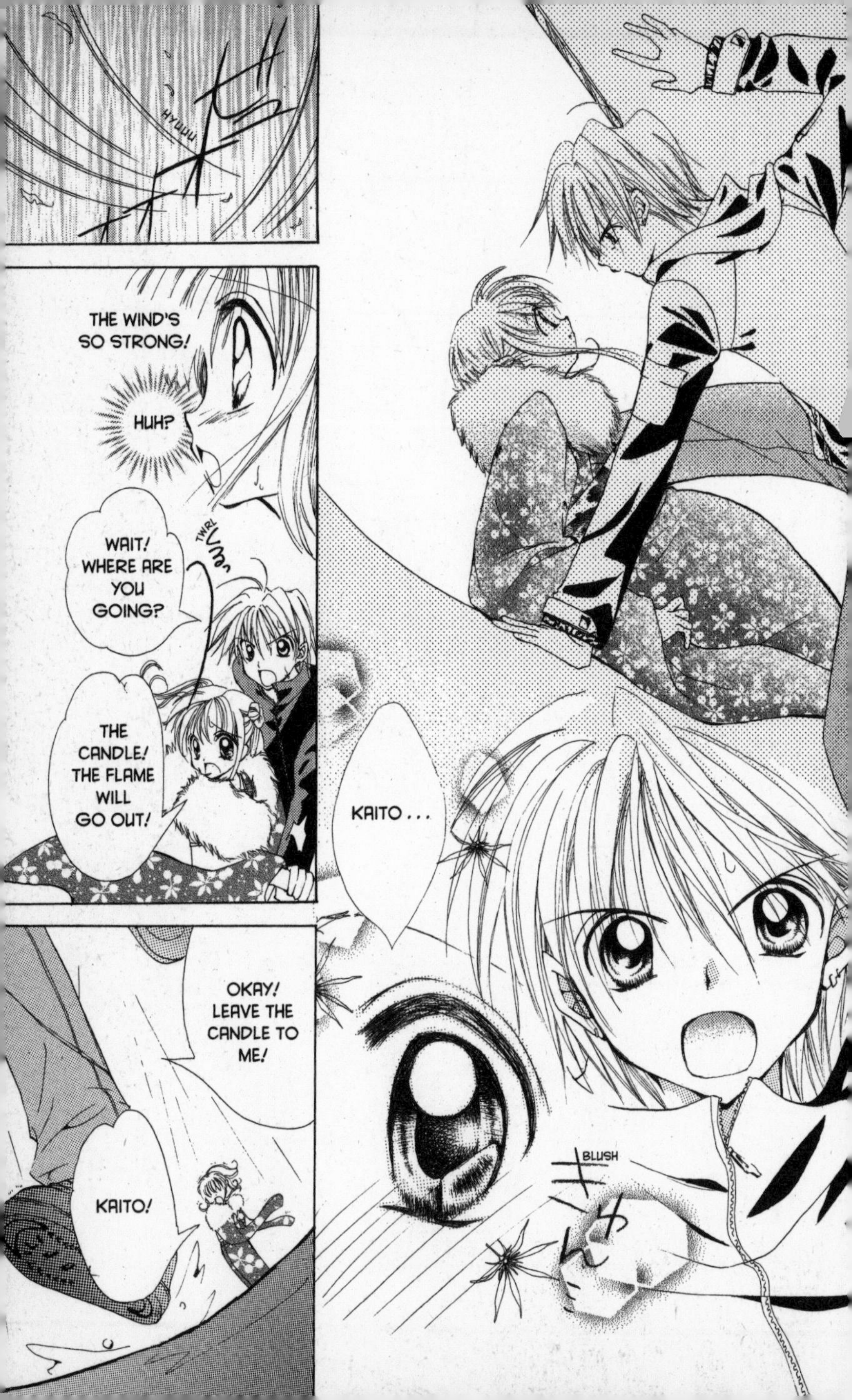
KAITO . . .
BLUSH
HYUUU
THE WIND'S SO STRONG!
HUH?
WAIT! WHERE ARE YOU GOING?
TWRL
THE CANDLE! THE FLAME WILL GO OUT!
OKAY! LEAVE THE CANDLE TO ME!
KAITO!

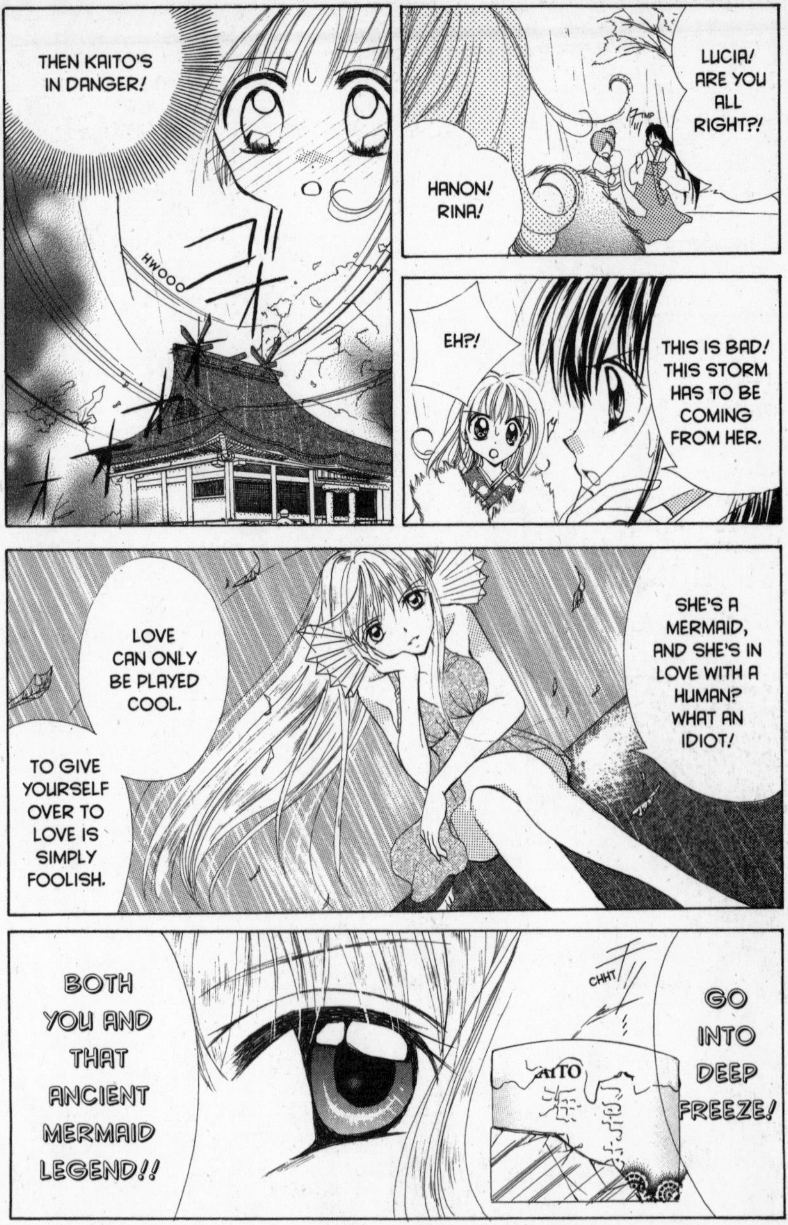
LUCIA! ARE YOU ALL RIGHT?!
HANON! RINA!
THIS IS BAD! THIS STORM HAS TO BE COMING FROM HER.
EH?!
THEN KAITO'S IN DANGER!
HWOOO
SHE'S A MERMAID, AND SHE'S IN LOVE WITH A HUMAN? WHAT AN IDIOT!
LOVE CAN ONLY BE PLAYED COOL.
TO GIVE YOURSELF OVER TO LOVE IS SIMPLY FOOLISH.
CHHT
GO INTO DEEP FREEZE!
BOTH YOU AND THAT ANCIENT MERMAID LEGEND!!

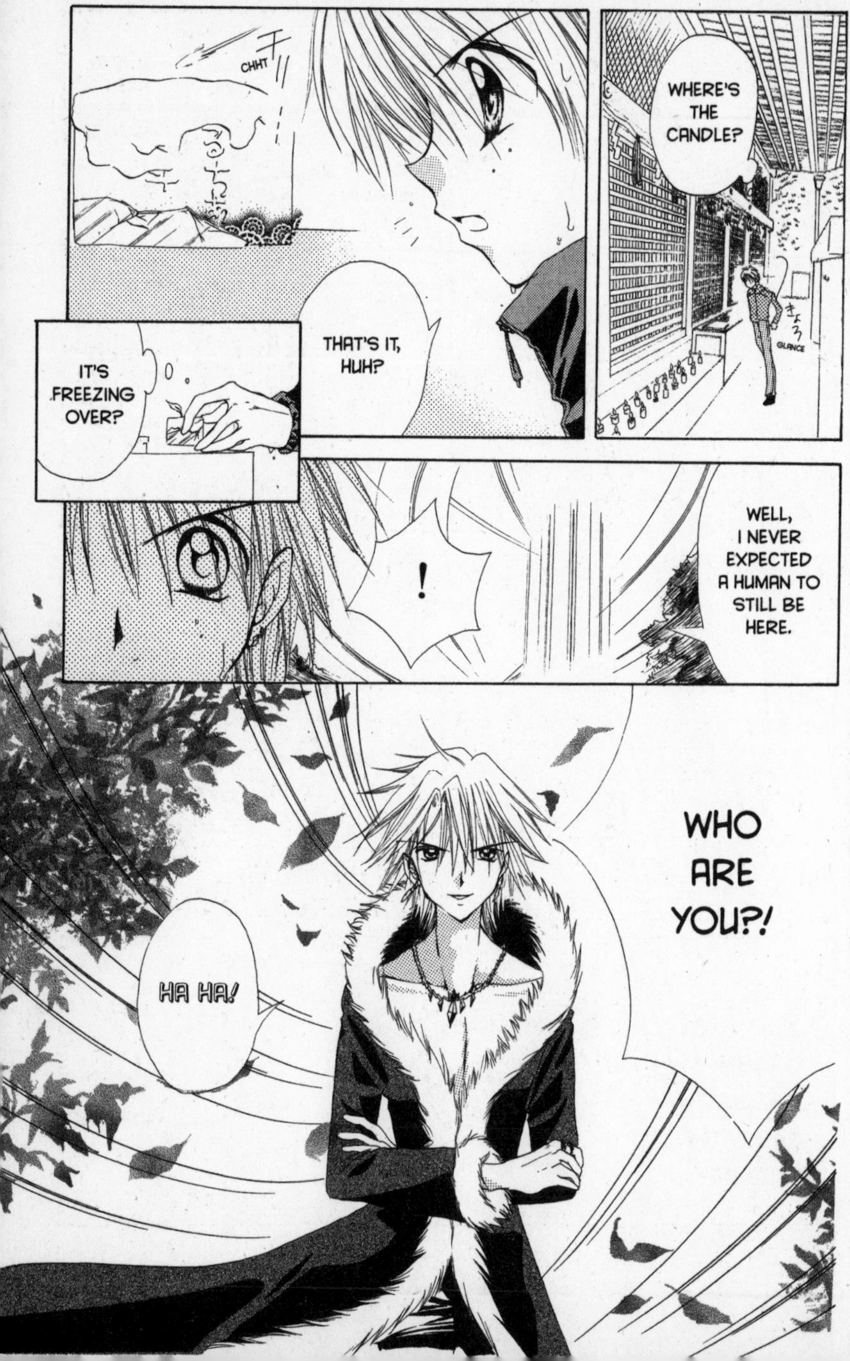
WHERE'S THE CANDLE?
GLANCE
CHHT
THAT'S IT, HUH?
IT'S FREEZING OVER?
WELL, I NEVER EXPECTED A HUMAN TO STILL BE HERE.
!
WHO ARE YOU?!
HA HA!

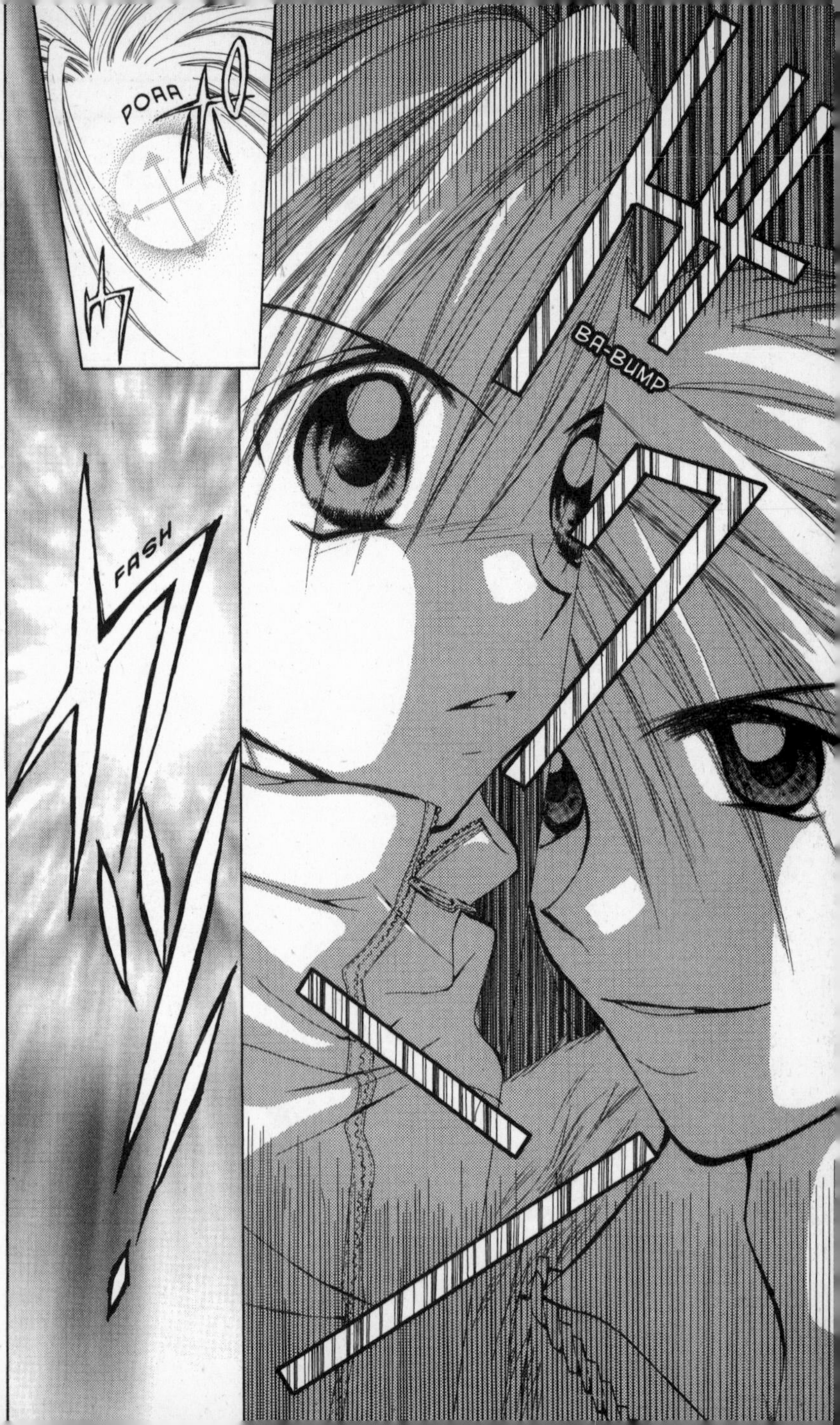
BA-BUMP
PORR
FASH

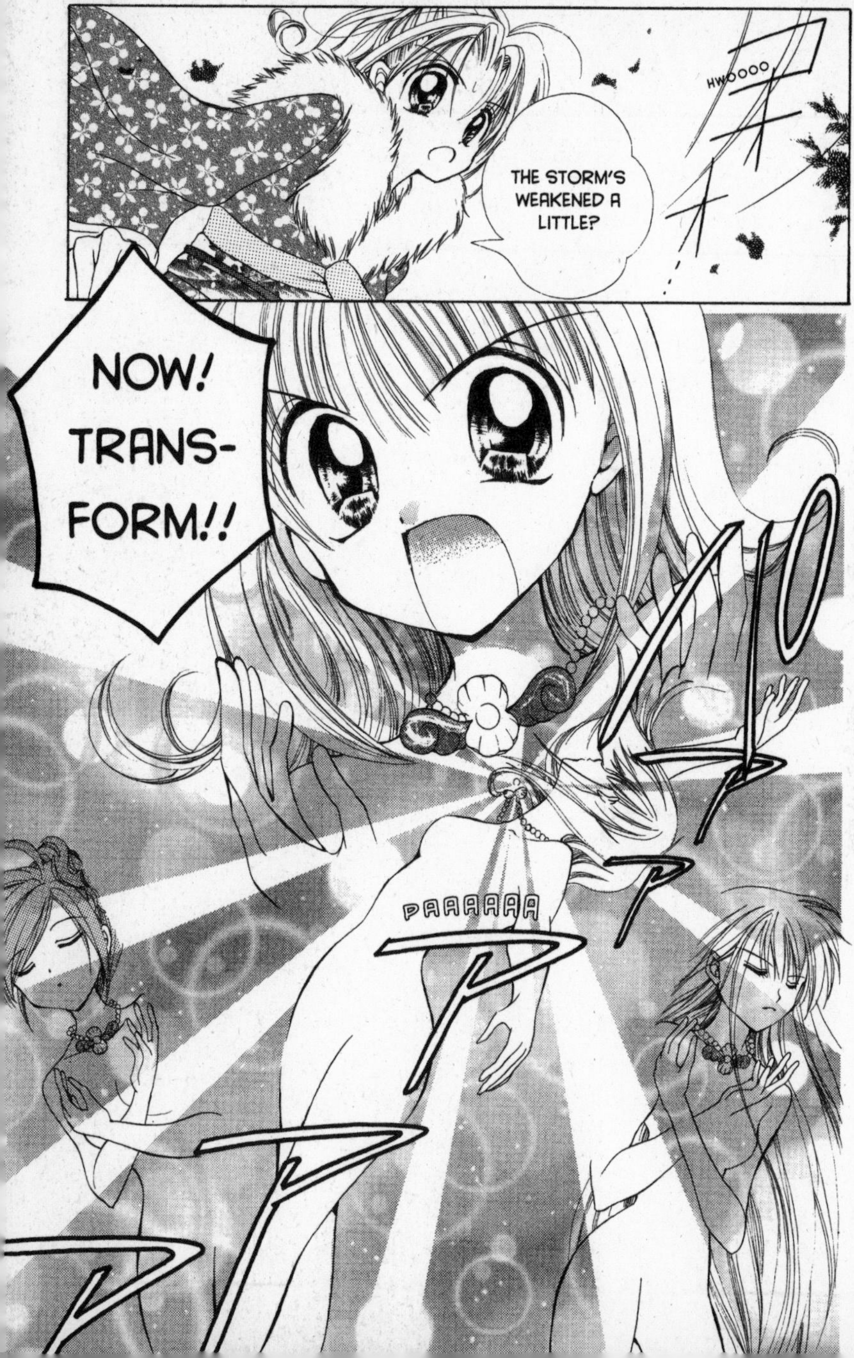
HWOOOO
THE STORM'S WEAKENED A LITTLE?
NOW! TRANS-FORM!!
PAAAAAA

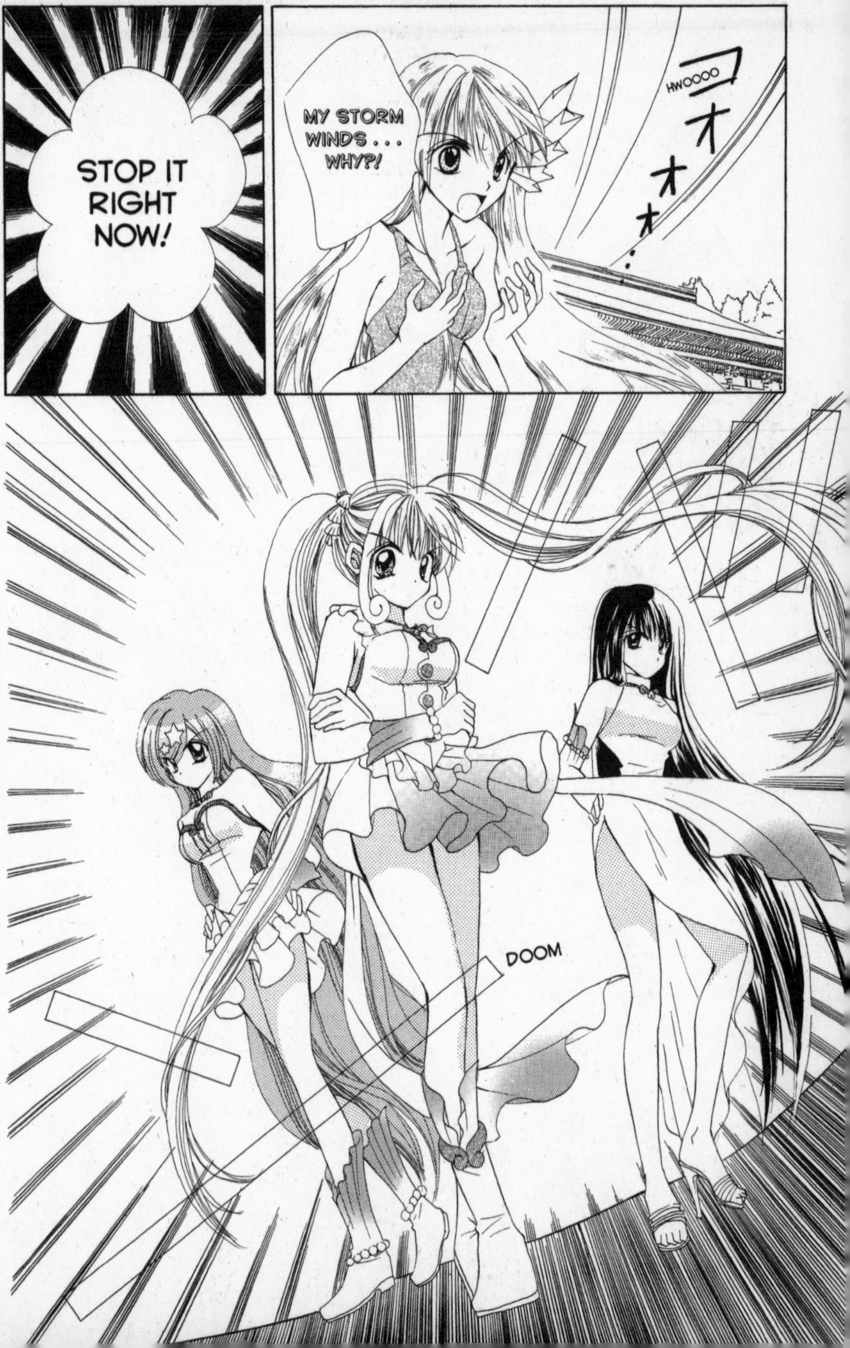
HWOOOO
コオオォ・・・
MY STORM WINDS . . . WHY?!
STOP IT RIGHT NOW!
DOOM

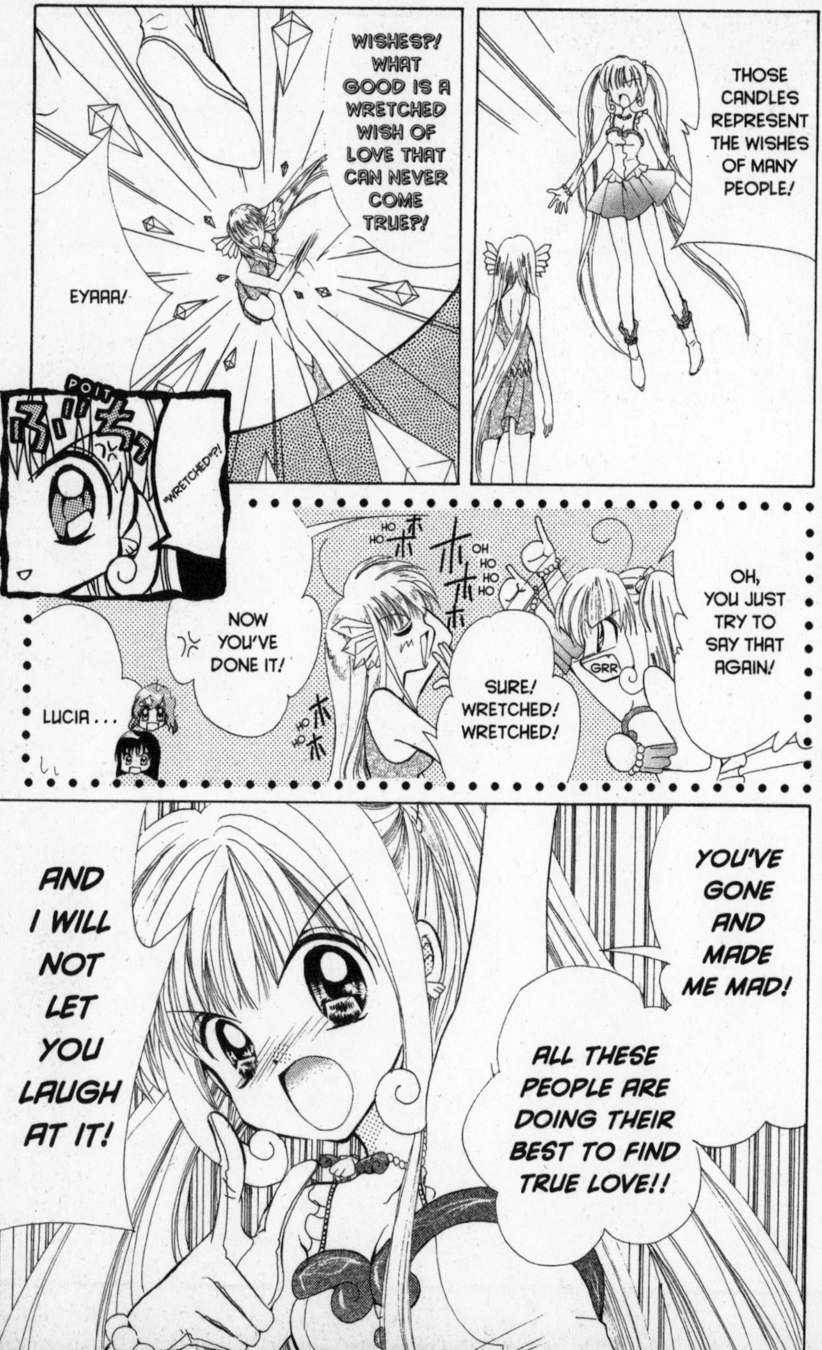
THOSE CANDLES REPRESENT THE WISHES OF MANY PEOPLE!
WISHES?! WHAT GOOD IS A WRETCHED WISH OF LOVE THAT CAN NEVER COME TRUE?!
EYAAA!
POIT
"WRETCHED"?!
OH, YOU JUST TRY TO SAY THAT AGAIN!
GRR
OH HO HO HO
HO HO
SURE! WRETCHED! WRETCHED!
HO HO
NOW YOU'VE DONE IT!
LUCIA . . .
YOU'VE GONE AND MADE ME MAD!
ALL THESE PEOPLE ARE DOING THEIR BEST TO FIND TRUE LOVE!!
AND I WILL NOT LET YOU LAUGH AT IT!

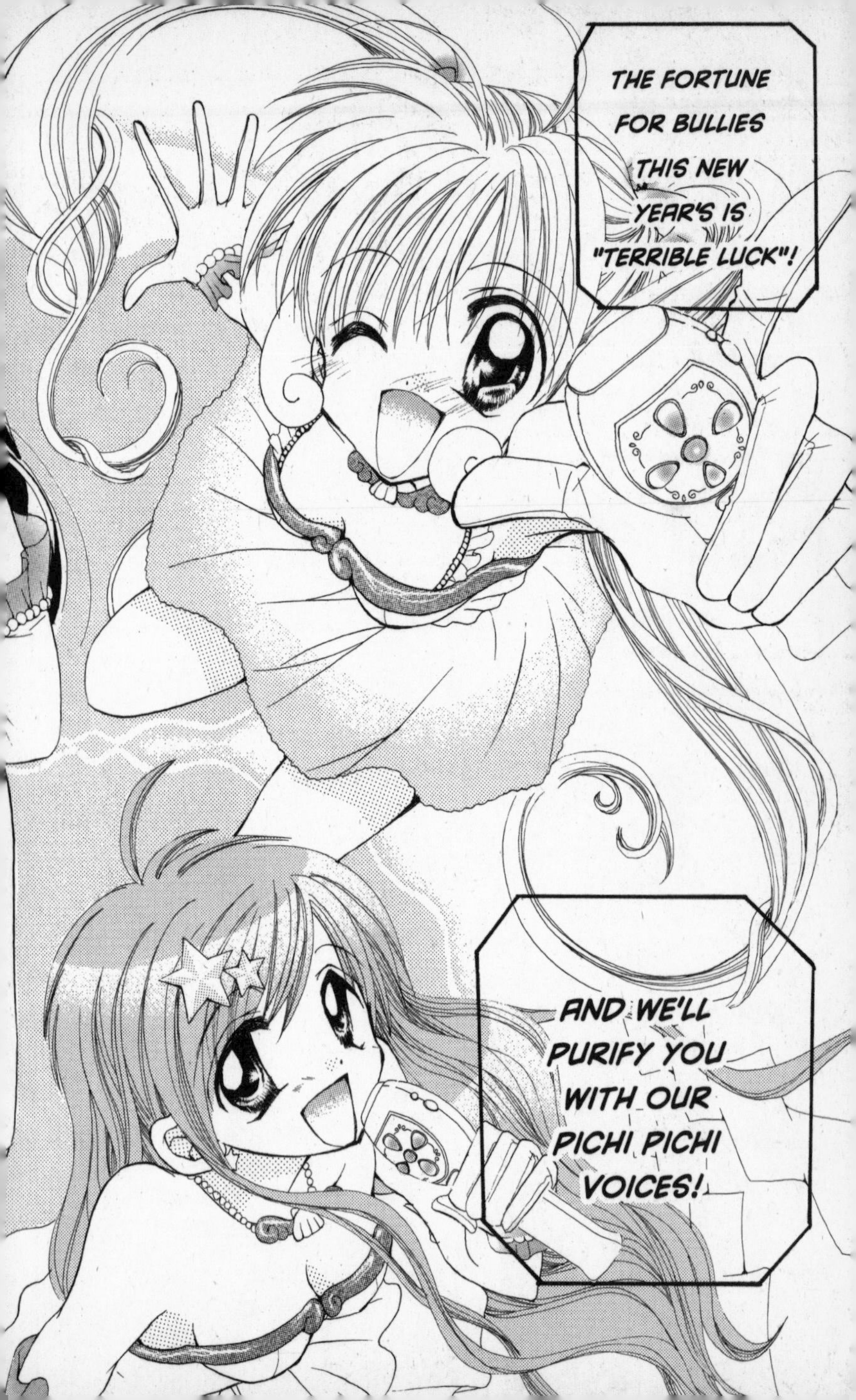
THE FORTUNE FOR BULLIES THIS NEW YEAR'S IS "TERRIBLE LUCK"!
AND WE'LL PURIFY YOU WITH OUR PICHI PICHI VOICES!

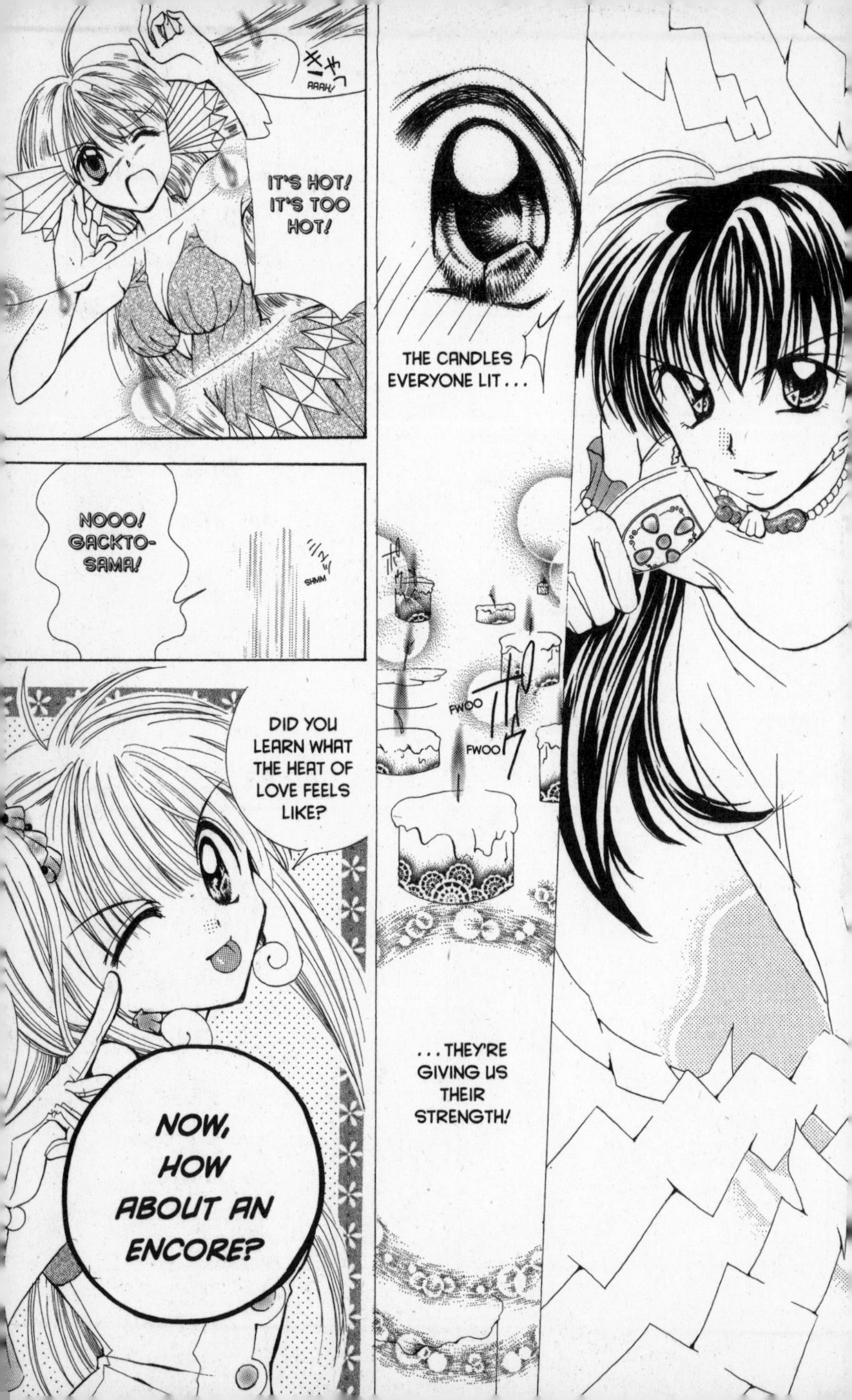
THE CANDLES EVERYONE LIT . . .
FWOO
FWOO
. . . THEY'RE GIVING US THEIR STRENGTH!
AAAH!
IT'S HOT! IT'S TOO HOT!
NOOO! GACKTO-SAMA!
SHMM
DID YOU LEARN WHAT THE HEAT OF LOVE FEELS LIKE?
NOW, HOW ABOUT AN ENCORE?

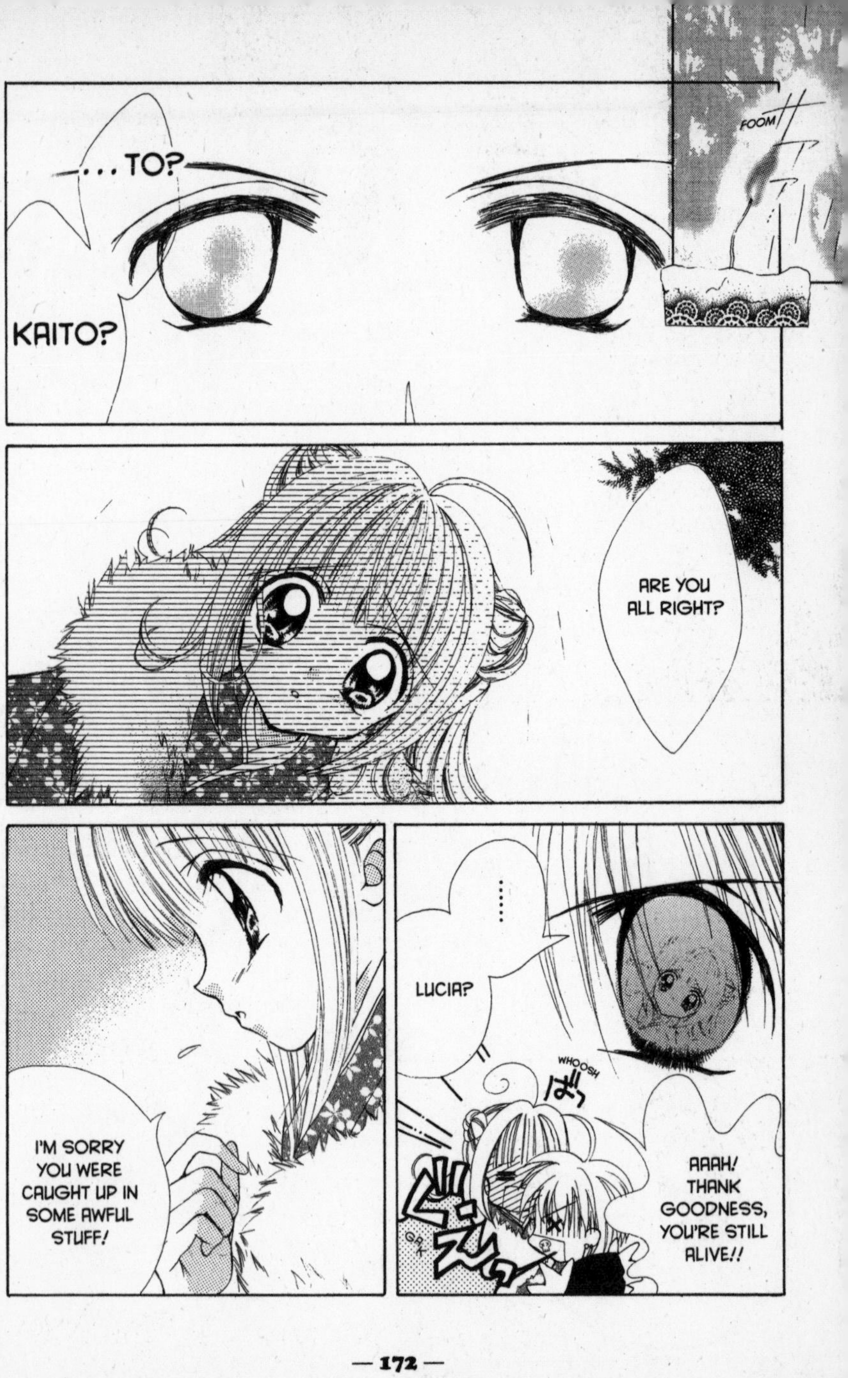

FOOM
...TO?
KAITO?
ARE YOU ALL RIGHT?
......
LUCIA?
WHOOSH
AAAH! THANK GOODNESS, YOU'RE STILL ALIVE!!
GRK
I'M SORRY YOU WERE CAUGHT UP IN SOME AWFUL STUFF!

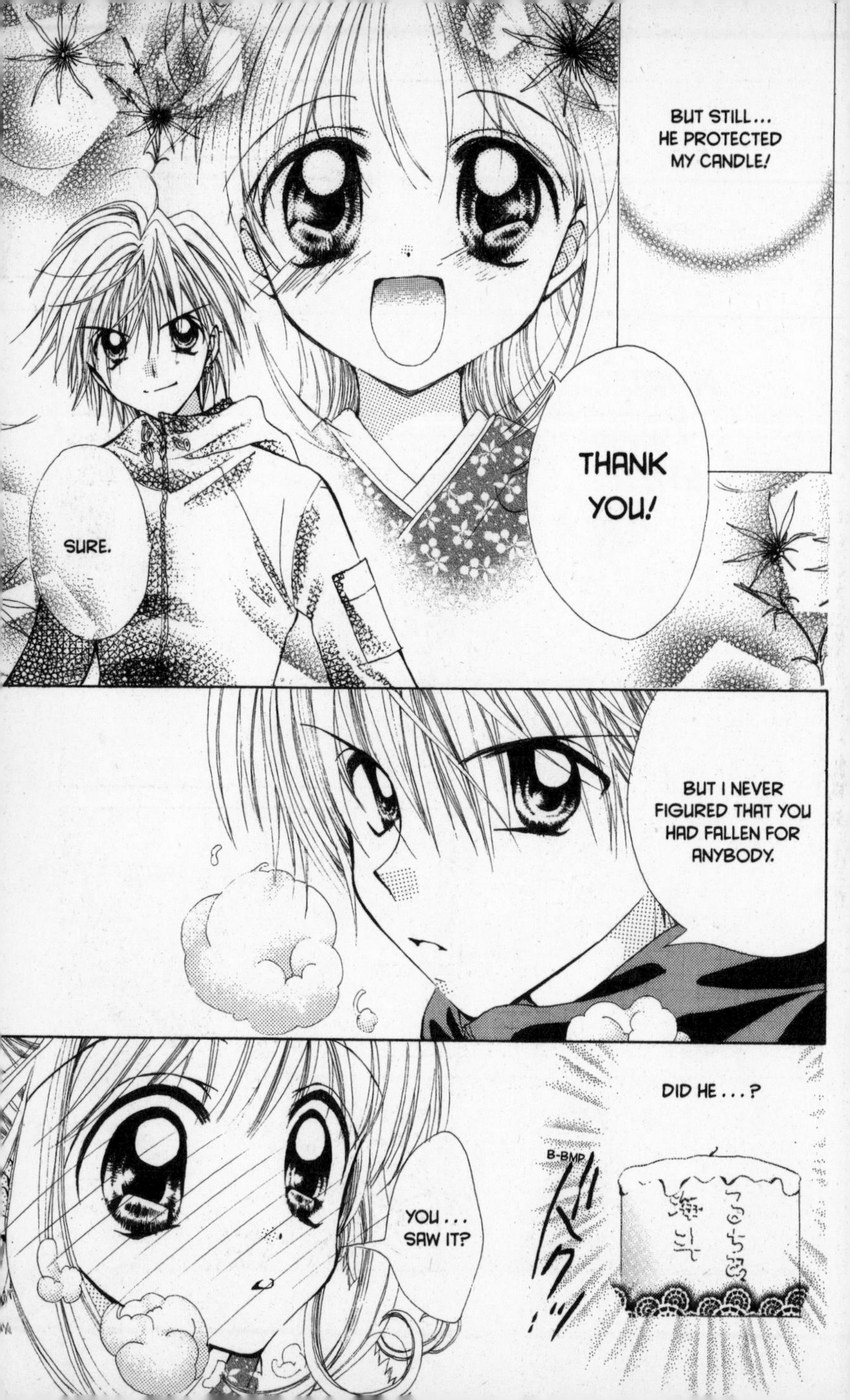
BUT STILL... HE PROTECTED MY CANDLE!
THANK YOU!
SURE.
BUT I NEVER FIGURED THAT YOU HAD FALLEN FOR ANYBODY.
DID HE . . . ?
B-BMP
YOU . . . SAW IT?

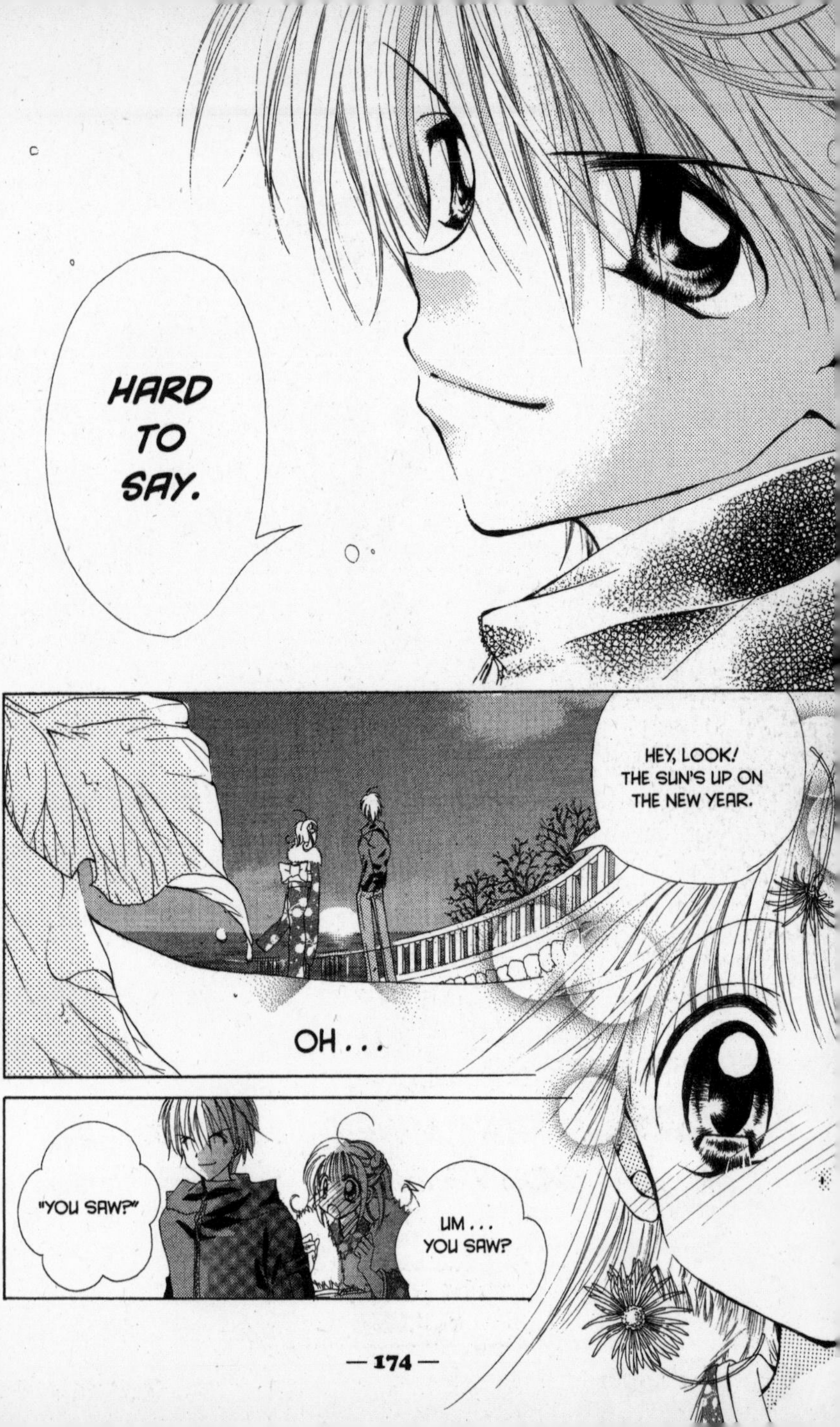
HARD TO SAY.
HEY, LOOK! THE SUN'S UP ON THE NEW YEAR.
OH . . .
UM . . . YOU SAW?
"YOU SAW?"

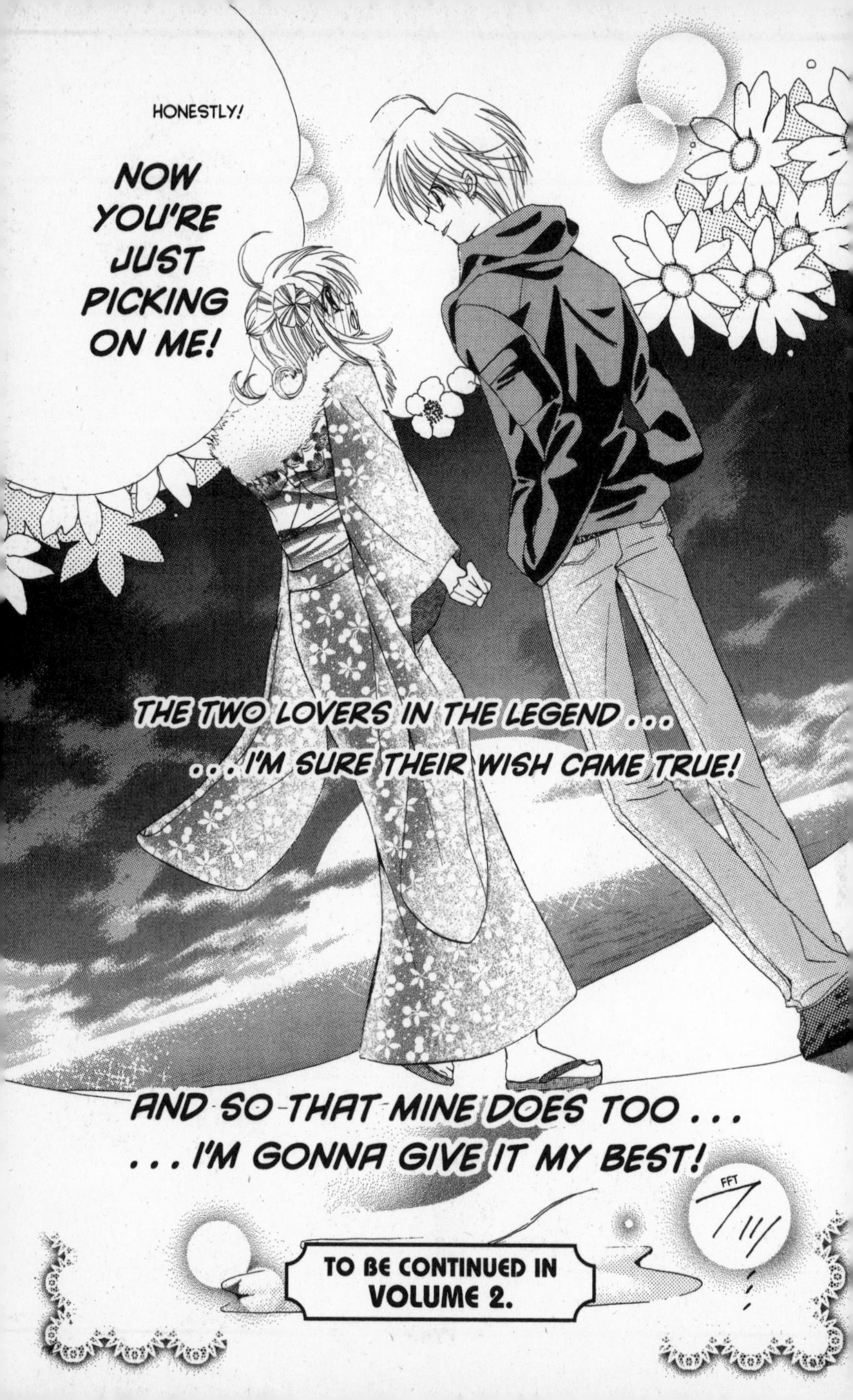
HONESTLY!
NOW YOU'RE JUST PICKING ON ME!
THE TWO LOVERS IN THE LEGEND . . .
. . . I'M SURE THEIR WISH CAME TRUE!
AND SO THAT MINE DOES TOO . . .
. . . I'M GONNA GIVE IT MY BEST!
FFT
TO BE CONTINUED IN VOLUME 2.

# About the Creator

**Pink Hanamori**

Born on November 5th in Shizuoka Prefecture; Scorpio, Blood type AB. Entered the 31st Nakayoshi New Faces contest with the manga *Miss Dieter Heroine* in the year 2000. Her debut work was *Nakayoshi Haru-yasumi Land* (Nakayoshi Spring Break Land) in the year 2001. Her signature work is *Mermaid Melody Pichi Pichi Pitch*. She loves to play with dogs and talk a lot.

# Translation Notes

Japanese is a tricky language for most Westerners, and translation is often more art than science. For your edification and reading pleasure, here are notes on some of the places where we could have gone in a different direction in our translation of the work, or where a Japanese cultural reference is used.

## Title: *Pichi Pichi Pitch*

*Pichi pichi* means lighthearted — it indicates the girlish exuberance that Lucia exhibits in her approach to life. *Pitch*, as will become pretty obvious, is the English word meaning a musical tone. (Sorry if anybody thought it was what a baseball player throws. Nope, that's an altogether different pitch.)

## Names

The characters in *Pichi Pichi Pitch* tend to have sea-based names: Lucia Nanami, for example. Artists around the world have depicted the saint, Santa Lucia, as a mermaid (the c in Lucia is pronounced as a ch sound), and the two characters that make up the name Nanami translate out to seven seas. We'll include the meanings of more character names in upcoming volumes.

## *Kyaa* and *Gyaa*

*Kyaa* is a girlish scream. Although it can be used when a character is frightened or surprised, it's usually heard as a scream of delight. *Gyaa* nearly always indicates real fright, embarrassment or pain, and hardly ever has a good meaning.

## Dôbutsu Uranai, page 4

Like the Western zodiac and the Chinese zodiac, *doubutsu uranai* (Japanese for animal fortune-telling) divides people into personality types based on the date of birth. It claims to be based on ancient Asian elements such as the Four Pillars of Destiny and the Five Elements, with social psychology and behavioral psychology  thrown in. The twelve animal types are Wolf, Panther, Koala, Fawn, Monkey, Sheep, Elephant, Raccoon, Cheetah, Pegasus, Tiger, and Lion. Elements of a "monkey" personality are dexterity, cheerfulness, a certain gullibility, susceptibility to flattery, and a desire to improve oneself.

## Johnnys, page 4

An agency that is so famous for putting together boy bands who stay together for decades (such as SMAP and V6) that it has attracted its own following of fans.

## Pearl Baths, page 5

Pearl Baths in Japanese is *Shinju-yu*, and is a *yu* or public bathhouse. Despite the attention given to mixed bathing in Japan, *yu* almost always have separate men's and women's baths. When going to a public bath, one brings a squat, plastic bucket made for bathing, along with soap, shampoo, towels, etc.; pays a small fee; washes oneself with soap and shampoos one's hair at the faucets and rinses off; and only enters the large hot-water baths for a soak. Maybe our readers have heard of *onsen: yu* that use hot springs rather than heating the water through boilers, as is normal for a town's public baths.

## Yobisute, page 19

As mentioned in the honorifics section, to leave off the honorific (*yobisute* in Japanese) is to assume a very close relationship. In this case, Hanon is indicating that she wants to be very close friends with Lucia.

## *Yokote-shi*, page 23

The honorific *-shi* is an honorific that is used if one is talking about a person one respects but that respected person is not a part of the conversation.

## Gackto, page 57

The character of Gackto is an obvious reference to the very popular J-Pop star and musician Gackt, who is said to have fallen off of a boat near Okinawa when he was a little boy. After he was rescued, he claimed to have seen things that nobody else has seen.

## Sneezing, page 85

It's a popular legend all over Japan that if you sneeze, it means somebody somewhere is talking about you.

## Panthalassa, page 91

Some 200 to 300 million years ago, all of the world's continents were joined together in one enormous continent known as Pangia. The globe-circling ocean that surrounded Pangea is called Panthalassa. The name of Gackto's clan comes from that ocean.

## Have a good day at school, page 110

In Japanese, what Nikora and Hippo said (*Itterashai!*) is a standard farewell to someone who is leaving the home. It is usually followed (or preceded) by the person who is leaving saying, *Ittekimasu!* Since English doesn't have these ritual phrases, the translation is an equivalent thing to say when one's family member is leaving for school.

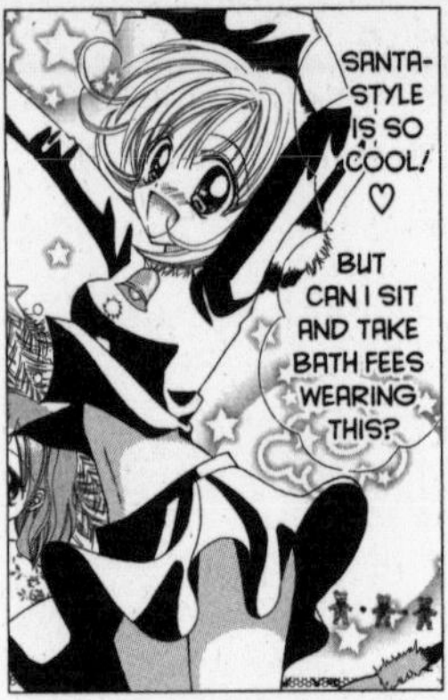
SANTA-STYLE IS SO COOL! ♡
BUT CAN I SIT AND TAKE BATH FEES WEARING THIS?

## Taking bath fees, page 114

There is usually a small counter set at the entrance directly between the men's side and the women's side of the public baths. That is where the baths' employee sits to receive the fees for entering the bath.

## Christmas in Japan, page 117

The spirits of Christmas and New Year's are reversed in Japan from the way those holidays are celebrated in North America. In Japan, Christmas is a party day, featuring huge fluffy Christmas cakes and small presents exchanged by people in close relationships. But Christmas has become very much a date night, almost rivaling Valentine's Day as a romantic evening for lovers.

## New Year's in Japan, page 147

New Year's Day is spent with family and close friends in quiet home-based tradition and religious observances. One of the religious events is to visit a temple or shrine. It is one of the few days left in the year when it is customary for Japanese women to wear full kimono. One usually approaches a shrine, makes an offering of money, rings a bell, and makes a wish or says a prayer. There are other traditions, such as buying fortunes (described below) and charms for luck, romance, a healthy birth, etc.

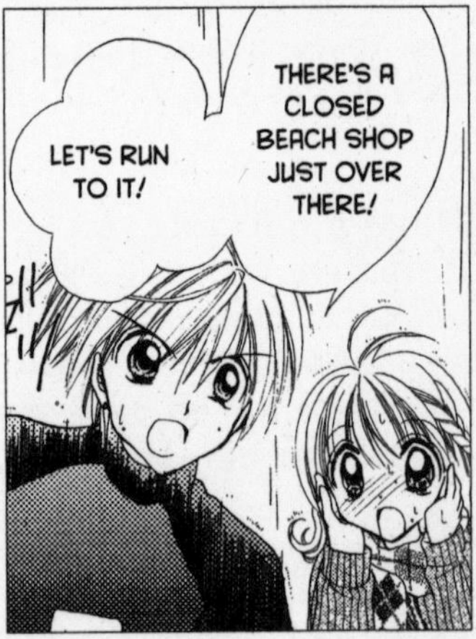
THERE'S A CLOSED BEACH SHOP JUST OVER THERE!
LET'S RUN TO IT!

## Beach shops, page 150

These are seasonal shops that open only during the busy summer months. Most beach shops, set up in temporary tentlike shelters, sell refreshments like shaved ice, sodas, beer, yakisoba fried noodles, cheap beach accessories, souvenirs, etc. Others can be quite elaborate bars and restaurants in fully enclosed wooden or sheet metal buildings. This chapter takes place in the dead of winter, so none of the beach shops would be open.

### Fortunes, page 170

When one visits a shrine or temple, one can usually buy a fortune from a special stand. The fortunes range from great luck to terrible luck (although the "terrible luck" fortunes are the most rare). Written on long scrolls of thin paper, the fortunes are then folded lengthwise and tied to the branches of trees on the shrine or temple grounds, making the bare limbs look as though they've sprouted white leaves.

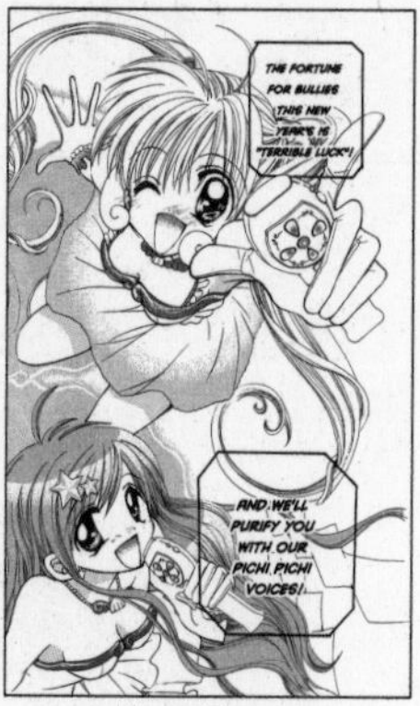
THE FORTUNE FOR BULLIES THIS NEW YEAR'S IS "TERRIBLE LUCK"!
AND WE'LL PURIFY YOU WITH OUR PICHI PICHI VOICES!

# Pichi Pichi Pitch

## Volume 2 is available
## in English now!

## Don't miss it!

# Manga is a completely different type of reading experience.

## To start at the *beginning*, go to the *end*!

That's right! Authentic manga is read the traditional Japanese way—from right to left. Exactly the *opposite* of how American books are read. It's easy to follow: Just go to the other end of the book, and read each page—and each panel—from right side to left side, starting at the top right. Now you're experiencing manga as it was meant to be!